NEW YORK
POLITICS

NEW YORK POLITICS

A Tale of Two States

Edward Schneier and
John Brian Murtaugh

M.E. Sharpe
Armonk, New York
London, England

Library of Congress Cataloging-in-Publication Data

Schneier, Edward V.
  New York politics : a tale of two states / Edward Schneier and John Brian Murtaugh.
    p. cm.
  Includes index.
  ISBN 0-7656-0064-1 (alk. paper) ISBN 0-7656-0065-X (pbk. : alk. paper)
    1. New York (State)—Politics and government. I. Murtaugh, Brian, 1937–   II. Title.

JK3416 .S25 2001
320.9747—dc21   00-053158

Printed in the United States of America

The paper used in this publication meets the minimum requirements of
American National Standard for Information Sciences
Permanence of Paper for Printed Library Materials,
ANSI Z 39.48-1984.

BM (c)   10   9   8   7   6   5   4   3   2   1
BM (p)   10   9   8   7   6   5   4   3   2   1

Contents

List of Tables, Figures, Boxes, and Maps

Tables

Figures

Boxes

Maps

Introduction

A Tale of Two States

The famous opening lines of Charles Dickens's *Tale of Two Cities* describe the people of France as living, on the eve of Revolution, in both the "best of times" and the "worst of times." Much the same could be said, on the cusp of the twenty-first century, about the people of New York. While it ranks fourth among the fifty states in per capita personal income, New York consistently exceeds the national average in the percentage of its citizens below the poverty line, and ranks eighth in the proportion of its residents on public assistance. It has 225 four-year colleges, far more than any other state, but also ranks second in prisons and spends more state money on prisoners than on college students. Nearly 10 percent of its citizens have advanced degrees, but 25 percent are high school dropouts. It is number one in health spending per family, but ranks eleventh in percentage of its population (20.8 percent) described as "medically under-serviced." While it is often depicted as a state low on traditional family values, it is tied for the fourth *lowest* divorce rate in the nation.[1]

"New York," as Sinclair Lewis once said, "is not America," to which the residents of many other states would add a fervent "Amen." Yet there is a simultaneous sense in which the Empire State is widely perceived as the quintessence, if not of the United States as it is, then of what it is about to become. From the highbrow humor of the Algonquin Round Table to the broader strokes of a David Letterman "top ten" list; from the Metropolitan Opera to the Broadway stage; from Madison Avenue to the Garment Center; and from the art galleries of SoHo to the publishing houses of midtown Manhattan, it has endured—for better or worse—as the cultural capital of the New World. Kodak, Xerox, and IBM made New York the early leader in the development of high technology industries. Wall Street remains the financial capital of the nation and its global economy. At the same time, upstate cities have remained virtually detached from the economic boom of the 1990s, farms are disappearing at an increasing rate, and the state's credit rating is among the nation's very worst.

New York's political history is studded with innovations: Al Smith's initiatives in passing minimum wage and worker safety laws anticipated the New Deal by twenty years; Robert Moses created an empire of parks and highways, and a governing structure to go with them, that became prototypes for all fifty states; and the state was a pioneer in creating the nation's first equal opportunity commissions. It has received its share of dubious achievement awards as well. The financial collapse of New York City in the 1970s, and the subsequent bailout of the city by the federal government, continues to serve as a symbol of urban decline. Although its state taxes are comparatively low, its combined state-local tax burden is among the nation's highest. The New York congressional delegation has distinguished itself neither by providing its share of national leaders nor for bringing barrels of federal dollars into the state. And for all of their putative sophistication, New Yorkers probably know less about their own state's government than do the residents of any other state. Voter turnout is shockingly low, and the state's election laws are Byzantine at best. The state's progressive policies are increasingly regarded less as prototypes of what ought to be than as cautions against the paving stones of good intentions. In the words of *The Almanac of American Politics*, "The noble aim of creating a public sector which would guarantee cheap rents, topnotch public schools and colleges, public hospitals, instead guarantees that none of these will be available. . . . The attempt to create a fail-safe society had produced a sure-to-fail government."[2]

This then, is a tale of two states: a state that is at once the richest and the poorest, sophisticated yet politically detached, liberal in intents yet slow to deliver. Our purpose in this book is to explain the politics of this dualism, giving particular attention to the changes in recent years that have challenged if not overthrown the Empire State's tradition of political liberalism. Is New York governed as badly as many of its citizens believe? How does the political system work? From our perspectives in the worlds of academic political science on one hand, and of practical politics on the other, what we have tried to write is a citizen's textbook, a book that at once tries to make sense of what is arguably the nation's most complicated and secretive political system.

Were New York a corporation, the state's finances would rank it eighth in *Fortune* magazine's ranking of the 500 largest corporations. Were it a country, it would be among the world's ten largest. Because it is part of the federal union of the United States of America, it neither can nor should be treated as a significant sovereign nation; but it is important, far more important politically and economically than many national governments that have received considerably attention both from the media and from academics. In part because New Yorkers tend to focus on a more national and global scale, and in part—more parochially—because the state does not require its high school or college students to take a course in New York government, there are almost no books available on the system. Our hope is to fill that gap.

Few governments have ever satisfied all of their citizens or done all that they could to satisfy their needs. Because of its enormous wealth and proud history, there is an expectation that New York is better positioned than most states effectively and efficiently to deliver the goods. The first half of this book is devoted to an analysis of that issue. What we hope to show is that despite its economic and cultural advantages, New York is an extraordinarily difficult state to govern. The bond of a common political culture, of the kind of basic underlying consensus on fundamental values that makes political discourse productive, is at best minimally in evidence in New York. The cleavages that divide the state ethnically, regionally, and economically, as we argue in Chapter 1, are sharper than in other states, less susceptible to compromise, and—in the final analysis—inimical to good government.

In Chapter 2 we turn to the federal system and to the state's standing as of one of fifty in a national union. Moving beyond the commonplace observation that New York sends more tax money to Washington than it gets back, we try to depict the many facets of the state's competitive disadvantage vis-à-vis the other states. We also examine the state's ridiculously complex system of local government, perhaps America's most bizarre and inefficient. In Chapters 3 and 4, we move to politics: to voters and nonvoters in Chapter 3; to interest groups, influence wielders, and unofficial centers of power in Chapter 4. The election of 1994 marked a watershed in New York politics that seemed to mark a sharp break with the state's liberal traditions. But, to the intense disappointment of Governor George Pataki's more enthusiastic backers, the changes effected in his two terms in office have been far less extensive than they either expected or hoped they would be. What we try to show in Chapters 3 and 4 is that the political system in New York is almost innately "conservative," not in the ideological sense so much as in the sense that it is structured to resist change. Every political system is paralleled by a shadow government of private centers, sometimes called the permanent government, to which it must generally defer on key issues. Electoral systems, moreover, are artifacts that can be and usually are structured in defense of those who have benefited from them in the past. In New York, both systems are almost uniquely ossified.

How does all this work in practice? In Chapters 5 through 7 we look at the actual process of governance. The election of 1994, while it produced fewer substantive changes in policy than it seemed to portend, marked a shift—not just from liberal to conservative in ideology—but in the basic ways in which the political system worked (or failed to work) at the state level. At a superficial level, there was a key change in what had become a stable pattern of party control in which, for the two decades of the Carey-Cuomo years, the Democrats had controlled the governorship and the state assembly while the Republicans ran the state senate. The change in party control of the governor's mansion altered the dynamic of the system only marginally: although Governor Pataki and Senate Majority Leader Joseph Bruno came in on the same wave, it was not long before that wave broke on the beach of political realities and the three-way pattern of shifting senate-assembly-governor politics typical of the Carey-Cuomo years reasserted itself.

Although the dynamic of partisanship remains much as it was, one of the arguments in this book is that both the substance and style of politics in New York has changed significantly. What we have seen in the past decade is the flowering of a new political paradigm that has its roots in the Cuomo years. It may or may not be permanent, but it has significantly altered the political landscape. New York, in ways that both parody and reflect national changes, has drifted toward a more conservative political agenda. This shift away from liberal democracy is a shift not simply in the substance of politics but of process as well. The substantive shift is perhaps best symbolized through a crude assessment of the legacies of the state's most prominent governors: George Clinton made the state the commercial center of the New World by building the Erie Canal; Al Smith virtually invented the welfare state; Roosevelt, Lehman, and Dewey created the parkway and thruway systems; Nelson Rockefeller built the state university. If Mario Cuomo and George Pataki leave such legacies it will be in the form of prisons.

Divided government has become the norm in New York politics. Not since 1974 have the executive branch and both houses of the legislature been in the hands of the same political party. More important, the divided legislature is frozen in place with the assembly almost unassailably Democratic and the senate firmly Republican. In almost no other state do incumbent legislators need to worry less about defeat, yet with their feet locked in the permafrost of permanent division, the two houses of the legislature continue to engage in a ritualistic show of partisan posturing that is too often devoid of real meaning. A system of tight party discipline that in theory could produce a responsible party government that simplifies complicated electoral divisions, and reaches out to the electorate by offering competitive visions of better public policy, seldom does either.

Two States, Two Systems, Two Authors

Social and economic cleavages in New York reinforce and confound each other. There are two New Yorks, both socially and politically; and the political system has become increasingly unwilling and unable to bridge the gap. The authors of this book—though we agree in our basic analysis—remain divided on its significance. Murtaugh, more the insider after two decades in the state legislature, believes that the system in the long run works fairly well, sometimes in spite of itself, and that New Yorkers get from their government pretty much what they want. Schneier, the academic, is less sanguine, seeing the bitter budget battles of the past decade as symptomatic of a system that is simply not working. We have diffused our arguments, melded them in some ways, and tried to write a book that leaves it largely to the reader to make the normative case. What we both think is clear, and what serves as the guiding theme of this book, is that patterns of cleavage and division in New York—regional, partisan, economic, and political—are so extraordinarily dualistic as to put traditional theories of government in the United States to a true test. We also are convinced that the diminished quality of political dialogue, the rise of posturing over substance, and the decline in common civility that others have found invading the halls of the U.S. Congress has gained a strong foothold in New York as well. Whether New York politics represents the triumph of politics over social adversity, or the failure of the system, we leave it to the reader to decide.

This book was Brian Murtaugh's idea. As a member of the state assembly asked to teach a course on state politics at City College, he was frustrated to find that there were no textbooks in print on the subject. As chairman of the department, Schneier—whose primary field of research was focused on the U.S. Congress—agreed to co-author a book on New York. While this might seem to be a classic collaboration between an activist and an academic, reality is more subtle. Murtaugh was inspired to write this book not by his political career, but by his three years as an adjunct professor of political science at the City College of New York. Schneier, professor of political science and chair of the department, became interested less from his academic orientation than from his experiences as an activist in Democratic politics, and as a lobbyist for progressive causes in the state legislature. We do not hide either our political liberalism or our strong Democratic party ties in the pages that follow. But unlike the few recent books published on New York politics, this volume is neither motivated nor funded by ideology. Our goal is more to explain than to advocate.

The outline of this book was in every sense a joint endeavor. Schneier did the bulk of the academic research. Together, and sometimes separately, we interviewed more than sixty present and former members of the legislature (including six party leaders), numerous department heads, budget aides, and lobbyists. Schneier wrote the basic text and we sat down jointly, and more than once on each draft, to work toward a final copy. One of our themes in this book, in which we discuss the increasingly closed, antagonistic nature of politics in New York, is not irrelevant to this discussion of research strategies. There is no doubt that Murtaugh's status in the legislature gave us access to people who would not otherwise have spoken candidly to academics or journalists. Even with this advantage, tight party discipline in the state makes it unusually difficult to get participants to speak on or off the record in such a way that they may somehow be identified. One state senator we interviewed in 1997 begged us not to include him in our list of interviewees when he admitted that party discipline was sometimes a very potent force. In general, however, the willingness of people like former senate majority leader Ralph Marino and former assembly speaker Mel Miller to be open, candid, and highly cooperative is what made this collaboration workable. To the citizens of New York we dedicate this book as an effort to facilitate their understanding of their government, what's right about it, what's wrong, and what the individual citizen can do.

To our wives, families, and friends, we owe the usual debts of forbearance and fortitude. Carolyn and Sean Murtaugh let their husband and father cancel out on more than one vacation activity for two summers running in Lake George. Maggie Schneier read the whole nine yards and let us know where we were getting too cute, too biased, or too arcane for a nonacademic reader.

We were lucky to have Patricia Kolb of M.E. Sharpe as our editor and Jeff Stonecash of Syracuse University as both a reader and a research ally. Our CUNY colleagues, especially Diana Gordon, Larry Fleischer, Ron Hayduk, and John Mollenkopf, were helpful with research advice and information. Murtaugh's Albany staff members and many of his legislative colleagues play key roles in giving us access to sources of information we might not otherwise have considered.

NEW YORK POLITICS

1

The States of New York

In 1524, a Florentine explorer, Giovanni da Verrazano, sailed through the narrows that now bear his name and "discovered" New York harbor. Despite his glowing reports, some eighty-five years went by without further significant exploration. As Mark Twain wrote of a comparable period in the history of the Mississippi, the Hudson and its magnificent natural harbor "was left unvisited by whites during a term of years which seems incredible in our energetic days."[1] Between Verrazano's first sighting and Henry Hudson's more fruitful venture in 1609, Copernicus revolutionized our view of the solar system, Shakespeare wrote most of his plays, Henry VIII divorced or executed all of his wives, and the Reformation began in Europe. In those same years, England, now under the reign of Queen Elizabeth I, defeated the Spanish armada; Ivan the Terrible began and ended his bloody rule as czar of Russia; Tokyo became the capital of Japan; Rubens and Rembrandt painted their greatest masterpieces; and Machiavelli's *The Prince* was posthumously published. By 1609, the Spanish and Portuguese conquests of South America were nearly complete, Europe had begun its colonization of Africa, and Magellan's feat of circumnavigating the globe had become almost commonplace. Only then did a small group of Dutch settlers arrive at the southern tip of Manhattan Island.

Growth and Development

Given the riches of North America, it is difficult retrospectively to understand why the Europeans took so long to appreciate them. Distracted, no doubt, by the more obvious wealth of the Incas and Aztecs, diverted by the lure of spices and other exotic products from climates radically different from their own, and encumbered by a series of religious upheavals and wars,

Europeans first came to North America almost as an afterthought to their age of exploration. The Dutch, in particular, seem never to have paid much attention to their New World outpost in the New Netherlands or its capital city of New Amsterdam, and indeed left its affairs largely in the hands of the privately held Dutch West India Company which viewed its outposts in the Hudson Valley essentially as points of contact for a lucrative fur trade with the Indians.

Box 1.1

The Purchase of Manhattan Island

The origins of most great cities are wrapped in stories and myths of heroic sacrifice and divine guidance. The enduring story of New York City is that of a mercantile transaction in which the wily Dutch supposedly "bought" Manhattan Island for $24.00. The amount and nature of this transaction have been questioned in a variety of ways. Since the Native Americans who allegedly made the deal had no tradition of land ownership, and were not even residents of the island they supposedly sold, it is not at all clear that the Dutch actually got the best of the deal.

Sometimes, however, the real meaning of myths and rituals is best discerned not by focusing on the stories and events themselves but on those who observe and recount them. The story of New York's purchase, as it contrasts the cunning of the white settler with the primitive lust of the natives for beads and trinkets, resonates enduringly with tales of the shrewd city slicker conning the rural rube. It also serves nicely to at least partially absolve subsequent New Yorkers from potential feelings of guilt: unlike other colonies, the tale implies, New York was founded in a commercial deal rather than violent conquest.

"Finally, however," as Burrows and Wallace point out, "as is usually the case with myths and legends, the notion that New York is rooted in a commercial transaction gets at a deeper kind of truth."* Unlike many of the world's great cities, New York was to become neither the military base of an empire nor the seat of religion or government. "Its civic chieftains would be merchants, bankers, landlords, lawyers; its mightiest buildings, office towers. . . . As the twenty-four dollar saga suggests, New York would become a city of deal-makers, a city of commerce, a City of Capital."†

---

*Edwin G. Burrows and Mike Wallace, *Gotham: A History of New York City to 1898* (New York: Oxford University Press, 1999), p. xvi.
†Ibid.

The Dutch were not settling on virgin lands: people had lived in what is now New York for more than five thousand years. Although it is tempting, as Thoreau did in his eulogy to Walden Pond, to contrast the ravages of European settlement with a golden age of unsullied wilderness, "The choice is not between two landscapes, one with and one without a human influence; it is between two human ways of living, two ways of belonging to the ecosystem."[2] The Indians first encountered by the European settlers—the ones from whom Peter Minuit allegedly "bought" Manhattan Island—were members of various tribes of the Algonkians, one of the most peaceable groups on the eastern seaboard. As they pushed up past Albany, the settlers encountered the feistier Five Nations of the Iroquois—the Senecas, Cayugas, Onondagas, Oneidas, and Mohawks—then approaching the height of their population and influence. Contacts between the Dutch and the indigenous peoples were seldom confrontational; but as the Europeans' insatiable lust for furs increased, conflicts intensified. European diseases, to which the Native Americans had no immunity, proved particularly devastating; and the more aggressive settlement patterns of the English and French eventually pushed the Iroquois and Algonkian Nations into a long period of numerical and economic decline.

Patterns of Settlement and Their Legacies

If the Dutch were slow to colonize and reproduce in the New World, their largely British neighbors to the north and east were not. By 1664, when the English captured New Amsterdam, the population of the city had reached barely 1,500; there were close to 50,000 settlers in New England, 9,000 in Boston alone. And while the Dutch confined their settlements largely to the 150–mile section of the Hudson River Valley area between Albany and New Amsterdam, the New England colonists were encroaching rapidly from Long Island, Connecticut, and Massachusetts, pushing the frontier west. When the British fleet in 1664 forced Governor Stuyvesant's surrender of the New Netherlands, it was as much a reflection of demographics as of military might.

The Early Settlements

Despite their minority status and rather swift assimilation into the dominant Anglo culture, the impact of the Dutch was substantial and their legacy continues to give a distinctive twist to both the city and the state. New York City quickly became one of the world's most cosmopolitan cities in which, as early as 1644, it was reported that eighteen distinct languages were spoken.[3] Unlike their fellow settlers in New England, the Dutch did not arrive or settle as religious communities and tended, as a result, to be more tolerant of diversity, more inclined to separate religion from citizenship. This spirit of tolerance would remain a defining characteristic of the New York colony—particularly in New York City—for generations to come. It was, moreover, a self-reinforcing tendency in which "the pluralistic nature of New York's social structure virtually assured a similarly heterogeneous immigrant population."[4]

From the Revolution to the Civil War

On the eve of the American Revolution, New York had already begun both to differentiate itself from the emerging new nation and to embody what it was becoming. Perhaps no colony was more ambivalent about the Declaration of Independence and the war that ensued. Once the war of independence had begun, the British sent their main force to New York and used the city, throughout the conflict, as its headquarters. The British chose New York as their base because of its strategic position midway along the seaboard, and the hope—dashed at the crucial battle of Saratoga—of moving up the Hudson Valley to Canada and cutting the rebel colonies in half. With New York City the principal seat of British power and the hub of Loyalist sentiment, and the Iroquois Indians allied throughout most of the war with the British,

> No other state suffered more for the cause of independence than did New York. Its frontiers blazed constantly in guerilla warfare. Armies marched and countermarched through its principal river valleys, strewing death and destruction behind them. Nearly one-third of the engagements of the war were fought on New York soil. New York City, which controlled most of the commerce of the state, was continuously in enemy hands from 1776 to 1783. Two major fires destroyed many buildings in the great seaport. After British evacuation the population of the city fell to ten thousand, half of what it had been on the eve of revolution.[5]

Both the city and the state were quick to recover. Large tracts of land, confiscated from Loyalists, were widely distributed. And the tribes of the Iroquois nation, loosed from British protection, had—by the end of the eighteenth century—surrendered, or had taken from them, virtually all of their claims to land.

If the Revolution brought independence to the former colonies, it did not dramatically affect the process of governance or the distribution of political power. A Constitution, adopted at the outset of the Revolution, created a strong, elected legislature and, of course, eliminated the veto power of the Royal Governor. It also secured the legal rights of citizens in conformity with the basic patterns of the English legal system. It was, however, silent on the issue of slavery, conferred no rights on Native Americans, and restricted the right to vote to a handful of male property owners. Nor did the newly independent state modify the increasingly resented system of aristocratic land distribution rooted in the Dutch patroon system of the Hudson Valley. While homesteaders were setting up small farms across the newly confiscated Indian lands in western New York, and some independent yeomen staked claims to the estate lands of fleeing Loyalists, one New York farmer in six was a tenant leaseholder. The huge family estates of the Livingstons, Van Rensselaers, Schuylers, and Clarks remained intact until the 1840s despite frequent rent strikes, political agitation, and occasional violence.[6]

The death of the leasehold system came less from political agitation than from the move West that superseded it. The trickle of New Englanders that began settling on Long Island and in Westchester in the 1640s became a torrent in the early nineteenth century. The amount of improved farmland increased from about a million acres in 1784 to 5.5 million acres in 1821, almost all of it on newly cleared, owner-occupied homesteads.[7] Meanwhile, urban areas were growing as well, exploding in size with the completion of the Erie Canal in 1825. Rochester quadrupled its population in a single decade and became the nation's first boomtown. Buffalo and Syracuse grew almost as rapidly once the canal linked the vast riches of the Great Lakes basin with the Atlantic Ocean; and New York City soon became the nation's largest metropolis.

The route connecting the Hudson and Mohawk rivers with the canal and Great Lakes has had a continuing impact on the demography of New York. Because the state's commerce developed along this corridor, it became the logical route, in the railroad boom of the 1840s and 1850s, for major rail beds and—a century later—for the New York state Thruway. Excluding Long Island, more than eighty percent of the state's citizens still reside in counties that lie along this inverted L-shaped route. Once it became the first state to burst through the Appalachian Mountains barrier that divided the coastal cities and ports from the rich farmlands and mineral resources of the Midwest, New York's ascension to a position of commercial and industrial preeminence was swift. By the eve of the Civil War, New York City's bankers had firmly established their supremacy in the world of finance, and "Whether one considers value of output, number of workers employed in manufacturing, or the diversity of industrial production, New York scored first."[8] Access to capital was an important factor in New York's rise, as was transportation; but nothing fed the industrial boom more assuredly than the steadily growing flow of cheap labor through Ellis Island.

As a commercial center for the whole nation, New York was as ambivalent about the Civil War as it had been about the Revolution. The state's black population, by 1860, had declined to less than two percent of the total, most of it centered in Brooklyn and Manhattan where they competed with immigrants for low-level jobs. Slavery had not been abolished in New York until 1827, and legal barriers to racial equality reflected and reinforced the biases of the white majority, which in 1846, 1860, and 1867, refused to approve a constitutional amendment giving blacks the right to vote.[9] Small wonder that the draft riots of 1863, which began as a protest against the ability of the rich to buy exemptions from military service in the Civil War, quickly turned into a lynch party. New York had its share of abolitionists, and as the largest and wealthiest state contributed more men and materials to the Union cause than any other; but the race tensions manifested in the draft riots are as much a part of the state heritage as its contributions to victory.

The Gilded Age

The Civil War intensified the process of industrialization and a growing cleavage between rich and poor. Although it served, if anything, to intensify racial differences in New York City, the war effort tended to diminish native prejudices against the immigrants and to solidify the identity of the newer immigrants with their adopted land. The Irish potato blight of 1845–54, which sent more than three million residents across the ocean, impacted with particular force on New York. Constituting nearly a third of the city's residents in the 1880 census, "The Irish were the first of New York's principal ethnic groups to arrive in large enough numbers to establish themselves as a coherent political force."[10] In 1880, William R. Grace, a self-made millionaire and native New Yorker, became New York City's first mayor of Irish Catholic ancestry, one of a growing number of immigrants and their offspring who had made it to positions of real wealth and leadership in the New World.

Few of his compatriots did so well. While the Irish and other immigrant groups were able to penetrate the city's political and economic elites, the gap between rich and poor loomed large; and a whole set of new immigrants flooding past the soon-to-be completed (in 1886) site of the Statue of Liberty in New York harbor kept the price of labor low. An 1860 allegorical engraving by Winslow Homer, titled "The Two Great Classes of Society," depicted what was to become an increasingly obvious set of dichotomies. On one side, Homer pictured a life of idle leisure: a well-dressed, pipe-smoking man sprawling in a chaise longue before the fireplace; couples in their finest clothes in a box at the Opera House, and a woman with her hair being done by a maid. "Those who have more dinners than appetite," the caption read. On the other side, a starving seamstress, a chicken thief, and two women hovering over a crude cradle as rats scurry through their basement hovel were shown under the banner of those having "more appetite than dinner."[11]

The contrast between the opulent wealth of the Rockefellers, Vanderbilts, and Morgans—most of it newly acquired—on one hand, and the miseries of the urban poor on the other, was probably as great in late nineteenth-century New York City as it has been in almost any society, anywhere in the world. At the same time, upstate New York—and to some extent New York City—was also the scene of a growth of the middle class that was perhaps equally unprecedented in world history. As the entrepreneurial rich rose to new heights of affluence, and the poorest of the poor sunk to new lows of squalor, many of New York's farmers had successfully made the transition from subsistence to commercial agriculture. "In 1870 New York led all other states in the number of farms and value of farm property. . . and its farm population of over one million constituted the largest single occupational group and nearly one-fourth of the total population of the state."[12] Even in the cities, there was a fast rising middle class of skilled artisans, merchants, and, especially toward the end of the century, clerks and junior executives in larger industrial and financial institutions. But it was manufacturing—labor intensive, increasingly productive, highly profitable industrial enterprise—that symbolized the future of the nation and increasingly characterized New York. In the census of 1880, New York became the first state to manifest an urban majority; the United States did not officially become an urban nation until 1920. For more than 150 years, New York, with its access to capital, public transportation, and cheap labor, was the nation's leading industrial state, sometimes accounting for as much as one-sixth of the nation's total output.[13] Those immigrants who lacked the resources to travel beyond their port of entry constituted an enormous reserve labor supply that further fueled an industrial revolution of incredible proportions. By the turn of the century, when the United States passed Great Britain and Germany to become the world's leading economic power, New York, truly now the Empire State, was the engine that pulled the train.

The Twentieth Century

The tremendous influx of industrial wage earners that was experienced throughout New York state in the nineteenth century was accompanied by a less visible but equally dramatic out-migration of farmers. By 1860, although New York was still the nation's number one farm state, "more than 800,000 New Yorkers (one-fourth of those born in the state as of that date) had resettled in the West."[14] A century later, New York had fallen from first to twenty-fifth in farm income. The flatter, more fertile lands of the Midwest, made accessible by newly developed rail and highway systems, made it almost inevitable that New York agriculture would be essentially reduced to such specialty crops as apples and grapes, and to dairy products and fresh produce aimed largely at local markets. But the decline in manufacturing that New York began to experience in the second half of the twentieth century has more complex roots.

In the 1920s, Congress virtually shut off the flow of new immigration to the United States and, of course, to New York. Many of the immigrants who had arrived in the 1890s and early 1900s, meanwhile, came out of the strong socialist and trade union movements of Central Europe, Germany in particular. As the supply of new labor diminished, and the militancy of the existing workforce increased, the state became both a cradle of an emerging American union movement and an incubator of legislation protecting the rights of working people. In the 1920s, even as the Harding and Coolidge administrations were taking the national government in a strongly pro-business direction, Al Smith, as governor of New York, put through a bill reducing the work week to forty-eight hours, a child labor law, and a workmen's compensation law described by Smith—with considerable justification—as "perhaps the most liberal statute of its kind in the world."[15] The Smith administration also funded dramatic increases in state expenditures on education, public works, and parks. Higher taxes were the inevitable result. Although the growth of government slowed in the early years of the Great Depression under the cautious governorship of Franklin Roosevelt, it took off again when Roosevelt became president and Herbert Lehman, his successor as governor, brought the so-called "Little New Deal" to Albany. Laws establishing a welfare system, strengthening organized labor, mandating public education until age sixteen, establishing a minimum wage, and regulating public utilities both complemented and extended similar programs adopted during the first four years of Roosevelt's New Deal in Washington.

The election of Thomas E. Dewey in 1943—the state's first Republican governor since World War I—did not significantly derail this progressive tradition. Extending the system of parkways developed by Robert Moses during the Smith, Roosevelt, and Lehman years, Dewey developed a system of modern highways (including the state thruway that now bears his name) that became a model for other states and eventually for the nation. A decade later, another progressive Republican governor, Nelson Rockefeller, brought New York up to the standards of many other state systems of higher education by making the State University of New York (SUNY) a major institution of scholarship and higher learning. Ironically, it was the Republican Rockefeller who put through the big tax increases that brought New York into the ranks of the nation's higher burden states.

The election of Hugh Carey as governor in 1975 began a period of twenty years in which the Democrats controlled the executive mansion. The Carey-Cuomo years were not marked by the kinds of policy initiatives that marked the tenures of Smith or Rockefeller, but they essentially continued the state's traditions of support for public works, social welfare, and higher education. The Carey and Cuomo years were also marked by a series of fiscal crises unmatched since the Great Depression. New York City's near bankruptcy in 1975 was the first shock wave of what has become an almost steady series of economic tremors at both the state and local levels.

New York in the "Postindustrial" Age

If the Industrial Revolution in the United States essentially began in New York, it ended there as well. Just as New York was the among the first states to have a majority of its workforce in manufacturing, it was also among the first to lose its industrial workforce and record the rise of a service sector majority. The massive and continuing shift away from the production and shipment of goods to the provision of services, and the accompanying shift from blue-collar to white-collar employment characteristic of what has been called "postindustrial society" hit New York first, and it hit hard. Its upstate cities, with aging industrial plants and rigid patterns of union-management relations, were ripe for the shift of manufacturing to the South, West, and overseas, helping to create the high-unemployment area of the northeast and mid-central regions known colloquially as the "rust belt." The total number of production workers in manufacturing industries in New York state fell from roughly two million in the 1960s, to one and a half million in the 1980s, and to fewer than a million in 1994.

Some upstate cities, most notably Rochester, were partially protected from the worst economic impacts of these changes by the employment practices of the Xerox and Kodak corporations.[16] The city of Buffalo, more typically, declined in population by 23 percent, losing more than 100,000 residents between 1970 and 1980 alone. General Electric, which once employed nearly 45,000 in Schenectady, now has more employees in Singapore than the fewer than 6,000 remaining in the place that still calls itself "the Electric City." Nowhere was the change to a postindustrial mode more rapid or dramatic than it was in New York City. By the mid-1990s New York City—once the heart of industrial America—had less than 10 percent of its workforce employed in manufacturing. The city's face has been transformed. "Uses and places associated with the industrial city and the poor declined heavily, while investment surged into office construction, the institutional expansion of hospitals and universities, the conversion of former loft-manufacturing areas, the gentrification of late-nineteenth-century upper class neighborhoods, and the growth of new immigrant neighborhoods."[17] The demography of the city also changed rapidly as a series of economic revolutions produced both new traumas and new opportunities.

New York has the dubious distinction of leading the rest of the nation in its industrial decline. In one frequently cited study, its "manufacturing climate" ranked twenty-third among the twenty-nine industrial states examined. "New York's negative rating," some have argued, "results from a combination of its high average hourly wages, high percentage of union workers, high unemployment and workers' compensation benefits, high state taxes, and poor education systems."[18] Without underestimating the roles played by each of these factors, reality is considerably more complex in the vortex of a massive worldwide economic transformation that is producing revolutionary changes in work, populations, and societies. Many of these changes hit New York first, and they have changed and are still changing the face of the state's population dramatically. We will deal at greater length with the nature of New York's economic transformation in later chapters. We introduce the topic here because of its connection with related demographic changes that are at least equally dramatic.

Race, Class, Geography, and Ethnicity

"Every important aspect of the U.S. demographic situation is linked to every other."[19] Immigrants came to New York because there were jobs; their presence as a pool of cheap labor created more jobs; their fertility rates, economic successes and failures, marriages, divorces, and death rates changed the roles of government and further altered the opportunity structures for new waves of immigrants. Throughout the United States:

> These demographic factors are intimately related to the evolution of our economic and social system, in matters such as the savings rate, the modernization of the South, the shift to a service economy, the gentrification of central cities, and the rate of advancement of employees within organizations. Finally, they are closely related to the economic and geopolitical positions of the United States in the world at large, in such terms as the emerging world division of labor . . . and technological advances in agriculture and medicine.[20]

At the national level, the policy consequences of such transformations—most notably in the connections between the aging of the population and the financing of Social Security, Medicare, and Medicaid—are receiving increasing public attention. As Washington continues to shift the financial burden and policy responsibility for such programs to the states, regional variations loom larger. The composition of a state's population—from the distribution of age groups to its overall educational levels—strongly affects its government's willingness, need, and ability to deal with policy problems. One set of challenges may offset or exacerbate another. New York's population, for example, is aging, not as rapidly as havens of retirees such as Florida and Arizona, but at a higher rate than the national average. As more people retire, the income tax paying workforce shrinks at the same time as the state's costs for programs for senior citizens grow. The aging of New York's native population has been largely offset by waves of relatively young immigrants. Only 5.8 percent of the state's Hispanics and 5.7 percent of the Asians counted in the 1990 census were over sixty-five years of age, compared with 15.9 percent of white non-Hispanics. The relative youth of the Hispanic and Asian cohorts, of course, raises other policy problems in areas like education because they have more school-age children.

Politically and economically, changes of this kind make for a volatile mix. While the young, largely foreign-born newcomers live mainly in the poorer sections of large urban areas, elderly, older immigrant groups are scattered throughout urban, rural, and suburban areas. The competition for government resources thus takes on geographic and ethnic as well as political dimensions.

Old Newcomers and New Immigrants

Of the millions of immigrants who came to the New World through the port of New York, a large number stayed within shouting distance of the Statue of Liberty. As recently as 1950, more than half of the city's residents were foreign-born or of foreign or mixed decent. But although New York City was the home of more than 70 percent of the state's foreign-born white inhabitants, upstate cities like Rochester (45 percent) and Buffalo (44 percent) were also the homes of large percentages of first- and second-generation immigrants. Even the smaller towns and communities outside these major metropolitan areas were almost one-third foreign born or second generation, this despite the restrictive laws adopted in the 1920s which had slowed the flow of new immigrants almost to a trickle.

The major ancestral groups succeeding the early Dutch and British settlers were largely German and Irish in the mid-nineteenth century; Italian and Eastern European around the turn of the century; and black and Puerto Rican in the years surrounding World War II. Liberalization of the immigration laws in 1965 brought a fifth wave of settlers dominated by Asians, Caribbean blacks, and a different, highly diverse group of Latinos. None of these groups have been randomly distributed either occupationally or in their places of residence. On the contrary, there are whole communities throughout the state that include virtually no Asians, Latinos, or blacks; others that are almost entirely Polish; still others that remain essentially English and Dutch.

No single census can render a full picture of the state's ethnic profile, and many citizens find it difficult to trace a distinctive foreign heritage; but the 1990 census question asking nonimmigrants to report their own perceived ancestries put Germany, Italy, and Ireland in a near tie for first, with England next, followed by Poland, France, Russia, and the West Indies.

In the decade of the 1980s, New York state's population was deceptively stable, growing by a modest 2.5 percent to 17,990,455 in 1990 from 17,558,072 in 1980. This seeming stability masks what was in fact a decade of enormous churning and mobility. As the number of Asians more than doubled and the percentage of Hispanics increased to 12.3 from 9.4, these two groups alone added nearly a million persons to the state's total, which means, by inference, that very close to that number of non-Hispanics and non-Asians left the state. Within the state, too, there have been dramatic shifts. One study, cited by Glazer, estimated an overall out-migration of 15 percent of New York City's population in just one five-year period between 1975 and 1980. The more successful of these emigrants, whites and Asians, by-and-large, moved "up," it appears, to nearby suburbs in New York, New Jersey, and Connecticut, while the less successful—largely black and Puerto Rican— moved backed to their Southern and Caribbean roots.[21] In both cases, it appears as if their places were taken by new immigrants who have settled almost entirely in and around the city: fully 90 percent of the foreign born counted in the 1990 census were found in the New York City metropolitan area, most of them in the city itself. There is little doubt, moreover, that the census seriously undercounts newer immigrants, undocumented aliens in particular.

Many of these new immigrants, presumably, will one day follow their predecessors to the suburbs and beyond. Or at least some of them will. Others, locked by tradition or economic necessity, will doubtless remain. A few of the earlier immigrant groups continue to reside largely in urban areas. As shown in Table 1.1, only 6 percent of those claiming Russian ancestry, and 7 percent of those describing themselves as Polish, live in rural areas, as contrasted with almost half of the Dutch. But the most striking demographic fact is the extent to which one of the later waves of immigrants—that which brought blacks and Puerto Ricans to the city half a century ago—remains largely locked in to urban areas (note the census category "West Indian" in Table 1.1), thus compounding the political and social impact of ethnicity. Economic differences further reinforce these differences.

Wealth and Poverty

The 1980s were hard on America's poor and good for the rich. While the incomes of the wealthiest 1 percent more than doubled, those of the poorest

Table 1.1

Percentage of Persons of Various Reported Ancestries Living in Rural Areas, 1990

Ethnic ancestry	% Rural
Dutch	47
English	37
French	39
German	28
Irish	22
Italian	12
Polish	7
Russian	6
West Indian	1

Source: U. S. Bureau of the Census,1991.

40 percent actually fell.[22] The same pattern appeared in New York state, but to an even greater degree. The real income of New York's poorest 20 percent—according to the Center on Budget and Policy Priorities—declined by a whopping 9.7 percent compared with a median national decline of just 2.8 percent. New York's wealthiest 20 percent, conversely, augmented their incomes by 20.3 percent, in this period, compared with a national average increase of only 8.3 percent.[23] The result, as summarized by one New York think tank in 1995, was that:

> The gap between rich and middle class families in New York was the 39th worst in the United States, and the gap between rich and poor families in New York state was the 46th worst. A 1994 study by Professor John Haveman of Purdue University found an even greater degree of inequality in New York relative to the rest of the nation. Professor Haveman used family income data for 1991, 1992 and 1993 to compare the mean incomes of the wealthiest 20 percent and the poorest 20 percent of each state's families. He found that except for Louisiana, New York had the most unequal distribution of income in the country.[24]

By 1997, the boom in the stock market combined with welfare "reforms," and continuing sluggishness in manufacturing and service industries increased these inequalities still further. In its most recent study, the Center for Budget Priorities found that, "The average income of [the] top fifth New York families is 19.5 times greater than that of the bottom fifth. This is the biggest difference of all states and is far worse than the national average of 12.7."[25]

These disparities, moreover, have important regional and ethnic correlatives. Long Island's suburban Nassau County, at one extreme, contains significant pockets of poverty, but its 1990 median household income of $54,283 was almost two and a half times that of the Bronx ($21,944), on one hand, and of rural Franklin County ($21,794) on the other. And the income differentials *within* these counties are equally striking: in Nassau the 1989 household median income ranged from $32,909 in Hempstead to $92,390 in Manhasset; in the Bronx, from $11,228 in the South Bronx to $29,825 in the west.[26]

Nathan Glazer, whose early studies of race and ethnicity virtually defined the field, recently reflected on his own work and others as follows:

> In the 1950s and 1960s, it was reasonable to project that the newest entrants into New York's complex ethnic mix, blacks and Puerto Ricans, would in time rise in the city's economic structure and become only modestly differentiated, in economic position and political power, from those who had preceded them—just as the Jews and Italians before them rose, in the economic and political spheres, to the level of the Irish and Germans who had preceded them. This was the expectation voiced by Oscar Handlin in *The Newcomers*, and it was my expectation in *Beyond the Melting Pot*. But it hasn't happened.[27]

Just as civil rights laws and attitudes were changing the job atmosphere for the better, and as the last wave of black and Puerto Rican migrants hit New York City, the nature of the job market shifted dramatically. Between 1950 and 1970, the number of jobs in the city increased by about 275,000, with a net increase in almost 575,000 jobs in the service sector more than offsetting—in gross economic terms—the loss of close to 300,000 jobs in goods-producing industries which were traditionally the main sources of employment for poorly educated immigrants.[28] The factory jobs that had served as springboards to the success of previous immigrant groups were simply not there for those arriving in this period. African Americans arriving from the South often lacked the educational background, and Puerto Ricans the linguistic ability, to compete for jobs in the growing service sectors. "At the other end of the economic distribution, the most rapidly growing and remunerative occupations in the advanced corporate services largely excluded blacks and Latinos,"[29] who, unlike some of the newer immigrants, did not have the capital resources to start their own small businesses.

New groups of immigrants—Asians in particular—have far outstripped both blacks and Puerto Ricans economically and in terms of educational achievement. More strikingly, newly arrived Hispanics have been doing better than Puerto Ricans, and new immigrant blacks are doing better than the blacks of native origin. These groups, as Glazer puts it, "have taken the kind of immigrant path that was projected for blacks and Puerto Ricans 20 and 30 years ago, but which for some reason they have failed to follow."[30] Although the experiences of recent immigrants would seemingly suggest that the traditional "queuing system" defined by Glazer still permits successive generations of first-generation migrants to "make it" in the larger society, some important caveats are worth noting.

Unlike earlier waves of immigrants, those admitted to the United States under the reformed immigration rules of recent decades have had generally to meet high standards of education and training, and to have sufficient resources or family ties to live on their own. Thus, the portrayal of Asian Americans as some sort of "model" minority because of their rapid achievement of middle- and upper-class status "belittles the significance of a simple historical fact: that in the 1970s two of every three previously employed Asian immigrants had a professional, technical, or managerial background. The fact of this extremely skewed cohort goes a long way toward explaining the Asian 'success' story."[31] Those Asian immigrants who came without educational degrees or family resources found very different economic realities in the textile sweatshops or restaurants of Chinatown, thus displaying a "bifurcation in the immigration flow . . . even sharper than for other groups."[32] But while there are substantial pockets of poverty among the new immigrants, many thousands of whom have been unable to put their professional training to appropriate use, and while rural white poverty is quite widespread, particularly in the north country, the low end of the economic scale in New York state is disproportionately filled with urban blacks and Puerto Ricans. And that low end is low indeed.

One measure of the gap between the very poor and the rest of the state is found in 1989 household income data compiled by school district by the state education department. Median household income for the state in 1989 was $32,965. There were two school districts, Chappaqua and Scarsdale in Westchester County, in which more than half of the families made more than $100,000; and at the other end of the scale, eighteen in which median income fell below $20,000. Of these extremely low-income districts, one includes the city of Buffalo, nine are in New York City, and eight are in rural areas, mostly upstate. As may be seen in Table 1.2, the poorest of these poor districts are in New York City and are largely black and Hispanic. One of the upstate high-poverty districts—Kiryas Joel in Ulster County—is a rather unique community of highly Orthodox Jews. Two others—Salamanca and Salmon River—include major Indian reservations. The five remaining rural districts testify to the fact that neither poverty nor welfare is race specific. A majority of New York's public assistance families are white, and many of them live in small towns like Herkimer. The rural poor, moreover, are almost as unlikely as their urban counterparts to go to college.

Table 1.2

The Face of Poverty in New York: Income, Education, and Ethnicity in the State's Poorest School Districts

Town or district	Median family income	% Welfare	% College graduates	% White	% Black	% Hispanic	% Other
Friendship	19,798	19	8	98	2	—	—
Salamanca	19,494	10	8	76	—	1	23
Margaretville	19,446	7	10	92	—	8	—
Buffalo	18,482	19	16	37	51	10	3
Brushton Moira	19,670	12	6	100	—	—	—
Salmon River	19,851	9	7	46	—	—	54
Herkimer	19,217	8	12	97	2	—	1
Little Falls	19,923	6	11	98	1	—	1
Kiryas Joel	14,702	18	5	90	—	10	—
Bronx 7	11,228	42	4	—	32	67	2
Bronx 9	13,604	36	6	—	39	59	2
Bronx 12	16,527	33	6	1	31	66	3
Brooklyn 14	18,241	25	8	9	21	68	—
Brooklyn16	15,990	28	7	—	89	10	—
Brooklyn 23	15,133	34	5	1	84	15	—
Brooklyn 32	16,256	33	5	1	30	68	—
Manhattan 4	13,495	37	9	2	35	61	1
Manhattan 5	14,939	22	12	75	24	1	—
State Averages	32,965	9	22	58	20	16	5

Source: The University of the State of New York, New York: The State of Learning (Albany: State Education Department, 1995), Appendix and Table 1.

When the job market for the unskilled was shriveling in the 1970s and 1980s, so was the government's "safety net" of job training, education, and welfare programs. In New York City, as a result of these trends, "Poverty rose from 15 percent in 1975 (about 20 percent over the national average), to 23 percent in 1987 (almost twice the national average.)"[33] There were, to be sure, similar trends in other parts of the state; and it would be highly misleading to conclude that high rates of poverty and high concentrations of racial and ethnic minorities could not be found in other parts of the state. Near suburbs such as Mount Vernon, New Rochelle, and Niagara Falls, for example, are less than 50 percent non-Hispanic white; and New York City as a whole has a mean family income that far exceeds that of most upstate counties. Upstate cities, such as Buffalo and Syracuse, have poverty, welfare, and unemployment rates that frequently exceed those of New York City. Yet there is really no question that upstate-downstate differences are as profound and significant in New York as in any of the United States.

Upstate, Downstate, and in Between

The north-south split in California is cultural, and increasingly ethnic, but has few economic correlatives; Michigan, Illinois, and Pennsylvania display significant conflicts between large urban centers with large minority populations, and surrounding rural and suburban areas of very different ethnic, economic, and political hues. But New York City stands alone among American cities in its relationship to the state of which it is a part. Size alone sets New York City apart: its population exceeds that of the nation's next two cities, Los Angeles and Chicago, combined, and has accounted for roughly half of the state's population for more than a century. In almost every way—in its wealth as well as its poverty, in its culture as in its crime—it is a force too large to ignore. More than one contemporary New Yorker would concur in the 1905 observation of George Washington Plunkitt that "The feeling between this city and the hayseeds that make a livin' by plunderin' it is every bit as bitter as the feelin' between the North and the South before the [Civil] War."[34] In the 1930s, when Abbott Low Moffat, the Republican chairman of the Assembly Ways and Means Committee invited a fellow committee chairman to visit him and his wife in the city, his colleague demurred. "Well, I tell you, Moffat, I ain't been in New York [City] for 30 years, and I don't intend to go there."[35]

Many of the dualisms that divide New York state are differences between state and city, but the boundaries between what New Yorkers mean by the terms "upstate" and "downstate" are surprisingly elusive. The core of New York City, Manhattan Island, is, relatively speaking, as small in population

Box 1.2

Ah, Wilderness!

While New York is among the most urbanized states in the union, even its own residents often fail to realize how vast and thinly populated much of the state is. There are more than 50,000 people per square mile living in Manhattan. Not counting tourists and commuters, each of them has a little over five hundred square feet, something like the space between the goal line and the fifteen yard line at Giant Stadium.

At the other extreme, there are 3.1 persons per square mile in Hamilton County. Folks in this area—just an hour or so north of Albany—could each put a thousand football fields on their share of the land, and still have room left for parking. These patterns are, of course, largely the product of economic and social choices having little to do with government. New York, however, was the first among the American states to choose to preserve its wilderness heritage. Article XIV, Section 1 of the 1894 constitution provides that more than two million acres in the Adirondacks and Catskills "shall be forever kept as wild forest lands." To this day, no other state has so sweeping and strong a land conservation provision inscribed in its constitution.

Not surprisingly, few other states—even those that are far more recently and thinly settled—have better preserved their wilderness areas. There are places within the Adirondack preserve where one can entirely escape the sights and sounds of human habitation. You can go so deep into the woods that you will neither see the glow of distant electric lights nor hear the faintest rumble of far-off trucks and trains. There is not another place east of the Mississippi River in which this is possible.

(about a fifth of the city's total) as it is large in image. Its surrounding boroughs are often as much at odds with Manhattan as in alliance, and the boundaries between eastern Queens and neighboring communities in Nassau County, or between the North Bronx and Westchester, are virtually indiscernible. The larger upstate cities, such as Rochester and Buffalo, moreover, have as much, if not more, in common with the Big Apple than with the small towns immediately surrounding them, while the city's smallest borough, Staten Island, identifies somewhat tenuously with the metropolis and has actually voted overwhelmingly to secede.

As difficult as it may be for a New Yorker to trace the precise geographic boundary between "upstate" and "downstate," the chances are that he or she has a fairly precise cultural concept of the division. A citizen of Staten Island, whatever his or her feelings about secession, feels a closer identity with Manhattan than, say, Buffalo.[36] And even the resident of Yonkers—though less than a mile from the New York City line—is likely to take a certain satisfaction in being from Westchester rather than the Bronx. There are important demographic distinctions between the state's two dominant regions. As noted, most of the extreme concentrations of poverty and wealth are found in New York City. Ninety percent of the newer immigrants live in its metropolitan area. Almost all of the state's substantial Jewish population lives within fifty miles of Times Square. And the bulk of the state's openly gay community is in the city, more specifically, in Manhattan.

Perhaps most important are the significant and long-standing political differences and distinctions between the two New Yorks. While the Democratic Party has significant pockets of support upstate, particularly in urban centers like Albany and Rochester; and while Republican candidates run well in parts of New York City—on Staten Island and in the Bay Ridge section of Brooklyn, for example—the centers of gravity of the two parties are clearly downstate and urban for Democrats, upstate and rural for Republicans. Thus in Governor George Pataki's 1994 victory over Mario Cuomo, he received only 27 percent of the vote in the five boroughs of New York City; 49 percent in the immediate suburbs of Nassau and Westchester counties, and in the upstate counties surrounding Albany, Buffalo, Rochester, and Syracuse; and better than 63 percent in the rest of the state. In the state assembly, only three of the 61 members representing New York City are Republicans; the rest of the members divide 52 Republican to 38 Democrats. Of the non-city Democrats, 16 are from suburban districts in Westchester, Nassau, Rockland, and Suffolk counties; 14 from the upstate metropolitan areas of Buffalo, Albany-Schenectady, Syracuse, and Rochester; and only 8 from all other parts of the state.

Demography and Politics

The separate and distinctive political loyalties of key blocks of voters have always played an important role in explaining New York politics. Regional differences, between upstate and downstate in particular, can be traced to the colonial period when they tended to overlap both with vestiges of the distinctions between Dutchmen and Yankees, and with growing economic differences between the increasingly commercial and industrial city, on one hand, and the agrarian countryside on the other. As newer immigrant groups began to arrive in significant numbers in the nineteenth century, the picture grew more complex. Lee Benson has argued that "at least since the 1820s, when manhood suffrage became widespread, ethnic and religious differences have tended to be *relatively* the most important sources of political differences."[37] What McNickle says of the city applies to the state as well: each of the "major ancestral groups to settle New York . . . brought a distinct cultural heritage . . . , and each responded differently to the environment it found, creating a unique ethnic identity in the process. Among the things that distinguish these groups from each other were their different approaches to politics, and the tendency of each to vote in a coherent pattern according to ethnic affiliation. As a consequence, the numbers of each group casting ballots in an election, and the nature of their voting patterns, explain electoral results in New York City with more power and consistency than any other form of analysis."[38]

Statewide, these ethnic patterns were slow to emerge. A political establishment—always Protestant, male, white, and largely of Dutch and British descent, though occasionally including Germans—consistently dominated elective offices, the higher levels of the bureaucracy, and the judiciary throughout the eighteenth and nineteenth centuries. With rare exceptions, the same small circle of men more or less continuously dominated New York state's major social and economic institutions since the early days of colonial Dutch rule. The first post-revolutionary governor of New York, who took office in 1777 and remained influential through the end of the century was, in a sense, the exception that tests the rule. George Clinton was wealthy, of British ancestry, and well-connected (he was a close friend and business partner of, among others, George Washington); but Clinton was never quite comfortable with the aristocracy, nor they with him: "family and connections," Philip Schuyler somewhat disdainfully wrote to John Jay in supporting Clinton's candidacy for governor, "do not entitle him to so distinguished a predominance; yet he is virtuous and loves his country, has abilities and is brave."[39] Far more typical of New York's early governors was Jay himself who actually left his position as Chief Justice of the United States in order to run for governor of New York. Through most of the state's early years, its governors were—like Jay—gentleman farmers, of English or Dutch descent, from the still rural parts of what is now the city or the nearby Hudson Valley.

Who Governs?

William Bouck, who was elected in 1842, has the distinction of being the first true dirt farmer and the first German-American to serve as governor; his successor, Silas Wright, was the first from upstate. Gradually, in the middle of the nineteenth century, the agrarian aristocracy of gentlemen farmers lost its hold on the governorship to the new captains of industry, and those with legal training. In rough terms, the socioeconomic evolution of the governorship parallels that described by Dahl in New Haven:

In the first period (1784–1842), public office was almost the exclusive prerogative of the patrician families. In the second period, the new self-made men of business, the entrepreneurs, took over. Since then, the "ex-plebes" rising out of working class or lower middle class families of immigrant origins have prevailed.[40]

The pivotal figure in terms of the modern governorship is Al Smith, who served from 1919 to 1920 and again from 1923 through 1928 when he ran, unsuccessfully, for president. Aside from the unfortunate William Sulzer—the only governor in the state's history to be removed by impeachment—Smith was the first urban, working class, non-Protestant to have reached the state's highest office. The product of Tammany Hall, New York's political machine, Smith not only won statewide elections four times, he won the somewhat grudging respect of those whose view of both the city and its politics was not generally favorable. Since Smith, and in part because of him, religion, region, and ethnicity have played a far less important role in statewide politics with the governorship going to wealthy, Protestant patricians like Rockefeller and Roosevelt; urban Catholics (Carey and Cuomo); a Jewish banker (Lehman); and a suburban white ethnic (Pataki). No woman, black, or Latino has ever won the nomination of a major party for governor, and comptroller Carl McCall's 1998 decision not to run was widely interpreted in the media as an indicator that prejudice against African Americans is still too strong in New York to make such a race winnable.

The demographic profile of the legislature has shifted dramatically, but it strikingly underscores the tendency of geographic and ethnic differences to be mutually reinforcing. Of the twenty-one assembly members of African-American descent in 1999, twenty were from the five largest cities, as were all six Hispanics. All nine minority members of the senate were from New York City. Women have increased their presence in the legislature to the extent that, with 18 percent of the overall membership, they are just under the national average in state legislatures of 21 percent. Looking just at leadership positions, in this case committee chairs in the state assembly, Leonard Ruchelman traced some rather striking demographic changes between 1931 and 1965. During this period, the percentage of farmers declined from 30 percent to zero, while "professionals" (mostly lawyers) went from 33 percent to 69 percent. In the same 35 years, the percentage of non-Protestants increased from 6 to 97. Those who Ruchelman labeled "ethnics" jumped from 3 percent of the committee chairs in 1931 to 89 percent in 1965.[41] We can attribute some of this change to a shift in party control: the Democrats, whether in 1931 or 1965, were considerably more likely to be non-Protestant ethnics and they had, by 1965, taken control of the assembly. Nonetheless, the shift is quite striking. Equally striking is the shift in occupations traced by Benjamin and Nakamura in the years since 1964. Looking at the official guide to state government in 1964, Benjamin and Nakamura found not a single member of either house listing his or her occupation as "legislator." "By 1988, however, more than two-thirds of Assembly members and more than half of Senators were describing themselves not as lawyers, business-men or consultants but as legislators, the trend more evident in both houses among Democrats than Republicans."[42] Alan Ehrenhart's description of members of the U.S. Congress is apt:

> The large number of lawyer-legislators obscures the truth about who these people are. They are not, by and large, successful lawyers who left thriving partnerships to run for public office. Rather they are political activists with law degrees. This does not mean that they are failures; it simply means that they are lawyers by training rather than by profession.[43]

Even more than in the Congress, moreover, legislators in Albany are vir-tually assured of reelection. In 1996, 97 percent of the state senators who ran for reelection won, as did 98 percent of the assembly members. In 1998, not a single incumbent in either house lost; only one, in 2000. The average ten-ure of a New York state senator, 13 years, or assembly member, 10 years, is considerably above the national average.

The professionalization of politics reflected in these figures is, superfi-cially, an historic reversion to form. In the days of political machines like New York City's Tammany Hall, literally thousands of people made their livings through politics, displacing the "amateur" patricians who lived either on inherited wealth or dabbled in politics during occasional interludes from their real professions. The machine afforded newer ethnic groups—New York's Irish in the case of Tammany—access to jobs from which they had previously been barred. From the water department and the police force to the higher reaches of city and state politics, immigrants used their numbers and organizing abilities to achieve what wealth and status had previously bought. The post machine professionals of modern New York politics, while not strictly patrician in their upbringing, tend to come from upper-middle class, professional backgrounds. They are more in the style of the suburban, Yale-educated George Pataki than the street-tough, Lower East Side Al Smith.

The literature on gender, ethnicity, and politics points to a variety of fac-tors ranging from prejudice on the part of voters to lack of confidence on the part of potential candidates to explain the under representation of various groups. In general, political representation lags behind group achievement in other fields that serve, more or less, as prerequisites to successful political careers such as higher education, professional status, and money. Women, for example, have only recently entered the legal profession in significant numbers; and since law has long served as a stepping stone to politics in the United States, the political under representation of women has roots that run deep into the socioeconomic fiber. Although nearly half of today's law school graduates are female, the comparable percentage for the 1960s when today's generation of elected officials was starting out, was less than 5 percent. Unlike in the time when Al Smith worked his way up in the organization, the road to politics today almost requires professional training and personal wealth, a situation that often gives women and minorities a double handicap. The problem is compounded in a state like New York where the professionalization of politics has lengthened the typical terms of incumbents, shrinking the available number of winnable seats in the legislature and in offices (such as city and town council seats) that are often the stepping stones to higher office.

New York, in most respects, is "unusual" only insofar as it fails to meet expectations that it might somehow be more diverse in its representation of minority populations than other states. Its history of bringing groups, like the Irish, into public office makes this disjunction more striking. The newest ethnic groups—most particularly Asians and non-Puerto Rican Hispanics—have been virtually shut out of elective office. New immigration rules that make it far more difficult for newcomers to obtain citizenship and the franchise are certainly a factor. Beyond the problem of fielding suitable candidates, moreover, the new minorities often lack cohesion: there is—in anything but the most abstract sense—no "Asian" or "Latino" community; there are Korean, Chinese, Filipino, Dominican, Puerto Rican, Ecuadorian, and other communities that may or may not have common identities. For these and other reasons, neither the Hispanic nor the Asian-American communities in New York have developed sufficient levels of what Torres calls "*community infrastructure*, the underlying foundation of organizations, networks, and traditional group practices that bind a group together"[44] to achieve high levels of direct ethnic representation. Even on the 51–member New York City Council there are no Asian-Americans and only one Dominican, despite estimates that put their shares of the population at roughly 7 percent.

Whether the gender and ethnicity of legislators has any important bearing on the nature of the representative relationship is a subject of continuing debate. One could argue that an experienced, sympathetic member of the city council or state legislature who knows what levers to pull can do more for his or her minority constituents than can a novice of any background. There is no doubting, however, the symbolic importance of politics in marking a group's social acceptance in society. The data on the social origins of

New York's elected officials are important indicators of assimilation that point up the nearly complete acceptance of third-wave immigrants like the Italians, the still-ambiguous status of African Americans, and the even more tenuous position of Asians, Hispanics, and women.

A New York State of Mind?

Ethnic distinctions aside, is there, as the song proclaims, "a New York state of mind"? It doesn't take much of an ear for language to distinguish the accents of Texans and Brooklynites. Beyond language differences are a whole set of subtle and not-so-subtle shadings of attitude, tone, and taste that most Americans more or less intuitively recognize and that have become the subjects of innumerable songs, stories, and jokes. Many of the political differences between the states—differences in voter turnout, party competition, and public policies, for example—have their roots in these kinds of distinctions, which political scientists call political cultures. Difficult precisely to define, they have nonetheless become an important part of the research strategies used to seek an understanding of how different systems work.

The Political Cultures of the Empire State

Daniel Elazar's widely cited work on the political cultures of the American states identifies three major streams of values that were spread across the country by diverse waves of immigrants and settlers. The states, in Elazar's classification, are primarily *individualistic, moralistic*, or *traditionalistic*.[45] In broad outline, the moralistic culture, with its roots in the Puritan communities of early New England, sees government as a positive force in the lives of citizens, and stresses the importance of citizen participation, issue-oriented campaigns, and high ethical standards in government. The traditionalistic culture of the South and Southwest has its roots in the plantation aristocracies of the Old South and continues to stress a role of government limited essentially to the maintenance of the existing social order. New York, Elazar suggests, belongs among the third group of states, those whose tradition is essentially individualistic.

Individualistic states, with their roots in commerce and industry, tend to limit government intrusions into private activities; to downplay the importance of participation in politics; and to be more than usually tolerant of political corruption. While New York has certainly had its share of scandals, and remains near the low end of measures of citizen participation, its governments in the twentieth century have been activists in the extreme. Elazar's schema, if it works at all in a mobile society, needs to be modified with regard to New York to take into account the coexistence of a competing, sometimes dominant, moralistic subculture that reaches back to the New Englanders who overwhelmed the Dutch nearly 350 years ago, and has been heavily leavened by the addition of a wide diversity of immigrant cultures. Using Elazar's classifications, George Pataki, in his determination to limit enforcement of laws encouraging voter participation, in his opposition to campaign finance reforms, and—most of all—in his agenda of dramatic cutbacks in state services and regulations, would probably be typified firmly in the individualistic mode, as such activist governors as Al Smith, Herbert Lehman, and Nelson Rockefeller were of the moralistic type.

This conflict of cultures, a continuing battle of both style and substance, is so persistent a feature of New York state politics that it makes it all but impossible to use the concept of an overarching "political culture" to describe the state. Dualisms, sometimes overlapping, sometimes not, have persistently punctuated politics in New York: upstate/downstate, rich/poor, native-born/immigrant, individualistic/moralistic, this is the stuff of politics in the Empire State. More important, even if we were to locate a dominant ideology or culture in New York politics, this is not to say that it would be reflected in public policy. Democratic politics is more a refraction than a reflection of public opinion: passed through the lenses of electoral politics, group mobilization, and the governmental process itself, public policy is at best a crude parody of public opinion. Public attitudes, at the same time, are important: they are the seedbeds within which group attitudes are nurtured and politicians grow up. They are the subjects of almost constant polls. Whether there is a dominant "political culture" in New York is an academic question; whether there is a "New York state of mind" is not.

Politics and Public Opinion

While there have been some successful attempts to use Elazar's concept of political culture to predict actual policy differences between the states,[46] and while there are states that can more readily be typed than New York, the concept is clearly more impressionistic than concrete. New York is not Mississippi, and Elazar's essential point—that the differences between New York and Mississippi are deeply rooted in different outlooks on the world—is well taken. It can, moreover, be described in relatively concrete political terms by comparing surveys of public opinion in the fifty states. Looking at this data for the years 1976 to 1988, Erikson, Wright, and McIver found that quite consistently New Yorkers were among the most liberal Americans surveyed, with the state ranking third (behind Massachusetts and Rhode Island) on a broad range of issues. Even when the authors controlled for socioeconomic

Box 1.3

Is New York Different?

Almost since the beginnings of the nation, foreign visitors and the citizens of the other fifty states have commented—usually in a negative manner—upon the distinctive characters of New York City in particular and the State more generally. Herewith a sample:

"New York, like London, seems to be a cloacina of all the depravities of human nature."

—Thomas Jefferson (1823)

"If there ever was an aviary over-stocked with jays it is that Yap-town-on-the-Hudson called New York."

—O. Henry (1920)

"The faces in New York remind me of people who played a game and lost."

—Murray Kempton (1963)

"New York is notoriously the largest and least loved of any of our great cities. Why should it be loved as a city? It is never the same city for a dozen years together. A man born in New York forty years ago finds nothing, absolutely nothing, of the New York he knew."

—*Harper's Monthly* (1856)

"City of the world! for all races are here, all lands of the earth make contributions here."

—Walt Whitman (1871)

"Every day sees visiting firemen in New York not only from the hinterlands of America but from the four corners of the emancipated globe, examining our work and asking for copies of our plans. Why are they here if there is nothing to see?"

—Robert Moses (1941)

"New York is not a finished or completed city. It gushes up. . . . I cannot forget New York, a vertical city, now that I have had the happiness of seeing it there, raised up in the sky. New York has such courage and enthusiasm that everything can be begun again, sent back to the building yard and made into something greater. . . . A city which will be replaced by another city."

—Le Corbusier (1947)

"New York is not America."

—Ring Lardner (1947)

"FORD TO NEW YORK: DROP DEAD."

—President Ford (as paraphrased in a New York *Daily News* headline, 1975) differences—by statistically eliminating the effects of New York's large minority populations and union membership figures—the state's political climate remained, comparatively, among the most liberal in the nation.[47] Even as the country turned to the right in the 1980s and 1990s, the turn in New York was slower to arrive and considerably less decisive than in most other states.

Two aspects of New York's turn to the right are particularly remarkable. First is the complete transformation of the state's Republican Party, which, in the days of Nelson Rockefeller, was both the symbolic and political engine of liberal Republicanism. The upset victories of Ronald Reagan and Alfonse D'Amato in the 1980 Republican primaries—with D'Amato's stunning upset of the incumbent Jacob Javits particularly notable—"rang down the final curtain on the Dewey-Rockefeller-Javits era of liberal Republicanism in New York."[48] With one or two exceptions among senior members of the state's congressional delegation and in the state legislature there are, quite simply, no moderate Republicans left.

The second important characteristic of New York's turn to the right is in the more muted liberalism of the state's Democrats. While their policies have not changed dramatically, Democratic candidates in the Carey and Cuomo years have talked of limiting the growth of government and cutting taxes. "Clearly," as White puts it, "there has been no party realignment in New York state akin to that produced by Alfred E. Smith and Franklin D. Roosevelt. Rather the political changes that occurred during the 1980s might be termed a rhetorical realignment. . . . Rhetorical conservatives are winning elections in New York. . . . Those who do not speak the new language face rejection by a fickle electorate."[49]

The obvious question, of course, is how a state like New York could take this kind of turn to the right. One answer is quite simply that New York was simply moving in the same direction as everyone else. Another possible perspective is that not much really changed either in the basic attitudes of New Yorkers or in public policy. For all of his conservative rhetoric, when it came to most important liberal programs in areas like health, welfare, mass transit, and—more reluctantly—education, Mario Cuomo was firmly in the progressive tradition of Smith and Roosevelt. And for all their fire-breathing conservatism, the Republicans in the legislature were remarkably inclined to work things out. While the legislative gridlock of Cuomo's last four-year term resulted in chronically late budgets and a seeming breakdown in the political process, the total differences between the Republican and Democratic bottom lines never exceeded 2 percent. The highly confrontational rhetoric of party leaders was, when you looked at the bottom line, much ado about almost nothing. Nor were the changes in Pataki's first four years as dramatic as his rhetoric might have suggested or as his conservative supporters might have hoped. Indeed his 1998, election-year budget proposed and produced increases in spending for education, mass transit, health, and even the arts that exceeded any such changes proposed by Cuomo. Finally, to the extent that New York actually has shifted to the right in its politics, the shift must in part be attributed to a changing economy, and in particular to the slow pace of the state's economic recovery in the 1990s with its corresponding threat to the government's already shaky finances. In terms of ideology or—if you will—the state's "political culture," the fact is that "when it comes [to] bread and butter issues like education, health care, the problems of the mentally ill, and mass transportation, most New Yorkers have not abandoned the old liberalism."[50]

2

New York in
the Federal System

The dichotomies described in Chapter 1—between upstate and New York City, between rich and poor, between the cultures of moralism and individualism—continue to play key roles in New York politics; but they explain only a part of the context within which the government acts. Although New York is larger in area, population, and gross domestic product than most members of the United Nations, it is not a fully sovereign state. As part of a federal system, in which power is shared between a strong central government in Washington, D.C. and fifty semi-sovereign states, New York is free to make its own laws about some things, shares its powers with Washington on some others, and has almost nothing to say about policies in such areas as foreign affairs. The Constitution of the United States offers considerably more detail on the respective powers of state and national governments than it does on most other topics; but the language the founders employed in defining this division of powers is, at best, ambiguous.

There is a third layer of government in the United States, a complicated mélange of cities, towns, villages, counties, and special districts. Legally, these local governments do not have the same independence vis-à-vis the state that the states have in the federal system. They are creatures of the state. With their powers derived from state charters, they have, in theory, no sovereign powers: the governor and state legislature of New York could—legally, at least—abolish Syracuse, give Staten Island its independence, or break New York City into fifty separate towns. The federal government cannot do likewise with the states.

The reality of intergovernmental relations in the United States bears only a passing resemblance to this legal ordering. Professor Morton Grodzins is famous for using the analogy of a swirled marble cake to describe the federal system in practice: "The federal system is not accurately symbolized by [a] neat layer cake of three distinct and separate planes. A far more realistic symbol is that of the marble cake. Wherever you slice through it you reveal an inseparable mixture of differently colored ingredients."[1] To make the analogy more accurate, we would need also to set it in motion, to give the mixing of policy powers a dynamic quality in which the relationships between federal, state, and local authorities is in constant flux. And this is pretty much what those who drafted the U.S. Constitution had in mind. "The proposed Constitution," as James Madison put it, "is, in strictness, neither a national nor a federal Constitution, but a composition of both."[2] And while the federal government may be stronger at some times, and the state governments at others, "The people, by throwing themselves into either scale, will infallibly make it preponderate. If their rights are invaded by either, they can make use of the other as the instrument of redress."[3]

The Changing Face of American Federalism

At the heart of the U.S. Constitution's definition of federalism are four key articles. From a states' rights perspective the key phrase is the Tenth Amendment's guarantee that "powers not delegated" to the federal government, nor "prohibited . . . to the States, are reserved to the States. . . ." Since the Constitution specifically enumerates relatively few federal powers, and prohibits the exercise of few state powers, it would seem as if most governmental powers might be "reserved to the states."[4] Although this position still finds an occasional adherent, and produces some powerful political rhetoric, it has little legal or practical standing in the face of three more forceful constitutional provisions and the changed nature of the American economic system. The first of these constitutional provisions is the last paragraph of Section 8 of Article I, the so-called "elastic clause." By giving the federal government the power to "make all laws which shall be necessary and proper to carry into execution" its enumerated powers, the Constitution left a large loophole made larger by the Supreme Court's long willingness to interpret federal powers broadly. Chief Justice Marshall set the tone for subsequent decisions in the landmark case of *McCulloch v. Maryland* where he wrote: "Let the end be legitimate, let it be within the scope of the Constitution, and all means which are appropriate, which are plainly adapted to that end, which are not prohibited, but consist with the letter and spirit of the Constitution, are constitutional."[5]

The second key source of federal power is the commerce clause, also in Article I, Section 8, giving the Congress the power "to regulate Commerce . . . among the several States." Justice Marshall's insistence that the definition of interstate commerce should be "comprehensive," extending to "every species of commercial intercourse"[6] has been carried to the fullest possible degree by subsequent courts, particularly since 1937. Finally, the division of powers between the federal governments and the states has been dramatically reshaped by modern interpretations of the Fourteenth Amendment to the U.S. Constitution. Seeking to avoid Southern retribution against freed slaves following the Civil War, the Fourteenth Amendment guaranteed all citizens—regardless of where they lived—the "equal protection of the laws." And in words that remain controversial, it suggested that the rights of the citizens of the United States would henceforth be the rights of the citizens of each individual state. The U.S. Supreme Court, particularly during the 1953 to 1969 tenure of Chief Justice Earl Warren, increasingly interpreted this to mean that the essential procedural and substantive rights protected against federal action by the Bill of Rights also apply to the states. The First Amendment, for example, says that *"Congress* shall make no law respecting an establishment of religion," thus rather clearly prohibiting a *national* law requiring prayer in schools. Since 1962, the court has said that the Fourteenth Amendment applies this prohibition with equal force to state governments: hence, state laws mandating school prayer, or abridging other First Amendment rights like freedom of speech, are not allowed either. More conservative courts in the 1990s have begun to allow more latitude to the states than they might to the federal government; but despite continuing controversies surrounding the Warren Court's interpretation of the Fourteenth Amendment, its essential limitations on state power remain very much in force. To put it another way, the ability of federal courts—and, with the courts' sanction—of Congress and the president to limit or encroach upon state powers has been very much enhanced by this modern reading of the Fourteenth Amendment.

Whether the Court's recent readings of the Fourteenth Amendment and the commerce clause was historically accurate continues to be a topic of academic and political debate. A strong argument can be made, nonetheless, that whatever the intent of the framers, the economic and social realities of the late twentieth century make many state powers obsolete. A mobile population expects to take its rights with it as it travels, knowing that a religious practice tolerated in New York is not forbidden in Texas. A changing economy has made most commerce "interstate" in nature, regardless of what the courts might say. And the globalization of economic and social forces has served, almost automatically, to enhance the powers of the national government. So has its growing access to money: by granting or withholding funds the federal government can virtually force the states to act in ways that no constitutional doctrine supports. In the 1980s, for example, Congress managed effectively to raise the legal drinking age in every state to twenty-one, this despite a general legal and scholarly consensus that the so-called "police powers"—laws governing crime and morality—are state and not national. What Congress did was simply threaten to deny federal highway funds to any state that refused to raise its drinking age. Within a year, every state had complied. (New York, incidentally, was one of the last and most reluctant: "We are doing this, said one member of the state assembly, "with a gun to our heads.")

Fiscal Federalism from the New Deal through Nixon

An old adage suggests that to understand political power you should "follow the money." One way, then, of tracing the locus of power between and among the different levels of government is to follow the funding trail and ask who spends how much for what? Until the later years of Franklin Roosevelt's New Deal, the bulk of the money spent on domestic government programs was spent by the states. In comparison with today, moreover, the amounts spent at all levels of government were—prior to World War II and the Cold War—relatively modest. Congress, along with presidents like Harding, Coolidge, and Hoover, was reluctant to involve the federal government in major programs, and a series of Supreme Court decisions that sharply divided the respective jurisdictions of the states on one hand, and the federal government on the other, tended further to limit them both.

All this changed with the New Deal. Working with President Roosevelt, Congress laid the foundations of the modern American welfare state, and in 1937 the Supreme Court reversed itself to accept the constitutionality of virtually the entire program. Some of these New Deal programs, like Social Security, were administered almost entirely by the federal government; many others used federal resources to subsidize state and local projects. State activities also expanded in the 1930s, as they too sought to combat the Depression. The result was an almost steady increase in what Hanson calls the "velocity" of federal, state, and local spending on domestic programs from 1927 through 1992.[7]

In cumulative terms, total domestic spending rose from just under 10 percent of the gross domestic product in 1929 to more than 30 percent in the 1990s. The rise in federal spending was particularly substantial. Even if we exclude military spending and national security—which accounted for roughly one out of every five federal dollars spent between World War II and today—the federal share of direct government spending rose as high as 18 percent of the gross national product. Direct state and local spending totaled nearly 15 percent, but much of this was actually money that came to state and local governments through intergovernmental transfers of funds, in particular federal funds granted to state and local agencies. Many of the New

Deal programs established in the 1930s involved what are known as grants-in-aid, and they have become an enormously important part of what state and local governments do.

Grants-in-Aid

A grant-in-aid is a fiscal device by which the federal government encourages state and local governments to do certain things, whether or not it might otherwise be constitutional for the federal government to do them. Grants-in-aid were not invented in the 1930s; but it was not until then that they moved to a prominent position in shaping the contours of the modern federal system. A classic early example of a grant-in-aid was the Morrill Land Grant Act of 1862 which gave each state 30,000 acres of public land for each of its representatives in Congress for the express purpose of establishing agricultural and mechanical arts colleges. Under the Morrill Act, the states could get the land only if they provided some of their own resources to meet certain minimal federal standards. The land was offered, in other words, as something of a bribe designed to get the states to do something the federal government thought they should do but was reluctant to do itself. An act of Congress establishing a system of federally funded colleges would almost certainly have been ruled unconstitutional, even if Congress had wanted to do it, but no such strictures applied to a simple transfer of land.

The number and scope of such grant-in-aid programs increased markedly in the 1930s as the Roosevelt administration cooperated with the states to combat the depression. During and after World War II, federal grants-in-aid accounted for an average of roughly 10 percent of state and local expenditures. Unlike the Morrill land grants, moreover, most of the New Deal programs were programmed to continue over a number of years, thus inculcating enduring relationships between state, local, and national administrators. The number and velocity of federal grant programs rose slowly in the years following World War II, dramatically in the 1960s. During Lyndon Johnson's administration alone, more than 200 new grant-in-aid programs were created. Even Richard Nixon, whose 1968 campaign call for a "new federalism" returning power to the states, continued the basic trend. Nearly 100 new categorical aid programs were created in the Nixon-Ford years, eight years in which the overall value of federal grants more than doubled. The Nixon years also saw the continuation of a trend, begun in the sixties, toward more direct relationships with local governments with grant programs sometimes bypassing the states entirely and putting federal funds directly in the hands of local officials. The three layers of government, which traditionally had remained relatively disconnected, increasingly came to resemble Professor Grodzin's marble cake.

The expansion of grant-in-aid programs that essentially began in 1964 as part of Lyndon Johnson's Great Society changed the nature of federal-state-local relations. Prior to 1964, as Walker puts it, the pattern of intergovernmental relations "was only moderately 'marbleized'" He goes on to note that:

> A full 92 percent of the aid funds in 1960 went to states, and four programs dominated the grant picture fiscally (highways, aid to the aged, [welfare], and unemployment compensation). . . . Only four state agencies were heavily involved with federal grant programs. Moreover, while all the grants were categorical, their conditions by current standards were quite reasonable—again facilitating federal intergovernmental administration. Most state programs and agencies and nearly all of their local counterparts were unaffected by this expansion of the federal grant role.[8]

By 1980, more than 25 percent of state and local expenditures were of funds derived from federal grants-in-aid leading one governor to complain that "four out of ten state and local employees are actually federal employees in disguise, marching like a secret army to the guidelines and regulations of Washington."[9] To many governors, mayors, and to a growing chorus of federal officials, grants-in-aid came increasingly to be viewed less as gifts to the states than as restrictions on their sovereignty. Former North Carolina governor Terry Sanford coined the term "picket fence federalism" to describe an evolving system in which vertical coalitions of professional administrators and policy advocates in the same fields cooperated across federal, state, and local lines to advance their own programmatic interests.[10] Categorical grants, particularly in such new areas of government action as air and water pollution control, forced state and local governments to create whole new agencies capable of meeting federal standards for aid. Often wedged uncomfortably into existing administrative structures, these state and local agencies—backed by "free" money from Washington—emerged as major players at the subnational level. These new subgovernments, uniting specialists at all three levels of government, sometimes proved highly resilient to control by elected officials. "Funds could be made to flow best by those most knowledgeable (the program professionals) at turning on the numerous spigots. Although cooperation was prominent during this period, it occurred in concentrated and selectively channeled ways."[11] At the same time, the growing pressures of program expansion emboldened and empowered federal middle-management grant administrators in ways that became increasingly unacceptable to top administrators, budget officials, and conservative politicians at all levels. With the policy experts at all levels finding ever-better ways to spend (and match) federal funds, overall levels of spending rose rapidly. The Nixon administration, for all its practical embrace of categorical grants, was simultaneously determined to break the power of these subgovernments, and slow, if not stop, the upward spiral of spending it helped produce. Working in conjunction with a number of state and local officials, Nixon planted the seeds of a philosophical reversal that has increasingly informed relations between federal, state, and local governments.

Revenue Sharing and Block Grants

The centerpiece of Nixon's "New Federalism" was a program of general revenue sharing in which the federal government simply allocated funds to states and localities according to their population and income. Guidelines on the use of revenue-sharing funds were left vague in a deliberate attempt to decentralize power. Some revenue-sharing funds went to the states, but the primary beneficiaries were municipalities, particularly the faster growing suburbs and small cities of the South which—not coincidentally—were an important part of the Republican Party's developing political constituency.[12] The losers ("victims," they would probably call themselves) were those sophisticated bureaucrats in big government states like New York who had become highly adept at maximizing their share of categorical grants.

It was also under President Nixon that the government began to move away from such *categorical* grants—federal funds earmarked for specific kinds of projects—toward more flexible *block* grants, federal funds with fewer strings attached. Block grants, the thinking was, would allow the president and Congress to encourage state efforts in furthering such national goals as pollution control, education, and social services without telling each state or locality specifically how to allocate its share of the funds. Despite the shift in administrative focus away from the Washington-oriented programs of the 1960s, there remained a bipartisan consensus throughout the Nixon-Ford years that most grant programs were worth retaining. "Federal grants," as one author described the consensus position, "have served as a stimulus to the development of state capabilities and, hence, have helped enhance their strength and vitality. Federal grants have helped the states in a positive way by broadening the programs they can offer their citizens and strengthening state administration of those programs. Conversely, the grants have prevented centralization of those programs and have given the states the ability to maintain their position despite the centralizing tendencies of the times."[13]

Many liberals, though sharing these basic goals, believed that Nixon's calls for greater state autonomy, and the shift to revenue sharing and block grants that accompanied it, was a smokescreen for the wholesale destruction of the programs themselves. Whether President Nixon's "real" agenda, however, the level of federal grant activity actually sustained in the Nixon-Ford years grew by substantial amounts. The conventional view of marble-cake federalists—that the federal government could give the states both money and power at the same time—still held; but the liberals' worst fears soon were to prove real.

Intergovernmental Relations and the New Federalism

The ongoing debate in American politics about *who* should govern—whether power should be lodged primarily at the local, state, or national level—tilted, particularly in the 1930s and again in the 1960s, toward Washington. In the Nixon years it began to tilt back toward the states, and Jimmy Carter, himself a former governor who had never held national office, continued the tradition. In his first two years Carter, like Nixon and Ford before him, increased domestic spending less by direct means than by channeling it through state and local governments. Midway through the Carter presidency, however, the often hidden subtext in the debate over *who* should govern—that is, the question of *how much* government in general is a good thing—reemerged. Nixon's New Federalism, as we have seen, showed that it was possible to increase the federal government's fiscal role in funding domestic programs while simultaneously giving state and local governments greater autonomy in deciding just how the money should be spent. Ronald Reagan campaigned for the presidency with a commitment both to scale back the overall level of domestic spending in government and to decentralize what remained. He was not elected until 1980, but in fiscal terms, the Reagan years really began in 1978 when Jimmy Carter began trying to preempt the Reagan position. As can be seen in Figure 2.1, 1977 marked the high water point in the importance of nonhealth federal grants-in-aid to state and local governments. Since 1978, the story of federal grants-in-aid has been, with one very big exception, a story of continuous stability and even decline. The exception, and it is a *big* exception, is Medicaid, "the 400 pound gorilla of federal aid to states and localities."[14] By 1996, Medicaid alone accounted for nearly 40 percent of all federal grants to the states, more than double the comparable proportion in 1978.

If we take Medicaid out of the equation, the declining federal role in the fiscal affairs of state and local governments is striking: in percentage terms, the role of the federal government is back to the levels of the 1950s. As the costs of state government continue to rise far faster than federal funds, the nonhealth federal percentage of state and local outlays—which peaked at more than 20 percent in the mid-1970s—was down to less than 14 percent in 1993, the lowest level since 1961. Most of this shift took place during the

Figure 2.1 **Federal Grants-in-Aid, 1950–2000**

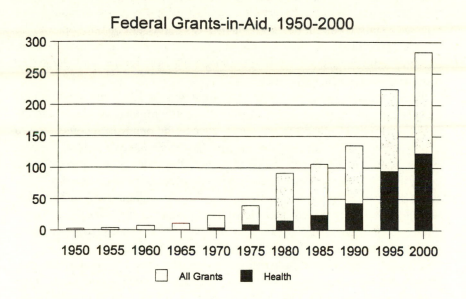

Federal Grants-in-Aid, 1950-2000

Source: Office of Management and Budget, *The Budget of the United States Government, Fiscal Year 2001, Historical Tables* (Washington, DC: Government Printing Office 2000), pp. 205–206. Figures for 2000 are OMB estimates.

1981–88 presidency of Ronald Reagan. Unlike Nixon, Reagan did not hide his belief that devolution would mean diminution: that cutbacks in federal grants would mean cutbacks in government spending at all levels. "It is far easier," Reagan argued, "for people to come to Washington to get their special programs. It would be a hell of a lot tougher if we diffuse them and send them to the states."[15]

Reagan did not get all of the cutbacks that he wanted: confronted by a Democratic House of Representatives throughout his eight years in office, and by a Democratic Senate for four years, he was able nonetheless to shift the terms of debate. Neither of his successors, Republican George Bush nor Democrat Bill Clinton, attempted in any significant way to restore a significant federal role in setting the direction of government spending. Indeed the election of Republican majorities in both the Senate and House in 1994 set the stage for even more dramatic devolutions and diminutions of federal power. President Clinton also came to office with a commitment, "to giving more responsibility to the states." As a former governor he admitted, in a

1995 speech to the Florida legislature, that he "loved block grants." But Clinton went on to warn against too uncritical an embrace of the concept: "The Congress," he said, "gives block grants primarily to save money. And now we're talking about block grants in areas that could be really painful to the high-growth states. So I ask you, think about what's attractive about it, but look at the details. . . . It can be a trap. So watch it, read it, look at the fine print, and stick up for your interests."[16]

What particularly concerned the president was the likely impact on politically weak groups in hard times. Although Clinton refused to side with many Democrats in predicting an immediate "race to the bottom," a contest to see which state could be toughest on the poor in the absence of federal requirements for public assistance, he signed a welfare "reform" bill that both decentralized funding and added new federal restrictions on state benefits. After twice blocking more drastic welfare bills, Clinton signed a bill in 1996 that effectively converted most income support programs into block grants, excluded legal aliens from coverage, and prohibited the states from providing public assistance to any family for more than five years.

Clinton's early reluctance to sign such a bill was grounded first in the argument that there is a *national* interest in providing a minimal safety net for the poor wherever they may reside; and, second, out of a practical concern about what might happen politically to these groups in hard times. "What happens," the president asked in a 1995 speech to the National Governor's Association, "the next time a recession comes down? How will you deal with the interplay in your own legislature if you just get a block grant for welfare with no requirement to do anything on your own, and the people representing the good folks in nursing homes show up, and the people representing the teachers show up, and the people representing the colleges and universities show up, and the people representing the cities and counties who have lost money they used to get for environmental investments show up? I don't know what your experience is, but my experience is that the poor children's lobby is a poor match for most of those forces in most state legislatures in the country."[17]

There is nothing hypothetical about the president's argument, for these are precisely the groups that had been hit hardest in the Reagan-Bush years, and—somewhat ironically—will probably be hit hardest by the welfare bill Clinton himself signed in 1996. Well-organized lobbyists for middle-class grant programs were far better able both to block devolution and diminution at the federal level and to get the states to pick up the slack locally. Senior citizens have been particularly effective at both the state and national levels in keeping their entitlement programs intact. Other groups, the urban poor particularly, were much harder hit by what John Shannon of the Advisory Commission on Intergovernmental Relations called the three Rs of the 1980s and early 1990s. The first of these dreaded Rs was the *reduction* in federal grant-in-aid funds. Second was the *recession* that plagued President Bush's tenure in office and simultaneously decreased government tax collections as it increased the demand for government spending on such programs as unemployment insurance, food stamps, and welfare. And finally, there was the *revolt* of the nation's taxpayers against what were increasingly perceived as excessive rates.[18]

Economic Dreams and Fiscal Realities in New York

The three Rs that hit the states in the 1990s hit with disproportionate force in New York. In the 1990–91 recession, employment nationwide dropped by 1.1 percent; the comparable figure for New York state was 3.8 percent. As the rest of the nation began to recover, moreover, New York's job picture remained bleak: between March 1991 and February 1994 employment rose by 2.1 percent in the rest of the nation but declined by 3.2 percent in New York. These high rates of joblessness have a twofold fiscal impact. On one hand, fewer workers means fewer taxpayers, fewer customers paying sales taxes, and less revenue for both state and local governments. High unemployment rates, on the other hand, usually mean higher costs for government in the form of unemployment insurance, welfare, Medicaid, and other need-based programs. Thus, in contrast with the more severe cutbacks of the 1980s, the slowed growth of federal grant programs in the 1990s were consequently more severe in their impact on New York.

In further contrast with the 1980s, the more recent round of cutbacks came at a time when the third R, the tax revolt that, symbolically if not literally had its roots in a tax-freezing referendum in California, also hit New York. Governor Cuomo pressed for politically popular tax cuts at the same time as the recession was peaking and as federal grant programs were being scaled back. These reductions in revenue both from Washington and from state taxes resulted in few immediate cutbacks in overall spending levels: hidden in fiscal gimmicks, passed on to local governments, transferred to capital debt, many of the cuts were not immediately visible. In the long run, however, they combined to make the state's fiscal position even more precarious.

Finally, it seems clear that few states had become fiscally more dependent on federal grants than New York, which continues to rank among the top five states in per capita federal aid to state and local governments and second only to California in total dollars.[19] There are three principal reasons why New York did so well in securing federal grants in the 1960s and 1970s, and was, conversely, so hard hit by later cutbacks. First, many of the largest categorical grant programs of the Johnson and Nixon-Ford years were targeted toward the kinds of problems endemic to New York: its old, deteriorating, and outdated infrastructure made it the cite of some of the nation's most serious housing, transportation, pollution, and toxic waste problems; and its disproportionate share of persons in need drew grants targeted at the poor and the sick. Second, New York's state and local bureaucrats and legislators became highly adept at the art of grantsmanship, of knowing just what kinds of categorical aid funds were available and how best to get them. The federal shift from categorical grants to block grants nullified this advantage.

Finally, New York benefited and later lost from its unusual willingness to participate in virtually all of the matching grant programs offered by Washington. Its policies with regard to Medicaid are typical. "New York," in the words of one close observer, "has sought consistently to maximize federal Medicaid dollars. For example, in addition to hospitalization, family planning and nursing-home services, all required under Medicaid, New York provides 26 of the 31 services that are categorized as optional. Most states impose limits on the use of optional services by Medicaid recipients; New York has almost none. In addition, more than 600,000 New Yorkers whose incomes exceed the welfare threshold receive Medicaid under a classification called 'medically needy.' Thirty-six states provide some Medicaid coverage to the medically needy; most set their income limits far above New York's. Finally, in 1988, the federal government established regulations to prevent elderly people from becoming impoverished because of a spouse's illness. New York chose the most liberal standards allowed by the federal regulations, allowing the spouse not institutionalized to retain the maximum allowable assets and monthly income."[20]

The 1996 welfare reform package signed by President Clinton was opposed by almost every New York politician for reasons that are almost a paradigm of New York's problems with cutbacks in federal aid. Because the block grant approach does not accommodate growth in the target population, because New York has an unusually high proportion of legal immigrants, and because its policies are more generous than those of other states, the welfare reform bill is expected to be unusually costly to New York. Whether a slightly more liberal Congress and a president freed from the pressures of reelection will modify the 1996 law, it seems likely that New York will continue to decline in its proportionate share of federal grants-in-aid. The fiscal crises that have plagued the state for more than a decade are likely to recur well into the next century.

Newt Gingrich Was Wrong. . . . Or Was He?

New York's uncommon dependence on grants-in-aid is what House Speaker Newt Gingrich had in mind when he charged in 1995 that the state's high-spending policies were costing the federal government and the nation's tax-payers more than their fair share. Gingrich's remarks set off a firestorm of protest from New York politicians, Republicans and Democrats alike, who argued that in fact it is the rest of the states that are living off New York. Daniel Patrick Moynihan, the state's senior U.S. senator, cited figures prepared for him by public finance specialists at Harvard's Kennedy School of Government that showed what Moynihan called a New York "balance of payments deficit" of $18.9 billion in 1994. New Yorkers, in other words, were paying nearly $19 billion more in taxes than they were getting back in federal funds, or more than $1,000 for every man, woman, and child in the state.[21] (The average resident of Speaker Gingrich's home state of Georgia, by comparison, received a net federal subsidy of $322.)[22]

There is no reason to doubt Senator Moynihan's figures: New York is a wealthy state with a number of wealthy citizens who pay a lot in federal taxes. It is, at the same time, a poor state with large welfare rolls, high medical costs, and numerous beneficiaries of special poverty programs. For many years, it has ranked among the top three or four states in per capita federal grants. One 1989 table, widely reprinted in textbooks and tracts on state and local government, shows New Yorkers getting an average of $763 dollars each in federal aid per year, compared with a national average of only $481.[23] It is this figure that Gingrich probably had in mind when he accused New York of living off the federal gravy train. New York, at the same time, does relatively less well in securing defense contracts, farm aid, and social security payments. Where the federal government's average per capita spending for procurement contract awards was $727 in 1990, New York's per capita share was only $440.[24] And on the other side of the coin, New Yorkers, or some New Yorkers at least, pay a lot more in taxes per capita than do the citizens of most other states (including former Speaker Gingrich's home state of Georgia). Thus in a sense, Senator Moynihan and Congressman Gingrich are both right: *some* New Yorkers are paying a lot more into Washington than they get back, *some* New Yorkers are getting a lot more from the federal government than people in other states. The ways in which the folks in Washington adjust these numbers up and down have a lot to do with the contours of politics and the range of available options in the state. In 1993, to summarize in quantitative terms, New York state accounted for 7.2 percent of the population of the United States. It received 11.1 percent of all federal grant expenditures; 4.4 percent of salaries and wages; 7.6 percent of direct payments to individuals; and a paltry 4.2 percent of federal procurement contracts. The net total: 7.1 percent of all federal expenditures.[25] On the other side of the coin, its citizens paid some $800 more than the state average in per capita in federal taxes, and the net imbalance has been growing steadily since 1984. Overall, "the net impact of the federal drain of funds from New York over the decade has been large. In . . . 1984 the flow of funds drained 2 percent of New York's incomes; by . . . 1994 that had risen to more than 4 percent."[26]

Mandates: Funded, Unfunded, and Underfunded

In the 1990s the concept of "unfunded" mandates became a hot-button issue in national politics. While there had been some earlier interest in the concept among scholars and local government officials, "The number of newspaper articles discussing 'unfunded federal mandates' jumped from just 22 in 1992 to 836 in 1994."[27] As part of its "Contract With America," the newly-elected Republican majority in Congress passed, and President Clinton signed into law, the Unfunded Mandates Reform Act of 1995 which sharply restricted the ability of the federal government to impose uncompensated financial burdens on state and local governments. The act was the product of a campaign led largely by political conservatives who argued that unwanted federal mandates were "putting a stranglehold on state budgets."[28]

In its baldest and most objectionable form, an unfunded mandate is an act of Congress that spells out a new direction in public policy without assuming any of its costs. In effect, the federal government gives orders to the states "as if they were administrative agents of the national government, while expecting state officials and electorates to bear whatever costs ensue."[29] The Americans with Disabilities Act, for example, requires that all public facilities be made accessible to the handicapped but provides no funds for the ramps and elevators needed to bring state and local facilities into conformity. The opposite side of this same coin is imposing restraints on certain kinds of action that have the effect of mandating more costly options. The marine protection amendments of 1977, for example, prohibiting cities from dumping sewage into the ocean, have been very costly to New York City, forcing it to ship tons of waste as far away as Texas rather than simply towing it out to sea.

Many of the most important mandate programs involve what are known as "pass through" mandates whose ultimate fiscal impact is at the local rather than the state level. The first of these pass-through mandates were established under the Water Quality Act of 1965, and they have been emulated many times since. Essentially what the act did was require each state to develop enforcement plans that met or exceeded the minimum national standards of the law. A state that failed to develop a minimally acceptable plan would forfeit its regulatory authority to the federal Environmental Protection Agency (EPA). While there is no doubt that the pass-through provisions of this act, especially those applying to wastewater treatment, have imposed significant costs on local governments, compliance has been spotty with some states enforcing compliance far more vigorously than others. The EPA itself has been slow in approving implementation rules, and many local governments have never been actually monitored. These different levels of enforcement and compliance make it virtually impossible to estimate accurately the "real" costs to state and local governments of unfunded mandates. "Estimating the costs to local governments of compliance with various environmental regulations—such as hazardous waste disposal and prevention of ground-water contamination—is compounded by the fact that many environmental mandates overlap."[30] And finally, the true costs of federal mandates are frequently obscured by the rather loose cost accounting systems of many municipalities.

The costs of such unfunded mandates are, nonetheless, both substantial and fast growing. One reasonably prudent 1992 study put the total cost of compliance with such regulations at between $8.9 and $12.7 billion a year, and some politicians have claimed even higher costs.[31] These costs would be higher still if we were to include the lost opportunity "costs" that derive from a wide variety of federal regulations, minimum standards, and prohibitions, some of them as old as the Constitution itself. By prohibiting the states from levying tariffs on goods imported from overseas, the Constitution deprives a port-of-entry state like New York of what could be a very lucrative source of revenue. When it required states to raise the drinking age to twenty-one or lose federal highway funds, Congress "cost" New York untold dollars of lost tax revenues from the sale of alcoholic beverages (though in the long run the "costs" from alcoholism, drunk driving, and medical care might far exceed these short-term revenues). Add to these the many grant-in-aid programs such as federal aid to education which have been cut back in the years since 1978, and it is clear that there are good reasons for state and local officials to feel somewhat beleaguered.

Not surprisingly, the state and local share of government spending has risen rather sharply in the 1980s and 1990s. As federal spending grew in the 1960s and 1970s, state and local expenditures had barely kept pace with inflation. Between 1983 and 1986, by way of contrast, "as the Reagan retrenchment and federalism policies took effect, state aid to localities increased by an average of 5.6 percent in real terms, i.e., adjusted for inflation. Total state spending rose by nearly the same percentage."[32] While there has been some slowing of this trend in the 1990s, the days when the states could look to Washington for monies rather than mandates are gone. The 1995 law will undoubtedly slow if not staunch the flow of unfunded mandates emerging from Washington, but the equally damaging underfunding of essential programs such as Medicaid means—in fiscal terms at least—about the same thing.

Aid to Localities

If Washington has solved some of its fiscal problems by passing the burden for essential mandated services to the states, Albany has done much the same to local governments in New York. Just as the federal government has increasingly passed the bill for basic services to the states, so has the state of New York transferred a growing fiscal burden to its towns and cities. In 1948 journalist Warren Moscow wrote that "the State is not just a money-grubbing miser. It returns to the cities, the towns, and the villages a major portion of its revenues."[33] "This statement," Zimmerman wrote in 1981, remains accurate as the state devotes approximately 61 percent of its budget to aid to local governments, the highest level of support among the fifty states. Of this amount, 75 percent is state aid for education and social services, and 15 percent is for general revenue and tax sharing."[34]

By 1994, by one set of figures, the state had become even more generous. According to the governor's 1994–95 budget estimates almost 70 percent of the state's general fund disbursements are in the category of "grants to local governments."[35] This figure, however, has almost no real meaning as many billions of these dollars are never actually transferred. In point of fact, New York requires its counties, cities, towns, and villages to shoulder more of the state's fiscal burden than does almost any other state. Depending on how you do the accounting (or who does it), the state could indeed be seen as Moscow's "money-grubbing miser." By nobody's measure is the state's level of support among the nation's highest, as Zimmerman described it just fifteen years ago. Indeed Gold and Ritchie's scholarly analysis of state aid figures for 1990 concluded that New York's fiscal system was "unusually decentralized," ranking "forty-eighth in state expenditures as a proportion of total state and local expenditures."[36] Looking at taxes rather than expenditures, the Fiscal Policy Institute reached a similar conclusion:

> In 1990, the most recent year for which such comparative data is available, New York ranked 48th among the 50 states in terms of the state percentage of total state and local tax revenue. Nationally, state taxes accounted for 59.9% of all state-local tax revenue. In New York, the state government's share (48.7%) was virtually the same as Colorado's (48.4%) and greater than only New Hampshire (31.8%). Since 1986, the state share in New York declined from 50.4%.[37]

By 1993, the State's share had apparently fallen still further to 47 percent.[38]

Because they are using different measures of fiscal effort, these various sets of figures are not strictly comparable. Zimmerman rather clearly was not looking at taxation figures when he described New York as being at the top of the fifty states in state aid. The general pattern, however, is abundantly clear: New York, increasingly and more than almost any other state, relies on local taxes to finance the everyday operations of the government. It ranks forty-eighth among the fifty states in the proportion of state versus local funds expended on highways, fiftieth on corrections. New York, moreover, is a major user of the "pass-through" device, requiring local governments to administer and provide the matching funds for a variety of federal grant programs. It is one of only ten states, for example, requiring its local governments to share the costs of welfare. Only twelve other states require a local share for Medicaid.

State "Mandates"

Beyond these deficiencies in state aid, local government officials in New York frequently fault what they regard as excessive efforts by the state to tell them what to do and how. Just as state and local officials complained about Washington's reliance on "unfunded mandates," New York's county and municipal officials have leveled the same charge at Albany. Elected officials in New York City have been particularly critical of what they often describe as the state's tendency to "micromanage" the smallest details of city government.

> Legally it makes no sense to describe state laws regulating municipalities in the same terms that are used to describe federal-state relations. In legal terms, New York has a "unitary" rather than a "federated" form of government. State and federal courts have historically denied local governments any "rights" to perform functions not specifically granted to them by the state. They have adhered quite consistently to what is known as "Dillon's Rule" after an 1868 court case in Iowa by a Judge Dillon which argued that a municipal corporation possesses and can exercise the following powers, and no others: first, those granted in express words; second, those necessarily or fairly implied in or incident to the powers expressly granted; third, those essential to the objects and purposes of the corporation—not simply convenient, but indispensable. Any fair, reasonable, substantial doubt concerning the existence of a power is resolved by the courts against a corporation, and the power is denied.[39]

While New York and the other states have granted varying levels of autonomy and "home rule" to local governments and agencies, they remain, following Dillon, "involuntary subdivisions of the state, constituted for the purpose of the more convenient exercise of governmental functions by the state. . . ."[40] No matter who actually puts up the money, "if a service is mandated, the funds come from the wallets of State taxpayers."[41]

Such legal niceties aside, New York asks more of its local governments than most other states do. One 1977 study conducted by a legislative commission on expenditure review, counted 2,632 statutory mandates to counties alone. The commission identified three kinds of mandates to local governments. Type I mandates are those which simply and directly require specific activities: every community in New York state, for example, must provide a system of public schools that meets an elaborate range of minimum requirements. Type II mandates are not legally binding, but are so popular politically that few local officials can avoid them. As former Albany mayor Erastus Corning said of a law allowing (but not mandating) municipalities to exempt senior citizens from various property taxes, "Here the Legislature gives a municipality an opportunity to help senior citizens, so you're damned if you do and damned if you don't. It's not a mandate, but you look like a bum if you don't do it."[42] Finally Type III mandates, in the commission's schema, are those that do not require particular services but set state standards for those that are provided. Towns and villages, for example, need not have their own police forces and may instead rely on county and state law enforcement officials; but if they do choose to have their own police officers, they must meet a long series of state standards as to training, equipment, and procedure.

As in our discussion of federal mandates, local governments in New York state have suffered as much from the *under*funding of established programs as they have from all three types of *un*funded mandates. While the state has followed the national trend of improving its public schools, it has put the fiscal burden of improved special education, computer training, higher teacher standards, and so on, squarely on the shoulders of local government. The share of local school costs financed by the state has fallen to less than 37 percent in 1995–96 from almost 43 percent in 1987–88. With schools accounting for roughly half of most local government expenditures, the impact on some communities has been staggering. Between 1985 and 1990, according to one study, local property tax collections in New York "grew about 40% faster than the economy while the [state] income tax grew about 40% slower than the economy." Twenty-six counties increased their sales tax one or more times in this same period.[43] "Between 1988 and 1994, every county in New York raised property taxes by more than 20 percent. Thirteen counties raised property taxes by more than 100 percent, including Saratoga County, which increased its property taxes by 295 percent."[44]

The Tangled Web of Local Government

The late Rube Goldberg was famous for his comic depictions of elaborate machines that accomplished relative simple tasks through incredibly bizarre mechanisms. His automatic sheet music turner, for example, began with a foot pedal that caused a bellows to blow a whistle that a goldfish was trained to regard as its dinner signal. By pulling on a worm suspended on a string in its bowl, the fish released a weight from a shelf on the wall that in turn activated a boxing glove on a spring. The glove hit an inflated punching bag into a spike, which forced the escaping air into a sail attached to the page of music needing to be turned. It would not be difficult to believe that Mr. Goldberg had something to do with creating the structure of local governments in New York. No state has a more elaborate, less efficient, or more expensive complex of local entities. Former Albany *Times Union* columnist Dan Lynch has pointed out that if you fired every single *state* employee in New York, leaving only local officials, there would still be more government employees per capita in New York than in neighboring Massachusetts.

This complex, often redundant, pattern has its roots in three strands of state history. The "New England system, in which the town is the dominant unit of administration" was brought across the Long Island sound and over the Berkshire mountains into the early Yankee settlements on Long Island and along the Connecticut, Massachusetts, and Vermont borders.

> Its essential feature, perhaps, is its simplicity. . . . Confronted with the unknown dangers of the new land, they settled in enclosed areas sufficiently large to produce the food required for their sustenance and yet compact enough to be adequately defended from hostile Indians. By the force of circumstances, the boundaries of their early communities were determined by their economic requirements.[45]

The second system had its roots both in the commercial and patroon systems of the Dutch, on one hand, and the surprisingly compatible English county system on the other. As in most Southern states, it is a system stressing relatively large units of local government in which "townships exist in name only or not at all."[46] Finally, there is a western element in New York's settlement with the Northwest Ordinance's creation of thousands of new settlements in the Adirondacks and Niagara frontier. Counties in this part of the state were divided into townships of thirty-six square miles each, some of which were quickly populated, others which were not. Local government in these counties ranged from strong to nonexistent.

As if this mixed pattern of local governance were insufficiently complex, the rapid growth of New York City (and to a lesser extent, Albany), led it to demand and receive special status. That special status continues to pertain in many cases only to New York City, and in even more cases to what are commonly known as the "Big Five" cities of Buffalo, New York, Rochester, Syracuse, and Yonkers. And in 1801, the legislature compounded the confusion still further by conferring the title of "village" on Troy and Lansingburgh, a designation that became increasingly independent of other boundaries to the extent that by 1995 there were 74 "villages" located in more than one "town." A resident of the village of Harriman thus pays local property taxes to the village, to Orange County, and to either the town of Woodbury or the town of Monroe.[47]

The picture becomes still more complex when we add to the mix the thousands of other government entities—school boards, water authorities, fire districts, highway and bridge authorities, park commissions, library commissions, development authorities, and so on—that sometimes overlap with other jurisdictions. Special districts for fire, sewers, street lights, and water are commonplace in New York and often have their own taxing authority. "Since these districts are formed to provide services to the inhabitants of a limited area of a town, their boundaries rarely coincide with one another or with the unincorporated area. There is, therefore, no uniform special district tax rate effective throughout the area."[48] Authorities, though funded by revenue bonds rather than taxes, also play an important role in local governance. The Metropolitan Transit Authority (MTA), to use one prominent example, controls the subways, most of the bus routes, and the major commuter rail lines into and out of New York City, yet it is not in any sense a part of the city's governing structure. Like most public authorities, the MTA has its own governing board and the power to borrow on its own, is exempt from taxation and civil service rules, and is isolated, in many respects, from control by the mayor, governor, and legislature.

> New York probably uses the authority form more than any other state. Beyond the usual political and financial arguments for the creation of authorities rather than ordinary line agencies, in New York there are additional constitutional factors: the state constitution limits the number of state departments to twenty; requires "full faith and credit" backing for state debt; and—very importantly—requires cumbersome statewide referenda for increases in state debt. The authorities escape these restrictions since they are separate, largely autonomous corporations that are not operating departments of the state.[49]

Finally, to confuse the picture still more, various state agencies and municipalities have set up a variety of quasi-independent public corporations that are often granted, paradoxically, "more flexibility than the jurisdictions which establish them."[50] The research foundations of the state and city universities, for example, provide college administrators with funds for programs and supplies that are not within the bounds of their regular budget authority. Most of the state's larger cities have local development corporations that can buy and sell property and broker deals between private corporations and mainstream government agencies. All of these local units, to be sure, are—following Dillon's Rule—creatures of the state and could, in theory, be abolished tomorrow. The political logic of localism is, however, as strong as its economic logic is weak. Attempts to "streamline" local government by eliminating smaller, less efficient units have generally failed. The state has for many years, for example, offered strong economic incentives for the merger of small school districts, but has found few takers. Small towns that could save money by contracting police services from the county continue, pridefully, to provide their own police forces. Municipal consolidations are rarities, and it seems to be in the nature of New York politics to create more rather than fewer governments.

Judicial Federalism

In New York, as in all fifty states, a federal court system exists and operates alongside, and in some senses, on top of, a system of state and local courts. Article VI of the U.S. Constitution seems rather unambiguous in declaring the Constitution, laws, and treaties of the United States "the supreme law of the land." In other federal systems, such as Canada and India, a single federal court system has the power to put similar supremacy clauses into effect, but the respective jurisdictions of state and national courts in the United States are far less clearly defined. As with issues of money and politics, federalism in the courts is a cumbersome and complex system of conflict, accommodation, negotiation, and compromise.

Questions of Jurisdiction

In broad outline, there are two basic kinds of courts: *trial courts*, which hear the evidence in specific cases and apply the law to such matters as divorce, personal injuries, crime, and housing; and *appellate courts*, which deal with disputed interpretations of the law and get into the game only when the losing party appeals the trial court's procedures or legal rulings. The U.S. Constitution established a Supreme Court that would function as a trial court in some extraordinary cases (such as those involving foreign diplomats), and as an appellate court with regard to virtually all other cases arising under the Constitution. It left it to Congress to limit and precisely define the Court's appellate jurisdiction and to establish any other federal courts. In the Judiciary Act of 1789, Congress refused "to bestow on federal courts all the jurisdiction to which the Constitution entitles them. At that time Congress was prepared to allow the state courts to handle a considerable part of what could have been federal court business. In particular, "federal question" suits were left to the state courts, and it was not until after the Civil War, in 1875, that the federal courts were authorized to exercise all the kinds of federal jurisdiction specified in the Constitution."[51]

Federal courts themselves—the Supreme Court in particular—have tended generally to expand the scope of what they are likely to consider "federal questions." As early as the 1816 case of *Martin v. Hunter's Lessee* the Court rather strongly asserted its power to review the decisions of state supreme courts. By slowly but steadily broadening its interpretation of the Constitution's commerce clause as to cover virtually any significant form of economic activity, the Supreme Court significantly expanded the legally sanctioned role of the national government and, by extension, of its own jurisdictional reach. And the Court's use of the Fourteenth Amendment to apply the Bill of Rights to the states, begun during the later years of the New Deal, but associated largely with the chief justiceship of Earl Warren (1953–69), expansively interpreted federal authority with regard to racial equality, freedom of speech, and a wide range of issues involving state criminal procedures and the rights of the accused. These decisions—particularly those in the area of criminal justice—expanded federal power into jurisdictional areas once patrolled almost exclusively by the states. These centralizing trends have been preserved if not extended during the supposedly more conservative chief justiceships of Warren Burger (1969–86) and William Rehnquist (1986–).

As a matter of general principle it remains true that in their interpretations of state law, federal courts are required to accept the opinion of the state's highest court as definitive. Where the issue is purely a state issue, in other words, where no important "federal question" is involved, the final say on issues of law resides in the state's highest court. Federal courts, moreover, will not normally intervene on a ruling based on state law unless it is clearly in conflict with federal law. In strictly legal terms, however, these limits on federal jurisdiction are relatively trivial. All that the loser in a case decided by his or her highest state court needs in order to exercise an automatic right to appeal to the federal courts is a showing that the case involves a "federal issue." Given the scope of the Supreme Court's interpretations of the commerce power and the Fourteenth Amendment, the potential scope of this right is enormous. In practice, the range of issues the federal courts will treat as involving "federal questions," is not nearly so extensive. As Pritchett puts it:

> Federal legislation provides a right of appeal to the Supreme Court from any decision of a state court of last resort declaring a federal law or treaty unconstitutional, and also from any state court decision upholding a state law or constitutional provision against a substantial challenge that it con-

flicts with a federal law, treaty, or constitutional provision. While in theory the Supreme Court must accept such appeals, in practice most of them are rejected for "for want of a substantial federal question" or on other juris-dictional grounds.[52]

In interpreting state law, the federal courts are required to treat the rulings of the states' highest courts as definitive. They will not generally intervene in the absence of a clear and unambiguous conflict with federal law. State courts, in theory at least, have no discretion: they "must not only give prece-dence to federal law over state law but also interpret that law in line with rulings of the U. S. Supreme Court."[53] Despite the presumed supremacy of federal law, noncompliance does occur. There is sufficient leeway in the interpretation of federal court rulings that it would be erroneous to "con-clude simply that the Supreme Court is the commanding officer and that a major state's highest tribunal is a usually obedient but occasionally recalci-trant private."[54] As with most questions with regard to the relations between the federal government and the states, in other words, judicial federalism is less a matter of doctrine than of evolving practice.

Federal Courts in New York State

In large part because of New York City's role as a center of business and fi-nance, New York state generates a disproportionate share of business for the federal courts. Only Washington, D. C. has a higher ratio of lawyers per capita than New York. At the appellate level, the country is divided into twelve regions (called circuits). New York is part of the second judicial circuit, embracing the states of New York, Connecticut, and Vermont, and generally one of the nation's busiest circuits. There are four federal trial courts in New York state: the North-ern District, with chambers in Albany, Binghamton, Syracuse, and Utica; the Southern District at the famous Foley Square courthouse in lower Manhattan; the Eastern District in Brooklyn; and the Western District which divides its sessions between Buffalo and Rochester.

The judges on these courts are appointed for life by the president with the advice and consent of the Senate. Through a long-standing tradition known as "senatorial courtesy," the reality is that the president cannot appoint any-one to a district court who is unacceptable to the majority party's senior senator from the state or circuit in question. What this practically means, in most cases, is that the real power of appointment lies less in the hands of the president than in that of the state's senior senator. Appointments to the appel-late bench, while not strictly subject to the rule of senatorial courtesy, can also be intensely political.

In addition to district and appellate courts, national legislation has also created a rich variety of specialized courts and administrative agencies that function in some ways as courts. U.S. magistrates help relieve the burdens of federal district courts by dealing with the less serious cases. Bankruptcy courts are the courts of original jurisdiction in most bankruptcy cases, and immigration and tariff courts do pretty much what their names imply. Increasingly, the national government has worked to relieve the growing caseload burden of the federal courts by delegating both rule-making and adjudicating powers to various administrative agencies. Jacobs argues that the "increasing prominence of administrative agencies in making and implementing the law and adjudicating resulting disputes is one of the most notable trends of the late twentieth century in American politics."[55] Although this trend has undoubtedly freed the courts from having to consider a large number of relatively arcane and technical issues that many judges are ill-prepared to consider, the growing linkage of administration and adjudication has, as Jacobs continues, "troubled many observers. Because administrative agencies are at least one step removed from the political constraints inherent in popular democracy, their power holds frightening potential. Agencies' quasi-judicial functions give them additional powers that courts may be unable to control because of the volume of cases that flow through administrative channels. And, unlike courts, administrative agencies are able to follow through on their adjudicatory decisions by implementing them without reference to another agency. Thus, executive branch administrative agencies have powers that neither a legislature nor a court can match. Those powers have the potential of transforming the legal system from a court-centered process to one that is administration-centered."[56]

The use of such administrative courts, at the same time, serves substantially to reduce the caseload of the federal trial courts, in itself a goal usually applauded. Increasing the number of federal judges, it has been suggested, is much like increasing and improving most highways:

> They solve short-term problems, but over the long run they cause more congestion. From a numerical and organizational perspective, the federal judiciary is becoming more bureaucratic and much more complicated. As judge and staff resources have increased over time, there has been an equal—if not greater—growth in the administrative work imposed on the courts. And, ominously, the pending backlogs of criminal cases and appeals have actually increased.[57]

Despite the rhetoric of decentralization currently in vogue, Congress seems more rather than less inclined to nationalize criminal justice issues. Each of its recent attempts to "get tough" on crime by making various terrorist, drug, and violent acts into federal offenses adds to the burden of federal trial courts.

This nationalization of the criminal justice process has enormously complicated the prosecutory process. Let us take the hypothetical case of a citizen of the Bronx who, unhappy with something he or she receives in the mail, shoots the postal service worker who delivers it.

Today, and throughout the history of the United States, a murder of this kind would be treated as a crime against the people of New York state. Following arrest, the perpetrator would be charged by a prosecuting attorney from the office of the Bronx district attorney and taken before a Bronx County judge for arraignment. Historically, the case would have proceeded from that point through the state court system where—unless some extraordinary procedural question arose—it would have been resolved. Since the 1980s, however, it has been a *federal* crime to murder a working government employee. Our enraged citizen, in other words, could now be prosecuted twice: once, in New York for the crime of murder; again, in federal court, for the national crime of killing a civil servant in the performance of his or her job. Since they are separate crimes, the rule of double jeopardy does not apply. In practice, the Bronx district attorney would almost certainly consult with his or her federal counterpart at the outset, and a decision would be negotiated as to which track—state, national, or both—to follow. The nation's long tradition of deferring to the states in the arena of criminal justice continues to prevail in most cases of this kind; but there is no question that the tilt in recent years is in a national direction.

The State Court System

Despite the political imperatives that have led Congress and the president increasingly to nationalize the issue of crime, and in the face of the federal court's expansive definitions of the commerce clause and Fourteenth Amendment, an overwhelming proportion of legal issues, more than 99 percent by one count, continue to be resolved at the state level. Indeed Stumpf and Culver estimate that New York's total case filings alone exceeded those of all federal courts combined by a ratio of better than 10 to 1.[58] The state court system, consequently, is considerably larger and more complex than its federal counterpart, though its basic structure is similar. At the apex the system is New York's counterpart to the U.S. Supreme Court, the New York Court of Appeals (New York and Maryland, for reasons no one can fully explain, are alone among the states in not calling their highest courts "supreme"). The Court of Appeals, whose seven members are appointed to fourteen-year terms by the governor with the advice and consent of the state senate is New

York's court of last resort and handles cases only on appeal. Most of its cases come to it on appeal from one of the four appellate divisions of the state supreme court. These appellate courts consist of two seven-member courts sitting in Manhattan and Brooklyn, and two five-member courts in Albany and Rochester.

As in the national government, the caseload of the courts winnows substantially as one moves from bottom to top. The decisions of trial courts are not usually appealed, and of those that are, only a small sample are given serious attention by the courts of the appellate division. Most decisions of the appellate division, in turn, are not appealed; and the Court of Appeals actually accepts jurisdiction in only a small proportion of those cases that are. For most citizens, most of the time, the courts that count are the trial courts.

What New York calls its "supreme court" is its trial court of general jurisdiction. It is composed of 322 justices elected from twelve judicial districts ranging in number from fifty-two (in the district covering Brooklyn and Staten Island) down to ten in the Binghamton area.[59] Most significant criminal and civil cases are tried at this level. At this point the system becomes more complex with different jurisdictions presenting different arrays of trial courts. At the very lowest level are some 2,327 town and village justices—who, in many New York jurisdictions, need not have backgrounds in the law—that handle most misdemeanor offenses, drunk driving cases, family disputes, traffic violations, and so on. The business of these "cafeteria courts," as they are sometimes called, "is to process large numbers of cases quickly and with an element of bureaucratic efficiency . . . much of the work occurs in private—meetings between opposing council, conferences with the judges in chambers, and so on."[60] In New York City and many of the larger urban areas these duties are usually parceled out among various specialized courts for traffic and parking violations, family disputes, probate, housing, and so on. More serious cases are referred in the city to the civil and criminal courts, to fifty-seven county courts upstate, or to district courts on Long Island.

Despite the apparent complexity of New York's judicial system, its essential features are those characteristic of state judicial structures throughout the United States. In Hurst's classic study of American legal history, these characteristics were identified as (1) localism: virtually every community, almost on a neighborhood basis, has some sort of judicial presence, usually in the form of a justice of the peace or local magistrate. These are supplemented by trial courts, both criminal and civil, within a day's ride (usually at the county seat); (2) hierarchy: a system unlike Great Britain's in which trial courts are considered "inferior" both in staffing and role to the "higher" courts of appeal; and (3) more than in any other nation, a proliferation of rights of appeal. To this list, Stumpf adds (4) surprising resistance to change. As in most states, the basic structure of the judicial system in New York is pretty much what it was in colonial times. And (5) the "paradox of unity and diversity": a system that despite its extraordinarily decentralized organization provides remarkably uniform outcomes.[61]

This uniformity of outcomes is attributable in part to the looming appellate jurisdiction of the higher courts. Even more important, however, is the Anglo-American common law tradition that makes precedent, or in its Latin form *stare decisis*, the controlling paradigm of legal practice. Legal research in the United States is deeply steeped in a tradition of finding comparable cases: a ruling in the first district becomes a key point in the brief submitted by lawyers arguing a comparable case in the eighth district. A ruling at the appellate level is more compelling, and the rulings of federal courts more so. And although there is no legal requirement that they do so, "the basic character of the American legal system encourages state supreme courts to consult and borrow from the decisions of sister courts."[62] Judges, defense attorneys, and prosecutors share an aversion to the time and expense of appeal: if the precedent is clear, so be it. On important issues of both substance and procedure, the congruence of laws between and among the several states is one of its most striking features: a lawyer trained in California is not likely to find it particularly difficult to pass the bar exam in New York.

At the same time, there are few policy arenas in which federalism and local customs count for more than in the courts. There are whole categories of important cases which almost never move beyond the state level, and in which the guiding principles of justice are set almost entirely by judicial precedent rather than statutory law. State courts, in effect, are the policy-making institutions in such important areas as divorce and child support, personal injury and medical malpractice, business contracts, real estate, and liability. And local courts, though theoretically constrained by precedent and the threat of appeal, are practically sovereign within their spheres. "The local judge who invariably sends drunken drivers to jail, the judge in the next county who throws the book only at youthful drug offenders, and the judge who sits in the courthouse making life miserable for errant spouses who have fallen behind in their child support and alimony payments—all are making policy."[63]

Other Intergovernmental Relations

Just as the courts frequently borrow from one another in deciding cases, governors, legislators, lobbyists, and bureaucrats pay considerable attention to what is happening in other states and localities. Organizations like the National Conference of State Legislators and comparable convocations of governors, mayors, and attorneys general provide formal mechanisms of communication. More important, issue specific groups—from welfare rights advocates to stockbrokers—frequently bring together lobbyists, legislators, and civil servants working in different states on the same issues. These "issue networks," as they are sometimes called, are an important source of policy initiatives in the several states. Beyond the informal borrowings of ideas that constantly take place at these and other forums, New York's governing bodies are involved in an enormous web of interstate and international institutions, arrangements, and formal agreements.

Most of the state's formal interstate relations involve agreements with the adjoining states of Vermont, Massachusetts, Connecticut, New Jersey, and Pennsylvania. In one way or another, however, New York has links with every state in the union. An alliance of states interested in protecting ocean resources, for example, connects New York with states as far away as Alaska and Hawaii. An interstate compact on the placement of children in interstate adoption includes forty-nine states and two territories. And the state has entered into numerous agreements with the adjoining Canadian provinces of Ontario and Quebec ranging from highly specific arrangements for the joint maintenance of bridges over the St. Lawrence River, to complicated compacts governing the state's purchase of hydroelectric power generated in Canada.

The Constitution of the United States contains three types of provisions on interstate relations. The first provides mechanisms for settling disputes between states and for establishing joint programs. The second governs the rights of citizens caught in conflicts of jurisdiction between differing state laws. And the third gives the Supreme Court original or trial jurisdiction in cases involving suits between states. This last provision has been rather sparingly used in recent years, as most states have been able to work out their disputes without resort to the courts. Beginning with *New York v. Connecticut*[64] in 1789, it was rather frequently used in settling boundary disputes in the early years of the nation. Most recently, the handful of state-versus-state cases coming before the court have revolved largely around issues of water rights. Even in this sensitive area, however, it is the exceptional case that actually goes to court. Typically, New York state has resolved a number of water issues with neighboring states through the device of interstate compacts such as the Champlain Basin Compact (1966) with Vermont, the Great Lakes Compact (1960) with the eight states touching the lakes, and the Delaware River Basin Compact (1961) with New Jersey, Pennsylvania, and Delaware.

Interstate Compacts

The Delaware River Basin Compact is interesting because it was initiated by Congress and makes the federal government a partner with the four states in solving the problems of the basin. In dry years especially, what New York's state and local governments do with the Delaware—both in terms of extracting its water and using it to dump sewage—dramatically impacts downriver communities in Pennsylvania, New Jersey, and Delaware. Sporadic attempts by the states to negotiate water use agreements had been largely unsuccessful until the federal government in 1961 forced the four states to come together. The Delaware River Basin Commission, created at that time, comprises members from the national government and each of the states adjoining the river. The commission has the power to regulate the river's flow by setting limits on how much water communities in each state can use and how. Similar federal-state compacts involve New York in the Appalachian Regional and Susquehanna River Basin Commissions.

The very large role played by the federal government in the establishment of the Delaware River Commission is somewhat exceptional but, at the same time, illustrative of the enormous political barriers that commonly prevent the more widespread use of interstate compacts. The classic interstate compact is one initiated and administered entirely by agreement between the affected states. Compacts of this kind typically require tentative agreement between the cooperating states, enactment into law by each of the participants, and the formal approval of Congress. The key political actors are the states in question, and it has generally been their inability to reach agreement that has frustrated their widespread use, particularly in recent years. One of the earliest and still most significant of these compacts is the 1921 agreement that created the Port Authority of New York and New Jersey. The Port Authority is an enormously wealthy and powerful institution, controlling more resources than many states.

What the Port Authority has been able to do, and what the states on their own almost certainly could not have done, is coordinate a number of transportation alternatives to the benefit of the region as a whole. In its direction of the major airports—Kennedy, Newark, and LaGuardia—it has produced a reasonably equitable balance of economic benefits and air transit efficiencies that interstate rivalries never would have achieved. Critics have argued that the Port Authority has tilted toward New Jersey in developing the area's maritime freight facilities. As with most bond-funded, independent authorities, moreover, the Port Authority of New York and New Jersey has not been a model of fiscal restraint. Its construction of the World Trade Center created a glut in the Manhattan real estate market that set the private sector back by a decade, at least, and significantly decreased the city's tax base; and because the Port Authority operates independently of the state, sewage from the Trade Center, unlike that of any other building in lower Manhattan, flows unfiltered into the Hudson River. Having essentially paid off the bondhold-

Box 2.1

Interstate Compacts and State Law

In order to form an interstate authority, states must agree and have the compact approved by Congress. Getting out of a compact can be more difficult.

In 1940, New York and seven other states entered into a compact to control pollution in the Ohio River. To develop and enforce regulations regarding sewage, they created the Ohio River Valley Water Sanitation Commission, consisting of three at-large members and three members from each state. In 1949, West Virginia—one of the eight states represented on the commission—got into a fight with the commission over an order banning certain kinds of pollution and refused to pay its dues. The supreme court of West Virginia upheld the state's position, arguing that the 1940 compact could not supersede subsequent state laws. The case was appealed by the other seven states to the U.S. Supreme Court where West Virginia lost. A compact, Justice Frankfurter wrote for the majority "is after all a legal document. . . . It requires no elaborate argument to reject the suggestion that an agreement solemnly entered into between States . . . can be unilaterally nullified, or given final meaning by an organ of one of the contracting States. A state cannot be its own ultimate judge in a controversy with a sister state. . . ."

> That a legislature may delegate to an administrative body the power to make rules and decide particular cases is one of the axioms of modern government. The West Virginia court does not challenge the general proposition but objects to the delegation here involved because it is to a body outside the State and because its legislature may not be free, at any time, to withdraw the power delegated. We are not here concerned, and so need not deal, with specific language in a State constitution requiring that the State settle its problems with other States without delegating power to an interstate agency. What is involved is a conventional grant of legislative power. We find nothing in that to indicate that West Virginia may not solve a problem such as the control of river pollution by compact and by the delegation, if such be necessary, to effectuate such a solution by compact. . . . The Compact involves a reasonable and carefully limited delegation of power to an administrative agency.*

West Virginia, in the Court's view, could not unilaterally withdraw from the compact once it was in force. This remains the prevailing law.

---

*State ex rel. Dyer v. Sims (1951) 341 U.S. 22, 27–28.

ers who financed construction of the Hudson River crossings, such as the George Washington Bridge and Lincoln Tunnel, the Port Authority has become a cash cow whose revenues both New York and New Jersey covet. Even its sharpest critics concede, however, that the Port Authority has produced a level of productive regional development that probably could not have been attained absent a formal agreement.

Despite the relative success of agencies like the Port Authority and the Delaware River Basin Commission, almost no significant interstate authorities have been created in the past three decades and the rush to sign such agreements appears to have peaked in the 1950s and 1960s. There are, to be sure, many less formal agreements between states, and numerous compacts that do not involve the kinds of separate governing bodies that the more prominent agreements involve. Numerous interstate compacts such as the 1965 driver's license compact, the 1960 placement of children compact, and the 1977 parole and probation compact, rather quietly operating at the agency to agency level, do much to facilitate relations between the states.

Full Faith and Credit

Many of the less visible interstate compacts, such as those governing drivers' licenses, are designed to deal with problems that arise when different states have different laws. Rather than invade the prerogatives of the states by developing a national legal system, Section 1, Article 4 of the U.S. Constitution attempted to balance diversity with sufficient uniformity to facilitate commerce and exchange between the states. It establishes the principle of reciprocal recognition by stipulating that "full faith and credit shall be given in each state to the public acts, records, and judicial proceedings of every other state." A contract signed in Massachusetts, in other words, or a driver's license issued in New Jersey, should be valid in New York. The "full faith and credit" section of the Constitution left it to Congress to "prescribe the manner in which such acts . . . shall be proved," but Congress has left the actual process pretty much up to the states and the courts.

An exception to Congress's general unwillingness to involve itself in defining the full meaning of the "full faith and credit" clause occurred in 1996. When a gay couple in Honolulu brought suit against the government of Hawaii charging that its ban on same-sex marriages was illegal, the possibility that the Hawaiian courts might sanction gay marriage was too much for many members of Congress. A law was passed exempting the other states from the necessity of honoring such marriages should they occur. This was an exceptional case. Generally, the meaning and extent of the full faith and credit clause has evolved through a long process of political accommodations and litigation.

Article IV of the Constitution also guarantees citizens the "privileges and immunities" granted by other states. A person living in New York, in other words, is as entitled to own property or do business in Vermont as is a native Vermonter. There are significant limitations on this right: a member of the New Jersey bar cannot practice law in New York without passing the New York bar exam, and it is perfectly legal for the city and state universities of New York to charge higher tuition rates to those who are not legal residents.

Finally, the states are also expected to cooperate in enforcing one another's laws. Through a procedure known as extradition, the authorities in one state can ask another state to return a suspected felon for trial. Although such requests are generally honored, New York sometimes refused to return black defendants to Southern states in the 1940s and 1950s when a segregationist system of justice made it unlikely that they would receive a fair trial. More recently, in 1994, Governor Cuomo refused to extradite to Oklahoma a man who had been accused of murder there and was already serving a life term for murder in New York. New York, unlike Oklahoma at that time, did not have capital punishment to which Governor Cuomo was philosophically opposed. One of George Pataki's first acts as governor was to extradite the man in question to Oklahoma where he was tried, convicted, and killed.

The U.S. Constitution, through the full faith and credit, extradition, and privileges and immunities clauses, imposes some loose degree of reciprocity and uniformity in state law. The realities of commerce and a more mobile life style make such cooperation even more cogent. And the law has in many ways been nationalized. Since 1897, when the West Publishing Company (St. Paul, MN) began indexing and compiling the decisions of state courts, legal precedents have flowed with growing frequency across state lines. Computerization has accelerated this flow, and federal statutes and court decisions have brought further uniformities to the judicial process. And yet:

> The struggle between uniformity and diversity, between centralism and localism, goes on without let and without end. . . . The basic issue is power: where it is placed, and who should exercise it. The structural features of the legal system reflect the distribution of power, and, at the same time, influence or perpetuate power. . . . In short, decentralization does not vanish, even in the teeth of the master trend of American legal history. . . .[65]

The Politics of Federalism

Former Speaker of the U.S. House of Representatives "Tip" O'Neill once said that "all politics is local," a phrase that has become an aphorism of

American politics. What is equally true, though less frequently acknowledged, is that *all local is politics*. It is not the Tenth Amendment, nor tradition nor philosophy, that sustains decentralization in American law and government, so much as it is the localized nature of politics in the United States. Even the Supreme Court has acknowledged that "state sovereign interests are more properly protected by procedural safeguards inherent in the structure of the federal system than by judicially created limitations on federal power."[66]

Professor Grodzins, in his essay developing the "marble-cake" image of federalism, argued that "the parties are responsible for both the existence and form of the considerable measure of decentralization that exists in the United States."[67] Whether parties continue to play as vital a role in sustaining federalism as they did three decades ago is not clear. What remains clear, however, is the local focus of so much of the dynamic of American politics.

3

Parties, Politics, and Elections

As fragmented as they are at their base, New York's political parties are remarkably cohesive, and, at one level of analysis, play a strong role in knitting together the state's disparate elements. The total number of bills defeated on the floor of the New York senate and assembly in 1995 and 1996 was zero. That's right: every bill that came to a vote—and the total was in the thousands—passed. This remarkable record of seeming consensus was not achieved because most legislators agreed on all the issues. On the contrary, the 1995–96 session was one of the most divisive in recent history. Rather, bills are not defeated in the New York legislature because the leaders of the majority parties have almost absolute control over what happens on the floor. As in the tightly disciplined "responsible parties" of Great Britain and many parliamentary democracies, the party leadership is able to exercise virtually total control over the formal process. Most of what happens on the floor of the assembly and senate has been carefully orchestrated in the secret meetings of party leaders.

As highly centralized as the parties appear to be in the legislature, New York's parties are not truly analogous to those of Great Britain, and fall far short of reform views of "responsible" parties. Horizontally, running across the three statewide elective branches, there is virtually no connection between the party systems that control, respectively, the two houses of the legislature and the offices of the governor, attorney general, and comptroller. As strong as assembly Democrats are in their chamber, or senate Republicans in theirs, they have virtually no influence (or desire to be involved) in the politics of each others' elections or, even less, in gubernatorial races. Candidates for governor, attorney general, and comptroller seldom coordinate their campaigns with each other or with fellow party members of the legislature. Vertically, there is comparable fragmentation, with individual legislative campaigns revolving more around local issues and personalities than the nuances of Albany politics. The six centralized campaign committees—the Republican and Democratic State Committees, DACC (the Democratic Assembly Campaign Committee), RACC (the Republican Assembly Campaign Committee), and their senate counterparts—are playing a steadily growing role in both bankrolling and managing key campaigns; but because the politics of primary elections is very much the politics of O'Neill's rule about all politics being local, they lack effective control over nominations. Nominations are won and lost not by permanent organizations of the faithful but by what students of campaigns call "candidate-centered coalitions."

The Organization of the Party System

The two major parties in New York—the Republicans and Democrats—have essentially monopolized the state's key political offices; but minor parties play a much more important role in New York than perhaps any other state. The Republican and Democratic parties in New York are allied in a loose sense with their counterparts in the other fifty states and with the national parties operating out of Washington. The national parties set the rules for their quadrennial presidential nominating conventions. All other rules and regulations, including those governing the selection of delegates to the national conventions, are set through state laws and state party rules. These laws, including those of New York state, give the parties a sort of quasi-legal status in which they remain private, self-funded organizations, but must follow a variety of specific rules of organization and conduct. Officially, the election code of New York state defines a political party as an organization that polled more than 50,000 votes for its candidate for governor in the last election. The two parties whose gubernatorial candidates poll the most votes are defined as major political parties.

Two Parties, Plus

Perhaps the most important quirk in New York election laws is that which allows parties to "cross-endorse" candidates. In contrast with most other states, New York law allows a party to nominate candidates already endorsed by other parties. In the 1994 gubernatorial election, for example, the Republican candidate (George Pataki) actually "lost" to the Democrat (Mario Cuomo) by a vote of 2,156,057 to 2,272,903. Pataki, however, won an additional 328,605 votes on the Conservative Party line, and 54,040 on a "Tax Cut Now" line, while Cuomo was able to win only 92,001 on the Liberal Party line. In a very real sense, the Conservative Party could (and did) claim to have made the difference in getting Pataki elected.

Candidates frequently use the gimmick employed by Pataki in 1994 of creating a unique, cutely named party like "Tax Cut Now" to broaden their appeal. While it requires effort to get such "parties" on the ballot, some campaign strategists believe that voters are more comfortable crossing over from their normal vote to something more neutral. Democrats, disillusioned with Cuomo, for example, might have been reluctant to vote Republican or Conservative, but could vote for Pataki on the "Tax Cut Now" line. Various "parties" like this appear and disappear regularly in New York, bearing such names as "Property Tax Cut," "Protect Seniors," "Taxpayers," and "Save Medicare." Other small factions turn out year after year to secure the petition signatures necessary to put their candidates on the ballot. Like the third parties in most other states, unofficial parties (unofficial in the sense that they have not reached the threshold of 50,000 gubernatorial votes specified in the election code) like the Prohibitionists, Libertarians, and Communists, seldom cross endorse and, even less frequently, win.

The most important and distinctive third parties in New York are those that have achieved more or less permanent ballot status. Currently—because they each received more than 50,000 votes in the 1998 gubernatorial election—there are eight parties that have the official recognition that automatically qualifies them for the ballot. Under the election law, the party receiving the most votes for governor, which, thanks to Pataki's overwhelming reelection margin in 1998 is now the Republicans, has its candidates listed under the first column (A) on all election machines in the state. The Democratic Party, second in the popular vote for governor, has column B. Column C is, at least until 2003, the Independence Party's; D is for the Conservatives; E for the Liberals; and F for the Right to Life. Two parties, the Greens and the Working Families Party, achieved ballot status by winning more than 50,000 votes in 1998. Their candidates will run in columns G and H.

The most senior of the established third parties, the Liberal Party was formed in 1943 with heavy labor union involvement and an explicit commitment to serve as a liberal balance to the major parties, keeping "Democrats liberal and Republicans honest."[1] The Conservative Party, essentially a mirror clone of the Liberals, was established in 1962 by a group of disgruntled Republicans who felt that the Rockefeller-led Republican Party had strayed too far to the center. The Right to Life Party is, essentially, a pressure group masquerading as a party. As its name indicates, its concerns are focused on the issue of abortion, and it becomes involved in campaigns only when abortion is an issue. Organizationally, the Liberal, Independent, Right to Life, and Conservative parties are rather hollow shells. The Conservative Party is the only minor party in recent years to have topped 100,000 in enrolled voters, an average of about seven in each election district. In most counties, the minor parties' executive committees, as one assembly member wryly puts it, "meet in a phone booth." The real power of these parties is their continuing

Box 3.1

How New York's Minor Parties Play the Game

- In 1980, a relatively obscure Nassau County Republican, Alfonse D'Amato, calculated that he could win the Republican primary against Senator Jacob Javits, who was seventy-six years old and, as D'Amato ads pointed out, "ailing and liberal."* The second, more difficult part of D'Amato's scenario—beating Democrat Elizabeth Holtzman in the November general election—became plausible when the Liberal Party backed Javits who, after losing the Republican primary ran again on the Liberal line. Result: D'Amato 45 percent, Holtzman 44 percent, Javits 11 percent. Neither Holtzman nor her strongest backers have ever forgiven the Liberals or the late senator Javits for "giving" the election to D'Amato.
- In 1978, as reported by Spitzer, "Republican gubernatorial candidate Perry Duryea sought the Conservative party line in his unsuccessful bid to unseat Hugh Carey. Since Duryea's conservative credentials were less than sterling, he struck a deal with Conservative party leaders that allowed the Conservative party to nominate one of their own, William Carney, for the U.S. Congress from the first congressional district (Duryea's home area) in exchange for granting Duryea the Conservative line for his gubernatorial race. Carney was later elected after winning the Republican primary." Duryea was not.†
- In 1989, the Liberal Party's disillusionment with New York City Mayor Ed Koch was strong enough that the party's leader Raymond Harding began actively to support the candidacy of Republican Rudolph Giuliani. Giuliani, in turn, began to fudge his more conservative positions, such as his previous opposition to abortion. Koch, meanwhile, lost the Democratic primary to David Dinkins; but Harding stuck with Giuliani and went down to defeat. Four years later, however, the Liberals and Republicans stuck by their 1989 deal and Giuliani became the city's first Republican mayor in more than thirty years. (It is worth noting that the city's previous Republican mayor, John Lindsay, actually lost the Republican primary in his second campaign but won reelection running as a Liberal).
- In 1990, no prominent Republican could be found to run against Democratic governor Mario Cuomo. The most enthusiastic and articulate candidate, New York University Dean Herbert London, was virtually unknown and far too conservative for most Republicans, who settled on the lackluster Pierre Rinfret as their candidate. The Conservatives nominated London, who turned out to be as energetic as Rinfret was inept.

Cuomo won handily, and the Republicans came close to losing their status as a major party with Rienfret getting only 22 percent of the vote to London's 21 percent. Four years later, Republican leaders, carefully consulted with the Conservatives before agreeing to run George Pataki against a far less popular Cuomo. They won.

---

*Michael Barone and Grant Ujifusa, *The Almanac of American Politics 1994* (Washington: National Journal, 1993), p. 862.

†Robert J. Spitzer, "Third Parties in New York State," in Jeffrey M. Stonecash, John Kenneth White, and Peter W. Colby, eds., *Governing New York State* (Albany: State University of New York Press, 1994), pp. 109–10.

ability to use the weapon of cross endorsements to work with and against the candidates of the major parties.

The elections described in Box 3.1 are illustrative of the different ways in which the minor parties, the Liberals and Conservatives in particular, have been able to magnify their electoral impact by cross-endorsement strategies. One study of New York's third parties, using data from all state senate races from 1950 to 1988, found them to be a significant force in only about three percent of the elections;[2] but these case studies show why they remain an important factor in the strategic calculations of candidates and party leaders. They derive disproportionate influence in no small part from the widespread perception that some third-party cross endorsements are at least superficially decisive in electoral outcomes.

This perception sustains the Liberal and Conservative parties in two ways. First, it leads major party candidates, particularly those in close races, actively to court cross endorsements. In state legislative campaigns in 1990, 43 percent of the Democratic candidates for the assembly and senate, and 60 percent of the Republicans also ran on the Liberal, Conservative, or Right to Life lines.[3] Second, the Liberal and Conservative parties have frequently reaped rewards of patronage in exchange for their support. McNickle describes the relationship between the former Liberal Party chairman Alex Rose and former New York City mayor Robert Wagner as one based in large part on Rose's ability to win commissionerships, judgeships, and scores of lesser jobs for Liberal Party stalwarts.

The relatively small number of registered Liberal party loyalists, and the high number of patronage positions Rose commanded under Wagner, meant that he could deliver more jobs per party supporter than any person in New

Table 3.1

Minor Party Endorsements of Major Party Candidates for New York State Legislative Races, 1990

Minor party endorsements	Democrats		Republicans	
	No.	(%)	No.	(%)
Conservative	16	(13)	107	(87)
Liberal	72	(96)	3	(4)
Right to Life	2	(11)	16	(89)

Source: Adapted from figures compiled by Robert J. Spitzer, "Third Parties in New York State," in *Governing New York State*, eds., Jeffrey M. Stonecash, John Kenneth White, and Peter W. Colby (Albany: State University of New York Press, 1994), p. 107.

York. The mayor himself once implied that the Liberals held up to five hundred important positions.[4]

City Liberals enjoy a similar relationship today with Mayor Giuliani, and the state Conservative Party has done quite well in securing patronage positions from Governor Pataki. There seems little doubt that these potential channels of access are as important in sustaining the organizational needs of the Liberals and Conservatives as are the ideologies reflected in their labels. "By 1980," as Scarrow puts it, "only Right to Life activists were known for their greater concern with the latter than the former."[5]

One of the most important functions of the minor parties is that of punishing the Republicans and Democrats when they deviate too far from the faith. As can be seen in Table 3.1, the Liberal Party almost always gives its cross endorsements to Democrats, the Conservatives and Right to Lifers to Republicans. The possibility that the Liberals might run a candidate of their own who would siphon away traditional Democratic votes is as unsettling to Democrats as a comparable threat from the Conservatives is to Republicans. The dilemma is compounded by an electoral calendar that gives minor parties extra leverage. It works like this: the power to allow a person (i.e., a Democrat) to run on another line (in this case, Liberal) is vested in the executive committee of the Liberal Party. Typically, it meets about a week before the process of qualifying candidates for the Democratic primary begins. Thus when one of the authors of this book (Schneier) decided to challenge an incumbent Democratic congressman, he had to decide whether to run as a Liberal *before* he knew whether he would win the Democratic nomination. Under the election law, there are only two ways a nominated candidate can get off the ballot: being appointed to a judgeship or dying. Schneier, unqualified for the bench and unprepared for death, wound up running a hopeless, third-party race in November that led some Democrats to charge him with trying to help the Republicans.

Patterns of Party Competition

Depending on how one looks at the question, New York has either one of the most competitive party systems in the country or one of the least. The strength of the state's minor parties often results in contests—like the 1994 gubernatorial race—in which the winning party receives less than a majority of the total vote. Statewide elections, moreover, have seldom been landslides. Yet "although New York continues to be highly competitive at the statewide level, it is equally true that most areas of the state are better described as being areas of one-party dominance."[6] The 1996 state legislative elections were relatively typical: in the state senate, party control changed in only two of 61 seats; in 51 of the remaining 59, the winning candidate received more than 60 percent of the vote; and there were fifteen candidates who ran without major party opposition. In the state assembly, only one of 151 seats changed parties; 132 were won by margins exceeding 60 percent; and thirty of these candidates had what amounted to a free ride. A total of three seats, all in the assembly, changed party control in 1998. Looking at the 1998 elections to the U.S. House of Representatives, the Center for Voting and Democracy's "democracy index"—a measure of the relative competitiveness of House elections—ranked New York 36th among the fifty states.[7] In Rosenthal's tabulation of state legislative turnover from 1987 through 1997, New York's senate ranked last, its assembly 48th of 49 lower houses.[8]

With significant exceptions, the pattern of party noncompetition follows a predictable path: Democrats win easily in New York City and in some upstate cities, Republicans win everywhere else. The exceptions—particularly in suburbs surrounding the city—are interesting and important, but as Jeffrey Stonecash has written:

> For much of the twentieth century the bases of political parties in New York have been simple and clear. Republicans dominated upstate and the suburban areas around New York City. Democrats dominated New York City and a few upstate urban areas. This division reflected the longstanding hostility of upstate to New York City. New York was regarded as "different"[9]

This sense of difference can perhaps be traced as far back as the early days of largely Dutch settlements downstate and English elsewhere, or to the Revolutionary War divisions between loyalists and patriots. Certainly it became manifest in the late 1800s when new waves of immigrants poured largely into the city. The political mobilization of these groups by Democratic Party organizations like New York's Tammany Hall and Albany's equally strong urban machine, "further convinced upstate Republicans that . . . Democrats were not to be trusted."[10] (Notwithstanding the fact that Republican machines were similarly dominant in many other parts of the state.) The increasing ability of Democrats to win assembly and senate seats outside of New York City has altered this regional factor significantly; but the upstate-downstate cleavage remains one of the most important defining characteristics of New York politics.

In the 1994 gubernatorial campaign, to cite an extreme but illustrative case, the winning Republican candidate, George Pataki, received 82 percent of the votes cast in rural Hamilton County (north of Syracuse), the mirror opposite of his performance in New York County (Manhattan) where he won only 18 percent. Mario Cuomo carried four of New York City's five boroughs (losing Staten Island by a narrow margin); but was able to win only one other county (Albany) in the entire state. Cumulatively, Democrat Cuomo won 71 percent of the vote in the city, 38 percent upstate.

Although upstate-downstate differences are important in other states, the political shadow cast by the New York City metropolitan area is unique. Pataki, whose roots in Westchester County place him in the area defined by the Census Bureau as comprising the New York Standard and Consolidated Statistical Area, kept alive the nation's longest-running regional victory streak: since 1960 every governor and U.S. senator elected statewide has come from New York City or its immediate environs. With his election in 1994, Dennis Vacco of Buffalo became the first upstate attorney general since 1928. Save for Buffalo's Ned Regan, every comptroller since 1950 has been from downstate. In Illinois, the Chicago metropolitan area has more than 60 percent of the state's population, Boston similarly dominates Massachusetts; yet "when each metro region's percentage of its state's population is compared with the area's share of the winners in the contests for governor and senator, New York turns out to have the largest regional imbalance."[11] Upstate, outnumbered by more than a million votes, also is highly fragmented. It has, for example, four of the United States's fifty largest television markets in Albany, Buffalo, Rochester, and Syracuse; yet the four combined total less than half the viewers of New York City. For the statewide candidate seeking media exposure, upstate is "a series of airports" encountered in an all-day "fly through" that will nonetheless yield less than half the media exposure of a single appearance in New York City. A local politician who makes the news in the New York City area "is regularly beamed into two-thirds of New York's households. His counterpart in Buffalo [the state's second-largest television market] has his local accomplishments broadcast to only 9.8 percent of the state's homes."[12] Big a fish as he or she may be in the home pond, the upstate politician is a minnow swimming among whales when it comes to comparative media exposure.

The legislature provides some balance. The Republican conference that controls the state senate draws only eleven of its thirty-five members from downstate. Democrats gained control of the assembly only when they began regularly to win upstate seats (particularly in the larger urban areas). And candidates for statewide office who cannot draw a certain base vote upstate will lose. The perceptive journalist Warren Moscow in 1948 criticized "a tendency to oversimplify the normal voting habits of the state electorate by explaining that 'rural' upstate, the fifty-seven counties outside the big city limits of New York, votes Republican and that New York City votes Democratic."[13] And there is even greater truth to Moscow's observation today. Within the city, Staten Island is competitive, with the Republicans often having an edge. The Bay Ridge section of Brooklyn, parts of the northeast Bronx, and many of the non-Hispanic, white neighborhoods of Queens are as reliably Republican as some rural areas. Many of New York City's suburbs are highly competitive, and upstate cities regularly send Democrats to the state legislature and vote Democratic for national and state offices. Many rural Republicans, moreover, are the kind of moderate Republicans who will support centrist Democrats like President Clinton for national office. In the 1996 campaign, Clinton won all but eleven counties. Only rarely, however, do most of these areas vote Democratic in state elections. Hostility to New York City is a staple of politics in upstate urban areas which might sympathize with its essential policy concerns, and the flogging of upcountry "hicks" is part of the ritual of New York's politics even among politicians who know better. Outside of the big cities, Democratic candidates upstate, and Republicans in New York City, tend to hide their party affiliations when they campaign.

More than in most states, regionalism has tended to distort the political demography of New York. Many working-class voters who might normally vote Democratic (and who often do so in national elections), vote Republican for state offices out of hostility toward the city. More affluent voters in the city, normally drawn more to the Republican Party, vote Democratic out of a feeling that Republicans do not understand the special problems of New Yorkers.

> Taken as a whole, upstate is far more Republican than states with similar proportions of urban, industrial, foreign-born, and Catholic population; similarly, upstate cities are more Republican than cities of equivalent size elsewhere in the country. Presumably the difference in partisan attachment

lies in the element that distinguishes upstate from other units, its location within the same state as a metropolitan center that threatens to dominate the state government by sheer force of numbers.[14]

New York, for its part, is not only more Democratic than most, but it actually tends to be more liberal on most issues. In part, it is a question of demographics. As compared with other large cities in the United States, "New York City is much less black, much more Latino, much less Protestant, much more Catholic, and much more Jewish."[15] But the city's liberalism transcends demographics: its wealthy, white Protestants are far more liberal than those polled in national surveys, its Hispanics more progressive than other Hispanics, and so on. As most upstate New Yorkers have long suspected, "the data support the hypothesis that New Yorkers have substantial policy differences with respondents in the rest of the nation even when compared within a given racial or ethnoreligious group."[16]

The very slow rate of turnover in legislative seats is one by-product of regional cleavage. Interparty competition for seats in the state legislature has become something of a rarity, and the gaps are widening. "Since 1900 the average margin of victory (percentage points by which the winner leads the loser) in legislative elections has steadily increased from a little over 20 to the current level of 54 percentage points."[17] Very few districts have close elections in November. In fact many legislators worry more about possible challenges from fellow party members in the September primary elections than they do about candidates of the opposite party in November.

The growing importance of primary elections has contributed to the growing fragmentation of the party system. Party discipline in the legislature exists despite rather than because of the parties' ability to control nominations. It is, at the same time, a legacy of the days when strong party organizations—both Republican and Democratic—very much dominated the electoral process. The old machines, fueled by patronage and their ability to control the nominating process, are either nonexistent or toothless shadows of their former selves. Yet their influence continues to be felt in the ways the parties are organized and go about their business.

The Shadow of Tammany Hall: Party Organization and the Rules of the Game

No organization better typifies the often-maligned urban political machine than New York City's Tammany Hall. At its peak in the late nineteenth century, Tammany seldom lost control of the city's government and was frequently able to elect governors as well. In the city its patronage powers extended to virtually all municipal jobs and contracts. If you wanted to work for or with the city you went through Tammany. If you wanted to run for political office, you apprenticed in the organization, turning out the vote, organizing the community, and delivering services. Those who supported the organization with their work, votes, or money received their just rewards. Others did not.

Critics of machine politics, and they are many, focused upon the morality of an electoral system based on a system of favor trading that was almost inherently corrupt. But the machine had positive functions as well: its capacity for personalizing politics and bringing it into every neighborhood, for providing channels of upward mobility to those ethnic groups excluded from more conventional pathways to success, and for integrating immigrants into the nuances of a foreign culture. Its role in organizing the dynamically changing political and economic life of the emerging industrial society, it could also be argued, helped make democracy work and cities governable.[18]

However one evaluates the roles of organizations like Tammany Hall, their influence pervaded New York state politics from the late nineteenth century well into the twentieth. Aside from Tammany, which dominated New York City's Democratic Party for more than a century, the Albany County machine of "Uncle Dan" O'Connell and Erastus Corning effectively ruled that area from the 1920s until quite recently.[19] Buffalo's Crotty Organization similarly dominated Erie County politics well into the 1970s. Cohesive Republican organizations dominated the politics of both Syracuse and Rochester at the turn of the century, and were a major force in such upstate cities as Utica and Schenectady as recently as the 1960s.[20] And remnants of the patronage-driven Republican organizations in Nassau and Suffolk counties can still be found at the local level and in the continuing ability of the party organizations to control nominations.

Periodic reform movements succeeded from time to time in displacing the machines; and in the early part of the twentieth century, reformers succeeded in enacting a number of laws designed both to curb abuses of power and weaken the party organizations. The most important of these reforms were those restricting the suffrage, establishing primary elections, and creating the civil service system. None of these changes were to prove immediately fatal to the better-situated machines. Most students of American political history see the rise of the New Deal welfare state as far more corrosive of the party organizations' main bases of power. It seems likely, moreover, that curbs on immigration combined with other demographic changes, such as increased access to education, played an important role in the eventual demise of Tammany Hall and its counterparts. With or without civil service reforms, growing affluence made municipal jobs less attractive; the welfare state displaced the precinct worker as the friend of the needy; and a better-educated electorate preferred to make its own decisions about how to vote—"favors, friendship, jobs, the Christmas turkey—lost their magic when compared to the rewards of middle-class life. Greater affluence gave the "new" middle class a higher stake in society, making its members more issue-oriented and less likely to swap a vote for a favor."[21] The development of the mass media, moreover, gave these new-style voters a direct access to candidates and elected officials that enabled them effectively to bypass the parties entirely.

The reform laws aimed at the machines, and the machines themselves, both continue to leave important imprints on New York politics. The basic structure of the parties, as codified in the state election laws, is essentially that of the old machines. In its most elaborate form, Tammany Hall constituted, as Moynihan describes it:

> . . . a massive party bureaucracy, which rivaled the medieval Catholic Church in the proportion of the citizenry involved. The county committees of the five boroughs came to number more than thirty-two thousand persons. It became necessary to hire Madison Square Garden for their meetings—and to hope that not more than half the number would show up as there wouldn't be room.
>
> [It was] a political bureaucracy in which rights appertained not to individuals but to the positions they occupied. "Have you seen your block captain?" It did not matter that your captain was an idiot or a drunk or a devout churchgoer who would be alarmed by the request at hand; the block captain had to be seen first. Then the election district captain. Then the district leader. The hierarchy had to be recognized.[22]

This essential structure is still embodied in the election code, which allows each of the state's approximately 13,000 election districts to select two members of each party in the primary election. Although the New York City machine was defeated more than thirty years ago, when reform Democrats won enough of these very local races to take control of the party organization, the reformers who control the organization in Manhattan continue to elect county committeemen and women throughout the borough, and to staff the hierarchy once dominated by Tammany.

The individual precinct or election district, commonly known as an ED, is at the base—in both law and practice—of the modern party organization as it was of the machine. Usually comprised of fewer than a thousand registered voters, each ED elects two party leaders (one of each gender) for each party. These election district leaders (known as county committeemen and committeewomen in New York City) are the building blocks of the party organizations. At the next rung up the ladder are the elected party officials variously known as ward leaders, district leaders, and town chairs. Typically, these party officials elect a county executive committee and a county leader. The modern county leader is the lineal descendent of the old machine boss. His or her power, like that of the boss, derives from his or her ability to maintain the support of those lower in the party hierarchy, although the term "hierarchy" seldom describes the relationships between leaders and led in organizations usually characterized as "porous," "ad hoc," and "permeable."[23]

Just as some bosses were more successful than others in keeping the diverse factions of the machine under control, there are important variations in the ability of contemporary county chairs to control their organizations. Although few would use the term "machine" to describe anything as fluid as most contemporary party organizations, Republicans in Nassau, Suffolk, and many upstate counties seldom experience competitive primaries and have been able, in general, to decide who can run as a Republican and who cannot. Similarly, in most of Brooklyn and in some upstate areas, the Democratic Party organization is as dominant in selecting candidates as Tammany ever was. The motivations of those who become party activists has changed. Usually motivated more by ideology than by dreams of patronage or other tangible rewards, "They use the party," as one study of Democratic district leaders in Westchester put it, "to achieve some version of their own visions of the future, playing the party's game to the extent that they agree with its goals."[24] As in the days of Tammany, the people who hold the party organizations together and give it continuity from one election to the next are those largely self-recruited individuals who toil at the election district and town committee level. They are at the base of an organization that is hierarchical in its formal structure but loose, amorphous, and—quite frequently—democratic in its actual operation.

Campaigns and Elections

In New York, as in most other states, we have moved increasingly toward a system of "candidate-centered campaigns" that bypass party organizations. It also is true, paradoxically, that the state's major party organizations—the Republican and Democratic state committees, and the assembly and senate campaign committees of the two parties—are better financed and more professional than at any time in modern history. The major parties are stronger in their ability to channel resources into campaigns than at any time since the heyday of the machine, but, unlike the old organizations, they have been unable to establish consistent effective control over the process of recruitment. Nor have they been able or interested in coordinating resources from one level of government to another, or between and among the two houses of the legislature and the offices of governor, lieutenant governor, attorney general, and controller. One of the keys to the effectiveness of organizations like Tammany was its vertical and horizontal integration: once the organization decided its policy, it had the ability to put it into effect. The hallmark of the modern party system in New York is its fragmentation. Despite the growing clout to the Republican State Committee under the recent chairmanship of William Powers, operationally, it is a multiparty system functioning under two labels.

Candidates, Parties, and Campaigns

New York state election law provides that in addition to precinct county committee members and district leaders, the parties in each county elect representatives to a state committee. The major party's state committeemen and committeewomen constitute the official governing bodies of the parties. The state committee does not get involved in races for congress, local office, or the state legislature, but it does have the power to set party rules not governed by the election code, and to endorse candidates for statewide office. Until 1967, endorsement by the state convention was the only way to get on the ballot, and it remains generally true that the state committees of the minor parties, and of the Republicans, have been able to choose the parties' nominees for statewide office with considerable regularity. Not so with the Democrats where endorsement by the party convention has been more a liability than an asset.

Under the 1967 primary law, any candidate supported by a majority of the state convention automatically appears on the primary ballot. A nonwinner who garners at least 25 percent of the vote on at least one ballot is not the endorsed candidate, but can appear on the ballot without going through the tedious process of gathering statewide petition signatures. In the 1974 Democratic primary, the voters rejected the convention's choices for governor, lieutenant governor, and U.S. senator. Since that fateful year, it almost has become a kiss of death for a nonincumbent to win the convention endorsement. While many reformers celebrate the independent spirit of the voters manifested in such rejections of party mandates, others see in the 1974 case an important cautionary tale. Where the state convention had gone out of its way to put forth a "balanced" slate, the Democratic primary voters selected one consisting entirely of candidates from New York City, one of them black and three Jewish. All but one (Comptroller Arthur Levitt) lost in the general election.

Both the Republican and Democratic parties regularly face a tension between the preferences of their core primary voters and the candidate attributes most likely to win elections in November. Because only the most dedicated partisans turn out for primary elections in New York, Democratic and Republican primary voters are unusually polarized ideologically as compared with the electorate as a whole. The reform clubs that took over from Tammany Hall in New York City in the 1960s were loosely organized into a citywide co-action called the New Democratic Coalition, or NDC. The real meaning of these initials, old-line Democrats liked to say was "November Don't Count," meaning that the reformers were more interested in making their ideological point in primary elections than in beating the Republicans in November. Whatever the truth of this charge, the tension between the dynamics of the primary system, where the only people eligible to vote are those already registered as Democrats or Republicans. and the general elections, where anyone can vote, is intense. It is compounded by the fact that primary voters are drawn from a very narrow cross section of the state electorate. In the competitive elections of 1992, Bill Clinton won both the Democratic primary and the November general election. The numbers are instructive. Of the roughly 12 million New Yorkers eligible to vote, 8,818,691 were registered. Of the registered voters, 4,140,794 were registered as Democrats and eligible under state law to vote in the April presidential primary. A little over one million actually did. In the November general election, Clinton carried the state with just under three and a half million votes. In the Democratic primary he won with 412,000, just about 10 percent of the state's registered Democrats, or about thirty people per election district.[25]

As one moves down the ballot to less visible races, the primary electorate shrinks still further. It is little wonder that Tammany Hall and other machines were not particularly hurt by the introduction of the direct primary system. Indeed the combination of primary elections and another key turn-of-the century "reform"—voter registration—made the machine's job of winning elections less difficult. In part, it was simply a question of numbers. In general elections in the 1880s participation rates sometimes exceeded 90 percent statewide. Thirty years later, even before the introduction of women's suffrage plunged the rates still lower, it had fallen into the 60 percent range. In the 1990s it is closer to 50 percent in November general elections for highly visible offices like president and governor, far lower in elections for congress and the state legislature, and lower still in primaries.

The unwillingness of many New Yorkers to vote in party primaries is quite remarkable, especially since those are elections that are usually decisive. A few recent examples illustrate the point. The 99th Assembly District, covering parts of Columbia and Dutchess counties, is so safely Republican that in 1996 no Democrat could be found to run against the incumbent Patrick Manning. But a local Conservative, Sean Donahue, who had run against

---

Box 3.2

Registering as an "Independent," or, How to Give Away Your Vote

In New York, as throughout the United States, a growing number of people prefer to think of themselves as "independents," unaffiliated with any organized political party. As in most states, a voter in New York—when he or she registers to vote—has the option of enrolling in any of the official parties or of refusing to state a party preference. How you register has nothing to with how you vote in November: in the secrecy of the voting booth a registered Democrat can vote for Liberals, Republicans, or whatever candidates on whatever lines he or she prefers. New York, however, has a *closed* primary system, an election law that allows only the enrolled members of a party to vote in its primaries. A registered Conservative cannot vote in the primary election of any party but the Conservative's. Voters who declare themselves independent by not checking a party preference when they register cannot vote in any primaries. By registering as independents, in other words, they have effectively disenfranchised themselves in what is often the most important election.

What if you change your mind? Suppose a person not registered in the Democratic Party had become interested in the campaign of one of the Democrats vying to challenge Alfonse D'Amato in the November 1998 election? Sorry, buddy, not this time: under New York law you can vote in a party primary only if you change your registration the year before the primary in question (that is, in 1997). Despite this fact, there were—as of 1997—close to two million registered voters in New York, more than 20 percent of the electorate, who had made themselves ineligible to vote in any party primaries in 1998 by refusing to state a party preference. In New York, political "independence" comes at a high price.

Manning in 1994, decided to challenge him in the Republican primary and was endorsed by a number of prominent Republicans. A total of 6,080 voted in the September primary, making Manning the Republican candidate, and an almost sure bet for reelection in November, by a margin of 3,755 to 2,325. Running on the Conservative line in November, Donahue alone got more votes (7,332) than the combined total cast in the primary but, as expected, lost by a margin of nearly 20,000 votes. In the 107th District, north of Albany, incumbent Arnold Proskin was the only Republican to lose his assembly seat in 1994. He lost it in the Republican primary by total votes of 3,321 to 3,604. His challenger, Robert Prentiss, went on to win in November with more than 24,000 Republican votes.

Both of these races received rather extensive coverage in the media, and were relatively well-financed. Manning spent more on his primary campaign than he did in the general election, and Prentiss about the same in both. Yet in both cases, they received *more than seven times as many* Republican votes in the November general election than they did in the more testing primaries. To put it another way, fewer than one Republican voter in three cast his or her ballot in the election that really mattered.

As a rule, the more visible the office, the less the gap between primary and general election votes. That is, more people vote in primaries for governor and president than in contests for Congress; more for congress than the state legislature; more for the state legislature than for judges or party officials. Even at the higher levels, however, New Yorkers are remarkably less likely to exercise their voting rights in primary elections than the citizens of most other states.

Who Votes and Who Doesn't

The United States is virtually unique among industrial democracies in the proportion of its citizens who do not vote. And New York state is increasingly distinguishing itself as a state in which voter participation rates are, even by American standards, unusually low. As far back as the 1920s and 1930s, New York ranked in the bottom third among northern states in voter turnout. The Voting Rights Act of 1965 was designed essentially to give the federal government a role in helping people to vote in areas where they had previously been disenfranchised. Aimed essentially at those Southern states whose segregationist politics had routinely prevented most African Americans from voting, the law targeted counties, almost entirely in the South, whose histories of nonvoting suggested systematic patterns of bias. New York is one of the three non-Southern states still under such federal jurisdiction. In the 1992 presidential election, New York ranked forty-first in the nation in voter turnout. Whatever it is that depresses electoral participation in the United States appears to operate with particular force in New York state. More important, given the noncompetitive character of many senate and assembly districts, there are few states in which turnout in primary elections is lower than it is in New York.

A long-running debate among political scientists about voter turnout features three principal explanations. One school emphasizes demographic variables. Noting a strong relationship between low income, youth, ethnicity, and—in particular—lack of education on one hand, and low voting rates on the other, a number of studies have suggested that nonvoting is best explained in terms of such factors as motivation, mobilization, and efficacy. Poorly educated people lack the information to make politics salient; the poor, more generally, are likely to lack a sense of political efficacy, or a feeling that their votes count, to participate in a process that seems remote from their everyday lives. Recent immigrants, it is sometimes suggested, are similarly detached from the system even when they are legally eligible to vote.

While the correlations between nonvoting and such characteristics as poverty are clear, other scholars have taken a more rationalistic approach: people, they argue, decide whether to vote pretty much as the economist's rational consumer makes market decisions. If the "benefits" of voting seem to outweigh the "costs," people vote; if costs outweigh benefits, they stay home. Emphasizing the "cost" side of the equation are those scholars who argue that nonvoting in the United States is largely the product of deliberately constructed impediments to voting, such as difficult registration requirements, inconvenient times and places of election, and aggressive efforts to intimidate and threaten potential voters. Looking at the other side of the equation are those who attribute nonvoting largely to the failure of the political system to offer meaningful choices to marginal voters. Stressing the failure of parties and candidates to reach out to the young and poor, the lack of meaningful competition in most areas, and the failure of politicians to address the real concerns of nonvoters, these scholars attribute nonvoting largely to the failure of groups like the Democratic Party and the union movement effectively to reach out to their natural constituencies.

Increasingly, students of voting are moving toward a theory that stresses the complementary interaction of these three factors.[26] There seems to be a self-reinforcing triangle that increasingly has the effect of driving lower status citizens out of the voting pool. Less educated people are more easily intimidated by paperwork and less likely to know how to go about filing the proper papers to vote. Because the young and the poor are less likely to be parts of communities in which friends and neighbors are active politically, they are similarly less likely to be encouraged and helped toward participation. Politicians, for their part, have little incentive either to seek the support of such citizens or to make it easier for them to vote; and the boards of elections, appointed under the patronage of these same politicians, seldom see their role as that of facilitating citizen participation.[27] Campaigns, quite naturally, are pitched toward the existing pool of registered voters; and those who run them are, as incumbents, leery of election law reforms that might dramatically alter the rules of the game that have worked well for them in the past. Nonvoters, for their part, correctly perceiving that politicians pay little heed to their communities, have still less incentive to become involved in the process.

A major consequence of this dynamic is the growing disenfranchisement of the poor. In 1994, New York's Voter Assistance Commission's district-by-district analysis concluded that each increment of $10,000 in median income was associated with a 3.7 percent increase in voter turnout.[28] Within New York City, the contrasts can be striking. On Manhattan's Upper East Side the general election turnout in the affluent 65th Assembly District (AD) was 38,359, nearly triple the vote cast in the impoverished 78th AD of the South Bronx where only 13,751 voters went to the polls. The contrasts are less dramatic, but still significant, upstate. The rural 149th AD, on the western edge of the New York-Pennsylvania border, covers two of the state's poorest counties (Allegheny and Cattaraugus). It sent 40,146 voters to the polls in 1994—more than *any* district in New York City—but 20 percent fewer than the 49,559 who turned out in Westchester County's 89th AD (Bedford/Mt. Kisco), one of the wealthiest in the state.

While income explains many of the variations in voting participation between different areas of the state, it does not account for the waning influence of New York City in state politics. The declining population of the city relative to the rest of the state has significantly reduced its ability to control statewide elections. Much of this decline can be attributed to population movements that have reduced the city's share of the state's population from 55 percent in the 1930 census to 41 percent in 1990. But New York's *political weight* has declined even more precipitously to the point where, in the 1994 gubernatorial race, the city cast less than 30 percent of the total vote. As can be seen in Figure 3.1, voter turnout rates in the city have consistently lagged behind the rest of the state; but while both rates have been declining steadily for more than forty years, the gap between New York City and the rest of the state has grown from an average of 7 or 8 percent to 11, 12, and (in 1980) as high as 17 percent.

A surprisingly small proportion of this decline is attributable to immigration. Clearly, one would expect New York City—because its population includes a higher proportion of aliens not eligible to vote—would have a somewhat lower voting rate than the rest of the state. Because Latinos tend to have higher proportions of citizens below the voting age, moreover, one would expect a further drop in participation. But these differences are not as significant as one would think: statewide, for example, "Latinos represent 12.31 percent of the total population and 11.20 percent of New York's voting age population."[29] Despite their formal eligibility to vote, however, few Hispanics have actually exercised the right. In New York City the gap is substantial: while 73.5 percent of voting age non-Hispanic white New Yorkers were registered to vote in 1993, the comparable figure for Hispanics was only 52.6. Asians were even lower at 25.2 percent.[30] African Americans, by way of contrast, have had unusually high levels of registration in the city, particularly since the 1980s when Jessie Jackson's presidential campaign

Figure 3.1 **Voter Turnout in Presidential Elections: Percentage of Adult-Age Population Voting in New York City and State (1952–1996)**

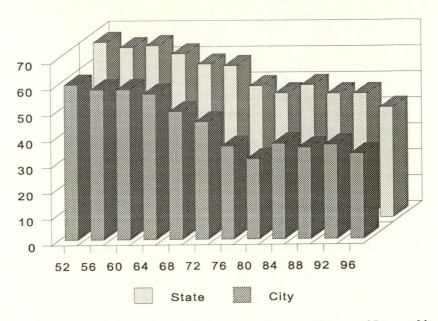

Source: Figures for 1952 through 1992 are taken from the 1994 *Annual Report of the New York City Voter Assistance Commission*, p. 35. Figures for 1996 are from the City and State Boards of Elections and census projections as calculated by the authors.

put a great deal of effort into registration drives, and the candidacy of David Dinkins for mayor in 1989 and 1993 sustained the effort. Although the effects of these events are beginning to erode, black registration levels actually exceeded those of whites in 1993 (76.8 percent to 73.6 percent).[31] Race would appear to be a less significant factor than class in predicting voter turnout. The key facts are (a) that eligible New York City voters are considerably less likely than their upstate counterparts either to register or to vote; and that (b) throughout the state the gaps in voter turnout between rich and poor are substantial and growing.

The gaps between New York City and upstate are in part the product of deliberate policy choices. The federal "motor voter" act required the states to provide easy access to voter registration forms for those applying for documents such as new driver's licenses. Although the law specifically mandated voter registration efforts in social welfare agencies, colleges, and high schools, as well as motor vehicle offices, this part of the mandate was largely ignored in New York; and one of George Pataki's first acts as governor was to defund enforcement of the program. Since only half of the city's voting age citizens have driver's licenses, as contrasted with more than 90 percent of those living outside the city, the predictable result has been a widening of the registration gap between New York City and the rest of the state.

That neither Governor Pataki nor the Republican state senate was enthusiastic about increasing voter registration is not surprising. The people least likely to vote are poor people from New York City, and these persons have generally been more inclined to vote Democratic. But although former governor Cuomo and the Democrats in the state assembly were supportive of an expanded "motor voter" program, they did not fight as hard for it as one might have imagined. What seems to have been at work here was a common reluctance on the part of most politicians to tamper with the method of election that got them where they are. New voters are wild cards, people who might support primary challengers, or even vote the "wrong" way (that is, against the incumbent) in the general election. Often there has been an unspoken bipartisan agreement not to risk whatever unpredictable consequences might flow from attempts to register the unregistered.

Districting and the Permanently Divided Legislature

Few things are more threatening to incumbent politicians than changes in the rules of the game. Changes in the laws regarding who can vote, how candidates are chosen, and what rules shall govern campaign finance, have usually come—at both the state and national levels—only after long periods of public agitation. There are few areas that more clearly demonstrate this inherent conservatism than those surrounding the periodic redrawing of legislative district lines.

One Person, One Vote

Every ten years, following the national census of population, the governor and the legislature must agree to plan for redrawing the lines of legislative districts to reflect changes in population. Although the state constitution requires periodic reapportionments, it does not mandate districts of equal size. Indeed the 1894 constitution (which is still in effect) was engineered by the upstate Republicans who controlled the convention to ensure that New York City would never be able to elect a majority of either house of the legislature. It did this by guaranteeing sixty of the state's sixty-two counties at least one seat in the assembly, and providing that "no two counties divided by a river— New York and Kings (Brooklyn) were in mind—could ever have half the Senate seats."[32] Demographic changes and the popularity of Democrats like Roosevelt and Lehman sometimes allowed the Democrats partially to overcome the bad hands dealt them by this malapportionment; but the decisive period in the history of New York's legislative elections had its dawn in a 1962 Tennessee case known as *Baker v. Carr* that was decided by the Supreme Court of the United States.[33] Although the Tennessee constitution—like that of the federal government and most other states—required the state to reapportion its legislative districts every ten years, it had not done so for more than sixty years. As a result, assembly districts in Tennessee ranged in population from a low of 3,454 to a high of 79,031. In a similar case in 1946 the court had refused to involve itself in what the majority called a "political thicket."[34]

In *Baker v. Carr* the court entered the thicket. By ruling the Tennessee case justiciable and enunciating the standard of "one man, one vote" the court placed itself on a track that soon revolutionized the process of legislative districting throughout the United States. By grounding its opinion in the federal equal protection clause rather than the Tennessee constitution, the court opened the door to challenges of the legislatures of almost every state. Baker was underrepresented because the Tennessee legislature had failed to keep up with population changes in drawing district lines. But what about a resident of New York City who was similarly "underrepresented" because his or her state constitution mandated it? The court's answer was not long in coming. Chief Justice Warren, writing for the majority in 1964, held that "the Equal Protection Clause requires that the seats in both houses of a bicameral state legislature must be apportioned on a population basis."[35]

Zimmerman and others have argued that ignoring these rulings in favor of strict population equality, while eliminating "rural over representation and urban under representation . . . made gerrymandering easier. . . . In other words, equally populated districts may have unfair district lines."[36] The term "gerrymander" originated in a journalist's description of a bizarrely shaped district designed in 1812 in Massachusetts by Governor Eldridge Gerry with the obvious intent of giving his party an advantage in the upcoming elections. In practice, the term is not easily defined. Oddly shaped districts most certainly predate the Supreme Court's reapportionment rulings, sometimes for nonpartisan reasons.[37] Prior to *Baker v. Carr* a legislature bent on gerrymandering could not only draw funny lines, but it could make some districts artificially small (or large) as well. And in fact it did. But even with districts of equal size, one person's gerrymander is often another's equitable apportionment scheme. Former Assemblyman Peter Berle argues, for example, that:

> The urban interests of persons in a city are not represented if legislative districts are drawn in pie shaped sections with the center of the city at the center of the pie. This condition persisted in Syracuse, New York under a

number of apportionment plans. In such a situation, the core city area is divided into a great many small pieces, each of which is lumped with a much larger population of suburban voters. . . . The suburban interests which predominate in number will elect representatives who . . . may be in direct conflict with their city dwelling neighbors.[38]

Berle's argument makes sense only if one accepts the premise that there is such a thing as "urban interests." Are the differences between people residing in downtown Syracuse so significantly different from those of people two miles away in Clay or Manlius that they deserve legislators of their own? Would a map that put suburban voters in a ring around the city be any less a gerrymander than one that mixed constituencies?

Ethnic Gerrymanders

This kind of question has become justiciably significant when the issue is race and ethnicity. Syracuse, it has successfully been argued in court, may or may not be a community, but blacks, Latinos, and Asians are. Beginning with a series of reapportionments in the 1970s, the legislature—the assembly in particular—began actively to create majority-minority districts, that is, districts in which minority groups were in a clear enough majority to elect more blacks and Latinos. This process was pushed from within by black and Latino members of the legislature and from without by the federal department of justice which, under the Voting Rights Act, had the power to veto any changes in voting laws that might affect minority voters in historically underrepresented areas. The justice department became involved in 1974 when a federal district court ruled that the Bronx, Brooklyn, and Manhattan—because of their unusually low minority voter registration rates—were eligible for review under Section 5 of the Voting Rights Act. In response to this 1974 suit, initiated by the NAACP Legal Defense Fund, the justice department voided the 1974 reapportionment and called for a new set of district lines.[39] Although the new lines resulted in an immediate increase of only one new minority member, taking the total from twelve to thirteen, the hidden hand of the justice department has been a player in every subsequent reapportionment deal.

Although the 1982 reapportionment plan had helped push the number of majority-minority districts up to twenty, pressure from the justice department reached a peak in the 1990s. A Republican administration in Washington saw that by linking itself to minority aspirations for greater representation it could also further its own legislative agenda. Since minorities, blacks in particular, tend to vote Democratic, any redistricting plan that concentrates minorities also concentrates Democrats. By conceding one seat to the Democrats by an overwhelming margin, the Republicans could remove enough Democrats from surrounding areas to virtually guarantee two, three, or even four surrounding seats to their own candidates. The districts created through this minority-Republican alliance served their dual purpose of substantially increasing the numbers of black and Hispanic legislators, on one hand, and of Republicans on the other. The most misshapen districts created out of this alliance were four newly crafted African-American districts in Florida, Louisiana, North Carolina, and Texas; and an Hispanic district winding across four boroughs of New York City in a shape vaguely reminiscent of the cartoon character "Bullwinkle."

Challenges to these districts, beginning with the landmark *Shaw v. Reno*,[40] eventually caused the Supreme Court to abandon its traditional reluctance to rule on the shape as opposed to the size of legislative districts, at least in cases where race could be shown to be "the predominant factor" in producing district lines. "Shape," the court held, "is relevant not because bizarreness is a necessary element of the constitutional wrong or threshold requirement of proof, but because it may be persuasive circumstantial evidence that race for its own sake, and not other districting principles, was the legislature's dominant and controlling rationale in drawing its district lines."[41]

Eventually, a challenge to New York's Bullwinkle district reached the courts and in 1997 it too was ruled unconstitutional: "all districting principles," a unanimous three-judge panel ruled, "must be applied in a race-neutral fashion."[42]

Protecting Incumbents

The Bullwinkle district's bizarre shape, the court made clear, was only one factor in making it constitutionally suspect: the legislative history of the redistricting process in 1992 "demonstrated that all traditional redistricting criterion were subordinated to race."[43] Thus although the case of *Diaz v. Silver* was specifically limited to the 12th congressional district, the reasoning of the court calls into serious question more than one district in the state legislature, and some of those cases are currently in litigation. There are no state senate or assembly districts quite as bizarre in shape as the congressional districts thrown out by the courts in 1997. There are districts, as author Murtaugh can personally attest, however, in which ethnicity was the primary factor considered in drawing the lines.

When the state legislature was redistricted in anticipation of the 1992 elections, Murtaugh's upper Manhattan district was little changed from the area he had represented for fourteen years. In June of 1992, however, the justice department vetoed that part of the plan including Murtaugh's heavily Hispanic district. Although the Legislative Task Force on Demographic Research and Reapportionment had provided figures showing that an overwhelming majority of the residents of the new district were of Dominican descent, the Justice Department ruled that a simple majority was insufficient. Because some Dominicans counted in the census are not citizens, because the percentage of Dominicans below the legal voting age is higher than among other groups,[44] and because eligible Dominicans are less likely to vote, an effective majority-minority district in upper Manhattan would have to be at least 70 percent Hispanic to meet the test. By snaking new lines down from Washington Heights, seeking Hispanic blocks and buildings in central Harlem, and avoiding non-Hispanic blacks, whites, and Asians wherever possible, the legislature was able to craft a district that met the justice department's criteria. The resulting key-shaped district, sixty-two blocks long, and for most of its length, no more than four blocks wide, was 77.7 percent Hispanic. Murtaugh was able, as an incumbent, to discourage opposition in 1992 and to defeat a relatively inexperienced Dominican candidate in the 1994 Democratic primary; but by 1996 he was overwhelmed by both demography and the emerging cohesiveness of the Hispanic community in northern Manhattan and lost by just under three hundred votes.

The courts' new willingness to challenge majority-minority districts stands in rather striking contrast to their general unwillingness to look at other kinds of gerrymanders. After size and ethnicity, it seems clear that, "Despite its conspicuous absence from any direct discussion, incumbency appears to have been the unacknowledged third-most-significant factor used when redistricting."[45] The New York constitution was amended in 1946 to incorporate compactness and respect for political boundaries into the factors that must be considered in drawing the lines for state legislative district; but these guidelines have never been clearly defined, and the legislature has often created odd-shaped districts which—if not quite as high on the bizarreness scale as the Bullwinkle district rejected in 1997—are anything but compact.[46] While some of these districts attempt to follow traditional community boundaries, and others implicitly protect minority groups not covered under the Voting Rights Act, the two kinds of gerrymanders most common in New York are those designed to protect (a) party advantages, and (b) incumbents in the state legislature. Since 1982, these two modes have largely coincided.

In its essence, the contemporary process of redistricting in New York boils down to this: the Democrats, who control the assembly, draw the assembly district lines; the Republicans draw the state senate lines; and the two parties—almost as an afterthought—fight over congressional lines (giving due respect to the protection of key incumbents). This process—almost unique in the fifty states—has been firmly established in New York since 1982. Once beyond the court-ordered fluctuations of the 1960s and early 1970s, it was clear, following the 1980 census, that neither the senate nor the assembly could have its own way. Unable to agree on a reapportionment plan that could pass both houses and satisfy the courts, assembly speaker Stanley Fink finally looked at senate majority leader Warren Anderson and said: "You don't quarrel with the way that I draw the Assembly and I won't quarrel with the way that you draw the Senate. I will pass a bill that has your version of the Senate if you will pass the same bill that has my version of the Assembly."[47] It has been done that way ever since. Aided by sophisticated computer programs, both assembly Democrats and senate Republicans have become increasingly adept at drawing district lines that maximize their respective party advantages.

While it is not always possible to predict how a given neighborhood will vote in future elections, party registration figures and past votes are good rough guides to future outcomes. The two parties' ability to utilize these numbers is nicely illustrated in Westchester County where party enrollments have been fairly evenly divided (in 1994 the proportions were: Democrats, 39 percent; Republicans, 33 percent; independents, 25 percent; and others, 3 percent.) In drawing their Westchester districts, assembly Democrats have concentrated as many Republican voters as they can find into the 87th AD where Republican Michael Spano has usually run unopposed. By spreading their own likely voters more evenly around the county, the Democrats have consistently won at least five of the remaining six seats in the county, and they currently control all six. Not to be outdone, senate Republicans have consistently won three of the four senate districts that their map makers have cut out of the same electorate. By connecting the heavily Democratic areas of Mt. Vernon to the South Bronx; building a donut-shaped, largely white, North Bronx/Westchester district around it; and by extending part of another district into heavily Republican areas of Putnam and Dutchess counties, the Republicans are nearly as solid in their control of the Westchester senate delegation as are Democrats in the assembly. Repeated throughout the state, such gerrymanders produce a Democratic assembly and Republican senate that are virtually givens of contemporary politics.

The Evolving Party System

For most of its recent history, the party system in New York has been relatively competitive at the statewide level, highly uncompetitive locally. While candidates for such statewide offices as governor and attorney general must be very much aware of both the other party's nominee and of the roles played by third parties, the only election that really matters in most legislative districts is the party primary. Once a member of the legislature has won his or her first primary, moreover, it is only under exceptional conditions that the seat will be significantly contested again. One of these exceptional conditions is after district lines have been redrawn and there has been a significant shift in population or a push to create new majority-minority districts. The other, and usually more interesting, times of electoral instability occur during episodic periods of major changes in the attitudes of the electorate.

Critical Elections in New York

Political scientists have used such terms as "partisan realignment" and "critical elections" to describe periods in which the dominant party has been displaced by a new constellation of political forces. Nationally, a realigning election is typically followed by a long period in which the new coalition dominates both congress and the presidency, not necessarily winning every election, but serving as the earth to the other party's moon for a long period of time.[48] The national election of 1932 was a classic realigning election, sweeping Franklin Roosevelt into the White House as the first Democratic president in twelve years, and displacing Republican majorities with Democrats in both the house and senate. Despite the elections of Republicans Dwight Eisenhower in 1952 and 1956, and of Richard Nixon in 1968, the so-called New Deal coalition forged by Roosevelt and the Democrats in the 1930s dominated the system for decades forcing both Eisenhower and Nixon to work with Democratic congresses for most of their White House years.

The national realignment of 1932 had begun to manifest itself in New York in the 1920s. After winning the governorship in 1918, losing in 1920, and winning again by a close margin in 1922, Al Smith's margins of victories grew with each subsequent election. His appeal to urban workers, particularly Catholics, transferred to Franklin Roosevelt in his 1928 campaign. By 1930, Roosevelt's opposition to Prohibition, combined with the beginning of the Great Depression helped Roosevelt to one of the biggest landslide victories in state history. On top of the 71 percent he won in the five boroughs, Roosevelt won 61 percent in the 58 counties outside of the city; and, most remarkably, 48 percent in the state's 21 rural counties. With Roosevelt at the top of the national ticket in 1932, Herbert Lehman won the governorship for the Democrats by an even larger margin, though his rural vote slipped, and neither Lehman nor any subsequent Democratic candidate for governor would again approach Roosevelt's 1930 performance upstate.

The New Deal realignment of the electorate was, despite Lehman's landslide victory, only partially reflected in state politics, for despite the fact that

Democratic candidates for the state assembly received 2,374,000 votes to 1,793,000 for the Republicans, the Republicans retained control of both the assembly and senate. There were, essentially, two reasons for continued Republican control of the legislature. First, the 1894 constitution's anti-New York City strictures on reapportionment and a series of Republican-sponsored redistricting plans had made the legislature virtually immune from significant electoral change. And second, the New Deal realignment in New York, despite FDR's temporary surge, proved to be a largely urban phenomenon. Building on Al Smith's enormous popularity as the first Irish Catholic from New York City to run for governor, Democratic enrollments among urban immigrants soared, in the metropolis and to a lesser extent in upstate cities. Despite, and in some ways *because* of, these trends, most upstate voters remained solidly Republican. Even in Roosevelt's landslide victory over Hoover in the 1933 presidential election, he carried only five counties outside of New York City. Indeed, the only county outside of the city that had a plurality of registered Democrats in 1932 was Albany.

The New Deal realignment, almost imperceptible upstate in 1932, began gradually to gather force, particularly in the urban centers, as both Lehman as governor and Roosevelt as president began to carve out new policy programs. As much as the Republicans schemed to rig the reapportionment of the legislature in their favor, by the 1940s "the Democrats had proved that they sometimes could win control of the Senate, if they are carrying the State by landslide or near-landslide proportions for other offices."[49] The growing weakness of the Republican majority was masked in part by the enormous popularity of Governors Dewey (1943–52) and Rockefeller (1959–72), but their successes were built in no small part on their abilities to transcend and overcome the rural conservatism of the legislature's Republicans. The very ability of rural Republicans to use their opposition to urban programs for New York City as a means of securing their own reelection began gradually to produce a backlash in urban areas upstate. Outside of the city, its northern suburbs, and Long Island, there were six upstate Democrats in the senate in 1997, two each from Buffalo and Rochester, one from Syracuse, and one from Albany. In the assembly, there were 19 upstate Democrats, 13 of them from these same four cities.

Increasingly, in the years following World War II, the battle for party control in New York state shifted with the flow of population to the suburbs. Whether the exurbanites who fled New York City by the millions were more conservative to begin with, or whether their new neighbors and circumstances changed their perspectives, there seems little doubt that they did not bring the overwhelmingly Democratic voting behavior of the city to their new communities. At the same time, suburban voters have not been as reliable a block of Republican votes as one might have predicted, instead functioning more as a swing group between the largely Democratic cities and the equally Republican rural areas of the state. In the 1997 legislature, to illustrate, the Long Island delegation in the state senate was entirely Republican, and there was only one Democratic state senator from Westchester, Orange, and Rockland counties; but 16 of the 35 assembly members elected from these same areas were Democrats. In keeping with the theory of political realignment, the strength of the Democratic Party upstate grew, not gradually, but episodically in two critical elections. The first of these realignments was in 1964. As a rule, national politics has but a faint echo at the state level, particularly since ticket-splitting—voting for parties of different candidates in the same election—has become more common among American voters. The 1964 and 1974 elections were exceptions to this rule. In 1964 Republican presidential candidate Barry Goldwater's hostility toward Social Security and civil rights, and his apparent willingness to use nuclear weapons, while it may have won the Republican Party some support in the South and West, was extraordinarily unpopular in New York. Many Republican candidates for Congress and the state legislature tried desperately to distance themselves from the top of the ticket, some successfully. But the magnitude of Goldwater's loss—he won just 31 percent of the total vote and lost every county in the state—was so great that districts that had not voted Democratic in living memory sent Democrats to Congress and the legislature. In 1974, after Richard Nixon resigned the presidency in the wake of the Watergate scandals, there was a similar drop in votes for Republicans at all levels. These so-called coattail elections, where particularly strong or weak candidates drag fellow party members to victory or defeat behind them, are becoming less common in American politics; but Goldwater's extremism and Nixon's ethical lapses put their fellow Republicans in difficult positions that many could not overcome. Some of the Democrats elected in these rather unusual elections were able to become something other than curiosities and actually hang on to their seats. One veteran Republican legislator described to us what had happened in an adjoining district that in 1974 had elected its first Democrat since the Civil War:

> Old X (the incumbent Republican) had been elected so easily, so often that he had long since stopped kissing babies, campaigning, or doing any of the things most politicians do. Essentially, he ignored his constituents. When the Democrat got elected, the first thing he did was to start touring the area in a mobile district office. He sent out newsletters, press releases, and never stopped going door-to-door. Well, hell, said a lot of those life-long Republicans, if this is the difference between a Democrat

and a Republican, maybe I've been making a mistake. And they've been voting for that guy ever since.

When coattails do impact local elections, the effect is usually temporary, and the Democratic surge in 1964 had relatively trivial long-term consequences. But 1974 was different. Of the Democrats net gain of 19 assembly seats, 14 were upstate. A decade later, 11 of these 14 seats were still represented by Democrats. "The 1974 transition," as Stonecash describes it, "was decisive. In subsequent years the Democrats were able to win even more seats upstate and expand their legislative base. The 1982 elections were particularly important. The Democrats increased their seats because they drew district lines as part of reapportionment. By 1991 they held 37 of 90 (41 percent) seats upstate. The Democratic party had become more of an urban statewide party than a downstate party."[50]

The Norm of Divided Government

Divided government, with a chief executive of one party and at least one house of the legislature controlled by the other party, has become more common both in Washington and in the states. As Fiorina has shown:

> The contemporary era of divided national government began with the first Eisenhower election in 1952, solidified when Nixon emerged as the choice of a badly split electorate in 1968, and became the norm by the 1980s. Although little noticed, developments in the states have been somewhat similar. Unified control in the states declined sharply after the 1952 elections, stabilized at a lower level in the late 1960s, and declined still further in the 1980s.[51]

Divided government began in New York long before Eisenhower. As can be seen in Table 3.2, every modern governor of New York, save Thomas Dewey in the years 1943 through 1954, has had to deal with a legislature with at least one house controlled by the opposite party. *Every* governor, since 1975, has faced at least one house controlled by his political opposition. As the table shows, the roots dividing government in New York state extend at least back to the New Deal, and in fact can be traced through much of the state's history. Al Smith compiled a remarkable record of legislative achievements as a Democrat in the years 1919–20 and 1923–28, yet the assembly in those years was always under Republican control, and the senate usually.

Whether divided government leads to deadlock and political stalemate is not as clear as conventional wisdom might suggest. At the national level,

Table 3.2

Divided Government in New York: Party Control of the Governorship, Assembly, and State Senate, 1933–1998

Years	Governor	Party	Senate majority	Assembly majority
1933–34	Herbert Lehman	Democrat	Democratic	Republican
1935–38	Herbert Lehman	Democrat	Democratic	Split[a]
1939–42	Herbert Lehman	Democrat	Republican	Republican
1943–54	Thomas Dewey	Republican	Republican	Republican
1955–58	Averell Harriman	Democrat	Republican	Republican
1959–64	Nelson Rockefeller	Republican	Republican	Republican
1965–66	Nelson Rockefeller	Republican	Democratic	Democratic
1967–68	Nelson Rockefeller	Republican	Republican	Democratic
1969–72	Nelson Rockefeller	Republican	Republican	Republican
1973–74	Malcolm Wilson	Republican	Republican	Republican
1975–82	Hugh Carey	Democrat	Republican	Democratic
1983–94	Mario Cuomo	Democrat	Republican	Democratic
1995–98	George Pataki	Republican	Republican	Democratic

Source: Various editions of the New York State *Red Book* (Guilderland, NY: New York Legal Publications, various years).

[a]With a system of annual elections for the assembly, the Democrats won a majority in 1935, lost in 1936, recaptured control in 1937, and lost again in 1938.

Mayhew's exhaustive analysis of the years 1946 through 1990 led him to conclude, in essence, that "Unified versus divided control has probably *not* made a notable difference during the postwar era."[52] The competing demands of constituency interests, among other forces, can produce unpredictable alliances regardless of party alignments. An interesting case in New York occurred shortly after George Pataki assumed the governorship in 1995. Despite Pataki's vociferous opposition to a bill increasing the pensions of retired state and municipal employees, it passed both houses of the legislature by veto-proof margins, and the governor was forced to swallow it. While passage in the Democratic assembly surprised no one, even the governor seems to have been caught off guard by the enthusiastic reception accorded the bill by the Republican state senate and its new majority leader Joseph Bruno. The main reason Bruno had unseated Ralph Marino to become majority leader, as one journalist put it, "was because the Senate's conservative Young Turks thought he was far more likely to do Pataki's bidding."[53] Yet here was Bruno, with strong support from the Young Turks, defying the governor before the honeymoon had even begun. The fact that Bruno himself came from a Capitol-area district that included thousands of state workers may have been a factor in the senate's stand against the governor. Far more important, how-

Box 3.3

Party Government in Action

In party government, voters can be reasonably confident that a party that wins an election will enact its campaign promises into policy. Even if party control over different branches of the government is divided, the responsible parties model suggests that the two branches controlled by the same party will be on the same page. A classic case of party government in action was on display in the 1995 session of the legislature.

Both the governor and Senate Majority Leader Joseph Bruno had promised to pass a bill legalizing casino gambling in certain areas. Knowing that some senate Democrats favored casino gambling, Senator Bruno had "let off" some of his own members. Thinking that he would win without them, in other words, Bruno had told a number of his fellow Republicans that party discipline would not be invoked and that they could vote their consciences. An hour before the expected vote on the senate floor, minority leader Martin Conner called a press conference to announce that because of the Republican's failure to go along on unrelated issues, senate Democrats would vote as a block against casino gambling. Bruno, who now found himself lacking enough votes to pass the bill, called his members into a hasty meeting.

A senior Albany reporter was standing in the hallway as the senate Republicans filed into their presession party conference, and, as he told us, "more than one of them told me 'There is no way I'm switching on this bill.'" Then the conference began, "and, lo and behold who comes around the corner but [State Republican Party Chairman] Bill Powers, [whom] you would not have seen so publicly before. He and Bruno did some heavy arm twisting."

The bill passed by a 34 to 21 vote with only two Republicans holding out in the end. It was, as one reporter described it, "a rare moment of public drama in this place. Everything was still done behind closed doors, but this time everyone knew what was going on back there. Everyone knew that people were getting beat up in that back room to vote with Bruno and the governor and this was a test of their leadership. They all came out in a row and went out to their seats and voted on that bill right away. I don't think there was even any debate. They just wanted to get it out and move on. They were really steam rolled."

If only to punctuate his point, Bruno stripped one of the remaining Republican dissidents of his committee chairmanship.

The bill, ironically, did not become law. A motley alliance of church groups, supporters of off-track betting, and Donald Trump (whose Atlantic

City casino would face new competition) forced reconsideration of the bill a few weeks later. The governor and Senator Bruno had apparently had enough, and Senator Conner released his senate Democrats to vote as they liked. The bill lost 41 to 19.

It is not unusual for a party leader in Albany to demand, and get, the absolute, unified support of his members on a key legislative vote. What was unusual was having that state party chairman—an ally of the governor—in on the action as well. The issue of casino gambling is still very much around in the legislature. The state party chairman is not.

ever, were the long-standing ties that the state's public employee unions had built with senate Republicans.

The fact, as this case illustrates, is that the major players in New York state politics have been accustomed to a playing field in which party control is divided; state legislators, in their turn, have become similarly accustomed to conditions of divided government. Although deadlock is sometimes a problem—chronically late budgets are often cited as symptomatic of a serious inability to govern efficiently—there are some observers who feel that governing has become a bit too automatic in New York, that the parties are so used to accommodating themselves to one another that they have overlooked real issues and become essentially incapable of change. There are ways, indeed, in which divided government serves each party well, making them more or less ritual enemies who use each other to shore up their own political positions. "One house bills" are commonplace in Albany. These are bills that pass either the Democratic assembly or Republican senate with no hope or expectation that they will become law. Bold new social programs, which even their sponsors know the state cannot pay for, emerge with considerable frequency from the assembly together with equally irresponsible tax cutting proposals from the senate. Democrats can thus take credit with their constituents for new initiatives and, while blaming the Republicans for bottling them up, remain free of any need to find the money to pay for them. Republicans play the same games in reverse. In a similar fashion, every governor since Hugh Carey has low-balled his budget request for education. Knowing that both houses of the legislature will fight to keep local school aid dollars flowing from the state, the governor is protected from the political consequences of actually cutting the education budget; but he picks up valuable bargaining leverage on other issues. Legislators, for their part, can go home to the voters and boast of their successful efforts to restore school dollars. Thus the road to reelection is paved.

New York's Vanishing Marginals

Students of Congress have filled thousands of pages exploring the amazing ability of contemporary members of the House of Representatives to win reelection. "Marginal seats," districts in which challengers have a reasonable chance of winning, have all but disappeared. New York too, as we have seen, has relatively few of its legislators at risk of losing any given election. As with Congress, it is difficult to isolate a single explanatory variable for this decline in electoral competition. Indeed there is evidence suggesting that incumbents running for reelection in New York have always done quite well. "The percent of incumbents (among those seeking reelection) winning reelection has remained in the 80 to 90 percent range since around 1900."[54] Careerism, the tendency of legislators to seek reelection and make politics a career "has increased dramatically in the last two decades."[55] As in national politics, moreover, state legislators have more resources at their disposal: more staff, bigger printing and postage budgets to keep their names in front of the people, and the ability of the legislature to deliver both symbolic victories (one-house bills) and real policies. As the party loyalties of the voters decline, moreover, more of them seem likely to take incumbency as a guide to voting. The impact of gerrymandering is also an important force in New York, particularly since the two one-party houses agreed to divide the job and acquired the computer resources to do it effectively. Finally, in New York, as in national politics, the continuing success of incumbents has tended to scare off strong challengers.

However each of these variables weigh in to the equation, the two houses of the legislature have become increasingly isolated from swings in the party preferences of the electorate. Table 3.3 charts the fluctuating fortunes of major party candidates for the state senate and assembly.

What is perhaps most striking about these figures is the sharp and growing isolation they show between swings in the popular vote and seats in the legislature. A dramatic surge in a party's vote—like the Democrats' jump from 48.9 percent of the total cast for assembly candidates in 1962 to the 57.6 percent they won in 1964—can produce a real change in the legislature, as it did. The Democrats' share of assembly seats went from 43.6 percent to 54.5 percent, taking them from minority status to a clear majority. Yet a jump of more than five points in the percentage voting Democratic for senate candidates between 1990 and 1992 resulted in no change at all in the senate's party alignment. And an even larger drop the next year—from 49.6 percent in 1992 to 40.2 percent in 1994—resulted in a net Democratic loss of only one seat.

Aggregate figures such as these can be misleading. Legislative elections are won on a district-by-district basis, and variations in turnout and patterns

Table 3.3

Seats and Votes in the New York State Legislature: Democratic Percentage of Assembly and Senate Seats Won, and Statewide Democratic Percentage of Total Vote, 1960–1994

Year	State assembly				State senate			
	Party division		% Democratic seats won	% Democratic total popular vote	Party division		% Democratic seats won	% Democratic total popular vote
	Dem.	Rep.			Dem.	Rep.		
1960	65	84	43.6	50.7	25	33	43.1	50.3
1962	65	84	43.6	48.9	25	33	43.1	48.1
1964	90	75	54.5	57.6	32	25	56.1	57.7
1966	80	70	53.3	51.0	26	31	45.6	49.5
1968	72	78	48.0	49.5	24	33	42.1	45.8
1970	71	79	47.3	49.5	24	33	42.1	48.2
1972	67	83	44.6	49.6	23	37	38.3	47.5
1974	88	62	58.7	55.9	26	34	43.3	53.5
1976	90	60	60.0	56.2	25	35	41.6	50.6
1978	86	64	57.3	52.5	25	35	41.6	48.2
1980	86	64	57.3	51.6	24	35	40.7	46.8
1982	97	52	65.1	58.4	26	35	42.6	46.5
1984	94	55	63.1	52.7	26	35	42.6	44.8
1986	95	56	62.9	54.5	26	35	42.6	45.0
1988	92	58	61.3	54.0	27	34	44.3	43.8
1990	94	56	62.6	52.8	26	35	42.6	44.2
1992	101	49	67.3	55.3	26	35	42.6	49.6
1994	94	56	62.6	51.5	25	36	40.1	40.2

Source: Figures from 1960 through 1980 are calculated from the *Red Book* (Guilderland, NY: New York Legal Publications, various years), which, unfortunately, stopped compiling vote totals. We are indebted to Professor Jeffrey M. Stonecash of Syracuse University for providing us with the aggregate popular vote totals from 1982 through 1994.

of competition can be lost in statewide totals; but the data seem rather clearly to underscore the importance of incumbency on one hand, and of redistricting on the other. Reflecting the importance of incumbency, the party holding a majority of seats in the assembly or senate has almost always been able to capture a statewide majority for its own candidates. Particularly since the institutionalization of divided government in the 1970s, the percentage of voters supporting Democratic candidates for the assembly has exceeded support for Democratic senate candidates by an average of nearly 8 percent. In 1990, when Mario Cuomo was trouncing the hapless Pierre Rinfret, and assembly Democrats were rolling up a 52.8 percent statewide vote, senate Republicans won more than 55 percent of the aggregate vote. In 1994, despite George Pataki's win, and in contrast with a Republican margin of nearly 60 percent in senate races, Democratic candidates for the state assembly still won 51.5 percent of the aggregate vote.

The importance of partisan redistricting plans is also evident in Table 3.3, particularly in elections since 1980. In the senate, the party ratio seems almost locked at 35–26, plus or minus one. 1992 aside, Democrats in the assembly seem unable to rise above 97 seats nor fall below 92 regardless of fluctuations in the popular vote.

New York City and the Cycles of Reform

In national elections, in most statewide contests, and in choosing its senate and assembly representatives in Albany, New York City has been overwhelmingly Democratic for the full century of its existence as a five-borough metropolis. For at least the past half-century, it has been almost as resoundingly liberal in its political orientation. Its members of Congress, state senators and assembly members continually receive high ratings from liberal groups and low ratings from political conservatives. Voters registered as Democrats have exceeded those registered as Republicans by a margin of at least three-to-one in every year but one since 1930. This quintessentially Democratic city, however, has had almost as many non-Democratic mayors as it has had Democrats. Even in the salad days of Tammany Hall, so-called fusion candidates, uniting dissident Democrats with Republicans and other outsiders against the machine, were a persistent, often successful characteristic of city politics. Some of the city's most famous mayors, including Seth Low, Fiorello LaGuardia, and John Lindsay, began as outsiders and Republicans.

From the late 1950s through the early 1980s the locus of reform politics shifted away from the traditional fusion model to a struggle within the Democratic primary. John Lindsay won his first campaign for mayor in 1965 as a typical fusion candidate running on the Republican and Liberal Party lines,

Box 3.4

Running to Lose

One of the more unique campaigns for mayor of New York City was that of magazine publisher William F. Buckley in 1965. The conservative Buckley, annoyed that Republican John Lindsay was as liberal on most issues as Democrat Abe Beame, sought the nomination of the Conservative Party in order to teach the Republicans a lesson by siphoning off enough votes to assure Lindsay's defeat. Eschewing such traditional urban campaign tactics as shaking hands at subway stops, visiting ethnic restaurants, and seeking the endorsements of other politicians, Buckley focused almost entirely on the media. What was most striking about the Buckley candidacy was his candor in admitting that he was not in it to win. Asked at his announcement speech if he wanted to be mayor, Buckley replied that "I have never even considered it"; and did he have a chance of winning? "No."

Somewhat later in the campaign, Buckley engaged in the following colloquy with a reporter:

Question: Why didn't you run in the Republican primary?
Buckley: Why didn't Martin Luther King run for Governor of Alabama?
Question: What would you do if you won?
Buckley: Demand a recount.

Source: Chris McNickle, *To Be Mayor of New York* (New York: Columbia University Press, 1993), p. 198.

and depicting his main opponent, Democrat Abe Beame, as a tool of clubhouse "bosses." Lindsay won by a narrow margin of just over 100,000 votes, polling 43 percent of the total vote to 39 percent for Beame and a surprising 13 percent for the Conservative candidate, journalist William F. Buckley. While Buckley succeeded in cutting deeply into New York City's Republican base, the key to Lindsay's victory lay in his ability to hold a significant proportion of this vote and add to it a substantial bloc (mostly on the Liberal line) of voters traditionally loyal in national politics to the Democrats. As mayor during a crucial period of rising racial consciousness, Lindsay came down squarely on the side of civil rights, thus consolidating his appeal to African Americans and traditionally liberal whites but badly alienating whatever was left of his base among white ethnics in the Republican Party. As he prepared for his reelection campaign and it became increasingly clear that he would have trouble holding his Republican base, the mayor increasingly sought and received the backing of prominent Democrats and the normally

Democratic leaders of the municipal labor unions. In the election, Lindsay won less than 20 percent of the largely Irish and Italian white Catholics but more than 80 percent of blacks. He and the Democrat, Mario Proccacino, split the Jewish vote, enabling Lindsay to win. A few months later, the mayor made it official and became a Democrat. So did many of his supporters.

For the next three decades, the real contests for mayor of New York tended to take place in the Democratic primary. With the organization splintered between competing reform and regular factions, Democrats in the legislature passed a law in 1969 requiring a runoff in the event that no candidate received more than 40 percent of the primary vote. The idea was that a consensus Democrat was far less likely than one chosen by a small splinter to lose to a fusion candidate in November. And that is essentially how it worked in the 1970s and 1980s as the winners of the Democratic primaries—sometimes with minor party help, sometimes not—became mayor. In retrospect, however, a more profound shift also began in the Lindsay years: the splintering along both ethnic and ideological lines of the old "New Deal" coalition that had made New York the penultimate liberal Democratic city. The alienation of the white ethnics and many Jewish voters—particularly in the outer boroughs—and the growing isolation of blacks and, to a lesser extent, Latinos was to become a persistent theme in city politics. "In the wake of the racial conflicts of the Lindsay era, many liberal whites, especially Jews, joined then-congressman Ed Koch in moving toward the more defensive, conservative positions already held by those who provided the social base for the regular Democratic clubs."[56]

As the reform movement that had united minority groups and liberal whites behind Lindsay began to splinter, the Republican Party began lurching to the right. Deserted by moderates like Mayor Lindsay, and paralleling the rise of the party's Reagan faction in national politics, New York's Republicans became increasingly unlikely candidates for fusion. Whatever mass base the Liberal Party had ever had, moreover, was gone. For the next four elections, from 1973 through 1985, the Democratic primary for mayor was, in essence, the only election that counted; and a badly splintered reform movement saw moderate and increasingly conservative candidates Abe Beame and Ed Koch win relatively easy victories. Splits between blacks and Latinos and various factions of the reform movement led one liberal candidate for mayor to observe that "if reform Democrats were asked to form a firing squad the first order would be to form a circle."

The Rise and Fall of Mayor Koch

The biggest of these circles was formed in 1977 when a record 900,000 primary voters narrowly selected Ed Koch over a field that included three members of Congress (Koch, Bella Abzug, and Herman Badillo), Manhattan Borough President Percy Sutton, Mayor Beame, and a novice candidate from Queens named Mario Cuomo. The gap between the top vote getter (Koch) and the lowest (Badillo) was less than 80,000 votes, with each candidate showing little ability to reach beyond his or her natural ethnic, ideological, or neighborhood base. By moving to the right, Koch was able to build a remarkably diverse coalition for his 1981 reelection campaign, winning the nominations of the Democratic, Republican, and Conservative parties with a popularity that cut across ethnic and ideological lines. Despite Koch's surprising failure to beat Cuomo in a statewide race for governor, Koch remained a powerhouse in New York City and rolled to any easy victory in the 1985 mayoral election. "His badly divided potential opponents were unable to put forward candidates who appealed strongly to their own constituencies, much less other constituencies."[57] Mollenkopf, dividing the city's assembly districts into five types, showed Koch, as expected, winning nearly 70 percent of the white Catholic vote and 65 percent of outer-borough Jewish votes. But even among white liberals (57 percent) and blacks (41 percent) Koch ran surprisingly well, particularly since he was facing both a black opponent and a white liberal.

And then, as quickly and unexpectedly as Koch had risen to power, his coalition fell apart. Following a series of bizarre revelations of petty graft involving, ironically, the party leaders Koch had opposed as a reformer, "the euphoria of victory was replaced by unfolding scandals that spread throughout the administration and reached into the inner rooms of City Hall. The press was soon comparing the administration to the dark days of Jimmy Walker and Boss Tweed."[58]

The 1989 election of New York City's first African-American mayor, David Dinkins, seemingly restored the liberal Democratic coalition that had dominated city government for so long. Dinkins, benefiting not just from the scandals plaguing the mayor, but from a series of incidents seeming to reveal an insensitivity on Koch's part to issues of race, ate into every part of the mayor's coalition. Between 1985 and 1989 Koch's support among outer-borough Jewish voters declined by 10 percent, and even among white Catholics it was down by 7.1 percent. Most strikingly, however, his support among blacks and Latinos dropped by more than 30 percent, and turnout in African-American districts was up almost 30 percent as well.[59]

Beyond Fusion: Rudolph Giuliani and the New
Republican Challenge

The general election pitted Dinkins against a former federal prosecutor, Republican Rudolph Giuliani. Unlike the typical fusion candidate, exploiting a split between the regular and reform wings of the Democratic Party, Giuliani seemed to have little chance of success. But as Mollenkopf says:

> Race, and more specifically, racially based mistrust, provided a new basis for whites who traditionally voted for the Democratic nominee to defect from their party. . . . White liberals, blacks, and Latinos (and by definition more strongly partisan voters) figured less heavily in the general electorate than in the Democratic primary electorate. In the general electorate, Republicans, independents, and whites were more numerous. . . . These conditions opened the way for Rudolph Giuliani to seek to reconstruct the Koch coalition of white Catholics and Jews along somewhat more conservative lines than Mayor Koch had pursued.[60]

Dinkins prevailed, thanks in large part to a massive get-out-the-vote drive that was particularly effective in black neighborhoods. In ethnic and ideological terms, Dinkin's victory was a traditional coalition triumph cutting across a variety of cleavages. "The Dinkins coalition," as Mollenkopf concludes, "resembled those that powered racial succession in other cities to the extent that it relied upon an extraordinary mobilization of his core constituency of blacks. But it differed from them in the degree to which it would have to rely on other constituencies as well. It had to include white liberals, Latinos, and indeed a significant number of the outer-borough Jews and white Catholics who had supported Mayor Koch. This black-led, biracial and multiethnic insurgent coalition constitutes a fundamentally new element in New York's political development, one that has few national counterparts."[61]

Giuliani's losing coalition was equally unique; and when Dinkins found himself embroiled in racially polarizing problems, the balance of power tipped enough to push him out of Gracie Mansion (the mayor's official residence) in 1993.

Although Giuliani had both the Republican and Liberal nominations, it was not a traditional fusion campaign. Unlike such classic fusion candidates as LaGuardia and Lindsay, Giuliani was not a champion of reform and did not campaign to the left of the regular candidate. It would be misleading to describe the shift from Dinkins to Giuliani simply in ethnic terms. Turnout declined slightly in black election districts and by a little more among Latinos, and there was some slippage in the mayor's support among white liberals. Turnout in white Catholic areas was substantially higher (particularly on Staten Island where there was a concurrent referendum on secession from New York City), and this helped Giuliani. But the shifts were small: having won by fewer than 50,000 votes in 1989, Dinkins lost by a comparable margin in 1993, a shift of less than 3 percent. In a nutshell, "Dinkins' difficulty was clearly related to the fact that many people, even among blacks and others who [had] supported him in 1989, had concluded that he had performed poorly as mayor."[62]

By 1997, the shoe was on the other foot, and Giuliani's first term—marked by a boom on Wall Street and a striking drop in the crime rate—won generally high marks from the electorate. Manhattan Borough President Ruth Messinger, after narrowly dodging the embarrassment of a runoff in the Democratic primary, was soundly trounced in the November election. Giuliani had essentially captured and built upon the old Koch coalition, a mixture of regular Republicans, white Catholics, power-tropic union leaders, the business community, and important fragments of the constantly fractionalized Democratic majority.

Although Giuliani is not in the traditional fusion mode, neither can his landslide victory in 1997 stand up to scrutiny as a major realigning election. New York City's peculiar combination of ethnic, partisan, issue, and power politics results in a continuing kaleidoscope of shifting coalitions that are only tangentially related to state and national trends. Even in the first Dinkins campaign, arguably the most racially polarizing in the city's history, "What is interesting . . . was not their degree of racial polarization, which was to be expected, but the degree to which they were *not* governed by race alone."[63] The Giuliani victory in 1997 was similarly unique in its ability to cut across traditional ethnic, partisan, and ideological boundaries. The mayor, despite a landslide victory, had no coattails, and Democrats retained a 46 to 5 margin in city council. Nor is it at all clear that the mayor, had he not dropped out of the U.S. Senate race against Hillary Rodham Clinton in 2000, could have translated his success in the city to a statewide race. No New York City mayor in the twentieth century was able to do so.

The Dilemmas of the Parties

Despite the frequent successes of Republicans in winning control of Gracie Mansion, even the most popular Republican mayors have shown little or no ability to build the party's strength in New York City. The number of Republicans elected to other offices in the city has been trivial. Except in such small pockets as Staten Island, the only elections that concern candidates for city council, judgeships, and seats in the state legislature are Democratic primaries. From a statewide perspective, the Big Apple remains the core of Democratic Party strength. Rural areas and the outer, more affluent suburbs are similarly central to the fortunes of state Republicans. Since 1974 the Democrats have expanded their city base to encompass urban areas in general and, to a lesser extent, some of the older, less-affluent suburbs; but in statewide Democratic primaries the city continues to cast roughly 60 percent of all the votes.

Statewide, the Republicans are almost the converse of the Democrats: their primary electorate is, essentially, upstate, conservative, and white. So is their majority in the state senate. The dilemma of both parties is that of escaping this inherent polarization, a task compounded by national trends. As long as the conservative, southern wing of the party controls its image, the party will have difficulty winning enough votes in urban areas to win a statewide majority. For the Democrats, the problems are at once ethnic and ideological: Jewish and other white city liberals together with blacks and other minorities have the votes to control most primaries; but the kinds of candidates they are likely to nominate will find it increasingly difficult to win statewide office. And the assembly's city-led Democratic majority has little interest in moderating its image, challenging Republican control of the senate, or working to elect statewide Democratic candidates.

Conclusion: The Roles of Parties in New York Politics

A potential candidate, surveying his or her chances of being elected in New York state, cannot ignore the historic and legal factors described here. To run for office in most parts of New York City, it helps to be a Democrat, which can be a near-fatal defect upstate. The support of the formal party organization, essential in most parts of the state during the heyday of the machine, is more peripheral today. There are four great contextual realities that define the parameters of politics in New York, and that distinguish it markedly from most other states. First, the Democratic and Republican parties in New York are essentially three parties loosely joined by a network of local institutions and a formal framework of little real significance. The parties that count are those that compete for control of the state senate, the state assembly, the executive branch, and, most important, the governorship. Within each of the major parties, they operate independently of one another and of the local Republican and Democratic parties that contest for municipal, county, and judicial offices. Second, these party systems are supplemented and sometimes swayed by a unique array of satellite parties—Liberals and Conservatives in particular—whose support is often significant enough to keep the major parties on their toes. Third, the kinds of demographic and economic variables that frequently explain electoral behavior lose their explanatory power in New York due to the continuing importance of region. More than in any other state, politics in New York is defined by a sharp line of cleavage that distinguishes New York City, and to some extent its suburbs, from everything else.

Finally, New York is different from most other states because its elected officials deliberately have worked to make it different. Electorates, as Schneier has argued elsewhere, are artifacts, "the product of political choices made by people who know what they are doing."[64] That the New York state assembly is as unassailably Democratic as the senate is Republican, that incumbents experience a high success rate of reelection, and that the voter turnout is spectacularly low in New York elections, are not just because of demography and change, but of a set of election laws crafted by incumbent politicians protecting their own interests. New York's election laws are by far the most complex in the United States, helping to account for the frequently cited fact that more than half of the election law cases filed in the courtrooms of the fifty states are filed in New York. Things that are relatively simple and straightforward in forty-nine other states can be quite complicated in New York. And they are complicated for a reason: the elected officials who make the laws that govern their own chances of reelection like it that way.

The late V.O. Key described the study of political parties in terms of three distinct but overlapping circles: the party in the electorate, the party organization, and the party in government. As on the national scene, the party in the electorate is harder to find in New York where nearly one voter in five refuses to register with a party, and where straight party voting is increasingly uncommon. Paradoxically, however, as one moves from voters to institutions, party lines are in many ways more sharply etched on the landscape of New York politics than in most other states.

The party organizations are, in the aggregate, weaker than once they were. One statistical study, using a variety of quantitative indicators, rated New York's party systems as the fourteenth weakest among the fifty states.[65] But if the days of Tammany and its counterparts are past, there are strong party organizations in New York. At the statewide level, the Republican Party continues to control nominations, raise money, and contest elections with every bit as much vigor as it did in the heyday of Dewey and Rockefeller. Unlike the Democratic State Convention—whose endorsement has proven a virtual kiss of death to potential candidates—the nominees of the official Republican Party have never been rejected in a statewide primary election, and almost never challenged. Potentially strong candidates have withdrawn in the interests of ticket balancing, as assembly minority leader John Faso did with his 1994 campaign for comptroller. And the party has been able to take virtual unknowns like Alfonse D'Amato and George Pataki and turn them into household names. The party organizations associated with the parties in the legislature, both Republican and Democratic, moreover, are considerably stronger than they have ever been.

Even in New York City, remnants of the old Democratic organization

Box 3.5

Electoral Realignment in New York

In statewide elections, New York remains a closely divided state. While individual officials can sometimes build substantial popular followings and win reelection without difficulty—as Comptroller Carl McCall did in 1998—it is never easy. Even George Pataki—riding a wave of prosperity and declining crime rates, with the state coffers brimming from the stock market, and with a little known Democratic opponent—won just over 51 percent of the statewide vote in 1998. The attorney general's race was decided by fewer than 25,000 votes. As always, Democrats won handily in New York City, lost decisively in rural areas, and broke even in the suburbs. But a closer analysis of election returns in the 1980s and 1990s reveals patterns of realignment that are quite striking. While the state electorate as a whole has retained the same sort of general balance, the overall numbers conceal significant changes.

In New York City and its surrounding suburbs, the movement of Catholics and Jews out of the Democratic coalition has accelerated. Catholics and non-Manhattan Jewish voters in the city—once among the most reliably Democratic voting blocks in the state—gave fewer than 30 percent of their votes to David Dinkins in his 1993 campaign for mayor.* While this defection has yet to threaten most legislative candidates, the trends are clear.

Equally striking, though less noticed changes have been taking place upstate, where "The historically strongly Republican population of . . . mostly English, better-educated areas have . . . grown increasingly disenchanted with the national Republican party since the 1950s."† It has, in Speel's term, been a largely "federalized realignment—more Democratic at the national level, solidly Republican at the local level,"‡ though there are interesting exceptions. Perhaps the most striking of these is Tompkins County—home of Cornell University and Ithaca College—which went from 22 percent Democratic in the 1952 presidential election to 64 percent in 1996.§ In 1998 its Democratic assemblyman, Marty Luster won with 64 percent of the votes. Luster is still one of a handful of nonurban, upstate officeholders, and it may be that tensions between New York City and upstate New York will continue to inhibit a full realignment; but the trends are striking.

---

*John Mollenkopf, *A Phoenix in the Ashes: The Rise and Fall of the Koch Coalition in New York City Politics* (Princeton, NJ: Princeton University Press, 1994), p. 211.

†Robert W. Speel, *Changing Patterns of Voting in the Northern United States: Electoral Realignment, 1952–1996* (University Park: State University of Pennsylvania Press, 1998), p. 136.
‡Ibid., p. 139.
§Ibid., p. 129.

continue to exert considerable clout in the outer boroughs where, to use Wolfinger's distinction, machine politics are still practiced in the absence of a well-organized machine.[66] As Mollenkopf puts it, "While they have much less influence over who wins the mayoralty than they once did, candidates supported by the Bronx, Queens, Brooklyn, and Staten Island organizations typically win elections for lesser offices and can absorb most of the few insurgents who win elections against them."[67]

These kinds of individually strong party organizations do not find reflection in the kinds of aggregate level, statistical studies that attempt to compare state party systems largely by focusing mainly on the state committees. When one takes into account the legislative party organizations and the continuing clout of many local leaders, the reality is that the parties as organizations in New York should be ranked in the top quartile rather than the lowest of the fifty states.

Finally, when it comes to the party in government, parties in New York have not declined in the slightest. As we shall argue in Chapter 6, the party organizations—particularly in the legislature—have become central guidance institutions in the shaping of public policy in New York state. Where once party leaders in Albany relied upon county leaders to push legislators into line, today it is local leaders who come to Albany as supplicants. In few states are the parties in government as strong as they are in New York, in no state are they stronger.

4

Power, Pluralism, and the Permanent Government

For years, students of both local and national government divided into two warring camps. On one hand, those described as *pluralists* emphasized the relatively wide dispersal of power in American politics, the existence of many competing groups and interests, and the role of government as an active arbiter of conflicts among competing interests. The *power elite* approach, on the other hand, viewed the system as essentially closed and tightly dominated by a small elite of powerful individuals who—whether they actually held positions in the government itself—were firmly enough in control of public officials that they could be described as a "permanent government."

Some of the force of the debate on power between these competing perspectives has been diminished by a growing recognition that the study of power cannot be effectively told if it focuses only on governments. Many private interests, business interests in particular, play vitally important roles in shaping society no matter who occupies the institutions of government. The study of politics, this argument suggests, is incomplete to the extent that it focuses only on government institutions that, whether pluralistic or elitist, must come to terms with key elements in the private sector. "Strong centrifugal forces," as Stone concludes his study of Atlanta, "characterize modern societies. Fragmented into myriad special roles, these societies lack an overarching power of command. The formal authority of government is limited, and substantial resources are in private hands. Especially at the local level, the power of public officials may be dwarfed by processes and activities entirely outside government control."[1]

Even in the absence of an active power elite, the revised argument goes, there are certain interests—too dispersed and disorganized to constitute an elite—that are too firmly embedded in the foundations of modern society to be defied. The very structure of a capitalist society forces all governments, local governments in particular, to be unusually deferential to the big mules who pull the economic cart.

One thing the pluralists and the structural elitists have in common is a tendency to be dismissive of traditional "democratic" forces. In the extreme argument, some pluralists depict elections as instruments too crude to provide meaningful mandates, while public opinion in the aggregate is insufficiently informed to be meaningful. Only when their attitudes are channeled through their areas of special concern and knowledge—essentially through interest groups—are ordinary citizens likely to be a significant political force. The extreme power elitists are similarly dismissive of public opinion and electoral politics as essentially peripheral to the real issues of society. While the people at large debate the trivial issues that the "real" power brokers assign them, major policy questions are resolved either by the ruling elite or the structural mandates of the prevailing economic order.

Most public officials, and a growing majority of political scientists, find it difficult to buy any overarching perspective on the nature of political influence. Yes, economic realities and the interests of key business leaders do set significant limits on the range of policies government can responsibly consider. At the same time, the boundaries set by these structural elites are quite broad, broad enough for politics to be significant to most people. And yes, within the areas of choice open to politicians, interest groups are important and power is, in many ways, specialized. But elections are also important: New York is a different city under Rudolph Giuliani than it was when David Dinkins was mayor, the election of George Pataki in 1994 marked a significant watershed in state politics, and the people who made these changes possible are not entirely drawn from either the pressure system or the power elite. Finally, public policy continues to be influenced to a considerable degree by public opinion. The mechanisms vary. Public attitudes matter more on some issues than others, but New York's conservatives—because they come from New York—will never be as conservative as North Carolina's. In sum, the field of forces that impinges on politicians in Albany is arrayed as a constantly shifting kaleidoscope of economic elites, competing interests groups, electoral forces, and general public attitudes.

Regime Politics in New York

Every government, however it is constituted, is part of a larger power structure or "regime" that is not fully reflected in its official government. Governing officials, elected officials in particular, must be cognizant of the limits of their capacity to intrude forcefully on the key interests of the regime. Whatever his or her ideology, a public official in Rochester does not need to be reminded that the city's prosperity is deeply intertwined with the prosperity of such major employers as Xerox and Eastman Kodak. Even at the state level, companies like Xerox, IBM, and American Express are so vital to economic prosperity that it would be almost unthinkable to challenge their core interests. As Pecorella writes:

> Because wealth production in the United States occurs largely in the private sector and because government at all levels depends on the producers of wealth for the resources it is charged with allocating, interests involved in large-scale wealth production are critically important to public officials. Such interests are particularly critical to officials at the subnational levels of government, where corporate mobility is often an option and operating budgets have to be balanced.[2]

Every politician knows that the businesses that create jobs and fuel the economy could, if sufficiently unhappy, move to New Jersey (or elsewhere). Business leaders are not shy about threatening such moves. All politicians, on the other hand, also see the larger and more prosperous enterprises in their jurisdiction as potentially enormous sources of tax revenue. When a company closes down or leaves the state, it stops paying taxes, its employees stop paying taxes, and they stop buying goods and services from other New York companies that also pay taxes.

Rivals for Power

As solicitous of business interests as most politicians may be, there are countervailing powers at work, particularly at the state level. With an economy as complex as that of New York, no single industry or sector of the economy has the kind of disproportionate clout that, for example, the oil companies might have in Louisiana, or the gaming industry in Nevada. While corporations in New York often have interests in common, they also compete with one another. New York, moreover, is a highly unionized state, and the unions have shown little reluctance to engage in politics. Real estate interests and land developers are well represented in New York state and city, but so are tenants. The reform coalitions that ended the rule of party machines also helped create government agencies—or bureaucratic "decision centers," as Sayre and Kaufman called them—that evolved into "new machines" centered around the protection and enhancement of their own roles.[3] The re-emergence of community, the wave of decentralization that Pecorella and others have associated with "postreform" politics, helped fuel the emergence of ethnic interests, on one hand, and of a more general focus on community groups on the other. So-called NIMBY ("not in my back yard") groups have shown increasing ability to frustrate powerful economic and political interests in the siting of roads, utility lines, stadiums, housing projects, and prisons. Finally, the general public, the mood of the state, the political culture—whatever one calls the usually inchoate set of attitudes, prejudices, media reports, and poll results that politicians believe to be reflective of reality—sets important limits on what political actors believe can and cannot be done.

It is interesting that the debate between pluralists and elitists has flowed almost exclusively through studies conducted in urban areas or at the level of national politics. Both pluralists and elitists have largely ignored the states, and students of state politics have, by and large, returned the favor by ignoring the question. Not surprisingly, elite theories have fared far better at the local level than the national. If, as most community power studies have suggested, New York City is more pluralistic than most cities, the most obvious explanation is rooted in size: New York is simply too big and complex to have a single governing interest or elite. At the state level, economic interests are still more highly diffuse. Students of urban politics have given more attention to nongovernmental powers in part because private interests frequently do play more visible and significant roles in local as opposed to state politics. There are lots of company towns but few company states. Local governments, moreover, often have powers that more directly challenge and confront certain kinds of businesses, such as real estate. While a state government can tax, regulate, license, or subsidize an individual business enterprise, it must usually direct its policies at the business as a whole, including a company's competitors. Both Coca Cola and Pepsi were against New York state's bottle return law, but neither suffered a competitive disadvantage from the requirement that they collect a five cent deposit on every bottle. But when New York City denies Donald Trump a variance to build a particular building on land he owns, Trump's injury is both direct and singular. It affects no other developer, and it affects Trump absolutely. Not surprisingly, studies of community power in urban America almost always include real estate developers high on the list of power wielders; yet they are not a major force at the national level and rank relatively low in most states.

The size and general liberalism of New York, both the state and the city, has long blended these forces in complex ways. Among students of urban politics, New York City has usually been depicted as unusually, if not uniquely, pluralistic. Paul Peterson's argument that urban areas must almost inevitably focus on promoting private investment while discouraging redistributive social services is persuasive *except* with regard to New York City.[4] Indeed, in his book *City Limits* Peterson devotes a separate chapter (co-authored with Margaret Weir) to an examination of whether New York really is different.

Whether it ever actually was, they conclude, the fiscal crises of the 1970s forced the city to confront the necessarily painful choices and conform to the model. "Aspects of the Koch Administration's policies," as Mollenkopf replies, "would seem to confirm this view." Acknowledging that Koch as mayor "vigorously promoted private investment in office building construction," and "de-emphasized redistributive spending," Mollenkopf nonetheless winds up affirming the view that New York is different. "In the final analysis," he says:

> The Koch administration did not pursue budgetary austerity. After the early 1980s it rapidly expanded all components of city spending. . . . By the late 1980s, the budget was rising as fast as it did in the 1960s under the supposedly profligate Mayor Lindsay, the burden of spending on value added was growing once more, and numerous social services were rapidly expanding. The Koch administration increased city employment expenditures, and taxation levels even after its private economy leveled off in 1988 and 1989 and began to decline in 1990. His actions thus ran flatly contrary to what theories of economic determinism would have predicted.[5]

What Mollenkopf convincingly shows is that the interplay between the economic "realities" supporting the "permanent government" in New York City and the "political" pressures from interest groups and the general public is far more complicated than structural elite theory would suggest. While we would argue that this is even more the case in state politics, the role of economic elites in defining the parameters of public choice, in both the city and the state, is not insignificant.

Pluralists, as a rule, have tended to overemphasize the importance of visible groups. Journalists too have tended to focus their attention on the activities of *organized* interest groups because their lobbying efforts are more directly and obviously political. And because the focus of this book is on the political process, we follow that tradition. A strong argument can be made, however, that many groups are active in politics more because they are vulnerable than because they are strong.

In a celebrated 1960 book on national politics, E.E. Schattschneider observed that, "It is the losers in intra business conflict who seek redress from public authority."[6] The ability of the most deeply established economic interests to escape adverse government action, and thereby avoid the need to lobby, has diminished since Schattschneider wrote. Government intrusions into such previously "private" areas as pollution control, worker safety, and consumer protection have forced almost all corporations to seek some form of political representation. If we confine our definition of public policy to decisions made by public bodies (such as governors, mayors, and city councils) many of the most powerful interests in society still have little reason to

Box 4.1

Group Representation in Albany

As in most states, lobbyists in New York are required to register. In New York, any lobbyist, group, or public corporation that spends more than $2,000 a year attempting to influence the legislature, the governor, or a state agency must register with the temporary state commission on lobbying. Although the fines for noncompliance (a maximum of $5,000 per offense) are relatively trivial for large interests, no one wants the bad publicity that might accompany failure to report. For a variety of reasons, however, the list of groups and corporations registered with the commission is not particularly representative of the realities of group power. In 1995, for example, some of the state's largest commercial employers—including Eastman-Kodak, Macy's, Sears, UPS, and Xerox—had either no registered lobbyists in Albany or were represented only part-time by a large firm.

At the other end of the scale are conglomerate enterprises, such as New York Telephone, that are vulnerable to government regulation and have multiple modes of representation. The champion of reported lobbying groups is probably Phillip Morris which—if we include its Miller Beer, and Kraft Food divisions—has its own office, is represented by eight different professional lobbying groups, and is a member of at least five trade associations that are registered to lobby. This spreading of the action is undoubtedly a question, at least in part, of image. Touting the health benefits of Kraft food products under the corporate symbol of a cigarette company probably is not a good idea. More generally, however, large conglomerates like Phillip Morris and NYNEX have diverse interests that may sometimes conflict with one another. Trade associations can also have this problem. To play it safe, most groups that have significant interactions with the government are represented in more than one way.

involve themselves in politics. Only a handful of the state's major banks and brokerage houses were registered with the state's lobbying commission in 1999. Other industries can go for years with relatively few problems until suddenly confronting a major threat. All of the major tobacco companies—threatened by proposals to increase taxes and ban smoking in various places—have become major players in Albany, a role they did not have to play when they were strong.

Schattschneider's caveat is important. Some very powerful social and economic interests are not adequately covered in a study such as this. Others—like the tobacco companies—are major players because they are weak rather than strong: absent a powerful lobbying effort they are almost sure losers in the group struggle. New York is a less liberal state than public opinion polls might sometimes suggest, in part because its public officials, no matter how liberal they are themselves, must honor the claims of key players in the permanent government. State and local politicians, as David C. Nice argues, "compete with one another in seeking to attract jobs, investment, and affluent citizens. This competition is most acute at the local level because of the small geographic reach of local governments. An individual or company wanting to locate in a given area can typically select from several local governments in that area. Moreover, relocating from one local government to another is relatively easy for affluent families. As we move from local to state to national governments, the difficulties associated with relocating from one jurisdiction to another increase. As a result, competition among governments for wealthy residents, business investment, and jobs is most acute locally and least acute nationally."[7]

States are, to be sure, less vulnerable on this account than localities, but the threat of relocation is an ever-looming reality. In the 1980s, Mario Cuomo began cutting taxes on corporations and higher income individuals not out of ideological conviction—indeed his rhetoric usually indicated great sympathy for redistributing income—nor as a result of any direct political "pressure," but out of a real concern for such movements of wealthy taxpayers and businesses. In advocating lower maximum taxes on personal income, Cuomo may have been playing an electoral card, but he was not responding to any of the traditional kinds of political pressures one associates with powerful lobbies. There was no "Citizens to Stick It to the Poor" group lobbying on behalf of wealthy taxpayers in Albany. There didn't need to be one.

Organization and Power

There are some groups whose connections with government are so strong and enduring, or whose legislative interests are so broad, that their presence as active lobbyists is permanent. The public employees unions, teachers, health care associations, and local governments have lobbyists who are as well known in the halls of the legislative office building as some legislators. Others are in and out of the system depending on how they view the policy stream. Table 4.1 compares the amount spent by the top ten groups in 1996 and 1997. The presence of the Trump casino interests on both lists is a relatively recent phenomenon as gambling issues have come to head only in recent years. Unions, always major players, were more active in 1996 than in 1997 because the issue of reforming workmen's compensation laws was high on the governor's agenda in 1996. And the rent stabilization group was active in 1997 because of a major Republican effort to change the law. What is most striking about this list, however, is continuity: the same faces, those representing public employees, local governments, teachers, and the health industry, show up over and over again.

Table 4.1

Top Ten Interest Groups Ranked by Reported Expenditures, 1996 and 1997 (in thousands of dollars)

	1996		1997
Civil Service Employees Association	1,074	Greater New York Hospital Association	898
Greater New York Hospital Association	1,037	New York State United Teachers	672
Emergency Coalition/Families' Health	794	Trump Hotel and Casino Resorts	672
Trump Taj Mahal	759	Rent Stabilization Association of New York City	633
New York State AFL/CIO	730	Healthcare Association of New York State	534
Healthcare Association of New York State	724	City of New York	495
New York State United Teachers	663	Public Employees Federation	471
City of New York	521	Civil Service Employees Association	432
Public Employees Federation	454	Conference of Mayors/Municipal Officials	428
Conference of Mayors/Municipal Officials	384	Association of Counties and Affiliates	408

Source: New York Temporary State Commission on Lobbying, *Annual Report* (Albany: Commission on Lobbying, 1997), Appendix H.

Three groups in the top ten—the City of New York, the Public Employees Federation, and the United Teachers—spent virtually the same amounts both years. If you trace down the list of major lobbying groups, this is not uncommon. Organizations as diverse as the League of Women Voters and the Sierra Club, the Motion Picture Association and the Wine Institute maintain a constant presence in Albany to monitor those actions of state government that group members want to follow. Lobbyists for these organizations, together with a large group of higher priced professionals who make their livings representing a variety of interests, form a sort of surplus staff—a reserve army of researchers—for the legislature. Every day that the assembly and senate are in session, each member receives upwards of ten to twenty memorandums from various advocacy groups touting their positions. While many of these quickly find their ways to the wastebasket, a surprising proportion are read by members and their aides, taken seriously, and often kept on file.

Just as in most studies of Washington lobbyists, legislators in Albany are more likely to feel helped by lobbyists than pressured. They rely on them to provide accurate indicators of the concerns of key constituency groups, and to provide guidance on technical policy issues. Lobbyists also play a vital role in communicating between and among members, at worst spreading rumors, at best bringing together people who might not otherwise know what they had in common. As one congressman once said about Washington,

> A professional lobbyist becomes part of the woodwork here. He becomes a source of information. A lot of people talk about the "invidious special interests," but we shouldn't engage in legislation without knowing who's affected by it, and usually the people who are affected by it are the best sources of information. There are a few guys up here who vote a certain way because they're bought, but most of us don't like to deal with people who only have a short-range interest in us.[8]

There are some important differences between Albany and Washington. The legislative community in Albany is much smaller and more intimate. It is not difficult to talk with the members without then being filtered through staff or given a cursory two-minute appointment. An Albany lobbyist can still buy a state senator a drink at Ogden's, join a group of assembly members for a late-night, after-session plate of pasta at Lombardo's, or a plate of Buffalo wings and a game of shuffleboard at McGeary's. At the same time, the lobbyist's job is more structured in Albany where the importance of party discipline makes the patterns of communication far less fluid. While no one totally ignores minority party members, there is little to be gained by spending much time with either assembly Republicans or senate Democrats. The dominating roles of party leaders, moreover, put most lobbyists a step away from real power: when you lobby an individual member on anything but a trivial issue, you are essentially trying to get the member in turn to "lobby" his or her party leadership to move the issue along.

Group Politics in Albany

Organization matters, and lobbying works. While we have almost never encountered a member of the legislature who would admit that his or her vote has been swayed as a result of organizational "pressure," neither would they suggest that most groups that hire Albany representatives are wasting their money. There are a variety of ways in which interest groups can be categorized. One is by noting how they get paid. At one extreme are literally thousands of volunteers who don't get paid at all. Traditionally, Tuesday is lobbying day in Albany and the halls of the legislative office building (or LOB, as it is commonly called) are thronged with busloads of citizens going from one legislative office to another to make their cases for and against abortion, coyote hunting, increased funding for the arts, and all manner of things small and large. These groups are rarely effective on their own: it takes a sound, experienced organization behind them to get the required numbers of people to Albany, to guide them to those legislators most likely to be influenced, and to brief them on what to say. Unless they arrive in surprisingly large numbers, these citizen lobbyists are seldom an important force. Indeed, most legislators welcome Tuesday lobbying days as opportunities to expand their own circles of potential electoral support. Legislators (and their staff assistants) are good listeners and have a way of appearing sympathetic (which they often genuinely are), even when there is nothing they intend to do.

The Lobbying Community

The difference between a professional lobbyist backed by large numbers of Tuesday amateurs, and the amateurs on their own, was neatly encapsulated many year's ago in the late congressman Clem Miller's classic tale of the walnut growers and the chicken farmers. In Miller's story, groups of chicken farmers and walnut growers descended upon Congress to explain their dire economic straits. Both make persuasive cases for federal help and aroused considerable feelings of concern. But when the chicken farmers went home, they went home leaving the ball in the congressmen's court; the walnut growers, far smaller in number, left a professional lobbyist in Washington to follow up, to propose a set of specific acts, to remind the busy members of their concern with the issue, to make sure that things got done. Gradually the members, busy with other demands on their time, forgot about the chicken farmers. The lobbyist for the walnut growers kept the issue alive and got his clients what they needed.[9]

A number of voluntary associations, recognizing the importance of such follow-up activities, have hired part-time lobbyists or had one of their members register with the lobbying commission. While such part-time lobbyists are seldom Albany based, they can help keep the momentum of lobbying days alive. A step up the scale from volunteers are professional representatives who "rep" a variety of clients on a contract basis. Individuals, companies, and law firms—often including one or more former legislators or staff persons—are paid on either an hourly or yearly basis to serve as a group's eyes, ears, and mouth in Albany. Sometimes these professional reps handle a rich variety of group needs: a representative of the state's chiropractors, for example, may lobby on issues concerning chiropractors, organize the association's annual meeting and banquet, collect member dues, maintain the mailing list, and produce a periodic newsletter informing individual chiropractors of goings on in Albany that might affect their lives. The same representative may also be performing similar services for a variety of other groups such as funeral homes, window-covering companies, and exterminators. The advantage of being repped by a professional such as this is, quite simply, that he or she is a professional. As much as such lobbyists may be pulled by obligations to other clients, and as little as they may know about your particular problems, they are generally among the best-connected lobbyists in the Albany community. Bolton-St. Johns, for example, which represents such diverse clients as Erie County, the Long Island Lighting Company, a union of government employees, and a hospital association, is made formidable by such key partners as former assembly speaker Mel Miller; Norman Adler, once a top union lobbyist, campaign consultant, and adviser to Governor Cuomo; and Armand D'Amato, brother of the former senator and himself a former assemblyman.

As impressive as some of these lobbying firms are, many organizations prefer to have their own "in house" lobbyists. Most major unions and a number of corporations have Albany offices that, presumably, combine political skills with a more detailed knowledge of the organization's needs. Since lobbying in the Capitol is not usually a year-round job, these in-house lobbyists frequently combine their political responsibilities with community affairs, philanthropy, and public relations. For some voluntary organizations, such as environmental groups and advocates for the poor, the executive director wears his or her lobbying hat when the legislature is in session and takes it off the rest of the week to focus on fund-raising and other organization-building needs.

An important part of the lobbying community comprises trade and peak association representatives. Groups such as the New York Restaurant Association, the Empire State Association of Adult Homes, and the Professional Fire Fighters Association serve the practitioners of these trades in a number of ways. The restaurant association, for example, keeps its members informed of changes in the tax laws that may affect their businesses, provides them with signs to post in compliance with laws, and updates them on new products such as computer programs. It also lobbies on behalf of the industry. Many small businesses rely heavily on such trade associations to keep them informed of new developments and to represent their interests, although there is some tendency for trade associations to be dominated by their bigger clients (e.g., Burger King in the case of restaurants). Peak Associations such as the New York State Business Council and the New York State AFL-CIO represent a whole variety of businesses or trade unions, large and small.

In New York, as in Washington, one of the more interesting developments in the interest group arena is the proliferation of so-called intergovernmental lobbies, groups of officials at one level of government hiring representatives to influence officials at another level. At the national level, Nice cites one study showing a rise in the number of such groups growing from five, prior to 1900, to eighty-six in the 1960s.[10] Some groups, such as the Committee for Modern Courts, are not really intergovernmental lobbies since they are privately funded; but the growth in this sector has been as remarkable in New York as it has in Washington. Individual cities, the state and city universities, school boards, and counties all maintain Albany offices, as do a wide variety of public officials such as the state school superintendents' association.

As we have already noted, the list of groups represented in Albany is by no means reflective of the range of interests with political concerns in the state. Some groups, as we have noted, are so unthreatened by government that they have no real need to lobby. And among organized groups, the pressure system clearly tilts against the poor. Not only are poor folks, students, welfare recipients, and so on likely to have no Albany representation at all, the representatives they do have are likely to be less skilled, less well paid, and part-time. Organized labor, to be sure, stands up for working people as a class; the professional staff congress works hard to increase funding for the city university and to keep tuition low; but the core concerns of groups such as these focus on their members. Forced, let us say, to choose between salary cuts for professors and tuition increases for students, there is no question where the professional staff congress (which represents the unionized faculty of the city university) would stand.

So-called public-interest groups that stand up for issues like consumer protection and the environment are growing in number. Often dismissed as "do-gooders," they can be effective. In order to keep their members happy and their contributions rolling in, groups such as these often confront a tension between the need to excite their members (often by trashing politicians or making outrageous claims), and presenting a serious, responsible face to the people they have just "dissed."

Until very recently, much of the literature concerning interest groups focused on voluntary organizations such as these. But a growing number of lobbies have no members. Look, for example, at some of the groups represented by Albany's biggest lobbying firm, Davidoff and Malito: the American Museum of Natural History, Coca Cola, the College of Podiatric Medicine, the Courtroom Television Network, and the Long Island Jewish Medical Center—institutions with interests, but hardly models for the system of pluralistic representation described by group theory.

Thomas and Hrebenar in 1994 used ten factors to rank the forty most influential interests in the fifty states. Their top five were: schoolteacher's organizations (which were rated "most effective" in 43 states), general business organizations (most effective in 37), utility companies (23), lawyers (26), and traditional labor organizations (22).[11] We asked a nonrandom sample of thirty-five legislators and staff aides which groups they regarded as highly influential in Albany. A majority mentioned the United Federation of Teachers and the New York State Business Council. No other group was mentioned by more than three respondents, though most were able to offer examples of groups with considerable issue-specific power, such as gun clubs, the public employee unions, and the insurance industry. Republicans, interestingly, were more likely to see unions as powerful interests while Democrats were similarly more inclined to mention business groups. While New York is not sharply distinguished from the national survey, it seems probable that its lobbying community is larger and more diverse than is the norm.

The Changing Locus of Group Politics

In the rosiest view of early pluralists, the group struggle was depicted as a relatively balanced battle for representation between elections, a mechanism through which the rather crude mandates of the electorate could be translated into specific policy proposals. There is, and always has been, considerable utility in this model. Few legislators at the state or national level ever feel "pressured" by lobbyists. Rather they tend to regard interest groups as service agencies that provide them with informed perspectives on important issues, and, in an important sense, "represent" important social groups. Who better to articulate the concerns of, say, dairy farmers than lobbyists paid by dairy interests to articulate their concerns?

The further the analysis of group politics has proceeded, the less this model seems reflective of political reality. While it is true that lobbyists can and often do effectively represent the interests of their clients, the pressure system is not, in the final analysis, democratic. The first problem with the pluralist model, as Schattschneider long ago pointed out, is that the range of organized group interests is not at all reflective of the general population. In Schattschneider's frequently quoted argument:

> The vice of the groupist theory is that it conceals the most significant aspects of the system. The flaw in the pluralist heaven is that the heavenly chorus sings with a strong upper-class accent. Probably about 90 percent of the people cannot get into the pressure system.[12]

Even among the groups that are represented in the system, moreover, there are serious questions about the legitimacy of the representative process. Almost a century ago, the Austrian sociologist Roberto Michels coined the term "iron law of oligarchy" to describe what he saw as the governing paradigm of Europe's supposedly democratic socialist parties. It was, Michels suggested, almost in the nature of voluntary organizations for the rank-and-file members to become increasingly disinterested in organizational business, and for the staff to become correspondingly independent. Michel's "iron law" applies with a vengeance to most contemporary interest groups. Most workers join unions either because they have to, or to advance their economic interests through collective bargaining. Most lawyers join the bar association so they can practice law. The lobbying efforts of the union, the bar association, the medical society, or the farm bureau are not high on the agendas of their rank-and-file members. Increasingly, interest groups are run by paid professionals, expert lobbyists, and administrators who may never have lived the lives of those whose interests they represent. As organization men and women, the leaders of most lobbying groups view themselves as career professionals not as carpenters, teachers, dairy farmers, or doctors; and it is precisely because they are professional lobbyists rather than farmers or workers that they were hired in the first place. Their desire to continue in these often well-paid positions combines with the apathy of the rank-and-file to sustain Michel's iron law. Beyond oligarchy, however, is the greater threat of what Lowi calls "the iron law of decadence." Increasingly, he argues, in every "highly organized element in modern society, there are organizational characteristics that dictate organizational maintenance over every other possible goal." In established groups "the goals of the organization have become intertwined with the needs of maintaining the organization, until the two have become indistinguishable and self-reinforcing."[13] The growing number of institutional lobbies, those that essentially have no "members," reinforces this tendency.

This institutionalization of group politics has also brought professional lobbyists into increasingly cordial relationships with their counterparts in

Box 4.2

Extreme Fighting: A Case Study in Lobbying

Extreme fighting, sometimes referred to as human cockfighting, puts two contestants into a ring where they then are allowed to pummel each other into a pulp until one of them becomes unconscious or surrenders, or until a doctor stops the action. Head butts, kicks to the groin, and kidney punches are allowed. How New York in 1996 became the first state to allow this "sport," and how it just as quickly banned it, provides some interesting insights into the sometimes murky legislative process, and how that process can be influenced.

In 1995, an extreme fighting match that had been booked for the Brooklyn Park Slope Armory was canceled by the mayor who quickly rushed a bill through city council banning the sport. Its supporters promptly proposed a state law preempting such local ordinances. They then hired one of Albany's shrewdest lobbyists to take their case. James Featherstonhaugh, whose firm represents clients like CBS, Goldman Sachs, Pepsi Cola, and the Tobacco Institute, is particularly known for his close ties to the Republican senate leadership, though he is liked and respected on both sides of the aisle. Rather than overtly call for legalization, Featherstonhaugh drew up a bill to "regulate" extreme fighting by putting it under the auspices of the New York State Athletic Commission. Not many legislators liked extreme fighting, and there certainly was no large organized constituency for it; but the potential constituency in opposition was not organized, and few legislators wanted to go on record opposing the "regulation" of so brutal a sport.

Mr. Featherstonhaugh was able to get majority leader Joseph Bruno to push the bill, helping it to enjoy a fast track through the senate. The Democratic assembly leaders seeing no organized opposition to block it, decided they could trade its passage for assembly bills that the Democrats liked but the Republicans were lukewarm about. So the extreme fighting bill was put on a "trade list" and passed without much debate during the end of session rush where many bills reach the floor during the late night marathon sessions the legislature is famous for just before it adjourns for the session.

The members of both houses were not told that they were actually sanctioning this kind of fighting, only that they were allowing it to be regulated by the state. Few if any knew that the effect of their vote would be to make New York the first state in the country to sanction this kind of fighting; and since the bill was placed by the leadership on the so-called Consent Calendar, where noncontroversial bills go through with little or no debate, it passed without difficulty. The governor then signed the bill using the interesting argument that "there was a large majority for its passage, so it had to be almost veto-proof and therefore his veto would have been overridden,"* something that almost never happens in New York.

When a match was actually scheduled for the Niagara Arena, the media picked up the issue and a whole series of editorials, church sermons, call-in show rants, and letters to the editor showed a decidedly negative tone. Governor Pataki quickly introduced legislation to ban such fighting state-wide, and a companion bill to allow local communities a final say on the issue. Not coincidentally, the state athletic commission (appointed by the governor) came out with its regulations, which required gloves, timed bouts, and basically made the sport similar to boxing. Two weeks later the embarrassed legislature outlawed the sport entirely. Senator Bruno was reported as favoring legislation that would give localities the option to allow the sport, but it was too late politically for that. Most lobbyists will tell you that they can have little influence on an issue when the public is aroused, but where most people know little and care less a good lobbyist can earn his or her pay. The extreme fighting case was unusual only in that it showed both sides of this coin in one six-month period.

---

*New York Times, January 17, 1997, p. B-1.

government. Subgovernments—triangles of influence linking bureaucrats, legislative committees, and lobbyists—are less visible in New York than at the national level. Instead, group leaders in New York have tended to link their fortunes increasingly to those of the parties in power. Much of this linkage is financial. Indeed the nexus between money and power in the form of campaign contributions is so important that it receives separate treatment later in this chapter. The point here has less to do with the amount of influence generated by lobbies than with its direction. Not only have the established groups been caught in Lowi's law of decadence, but they have become so enmeshed in their defense of the existing order of things that they are reluctant to call for change *even when it would appear to be in their own interest to do so.* They have, in a word, become power-tropic, leaning toward the party in power as plants lean toward the sun.

Take, for example, the United Federation of Teachers (UFT), which makes most people's lists of the most powerful groups in the state. The UFT's political action committee always ranks among the top campaign contributors in state elections. To whom does it give? In 1996 every incumbent running for reelection to the state senate and assembly, *every one of them* (except Robert D'Andrea, Republican from Saratoga, who claims to have refused their money) received an endorsement and contribution from the UFT. What did the union get for its support? In institutional terms it was and has been enormously effective. Its effectiveness, however, is defined almost entirely in institutional as opposed to programmatic terms. Like many groups in Albany (and in Washington) it has become what the late Aaron Wildavsky called a political aircraft carrier. An aircraft carrier, Wildavsky would point out, cost, say, $5 billion to put to sea. Of the $5 billion, $1.5 billion went for sophisticated radar and sonar systems, double hulls and special plates to protect the carrier from attack. Of the $1 billion worth of planes on the carrier, roughly half were there to protect the aircraft carrier. Its guns—half a billion worth—were there to protect the aircraft carrier. And it went to sea with a flotilla of four other boats (cost: $1.5 billion) whose function was—are you getting the idea?—to protect the aircraft carrier. Net result, you spend 75 to 80 percent of your resources defending yourself against potential attacks. The UFT, to be sure, lobbies for better schools; but its real mission is to protect the UFT: to fight against attacks on tenure, to oppose charter schools (unless they are prohibited from hiring nonunion teachers), to protect the pension system, to protect the aircraft carrier.

We single out the UFT largely because of its size. Among "liberal" groups in Albany it continues, more than most, to fight the good fight. Like many other organizations represented in the state capital, it is caught in the middle of a system stagnated by the institutionalization of divided government. In a system that is dominated by strong parties, like New York's, interest groups that want to be effective will find it necessary to work through the parties to achieve their objectives. Groups with too strong an identity, in either ideological or partisan terms, can be frozen out of one party conference or another. There are, to be sure, a number of issues on which the parties have not staked out clear positions, and the array and tactics of interest groups in areas such as these is probably pretty much the same in New York as in most other large states. The general proposition that states (or countries) with strong party systems tend to have weak pressure systems is not entirely borne out in New York.[14] "The major parties in New York," as Cingranelli argues, "are not particularly ideological, and that fact increases the access that most groups have to the elected representatives of both parties. . . . Parties need to have the active support of interest groups in order to maintain and enhance their legislative majorities and to capture the governor's seat."[15]

Yet a group that becomes too active in supporting one party risks so alienating the other that all of its legislative victories are doomed to be one-house bills. Thus Thomas classifies interest groups in New York as "complementary," that is, where they "tend to have to work in conjunction with or are constrained by other aspects of the political system."[16]

While most researchers share the view that the interest groups in New York are weaker than those in most other states, and, in a general sense, more constrained by the strength of the party system, the study of state lobbying is in its infancy.[17] The so-called reputational approach, which we used in simply asking informed policy makers which lobbyists they thought were most powerful, runs the danger of mistaking rumor for clout. A strong reputation is nice to have, but it doesn't always win fights. The United Federation of Teachers, for example, makes almost every New Yorker's list of powerful groups; yet it was badly beaten in the 1998 special session when the party leaders in effect bought the governor's approval of a legislative pay raise by passing his nonunion charter schools bill.

The Party System, the Pressure System, and the Locus of Power

In his award-winning discussion of agenda setting, John Kingdon used the concept of a policy "stream" to describe the balance of organized forces that can move an issue onto or off of the political agenda. "If important people look around and find that all of the interest groups and other organized interests point them in the same direction, the entire environment provides them with a powerful impetus to move in that direction."[18] If there is conflict in the environment, conversely, there is almost invariably a reluctance to act. On major statewide issues, New York's entrenched system of divided government almost invariably traps some organizations into alliances that blend policy streams, on one hand, as they make them conflictual on the other. Organized labor, for example, frequently finds itself in close alliance with the Democratic Party. In the 1996 fight to reform the Workmen's Compensation Law it was labor and the Democratic majority in the state assembly against the governor and the Republican state senate. For Democrats in the assembly, the streams ran together: voting with labor, for the working man, with their party, and in accord with their personal beliefs was easy.

The problem for labor was with its allies. By linking the Workmen's Comp issue with the budget, the Republicans in effect held other groups hostage: to the extent that teachers wanted more for schools, that advocates for the poor wanted more for social welfare, they had to deal with the Republicans by letting labor go it alone on its big issue. Labor could win only by tying itself still more tightly to the Democrats, hoping to keep the assembly leadership from cutting a deal. In the end, their act could not be sustained: conflict in the environment—in this case the budget needs of other groups—forced the Democrats to blink.

Many groups—the UFT and the public employees unions in particular—are capable of a "two-stream" strategy, floating with one current on the senate side, with another on the assembly. But groups like the AFL/CIO, both sides on the abortion issue, and the gun lobby are locked into one party and one house of the legislature. This means that they can usually block actions that hurt them, but they have virtually no power of initiative, no ability to compromise. Interestingly, one study attempting to assess the relative power of interest groups in New York politics classified labor as less effective than some other groups during routine legislative sessions, but found that "legislators thought unions were the most effective interest groups as elections approached."[19]

Campaign Finance: Meeting Ground of the Party and Pressure Systems

New York's campaign finance laws are, on paper, quite restrictive. All candidates for state office in both primary and general elections must file detailed reports with the state board of elections listing all contributions of $100 or more. The maximum amount that a single contributor can donate to a statewide candidate is one-half cent per registered voter. Thus in 1994, when there were roughly 8,800,000 registered voters statewide, a single donor could have given a candidate for governor or attorney general no more than $44,000 for his or her general election campaign. In the primary, he or she would have been limited to about $20,000 for a Democrat (half-cent for each of the approximately four million enrolled Democrats), $13,500 for a Republican, and $365 for a Liberal. In a primary or general election for other than statewide office, the limit goes up to five cents per voter or $50,000, whichever is less. Each donor must be clearly identified in reports filed regularly with the board of elections during the campaign.

Real Money and Reported Money

To say that there are loopholes in these finance laws is like saying there are holes in swiss cheese. The so-called soft money scandals that attracted so much media attention in the wake of the 1996 presidential campaign are more than matched by the less closely followed evasions of campaign finance rules practiced in New York. Despite attempts by legislators and journalists to learn who gave how much to Governor Pataki's "inauguration committee," no one knows how much was spent on the party (celebrating the governor's inauguration) and how much was spent on the Party (trying to elect a Republican legislature two years later). In the 1996 campaigns there were a lot of television ads, not reported as candidate expenditures, targeting vulnerable Democrats and paid for either by independent groups or from soft-money accounts like the inauguration fund. Democratic candidates for their part were frequently helped by independent expenditures (not covered by reporting requirements) that, presumably, were paid for largely by labor unions. Finally, money not subject to contribution limits can be and is transferred from other accounts to state campaigns. As chairman of the U.S. Senate Republican Campaign Committee, for example, Alfonse D'Amato transferred funds to the campaigns of two judicial candidates in the Capitol region. It is probably not a coincidence that these Republican judges (who won in close races) now sit on the court that decides most election law cases in statewide races (Senator D'Amato was himself up for reelection in New York in 1998).[20]

Reporting requirements can also effectively be evaded or at least made difficult to trace. Few filings in New York are computerized and the paper trails of some campaigns are at best confusing. One list produced by the Pataki for Governor Committee was alphabetized by first names instead of last. Candidates sometimes, quite legally, file reports under two or more different organizational names (a practice facilitated by third parties' cross-endorsements). So-called in-kind contributions, where unions, for example, donate phone banks, have not been effectively audited or regulated in New York. Incumbents in the legislature have access to very sophisticated maps of their districts, which, while technically in the public domain, are not widely known to exist. Employees of the legislature, though increasingly scrupulous about doing so in their spare time or on leaves of absence, regularly work actively in campaigns. In short, when we look at the official numbers accessibly filed by campaign committees in New York, it is not really possible to say whether we are seeing nearly all, most, or only some fraction of the amount actually raised and spent in that election. From personal experiences and our conversations with a number of public officials, we would say that most—meaning 80 to 90 percent—of the funds spent in most campaigns are honestly, reliably, and accessibly reported. But it is also clear that the numbers and kinds of evasions are growing fast.

The Role of Political Action Committees

Most major lobbying groups have political action committees or PACs, as they are commonly known. While the term itself does not appear in either federal or state election law, a political action committee is generally defined as a nonparty organization that takes money from a number of individual contributors and gives it to more than one candidate. Frank Sorauf divides PACs into "two broad types depending on their organizational structure: the connected and the unconnected."[21] Connected PACs, in Sorauf's classification, are those that are linked to a parent organization—frequently a lobby—and can solicit funds only from members of the group. Unconnected PACs, including the so-called leadership PACs of many party leaders, are free to solicit contributions from anyone but must pay their own expenses out of those contributions. Most PACs in New York are connected, and a look at a sample of 1996 filings indicates that these organizations accounted for considerably more than half of the money raised by most candidates for the legislature.

It is now practically routine for most members of the legislature to host a reception in Albany sometime during the session. The asking price for such receptions has been going up with $100 being the floor, and top policy makers—such as the chairs of important committees—charging as much as $500. Monday and Tuesday nights in Albany find lobbyists and legislators doing the circuit from rooms in the Omni Hotel to the top of the Corning Tower, to the Sign of the Tree (a restaurant in the Empire State Plaza). Sipping soda water (you can't start on alcohol too early when you've got to get to six receptions between 5:30 and 8:00), picking through the cheese plates and dips trying to find a reception that still has shrimp, the key thing is to show your face. No one acknowledges any kind of quid pro quo in these encounters, but it just wouldn't be smart for a lobbyist dealing with transportation issues not to be at a reception for the chair of the transportation committee. A health lobbyist who has a Tuesday appointment to talk about a bill with the chair of the health committee knows that it is smart politics to be seen at the chairman's Monday night reception.

There is not a lot of lobbying that takes place at these receptions; but the opportunities they provide for networking, for keeping up on the latest in political gossip, and for, quite simply, establishing and cementing personal relationships, have made them a favorite target of reformers. Since the invitation lists to these events are culled almost entirely from the files of the Lobbying Commission, it would be difficult to find a more blatant example of "special interest" money at work. But as much as there is a ritualistic quality to these receptions, and as much as both legislators and lobbyists groan about the need to do the circuit again and again, they are unlikely to be reformed away. For most legislators with safe seats—and that means most legislators—these annual receptions may provide most of the funds they need to go to the receptions of other members, to fund their campaigns, or simply to keep themselves in the public eye.[22] For lobbyists, there are few better ways at once to make favorable impressions on the right people and to get to know key members.

Through his or her connected PAC a lobbyist with money can attend the important receptions, make contributions (within the legal limits) to individual campaigns, and make contributions to other organizations such as the state committees, legislative campaign committees, and various leadership PACs that can them pass them on (beyond the legal limits) to individual candidates. Rosenthal summarizes the problems raised by this system as follows:

> Reformers allege that even if money does not actually buy votes, it buys access. It gives the contributor the chance not only to speak with a legislator, but to be listened to as well. That is the least thing contributors get. . . .
>
> A campaign contribution, by offering support to a legislator in his or her time of need, creates an "attitudinal tendency," in the words of a former Ohio legislator, on the part of a receiver toward a donor. . . .
>
> It operates in the interstices of the process at the margins. Under most circumstances, a sense of obligation does not sway votes, but it probably earns from legislators the willingness to consider a case or even some slight change in their behavior.[23]

The amount of money it takes to mount an effective campaign in a competitive district is both enormous and growing. Perhaps the most important change in campaign finance in the past three decades has been one of sheer magnitude: PACs are more important, legislative campaign committees are more important, and incumbency is more of a factor quite simply because it is almost prohibitively expensive to go up against an incumbent.

Beyond these electoral effects, students of campaign finance have traced four other kinds of relationships between money and politics. First, as Rosenthal suggests, money buys access, the chance to at least make your case. Second, as the quotation from Rosenthal also suggests, it can buy attentiveness, a greater willingness to work actively on behalf of a cause to which a generally sympathetic member might move from passive to active support. In one study of Congress, it was clear that campaign contributions "bought time," increasing member activity in pushing legislation through committees and on the floor.[24] Although the ability to gain such access and mobilization does bias the system in favor of the more affluent, many scholars and politicians regard this kind of bias as relatively benign. Even without campaign contributions, the argument usually goes, a group with solid public support and a good argument can obtain similar access. More troubling are two other kinds of relationships between campaign finances and legislative politics, one where members tailor their legislative interests and activities in anticipation of its monetary value; the second where he or she actually changes the direction of a vote. Twenty years ago it was uncommon for a legislator to seek a committee assignment because it was a good place from which to raise funds, or to introduce a bill in the hopes of attracting the interest of a PAC. And if there were members who changed their votes with campaign contributions in mind, almost none would admit it. Neither is uncommon today. "I really liked lobbying on the issues," one Albany lobbyist wistfully told us, "but now it's just more and more about money."

Parties, Party Leaders, and Campaign Finance

Until the widespread proliferation of PACs, which began, ironically, with the first attempts at federal campaign finance reform laws in the 1970s, legislative campaigns in New York were funded largely by local party organizations, by wealthy individuals, and by a few key interest groups such as labor unions. Republicans had the additional advantage of having Nelson Rockefeller in the governor's mansion. When Rockefeller's money was no longer there, the party set up the state's first legislative campaign committee.[25] The Republican Assembly Campaign Committee was also established, as one former Speaker puts it, because legislative leaders "didn't feel that the county organizations were giving us the right kinds of candidates or supporting candidates in the manner in which they should."[26] Soon there were four such committees, one for each major party in each house. Through these assembly and senate campaign committees, the process of fund-raising has become increasingly centralized within each house of the legislature.

The two manifest functions of these campaign committees are: (1) to reallocate contributions to those campaigns that the leadership feels can best use them, and (2) to professionalize campaigns throughout the state by offering electoral analyses, polls, help with newsletters and campaign brochures, issue research, research on the opposition, and so on. Their latent functions are (1) to divorce special interests from individual candidates by pooling PAC funds in such a way that no candidate can really know who—except the party committee—is funding his or her campaign; (2) to give the party leaders in Albany a great deal of control over the question of whose campaigns are going to be viable; and (3) by giving them that power, to make the speaker, and the majority and minority leaders even more powerful. Except for those with enormous personal wealth, it is almost impossible for a novice candidate to marshal the resources to run a viable campaign without such help. How do the parties allocate their funds?

One strategy, as Stonecash suggests, might be to use the money to enhance their own powers by rewarding their most senior members. "Or they might help challengers, newer members, and those in marginal contests." Party leaders, to be sure, sometimes direct PAC contributions to senior members, especially if they are facing any kind of potential challenge; but their clear focus is on "helping marginal and newer members, challengers, and those running in open seats," a strategy which, as Stonecash says, "could promote party unity and build the party."[27] The roles of DACC (the Democratic Assembly Campaign Committee), RACC (its Republican counterpart), and the major parties' senate committees vary almost entirely according to electoral marginality. Safe seat incumbents, and those challenging safe seat incumbents, receive virtually no help at all. Most other incumbents—except those from extremely marginal seats—are pretty much on their own unless and until they can show that they are really in trouble. One urban Republican who won a previously Democratic seat with the very active financial and strategic help of RACC was told two years later that she was on her own. Another, from a suburban area, was told the same thing until he produced a poll showing that he was in danger of losing. RACC not only provided needed funds but sent in campaign experts from Albany to work in his campaign. Little wonder that, as one party leader lamented to us, there are members who actually lie about how good their opponents are and how likely they are to lose.

Despite a long tradition in American politics of party leaders staying out of interparty fights, New York's legislative campaign committees have become increasingly active in support of *all* challenged incumbents, even when that challenge comes from a fellow partisan. Many New York politicians believe that the antagonism between George Pataki and Ralph Marino— which led ultimately to Marino's being overthrown as senate majority leader— had its roots in Marino's aggressive support of Senator Mary Goodhue against a primary challenge from Pataki in 1992.

There are some important differences between and among the four legislative campaign committees. In the assembly, as Stonecash has shown:

> The strategies of the two parties reflect their different situations. As the dominant party, the Democrats are concerned to maintain that position. They have allocated more of their money to protecting incumbents because they must do so to retain power. The Republicans, as a party that must make some dent in the Democratic majority in order to regain control . . . cannot afford to devote money to incumbents.[28]

While we do not have the kind of systematic data for the senate that Stonecash gathered for the assembly, the same logic apparently applies with the majority Republicans adopting an essentially defensive, proincumbent strategy and the minority Democrats more aggressively backing insurgents.

Centralization or Balkanization?

There is no doubt that party leaders, for many years, welcomed and embraced every step on the road to centralized fundraising. One senior Democrat even lost his chairmanship of a major assembly committee because his friendly interactions with the groups interested in the committee's work had given him the personal ability to raise large sums of money both for his own campaigns and for other Democrats. For Democrats, the centralization of fundraising helped free the assembly speaker and the majority or minority leader from having to deal with county chairmen in trying to put together legislative majorities. Republican speakers and leaders also welcomed such growing independence and in addition were able to establish greater independence from the governor and the state committee. Legislative campaign committees, as Daniel Shea concludes, "represent a means for legislative leaders to control external resources—to collect and control campaign funds, to free their members of damaging elements of the party, and to augment their caucus regardless of the party's status in other branches."[29] Many of the members we talked with, however, and even—to our surprise—some party leaders, expressed growing reservations about the system. To understand their reservations, we must briefly return to the "responsible parties" model we discussed in Chapter 3.

The essential argument for strong parties is that by centralizing power they focus responsibility thereby letting the electorate know precisely who is to be blamed or given credit for changes in public policy. A strong party system, it follows, can prevent the fragmentation of the system into subgovernments and thereby sharply diminish the often hidden influence of special interests. A strong party system by clarifying differences between the parties brings issue differences before the electorate and thus facilitates what is called a "rational choice" model of politics. "At first glance," as Shea concludes, New York's legislative campaign committees would appear to fulfill at least some of the conditions of this model. "But on closer inspection even this notion is tenuous. Units designed to capture seats only within one branch of a legislature, holding little or no affinity for broad-based or long-range activities, may strain even the most inclusive view of 'party.'"[30]

Money follows power. In a strong party state like New York this means that it flows largely to and through party leaders. To the extent that groups have ideological agendas this tends to mean that as they cement relations with one party they destroy their ability to work with the other. Political action committees representing gun owners, some real estate interests, and some health insurers give vastly disproportionate amounts to Republicans. Some unions are similarly tied to the Democrats. In practice what this tends to mean is that absent a very strong push from the governor or from public opinion, these groups have veto power over policies that might affect them but little or no ability to change existing law. Groups aligned with the Republicans can initiate or block bills in the senate but fail in the assembly.

Democratic groups are equally assured of success in the assembly and failure in the senate.

To avoid these pitfalls, many of the more powerful groups in New York give heavily to both majorities. As Robert Haggerty, a former director of the Republican campaign committee says, "The major players in the money area don't play philosophical politics. They play majority politics."[31] Majority politics is almost by definition moderate politics. It is a politics that, like the politics of deadlock, produces few new initiatives.

When the governor's campaign operations are also totally independent of the legislature's, as they were in the Cuomo administration, there is a still further fragmentation of responsibility. The Pataki administration, aided by a revitalized Republican state committee and U.S. Senator Alfonse D'Amato with legendary fundraising abilities has shown some interest in and ability to cut across these lines. Publicly led by the conservative group CHANGE-NY, and quietly funded by a small group of businessmen from the right wing of the party, the Pataki campaign from its opening challenge to the moderates in the 1994 Republican primary exhibited an ideological consistency and willingness to involve itself in legislative politics that is reminiscent, in some interesting respects, of the Rockefeller era. Although it seems unlikely that Pataki can ever achieve the kind of influence Rockefeller had (it was once said that Rocky owned one house of the legislature and had a long-term lease on the other), there is little doubt that the conservative wing of the Republican Party is firmly in control of two of its three key components—the state committee, and the party's assembly leadership—and very strong in its senate team. The edge of confrontation with assembly Democrats was somewhat dulled by Democratic acceptance of many Pataki initiatives in 1995, when a stunned assembly leadership looked at the election returns and their polls to navigate a turn to the right. And the budget surplus in 1998 further dulled the level of confrontation. But the fundamental challenge to the Republican right, and to advocates of responsible parties more generally, is structured into the system of divided government and the coincident pattern of campaign finance and interest group politics we have just described.

The Media in New York Politics

New York state has 88 daily newspapers, 12 with daily circulations in excess of 75,000, plus nearly 600 weeklies, bi-weeklies, and semi-weeklies. It has 34 television stations and 274 radio outlets.[32] In the press offices in the Capitol, however, there are representatives of only 29 media outlets and wire services.[33] The overwhelming majority of New York's outlets are thus getting whatever stories they run either from wire services or from the press offices of politicians and interest groups. Even among statehouse reporters themselves, there is widespread agreement that state politics in general and legislative politics in particular are not well covered.[34]

Journalists and Partisans

For the legislature, the problem of poor coverage is not unique to New York. Martin Linsky identifies four general sources of tension between journalists and state legislators that often result in gaps in understanding. First, there is the collective, unfocused nature of the legislative process which—even in a centralized legislature like New York's—makes it hard to give journalists the personalized, focused kinds of action portraits that tend to make interesting stories. Second, the legislators that politicians call show horses—as opposed to the workhorses who do most of the real policymaking—are easier to cover and tend to dominate the news with material that is really peripheral to the real work of the legislature. Third, the kind of compromise and bargaining that makes the process work is often not very interesting to write about: "Good legislating is often done without publicity, or else it would not, and perhaps could not, be done. . . . When good work is done that way, the result is sometimes very unappealing from a news perspective." Finally, "the mix between politics and the substance of legislation" sometimes gives legislators reason to avoid coverage if they can. The kind of flexibility that allows effective bargaining to take place is difficult to explain to a wider public.[35]

Beyond these general sources of tension, there are reasons specific to New York that make for bad coverage. One is simply that of competition: there are just too many things going on in New York for state politics to command ink. This is particularly true in New York City where "Albany political news is competing with the political news that comes out of a major metropolis that people have been studying and reading about for years and where all the politicians are celebrities."[36] There are enormous variations between the various media and their coverage of state politics. Outside of the capital district, television almost never gets into the act. For stations in New York City, Syracuse, Buffalo, and Rochester it takes a full working day for a news and camera crew to set up in Albany. Quite sensibly, their producers send them only when there is some certainty that a newsworthy event will take place. Newspapers vary. In Morgan's study, the percentage of news space given to state as opposed to local, national, and international affairs ranged from a high of 52 percent in the Albany *Times Union* to a low of 11.6 percent in the *New York Times*.[36] For the *Times Union*, what happens in state government is in a sense local news. Its reporters know that what they write will probably be read by most legislators and their staff aides, and by large numbers of civil servants whose jobs may sometimes depend upon the goings on in government. The *New York Times*, with a national audience and a tendency to view itself as the newspaper of record, weighs state issues against a flow of national and international events that tend to receive only cursory coverage in papers like the *Times Union*. At the same time, reporters from the *New York Times*, knowing that they have a more educated, upscale readership than many other papers, can give more serious, thorough coverage to certain kinds of issues. In 1998, for example, both the *New York Times* and the Albany *Times Union* gave rather extensive coverage to the revised budgetary process. Some other papers—the Syracuse *Herald-Journal*, for example—covered the change with particular reference to a local angle; but most barely mentioned it all. As one reporter for a New York City tabloid put it, "If it doesn't involve sex or the lottery we don't print it."

Weeklies and the smaller local papers will occasionally run wire service articles on major issues, particularly if they have a local focus. Almost every paper in the state will run an article every year on the potential impact of various budget scenarios on local property taxes. And these smaller papers quite frequently run the press releases of local assembly members and state senators as if they were regular news stories. Whether they represent small towns or parts of big cities, getting mentioned in the press is an important goal of most legislators. And for interest groups and bureaucrats with policy agendas, media attention is a major step on the road to influence. Because small town and neighborhood papers, weeklies in particular, do not have the staff to research the sources of press releases from politicians and others, they tend to be far less critical in their coverage; but tensions between journalists and public officials are very much a part of the system at all levels.

Perhaps the biggest source of frustration for Albany journalists is the essentially closed nature of the process when it comes to making key decisions. Journalists thrive on conflict, and as one told us, "it is rare that we have any drama around here." In the typical budget negotiations, where a growing number of key decisions have been made, the Albany press corps sat outside a room where the governor, speaker, and majority leader were making the deals that counted. From time to time a staff aide might enter or emerge, politely refusing any comment on anything they might have seen or heard. As the leaders emerged you "felt as if you had gone through about the lowest for journalism that you could get." For anywhere from fifteen minutes to two, three, or more hours, twenty or thirty reporters would sit on little metal folding chairs, talking with each other or with staff about anything but what was going on inside—the Yankees, the weather, good restaurants—"they weren't even doing spin control." Finally, the great men would emerge.

They would all give you the, you know, whatever the response was that day. In their own words they would all say the same thing. And then Cuomo would have you into his office and we'd talk forever and ever on anything from what they had just talked about in the budget to presidential politics. It was all close to the vest, but we talked. Now [with Pataki] it's a telephone thing going on. Cuomo was real in person, you know, let's get this thing negotiated. Now George [Pataki] and Shelly [Silver] barely meet.[38]

Either way, it can be enormously frustrating to journalists. During the Cuomo years, a perceptive journalist might be able to craft a story out of some nuance in the ways in which the respective leaders made their cases; but there was always a feeling among experienced journalists—particularly in dealing with the governor—that they were not being treated with respect. Because party discipline is strong, moreover, a reporter cannot usually stir up a story—as he or she might in Washington—by going to a disgruntled member of the speaker's party, or to a bureaucrat trying to protect his or her agency from rumored cuts. Few even try.

Managing the News

Politicians and journalists need each other, but they need each other for such different reasons that conflict is inevitable. There is a school of journalism that operates on the premise that all politicians are essentially corrupt and that it is a prime function of the media to expose that corruption to the public. Even journalists who know better are not above taking what legislators consider "cheap shots" at the institution and its members. The late Bill Passannante—who served more than thirty years in the state assembly—took particular umbrage at the ritualistic articles, which almost every paper runs from time to time, blasting legislators as overpaid fat cats. At the fortieth reunion of his Harvard Law School class Passannante had discovered that he was the lowest paid member of his class. City newspapers delight in making fun of rural projects, an upstate cheese museum being a favorite target, while upstate journalists invariably find something to outrage their readers in grants to New York City artists. Needless to say, the city papers are as seldom likely to hold art grants up to criticism as their rural counterparts are to criticize local dairy farmers. As much as the legislature often deserves to be criticized for late budgets, for the invariable sloppiness of session's end, for occasional corruption, and for excessive secrecy, "the degree of bad conduct by legislatures does not seem commensurate with the bad press and the low esteem in which the institutions are generally held."[39] There is nothing very newsworthy about a competent legislator going about his or her job; there is a lot that is newsworthy about a legislator caught

Box 4.3

Governors and the Press

It is not an exaggeration to say that few Albany-based journalists were fond of Mario Cuomo. Cuomo, more than one reporter told us, would "call you in the office, call you at home, call your editor" if you didn't report a story the way he wanted it reported. He would, apparently, refuse to recognize certain reporters at his press conferences or refuse to answer their phone calls after they had printed something he didn't like. Rather than answer a hostile question, Cuomo would often lecture the reporter on his manners, her syntax, or his motives. His press secretaries often spent hours working as intermediaries between an angry governor and an individual journalist. What made their dislike for Cuomo particularly frustrating for many journalists was the governor's teflon-like ability to resist letting anything stick. No matter how serious his mistakes, he always came out looking good, particularly on television.

George Pataki is, paradoxically, far better liked yet far less accessible. Where Cuomo courted coverage and seemingly read or watched almost everything the media said about him, Pataki's staff goes to great lengths to keep him from personal encounters with journalists. The second floor of the Capitol, where the governor and his top staff people have their offices, has become a protected enclave open by appointment only, with the elevator operators instructed not to stop there without prior clearance. In dramatic contrast with Cuomo, Pataki is always affable, always personable when his staff allows access. While Cuomo's press aides were constantly apologizing for the governor, Pataki plays the role of good guy to his feisty staff. One journalist describes an incident in which he was attempting to get a more concrete answer than the governor wanted to give to an embarrassing question. As the governor fumbled for words, his then press secretary, Zenia Mucha, started yelling at the reporter and pushing the governor back toward his office. As the entourage of the retreating governor, his shouting press secretary, and a couple of dozen reporters moved down the hall, the reporter attempted to press his question. Finally, the governor stepped between Mucha and the reporters, apologized for *her* behavior, and tried to calm everybody down. "How," our reporter friend asked, "can you keep pushing a nasty question with a guy who has just done you a favor like that?"

stealing, or about the chair of the Alcohol and Substance Abuse Committee being arrested for drunk driving. While such acts are far from typical, a public that receives most of its information from stories such as these may become unduly cynical about an important institution.

Bureaucrats are perhaps the worst abused of all public servants if only because they have almost no ability to fight back. Governors, and other state-wide officials like the comptroller and attorney general, get into interesting sparring matches with the press. Ever since the 1940s when then-governor Thomas E. Dewey hired a press secretary, statewide officials have sought to put their own spin on stories out of Albany. Even in the legislature, press offices are among the largest and best paid. Public officials, governors in particular, have long "sought and expected to get a large share of the credit for policy successes and tried to minimize their responsibilities for policy failures. . . . In pursuit of these goals, executive and legislative branches built up a highly professional public relations capacity that gave them, and especially the governor, maximum publicity. As seen by the press it also provided a potential for the manipulation of the media, or for their co-optation."[40]

No professional journalist likes to be the target of such manipulation, although that, in a manner of speaking, is what every politician would like them to be. No politician, conversely, likes to be caught off guard by stories they didn't script or at least anticipate.

For every incident in which politicians attempt to rebuff reporters there are probably twenty in which they seek them out. "The seeking out," as Morgan says, "takes a variety of forms—hand-delivered press releases, letters, telephone calls, personal visits; the press room at the capitol is often as congested as a busy airport terminal. The staffs of the Governor and of legislative leaders are frequent callers. Most journalists identify legislative staffs as more assiduous callers, though not more successful, than a variety of people who come from the agencies."[41]

Interest groups too seek press coverage, if only because, as one lobbyist put it, "getting your argument in the right papers is like home delivery, you put it right in the hands of the people you want to see it." There is also a sense in which something that appears in the media is more authoritative than the same idea conveyed in a lobbyist's memorandum or a politician's letter.

Because their words tend to have this authoritative character, most journalists are acutely sensitive to the problem of being "used." There is a whole ritual set of guidelines as to how certain statements from politicians should be reported: when a politician goes "off the record," for example, it means that what he or she is about to say should not be part of the published story; statements issued "on background" may be used so long as they are not attributed to the person making them; statements "on deep background" can be used but only in such a way that most people couldn't even guess who was making them. Specific terms and meanings differ from one state capital to another and across generations; but the nuances of the relationships between politicians and journalists that they suggest are a constant. One story, widely circulated among Albany reporters in 1998, is nicely illustrative of this dynamic. On the day that lieutenant governor Betsy McCaughey Ross announced that she was planning to run against the governor, a number of reporters received phone calls from somewhere in the capital alleging—"off the record," of course—that Ms. Ross was illegally using staff and office resources for partisan political purposes. Those reporters who checked the story out discovered that it simply was not true, and it appears to have run in only one tabloid; but it illustrates clearly how and why journalists fear being "used."

The dynamic does not end here. Whoever the source of the putative story on the lieutenant governor was, there is no doubt that he or she lost credibility. A reporter once burned by a source is going to be very skeptical the next time around. (Fool me once, as an old saying goes, shame on you. Fool me twice, shame on me.) Had the story been true, on the other hand, he or she might have gained credibility, particularly if one reporter got it as an exclusive. Albany correspondents do not always agree on what is news: actions affecting, say, the Erie Canal or the Adirondacks that get front-page treatment upstate may be totally ignored on Long Island and in New York City. Changes in the policies of the lottery or off-track betting corporation that make the front pages of the *Daily News* and the *Post* are likely to be ignored by the *New York Times*. There are some stories, though, that are *stories*; reporters who missed the McCaughey-Ross story (had it been true) would have felt bad, even if their editors didn't remind them that they should. At its best, the tendency of most reporters to run the same stories reflects a true consensus on the nature of news. At its worst, in what its critics call "pack journalism," it reflects an ingrained laziness in which everybody follows the most obvious events to make sure that they aren't being scooped by someone else. It is particularly easy for Albany journalists to fall into this latter mode because so much of the real conflict and compromise in New York politics takes place behind closed doors.

Powers and Roles

Building on the unquestionable fact that most of the people who own newspapers and broadcasting stations are rich, elite theorists have generally depicted the media as lackeys to, or coconspirators with, the powers that be. In terms of their editorial policies, most of New York state's newspapers undoubtedly represent the relatively conservative leanings of their publishers. Frequently moderate to liberal on social issues, mixed on questions of equality and civil liberties, and probusiness on issues involving labor, taxes, and government spending, the state's media tend to reflect the old-family, largely Protestant, upper-income attitudes of their owners. Whether there is a truth in the countervailing hypothesis that the working press is hopelessly liberal and slants the news in that direction is a question of long-standing and possibly unresolvable dispute.

The most important fact about the media in New York is that it is media: it mediates between and among people, politicians, and power wielders; it communicates facts, hearsay, opinions, and attitudes. Despite complaints from almost everyone involved in politics about the alleged biases of the press, the more serious problem is one of diversity. Whether because of pack journalism or the relatively closed nature of the process in New York, it is truly unusual for journalists in New York to go beyond ritualistic "exposés" of "overpaid" legislators, inflated "pork barrels," and "three-men in a room" politics into really meaningful analyses of state politics. While this critique could probably be made in almost any state, and in national politics as well, it is particularly damning in a state like New York where state news so seldom receives significant coverage. Whatever its ideological tilt, the tilt that matters most is toward the status quo: the press in New York seldom moves beyond party leaders and toward those stages in the political process where the essential decisions have already been made. Too many journalists, as Stonecash suggests, "don't like the conflict, politicians and the messy legislative process. Their hostility distorts their judgment. For whatever reasons, journalists have misled us with a myth. They have failed to explain how the legislative process works and why decisions are so difficult to reach. What is ultimately so unfortunate, and puzzling, is that in the name of saving democracy, journalists have continually failed to communicate how democracy works."[42]

Continuity and Exchange: Politics and the Power Structure

The desire to get a handle on things, to understand how politics "really" works, can lead to penetrating insights or, with equal frequency, ridiculous distortions. The early pluralists made an important contribution to the study of politics both by underscoring the importance of interest groups, and by showing that electoral politics and the politics of governing were not one and the same. Elite theorists awakened us to the fact that on some very basic issues there is a "permanent government," a set of core economic interests, that made both the group struggle and electoral politics more or less irrelevant to what happens on some issues. Finally, if we can revert to the discussion of "political cultures" raised in Chapter 1, there is probably a case to be made for the general influence of public opinion in the crafting of public policies.

For politicians all of these forces are important. Politicians operate in a world of stimuli that is far more complicated than most of us realize. So many incumbents in the legislature have "safe" seats that it seems almost ridiculous to imagine any of them worrying about the next election; yet there are almost none who do not. The party leaders of all four legislative parties, Republicans and Democrats in both the assembly and senate, are almost constantly surveying public opinion, as is the governor; and the results of their opinion polls weigh strongly both in how they explain their stands and in deciding how they actually stand. And finally, as we have noted, there are certain key interests, and certain economic realities that are so compellingly important that they need no organizational advocates. This field of forces within which politicians operate is not stable. Politicians themselves, moreover, have policy preferences of their own that serve as lenses through which they view their political universe.

Despite the complexity of this field of forces, what is perhaps most remarkable about politics in New York is the ways in which they coincide. The election of 1994 was as dramatically an unsettling event in state politics as the fiscal crises of the 1970s were to New York City; yet in both cases the policy consequences turned out to be relatively trivial. More than two decades of divided government have given the major players in state politics growing disincentives to change the system to which they have become accustomed. Interest groups that "should," in ideological terms, be supporting Republicans have found it easier and more convenient to make peace with assembly Democrats. For more liberal groups, the same game works with senate Republicans. The incentive to show up the opposition, to make the other party look bad, to come up with new policy ideas that point up the differences between the parties is consequently less present in New York than the responsible parties model suggests it should be. Broader appeals to public opinion that might bring ideological concerns back into citizen consciousness are frustrated by a pressure group system that is afraid to shake the status quo, and by a press that is rightly suspicious of posturing of any kind.

The elections of 1994 did produce some changes in these dynamics that may prove significant. Fights over the budget in 1998 were conducted under different rules of the game. Although these changes had—as we shall see in Chapter 8—relatively trivial public policy impacts, they have opened the way for a very different dynamic in state politics. Before exploring these dynamics, however, it is important to understand the constitutional and legal structures within which these struggles for power take place. In politics, as in sports, the strengths and weaknesses of the different teams are important, but so are the rules of the game.

5

The Living Constitution

The constitution of a state or nation is usually described as the fundamental document that defines the structure of government and the extent of its powers. In the narrow sense, it is a text—a folio of parchment or paper signed by appropriate dignitaries and ratified by some proportion of the populace—that guides succeeding generations of public officials. The "true" constitution of a political system, however, is seldom described simply by a text. It is instead a body of traditions, statutes, local laws, judicial opinions, and related texts that simultaneously reinforce, supplement, constrict, and sometimes even nullify the basic text.

The New York Constitution sets the voting age at twenty-one, requires ninety days of residence in the state, and mandates literacy in English. In actual practice, the voting age is eighteen, there is no literacy test, and the required period of residence is thirty days. The superseding federal laws that mandate these requirements have not changed the *text* of the New York Constitution; they have changed its meaning. Eighteen-year-old New Yorkers vote despite a constitutional text which still rather plainly states that they cannot.

In a related vein, the state constitution mandates a balanced budget. But while the state's highest court has recognized the obligation this imposes upon the governor "to *propose* a balanced budget . . . at no time has the Court suggested that, once plan is enacted, revenues and expenditures must match throughout the fiscal year. . . . There must in every year be either a deficit or surplus."[1] Thus, although the text of the constitution would seem to mandate a balanced budget, economic realities and the state's highest court have co-conspired substantially to loosen the seemingly inflexible language of the formal document.

Our description of the formal organization of the government of New York begins with its constitution, a text to be sure, but also a penumbra of custom, law, and political realities that constitute the true constitution of the state.

New York's Constitutional Tradition

The Constitution of the United States runs about 8,000 words. State constitutions, save that of Vermont, are more verbose. New York's, at more than 47,000 words, is a little above the national average. Theoretically, the long-windedness of the states is attributed to the greater potential range of state powers and the consequent need to detail precise limits. More important, frequent amendments and revisions of state constitutions have provided numerous opportunities to make constitutional policies that would appear in statutory form at the national level. The fifty states, by one count "have had 146 constitutions, for an average of nearly three per state."[2] Since its colonial charter was replaced by the constitution of 1777, New York has adopted three new texts, in 1822, 1846, and 1894. It has, moreover, held five other constitutional conventions—in 1801, 1867, 1915, 1938, and 1967—which, although they did not produce new documents acceptable to the voters, frequently resulted in significant amendments. The prevailing text of 1894 has been amended more than 200 times.[3]

Until the Revolutionary War, New York was governed under the terms of a charter granted by the King of England to his brother the Duke of York that gave the duke virtually dictatorial powers. Attempts by the colonists to liberalize the formal charter by giving some consultative local powers to an elected assembly were vetoed by British monarchs in 1685 and 1697; "but its rejection," according to Peter Galie, "did not prevent the principles and practices embodied in the charter from being implemented."[4] Prudent governors found it increasingly convenient to consult with locally chosen officials, making the absolutism of the formal charter essentially a fiction, or, as Gailie puts it, "a 'charter' that was not a charter."[5]

In 1777, as it became increasingly possible that the colonies might win independence, the need for a new constitution could not be ignored. Some states, most notably Connecticut, had negotiated charters so tilted toward self-government that few or no changes were needed to adopt them to the needs of a sovereign polity. New York was at the other extreme. Although many of the traditions, institutions, and sociological factors favoring self-government were firmly established, especially at the local level, there was no text, no constitution worthy of an independent state.

The Constitution of 1777

At once a war-time legislature and a constitutional convention, the "Convention of Representatives of the State of New York" convened in White Plains on July 10, 1776. That it took nearly a year to produce a text is not surprising since British troops controlled New York City and the convention itself was forced to move first from White Plains to Fishkill and finally, 60 miles up the Hudson, to Kingston to keep ahead of the advancing British army. Compared with the constitutions of the other twelve rebellious colonies, most which had been adopted in 1776, the 1777 New York text has usually been described as among the most conservative. It had no separate bill of rights, and the few rights specifically enunciated, such as trial by jury, were well established in the common law. The franchise was, even by the standards of the day, limited, with only white, male property owners allowed to vote. And at a time of rebellion against the Crown—when executive power was generally suspect—New York was alone among the thirteen original states in creating a strong office of governor. Unlike the New England states, moreover, the original New York Constitution gave relatively trivial powers to local governments, and made most local officials appointees of the governor.

If the structure created in 1777 both reflected and extended the powers of New York's landholding elite, the rise of political parties in the 1790s, particularly the somewhat more democratic Jeffersonian faction, made many of the gentlemen's agreements it embodied unworkable. A series of deadlocks between Federalists and Jeffersonians over the relative roles of the governor, legislature, and a long-forgotten body called the Council of Appointment resulted, in 1801, in the call for a new convention. With the legislature that called the convention dominated by Jeffersonians, the successful referendum that brought the convention into being was, quite notably, based on universal male suffrage. Despite its democratic origins, the body itself was not particularly bold. After weeks of rather aimless debate it resolved the two main issues it convened to deal with—reapportionment and the role of the Council on Appointment—and then adjourned.

Nineteenth-Century Roots of the Modern System

After a series of false starts in the early 1800s, the question of whether to have another, less narrowly focused convention was put on the ballot in 1820 and passed by a vote of 103,396 to 34,901. This time, reflecting the restricted suffrage laws in force, the vote represented roughly 10 percent of the state's population. The 1821 convention, nonetheless, was the one that marked the full emergence of the state from its colonial heritage.[6] A clearly defined separation of powers between legislative, executive, and judicial powers was delineated; the convention adopted a bill of rights; nearly doubled the eligible electorate; and made thousands of local offices elective. It required periodic reapportionment of the legislature based on population and established a fixed process for amending the constitution. Although it did not go

Box 5.1

New York's Landed Aristocracy

Unlike the New England colonies, settled largely by corporations and religious dissidents, New York inherited and built upon the Dutch patroon system in which an aristocracy of large landholders dominated both the economy and the government. Although many of the freeholders on Long Island and what is now Westchester had established New England-like self-governing villages, most of the colony's rural inhabitants worked as tenant farmers. When the British ousted the Dutch from New Amsterdam, "New York was a colony of conquest; to the victor went the right to establish political ground rules."*

New York's seventeenth-century royal governors recognized and extended the patroon rights of the wealthy and took some for themselves. Thomas Dongan, appointed governor in 1683, added a total land area larger than Manhattan to the existing manors of the Van Rennselaers in what is now Columbia County, and the Van Cortlands in the Bronx. He also added 250,000 acres to Livingston Manor, and established new family estates in what became known as Pelham Manor, Cassilton Manor, Lloyd's Neck, and, of course, Dongan Hills. Dongan and his successors did concede such basic English rights as jury trials to the colonists, and representative assemblies continued to meet in many towns, but the manors of Livingstons, Von Rennselaers, and Schuylers were essentially medieval fiefdoms "over which their 'lords' received quasi-feudal legal and governmental powers subject only to the authority of the governor."†

The *men* (no women allowed) who drafted New York's first constitution were anything but a representative cross section of the population. The convention essentially convened those wealthy landowners who supported the cause of independence; and the document they drafted—though remarkably progressive in extending the suffrage, guaranteeing basic civil rights, and separating church and state—was deliberately protective of their interests. Only the wealthiest landowners, for example, could vote for governor; and the powers of the more democratically elected state assembly were further checked by a senate, a council of revision (with the power to review and veto legislative bills), and a council of appointment. Not surprisingly, the manor system survived well into the nineteenth century.

---

*Alan Tully, *Forming American Politics: Ideals, Interests, and Institutions in Colonial New York and Pennsylvania* (Baltimore: Johns Hopkins University Press, 1994), p. 15.

†Edwin G. Burrows and Mike Wallace, *Gotham: A History of New York City to 1898* (New York: Oxford University Press, 1999), p. 92.

as far as some states in expanding the suffrage or increasing the power of the legislature, it was, by comparison with the document it replaced, a reasonably democratic constitution. Numerous checks on popular sovereignty, including a still very limited electorate, are found throughout; but what is more significant, in Galie's words, "is the extent to which the 1821 Constitution was modeled on the United States Constitution in both its structure and its essential theory."[7]

A series of amendments between 1821 and the Civil War gradually extended the suffrage to include virtually all adults save women and African Americans. More important, an 1846 convention produced what has been called the "People's Constitution," both because of its broad-based membership and its devolution of power to the voters. Under its terms, the powers of local governments were greatly increased, and virtually all significant state and local offices—from judges to sheriffs, from the state attorney general to court clerks and canal commissioners—were to be chosen by popular election. Despite the convention's refusal to extend the suffrage to African Americans or women, there is considerable truth to Galie's suggestion that "the 1846 Constitution represents the apogee of participatory democracy in New York."[8]

The Constitution of 1894

Since 1846, the constitution has required the question of whether to have a constitutional convention be put to the voters every twenty years. Following the failure of an 1867 convention to produce an acceptable text, the voters again chose to convene a convention in 1894, and it was this convention that produced the basic document under which the state is still governed. Subsequent conventions have offered substantial revisions, many of which were adopted by the voters, but they have not substantially modified the fundamental text.

Although the convention of 1938 did not alter the basic structure of government erected in 1894, it did attempt some interesting changes. Students of the convention have characterized it largely in terms of its domination by interest groups and by its moderate to conservative ideology.[9] It also was notable in going beyond either national policy or the constitutions of most other states in guaranteeing a new set of social and economic rights. Because of its work, New York remains the only state with a constitutional guarantee of "the aid, care and support of the needy." It also marked the first constitutional affirmation of a public role in housing. Its guarantees of labor's right to organize and of a state role in public health also went far beyond existing national policies or those of most states. Finally, the 1938 convention expanded the bill of rights. Long before the U.S. Supreme Court interpreted the Fourteenth Amendment's equal protection clause to protect racial equality, the New York Constitution specifically prohibited discrimination against civil rights on the basis of race, color, or creed. The 1938 convention also added language, similar to that of the federal Constitution, prohibiting unreasonable searches or seizures, and made New York the first state in the United States specifically to recognize wiretaps as a potential threat to liberty. Unlike most previous (and subsequent) conventions, the 1938 gathering submitted its work to the voters as a series of amendments rather than in the form of a new constitution, and the bulk of its recommendations were passed.

Numerous amendments to the state constitution, approved by the voters since 1938, have done little to alter the basic text. A 1967 convention offered a number of significant revisions, but when put to the voters as a complete package it went down in overwhelming defeat. Two of the convention's recommendations were particularly controversial with the voters: one was the repeal of a provision in the 1898 constitution known as the Blaine amendment, which prohibits use of state money by religious schools; the other, infuriating fiscal conservatives, would have eliminated the requirement that state debt extensions be approved by the voters. Some of the convention's proposals have been added as amendments, most notably a conservation bill of rights, a reorganization of the courts, and a provision allowing the legislature to call itself into session. Others have simply disappeared into the dustbins of history, such as an article requiring the state to pay for college tuition for all state residents.

The Governor and the Executive Branch

In colonial days, during the war of independence, and as we enter the twenty-first century, New York has had, and will continue to have, strong governors. Even if the written constitution did not provide the office with significant formal powers, the preeminence of the state almost automatically confers upon its chief executive an aura of influence. The governor of New York is almost automatically treated by the media as a potential president, and in fact, ten of the state's fifty-three governors have been major party candidates for the presidency, four (Van Buren, Cleveland, and the two Roosevelts) have won, and six have served as vice president.

New York's Constitutionally Strong Governors

In comparing state constitutions, political scientists have long distinguished between strong and weak governors. Strong governors, the literature suggests, are armed with the following key powers:

- First, they are elected for four- (as opposed to two-) year terms and can run for reelection as often as they choose. In the 1960s, sixteen states had two-year terms, and twenty-four restricted their governors to one or two terms. New York was one of only twelve states with no restrictions. While three states now have elections every two years, New York still is among only eleven states with unlimited four-year terms.
- Second, the governor is one of only four statewide elected officials. Aside from the lieutenant governor, comptroller, and attorney general, he or she appoints—and can fire—all of his or her cabinet members. New York's governors have almost always been relatively free of potential rivals for executive power; nationally, the states elect an average of 10.2 executive officials.[10]
- Third, New York's governor not only has the power to draft the executive budget, he or she has the power to veto specific items added by the legislature. Most states now grant both of these powers to the governor, but there are few in which the process has become so deeply institutionalized as in New York.

Beyle has quantified various aspects of these institutional powers on a scale of one (*very weak*) to five (*very strong*) in comparing governors. With an overall state average of 3.4, the nine governorships with the most institutional power, scoring 4.0 or higher, include New York.[11]

In most important respects, the formal powers of the governor in New York closely parallel those of the president in Washington. They include the powers to "take care that the laws be faithfully executed"; to grant reprieves and pardons; to appoint—with the advice and consent of the state senate—members of the Court of Appeals, supreme court, and most important executive agencies. As with the presidency, moreover, the powers of the governor are checked and balanced by the legislature's ability to override vetoes (by a two-thirds vote), to approve major appointments, to reorganize the executive branch, and, of course, to make the laws. As in Washington, the real powers of real governors in Albany flow largely from their abilities to use effectively the parchment powers granted them by the formal constitution.

New York's Really Strong Governors: The Exercise of Power

Beyond the legal powers that inhere in the state constitution, the governor of New York has resources at his or her command that significantly extend and enhance his or her formal authority. In what Albany insiders call "the second floor," those parts of the capitol building housing the governor's office, there are more than 200 directly appointed members of his or her personal staff.

This is by far the largest such staff of any governor and far exceeds the national average of fewer than forty.[12] New York's governor, moreover, directly appoints more than 2,500 high-level officials and has considerable influence in the selection of thousands of other bureaucrats classified as "exempt" (from civil service regulations). The ability of New York governors to shape their own administrations is not only extensive but has tended to be remarkably free of legislative impediment. In 1977, when the Senate Committee on Corporations, Authorities, and Public Utilities voted not to confirm Governor Carey's nomination of Republican-turned-Democrat Peter Peyser to a position on the Public Service Commission, it marked the first time in memory that a nomination did not sail through the normally perfunctory confirmation process. While the process of confirmation became less automatic in the Cuomo years, it remains largely true, as Zimmerman wrote in 1981, that, "One of the unwritten rules of Empire State politics is that the Governor is free to pick the top members of his administration provided they are competent and honest."[13]

A second source of informal power for New York governors derives from their almost unique access to key media. They play in the home parks of the *New York Times* and the *Wall Street Journal*; of Don Imus, Howard Stern, and David Letterman. They, together with the governors of California, are the ones most talk show hosts and late-night comedians read about in their morning papers. Like the governors of California and Texas, they are national figures simply by virtue of the size of their electoral constituencies.

Third, candidates for governor in New York typically run expensive, highly visible campaigns. The size and wealth of the business community remains unmatched, and while it certainly tends to be heavily Republican there is a strong progressive element as well. For Democrats, moreover, the state's high rate of unionization helps assure a steady flow of campaign dollars. By the time they are elected, most New York governors are well known to the voters.

Fourth, party discipline in the legislature has more than a faint echo in the governor's mansion. As long as the governor's party maintains more than one-third of the seats in one house of the legislature, it has proven almost impossible to override a gubernatorial veto. Arguing that it could only embarrass the whole party, Democrats and Republicans alike have been able to keep their troops in line to protect the tradition of letting vetoes stand. Sometimes, as we shall see, legislative leaders extract their price, and governors must be careful not to push their veto power too far; but the remarkable fact is that only two gubernatorial vetoes were overridden in the entire twentieth century. An equally important, somewhat paradoxical, consequence of party control in the legislature is the parallel line of control it extends to the governor and the bureaucracy. Centralized power in the legislature prevents the

Box 5.2

Nelson Rockefeller and the Modern Governorship

Few New York governors introduced more social and political innovations than Al Smith, and Thomas Dewey was perhaps the quintessential party leader, but none loom larger in the history of the state than Nelson Rockefeller. Whether he was, as one of his biographers asserts, "the best governor in New York's history,"* his sixteen years in Albany defined the modern governorship.

Whether Rockefeller was a "liberal" or a "conservative," what best describes his politics was desire to get things done; above all, to get things built. The huge Empire State Plaza that dominates downtown Albany is commonly described as a fitting monument to Rockefeller's "edifice complex"; but he also built the State University of New York (SUNY) from a collection of teachers' colleges to a major university. He once described his attitude toward governing to a small uptown audience as follows: "You could plop me down in a town of two hundred people, and the first thing I'd do is to start solving their problems." A few days later he got a letter from one member of the audience saying, "Thank God our town is too small for you plopping."†

Despite the growing hostility of conservative Republicans, particularly at the national level, Rockefeller never lost his ability to win upstate votes and work with the most conservative Republicans in the legislature. What best defines his governing style, however, was his ability to reach across the aisle and make deals with Democrats. Using a blend of personal charisma, media appeals, and raw power, Rockefeller seldom lost a legislative fight. He was especially proud of his ability to horse trade. Once, needing two Democratic votes to get a bill through the legislature, Rockefeller promised them high-level jobs in his administration. A few months later, when the appointments were publicly announced, an aide to the governor was asked if they were the products of a political deal pushed by Rockefeller. The answer was simply, "Of course."‡

---

*Joseph E. Persico, *The Imperial Rockefeller* (New York: Simon and Schuster, 1982), p. 200.

†Ibid., p. 201.

‡Ibid., p. 210.

---

kind of fragmentation, common in most American legislatures, that allows individual legislators and committees to establish the strong and enduring links with key bureaucrats that enable them both to elude central direction. Beyle combined a variety of measures, including standing in the polls, electoral margins, and a 1994 survey of elite opinions, to compare the personal (as opposed to institutional) powers of governors. As in his rankings of institutional powers, New York's governors came out near the top, scoring four on a scale of five, among the fourteen strongest in the fifty states.[14] Since these figures were compiled during the last, fading lights of the Cuomo governorship, they serve vividly to underscore the comparatively strong role of New York governors in the system. Much of this strength derives, quite simply, from the qualities of leadership that such individuals as Mario Cuomo, Nelson Rockefeller, and Franklin Roosevelt brought to Albany. These are strengths that cannot be measured in a study such as Beyle's, though they derive in no small part from the power that inheres in the office itself. "Great men," as Nelson Rockefeller once immodestly observed, "are not drawn to small office."[15] Because for so long it has been the nation's commercial and legal center, the state has never been short of talented men and women. That they can be tempted to leave positions of great power in the private sector, or in public affairs, is in part due, as Rockefeller suggested, to the fact that the formal powers of the governor "comprise a substantial grant of authority. And because our governors possess this authority, we have enjoyed leadership that has established New York as a pioneering, innovative, and eminently successful state."[16] From a broader, national perspective, one 1982 effort to choose ten members of an all-time, all-state, gubernatorial hall of fame would have listed five New Yorkers were it not for a deliberate attempt to achieve geographic balance. As it was, three of the ten governors selected (Al Smith, Thomas Dewey, and Nelson Rockefeller) were New Yorkers.[17]

The Governor's Rivals for Executive Power

There are states in which virtually the entire cabinet is separately elected. Running in the same statewide constituency as the governor, and able to cultivate strong support among the groups whose interests their departments affect (such as farmers in the case of an agriculture commissioner), these officials often emerge as the governor's key rivals for power. Because they cannot be fired, and because they have their own electoral bases, separately elected department heads tend to diffuse gubernatorial authority. New York's governors are characterized as strong governors in part because they have few such rivals for power.

The Lieutenant Governor, Comptroller, and Attorney General

In New York, only the comptroller, the attorney general, and the lieutenant governor are, as statewide elected officials, the governor's potential rivals.

One lieutenant governor in recent history (Mary Ann Krupsak) ran in the Democratic primary against the man (Hugh Carey) who had been her running mate just four years earlier; another (Betsy McCaughey Ross) ran, as a Democrat and Liberal, in 1998, after having been George Pataki's Republican running mate in 1994. And although most of them eventually back off, it is almost a reflexive action to put the sitting attorney general and comptroller—both of whom have demonstrated the ability to win statewide elections—on the short list of potential candidates for governor. Given this logic, one of the more interesting paradoxes of New York politics is how *infrequently* the state's other statewide elected officials have actually run for governor. Part of the reason is probably rooted in historical accident. For a cumulative total of forty-four years, the offices of attorney general and comptroller were held, respectively, by Republican Louis Lefkowitz and Democrat Arthur Levitt, neither of whom seemed to have higher political ambitions. They not only established a tradition of keeping the offices out of a career track aimed at the governorship, but they conducted their offices in such as way as to avoid policy decisions that might bring them into conflict with the governor, a tradition that has, essentially, endured. A second reason for the comparative insignificance of these officers as rivals to the governor inheres in the written constitution, which is uncommonly spare in defining their powers. The comptroller's constitutional power is defined largely in terms of the unglamorous accounting chore of approving all state vouchers, and auditing state and local government accounts. While such audits can be embarrassing to a corrupt or incompetent administration, in the normal order of things they carry little political weight. Similarly, the comptroller's role as guardian of the pension plans of almost a million present and former state and local employees is an awesomely important job that receives little public attention.

If the state constitution is terse in its definition of the powers of the comptroller, it is virtually silent on the powers of the attorney general. Aside from putting the office at the head of the department of law and requiring him or her to report to the legislature on the legal implications of proposed constitutional amendments, there is no formal power inherent to the office. In practice, the legislature and more aggressive occupants of the office have substantially expanded the role and size of the law department. Robert Abrams, who served as attorney general from 1979 through 1990, vigorously expanded the office's reach into such areas as consumer protection, prosecuting white-collar criminals, and using litigation as a tool for fighting environmental pollution. Some of the law department's expanded activities, such as its pursuit of certain kinds of criminal activities, were founded in powers long latent in the office; others—particularly in such areas as consumer protection and civil rights—were expanded as a result of Abrams's lobbying the legislature to give his office new powers. The powers of the attorney general also have important roots in the common law that can be traced to the origins of the office in colonial New York in 1684. As early as 1868, an appellate court enumerated some nine powers which it suggested inhered not in the formal constitution but in the common law.[18] The Department of Audit and Control (the formal name of the comptroller's office) has been less able to expand in large part because Article 5 of the state constitution specifically provides that the legislature may not assign additional duties (beyond those of audit and control) to the office. Unlike the attorney general the comptroller had no common law counterpart.

Commissioners and Department Heads

Because the constitution limits departments to twenty in number, there are only twenty appointed executives with the formal title of commissioner. In practice many units not called "departments" are located in the "executive department" and are of comparable importance. The executive department's division of housing and community renewal, for example, has a larger budget than many of the formal departments. The divisions of human rights, parks and recreation, and the state police are departments in all but name. Whatever they are called, the centrifugal forces pulling agencies away from the center is strong. As policy problems become more complex and technical, the ability of career experts to isolate themselves from control by elected neophytes expands. Most career civil servants are highly protective not just of their own jobs but of their agencies' missions as well. Unionized employees, and most New York state civil servants are union members, have the extra organizational clout of the union movement behind them. And every agency has strong supporters in the private sector, in the legislature, and in parallel federal agencies. In describing the federal government, Louis Galambos expresses what most informed observers believe to be true in Washington. Although nominally in charge, Galambos says:

> The president's grip on the executive branch is weaker than most Americans think. He can place his own political appointees in departments and agencies, but where well-entrenched administrative officers are in charge of programs specifically authorized by statute, even the president can do little to influence their performance. Moreover the bureaucracies have in some instances acquired a virtual monopoly on expertise, on knowledge about their specific programs and their implementation. . . . Bureaucratic decisions have in many cases replaced legislative or executive decisions as the key factor shaping the specific content of our national policies.[19]

The size and complexity of New York government makes it almost inevitable that there will be a substantial degree of bureaucratic discretion. The decision as to how best to combat AIDS or to neutralize a toxic waste site is not likely to be centralized in the office of an elected politician. Many state bureaucrats, moreover, have access to a number of "pass-through" powers derived from federal rather than state law: the air resources division of the New York state department of environmental conservation is a state agency with important responsibilities under the state's clean air compliance act, but it is also responsible for enforcing federal rules in New York state. Since New York's air quality standards often match or exceed those of the federal government, this is a less important source of bureaucratic discretion than it might be in a less liberal state. One of the defining characteristics of New York state government, moreover, is the extent to which most day-to-day issues of governance *are* centralized. Whatever its formal position on an organizational chart, the typical department or division is firmly under the governor's control. While the senate has the power to approve or disapprove initial appointments, the governor alone has the power to dismiss. Appointed bureaucrats, in other words, serve at the pleasure of the governor. The governor's office on the second floor of the Capitol—known officially as the executive chamber, more frequently as just "the chamber," or "the second floor"—has a number of less stringent mechanisms in place for controlling and coordinating administration policies. Different governors emphasize different mechanisms and display different styles of leadership making it difficult, as one study put it, to describe a "generic administration."[20] But both the formal structure of the governor's office and the realities of New York politics combine to give to the chamber a degree of influence over the bureaucracy that is perhaps second to that of no other governor, and certainly far stronger in relative terms to that of the president.

There are three formal institutional mechanisms through which policy direction radiates from the second floor to the agencies. Every year, usually in the early fall, each agency must clear its legislative agenda through the program office under the guidance of the director of state operations. These proposals are circulated for comment among other agencies that might be affected, and then checked, as one program officer put it, "to make sure that these bills support, or at least don't work counter to the Governor's priorities."[21] Agencies also are expected to check regularly with the program office on their routine activities. The Cuomo administration regularized this form of management control by requiring one quarter of the agencies to submit monthly reports to the second floor each week. Finally, the Division of the Budget (DOB), though not formally a part of the executive chamber, plays a significant role in monitoring agency policies. The DOB's primary role is that of developing the executive budget, but it also has its own lines of access to the governor and the agencies. The line between money and policy is a thin one, and the policy of recent governors has been to bring them closer together. Robert Margado, secretary to Governor Carey, claims to have "brought the first floor up to the second floor. That was difficult. I made the Budget Division part of the central policy process, a participant in the executive process. I forced them to understand the political judgments as well as financial judgments in ways they were not previously prepared to do."[22]

Since Carey, the budget division has been very much a part of the policy process and a very strong force in enhancing the chamber's control over agency programs.

New York's budget is more policy focused than that of the federal government or that of most states since it makes no real distinction between program authorization and appropriations. In Washington and in many states it is—technically at least—illegal to legislate in an appropriation bill: that is, you cannot budget funds for an agency or program that has not already been established in a separate law. In New York it is commonplace for the governor and legislature to create all kinds of new policies in the budget. Thus even before Governor Carey brought the DOB "up to the second floor," it was, almost by definition, a very important part of the policy process, and it continues to become more and more central. The 1997 budget, in particular, was a sort of legislative black hole, a celestial phenomenon that sucked virtually everything around it into its voracious embrace.

Governors still have one other device for influencing the flow if not the substance of policy. By reshuffling components of the executive chamber, or by getting the legislature to authorize the full-scale reorganization of executive departments, a governor can refocus the level and nature of administrative attention a policy proposal is likely to receive. "Every bureau or agency in the government," Don Price once observed, "wants to be absolutely independent of everybody else or to be established in the Executive Office."[23] Divisions of the executive department, such as the arts council, the division of criminal justice services, and the division for women are thought to have greater visibility and access to the governor than they would if located further down the hierarchy in a traditional department. Under governors Carey and Cuomo, a number of offices were created in the executive chamber whose functions closely paralleled those of existing departments. The commission of quality care for the mentally disabled located in the executive department, for example, has a different set of responsibilities from the department of mental hygiene; yet there is sufficient overlap between the two that a governor can, if he or she chooses, play one against the other. Governors Carey and Cuomo were apparently more comfortable with these kinds of overlapping jurisdictions than is Governor Pataki who has moved to consolidate a number of such units.

Within the first four months of his inauguration Pataki abolished the state energy office, the office of voluntary service, the division for women, the Martin Luther King commission, the office of gay and lesbian concerns, and the offices of black affairs and minority affairs. It does not take an astute student of electoral politics to see something more than a desire to streamline government in these choices: just as Carey and Cuomo had created chamber offices to facilitate the access of important supporters such as gays and blacks, Pataki felt no particular obligation to continue them. His more ambitious restructuring agenda, because it involves the consent of the legislature, has been slower to evolve. All of the executive chamber offices and such departments as social services, health, and labor that were involved in various aspects of implementing federal welfare laws were dramatically impacted by the 1996 changes in federal rules, and the state has been forced to respond. On his own initiative, Pataki has pushed the legislature to consolidate the state's economic development efforts, and to consolidate a variety of offices and agencies into a new department of children and family services. Perhaps his most ambitious reorganization effort has been directed toward the numerous divisions, agencies, and a variety of semi-autonomous public authorities and corporations whose purposes are to attract or keep businesses in the state. Pataki's commissioner of economic development, Charles Georgian, elected not to go to the legislature to effect a formal consolidation of these disparate offices. The three major development offices, and a variety of minor ones, "still exist today—on paper. In reality, however, all of the state's economic development efforts are now under the auspices of the Empire State Development Corp. and under Georgian's immediate control."[24]

Quasi-Independent Authorities, Commissions, and Boards

One of the interesting and ironic aspects of Governor Pataki's attempted consolidation of economic development activities is that it is being undertaken under the aegis not of a line department or an executive office but, rather, by a semi-autonomous government corporation. The irony of this use of a government corporation to consolidate governing authority is that most such independent agencies were created to *isolate* them from political control. "It is clear," says Keith Henderson, "that authorities are not held to the same standards as general-purpose governments. As in other states, the legislative and gubernatorial intent to establish 'business-like' agencies with the power to issue tax-free bonds has resulted in a profusion of authorities removed from direct accountability to the public."

Ironically, as Henderson continues, those authorities that "have taken advantage of their position" to "directly thwart the public will," have usually done so "with the collusion of the governor."[25]

There is a continuing danger of such independent authorities becoming rogue elephants capable of trampling lesser creatures. Because their finances do not, as a rule, go through the standard budget process they are little influenced by the DOB; and because they often have self-perpetuating boards of directors, they can frequently free themselves from control from the second floor more generally. Nonetheless the incentive to create such independent agencies is strong. By limiting the number of departments to twenty, the constitution prohibits the governor and legislature from expanding the cabinet. More important, the constitutionally mandated balanced budget makes it almost imperative to put capital-intensive agencies like the thruway authority and the Empire State Development Corporation off budget; that is, in a position to raise their own funds through borrowing and fees. The Rockefeller administration was particularly fond of creating new authorities to the point where their total operating budgets were "nearly half the size of the state's own budget for operating its departments and agencies."[26] Some of the more ambitious of these independent agencies came to grief in later years when a shrinking state economy made them unable to pay back their accumulated debts. On the day he was sworn in as governor in 1975 Hugh Carey was faced with the imminent collapse of the state's urban development corporation and forced to devise a bailout plan. Carey and his successors, moreover, have found it difficult to exercise firm control over many of these corporations and authorities. As Benjamin and Lawton have written:

> Though firmly controlled by Rockefeller, the governor who created them and made the initial appointments, the board members of some of these agencies who serve fixed terms, were less responsive to Governors Wilson and Carey. Although Mario Cuomo has had nearly twelve years to put his own stamp on New York's authorities through appointment and reappointment, his control has yet to approach that exercised by Rockefeller.[27]

New York was one of the first states to make extensive use of independent authorities and government corporations, but it has been slower than others to privatize or contract government services out to nonpublic agencies. The movement to "reinvent" government, to bypass state bureaucracies and leave the task of implementing public policies to the private sector,[28] has gained few victories in New York in part because its highly unionized public employees have had enough allies in the legislature to resist. A growing number of local governments in New York, conversely, have turned to private corporations for such functions as trash collection.

One unique New York institution that merits special attention is the Board of Regents of the University of the State of New York (USNY). As described in a press release from the board:

> USNY is perhaps the most comprehensive educational organization in the world, including within it all public and nonpublic elementary and secondary schools; all postsecondary institutions including the State University of New York, the City University of New York, and all independent and proprietary schools; vocational education entities serving individuals with disabilities; all museums, libraries and historical societies, and jurisdiction over 38 licensed professions.

Unlike the other independent agencies, the state education department is subject to budgetary controls. The governor and the legislature, in other words, can tell the board of regents how much they can spend each year on what. In most other ways, however, the board is free from gubernatorial control. Its sixteen members are elected by the legislature, sitting in joint session, with one member from each of the state's twelve judicial districts and four at large. The board of regents, in turn, appoints the commissioner of education who sits at the pleasure of the board.

The Legislature

The constitution requires that the laws of the state must pass both houses of the legislature, an assembly of 150 members and a senate of 61. The constitution of 1777, though less focused on the legislature than were the constitutions of the other twelve emerging colonies, provided for a strong, independent legislature. A long series of scandals in New York and other states brought the institution into growing disrepute. When the distinguished student of American politics Lord Bryce wrote in 1906 that "the state legislatures are not high-toned bodies" he was expressing both the prevailing public view and the concomitant reality.[29] The response, over the past two centuries has been a series of amendments and redrafts of the constitution that gradually eroded the powers granted to the legislature in 1777, or that imposed procedures designed to check specific kinds of abuse. In 1847, for example, the senate was stripped of its power to sit as part of the court of final appeals. Also added to the constitution were a number of procedural rules such as the requirement that local and private bills be confined to one subject to prevent the legislature from sneaking special provisions into otherwise innocuous laws. Legislation by reference was also prohibited in 1847: that is, a bill may not simply incorporate the language from another law into a bill without specifying exactly what it says. The constitution also lists fourteen kinds of local bills the legislature cannot enact and—by the terms of the so-called Blaine amendment—forbids public assistance to religious institutions. Bills in the legislature—unless given a special waiver by the governor (called a message of necessity)—must "age" for at least three days before a final passage. Most important, the power to initiate the state's budget was transferred in 1927 from the legislature to the governor.

Partly as a result of these changes in formal rules, partly as a consequence of electoral politics, and partly because strong governors—Smith, Dewey, and Rockefeller in particular—tended to dominate the system, the legislature by the middle of the twentieth century was not a strong institution. In the 1950s Governor Dewey would sometimes wait until just a few days before the deadline to submit his budget to the legislature which usually passed it virtually unchanged. Nelson Rockefeller, it was sometimes said, owned one house of the legislature and had a long-term lease on the other. No change has been more striking in recent New York politics than the reemergence of the legislature as a key policy actor. With no significant changes in the written constitution, the rise of the legislature as an equal branch has been remarkable.

The Institutionalization of the Legislature

In a widely reprinted 1968 essay, Nelson Polsby delineated three characteristics of what he called an "institutionalized" organization. Referring to the U.S. House of Representatives, Polsby suggested that an organization achieves institutional status to the extent that it (1) is differentiated from its environment, (2) is relatively complex, and (3) has fixed rules and procedures that shape its behavior into relatively predictable patterns.[30] The institutionalization of the house was manifest most clearly between 1890 and 1910; similar patterns can be discerned in Albany largely between 1950 and 1970, when the contemporary legislative system flowered.

The Establishment of Boundaries

"In an undifferentiated organization," Polsby writes, "entry to and exit from membership is easy and frequent."[31] In the U.S. House of Representatives, more than 40 percent of the members elected in most years prior to 1890 were in their first term. Since 1910, the percentage of freshman has seldom exceeded 25 percent, and the average number of years served increased from four to six years in the nineteenth century to more than ten years in recent years.[32] There has been a similar change in Albany. The percentage of freshman legislators in the assembly declined from 56 percent in the 1890s to 26 percent in the 1920s, to 13 percent in the 1980s. In the senate it went from 59 percent in the 1890s to 30 percent in the 1920s, to 10 percent in the 1980s. Although legislative salaries remained low, "the legislature became a very attractive place to return to by around 1930,"[33] and it apparently has become even more attractive since. In 1990, the average New York state legislator had been in office for 14.7 years,[34] and a majority of legislators had come to consider membership as a career. Instead of the citizen-legislators who moved in and out of the legislature to resume their "real" occupations as farmers, lawyers, or businesspeople, "there is not a very high proportion [today] who have full-time occupations outside the legislature."[35] In their biographies "in 1964 not a single member of either house listed their occupation as 'Legislator' in the official guide to state Government. . . . By 1988, however, more than two-thirds of Assembly members and more than half of Senators were describing themselves not as lawyers, businessmen, or consultants but as legislators."[36]

Another sign of the legislature's growing sense of itself as a distinct institution has been manifested in growing control over its own leadership and governance. The first Speaker of the assembly to serve for more than two consecutive terms was S. Frederick Nixon in 1899–1905. Four to eight years has been the norm in recent years. In the senate, between 1880 and 1920, sixteen men served as majority leader, only one for more than two terms. In a comparable time span of forty years between 1954 and 1994, five men held the same job with one—Warren Anderson (1973–88)—holding the post for sixteen years. More important, the legislative parties in both houses have chosen their own leaders. An important source of Nelson Rockefeller's legislative power was the influence he was able to exert in the elections of party leaders in both houses, even, in one case, in the Democratic Party. Other governors, prior to Rockefeller, may not have actually involved themselves in the process of leadership selection, but the legislative leadership clearly viewed its role in subordinate terms. Many participants cite a 1981 fight over the financing of the metropolitan transportation authority as marking a crucial turning point in defining the independence of the legislature. In the words of former Speaker Stanley Fink:

> When this major institution was on the verge of collapse, and an Executive attempt to solve the problem was abandoned, I believe that [Senate Majority Leader] Warren [Anderson] and I jumped into the breach. . . . We put the budget together that year, and I think that this gave birth to the sense that the Legislature had finally achieved the capability of developing its

own financing plans and had the courage to put into place unpopular taxes when people said no one could do it. I think that the whole MTA era was a turning point in Executive-legislative relations.[37]

Also contributing to the autonomy of the legislature were some of the changes in state politics discussed in Chapter 3. The decline of party machines helped produce a legislature far freer of external influence. In comparison with the legislator of the sixties, one member said:

> Today the member is the organization. Each one of us becomes a party within him or herself, whereas years ago we couldn't get to first base without being in the party. You have got 90–some-odd Democrats in the assembly, and I would say that maybe 85 of those Democrats are elected by virtue of the fact that they are an island unto themselves.[38]

Most important, perhaps, was the professionalization of the legislature, which came in the wake of completion of a separate legislative office building in the Empire Plaza. Stonecash shows that in constant dollars the budget of the legislature increased tenfold from the 1900s to the 1980s, with the bulk of the increase coming after 1950.[39] "During the Rockefeller era the legislature . . . was incapable of making policy initiatives in most areas. It was more often in a position of responding to gubernatorial initiatives than proposing its own."[40] In the contemporary legislature, each member has a district office with a minimum of two paid assistants, and an Albany office with a minimum of one. Each committee has both its own counsel and staff aides plus the help of a counsel appointed by the party leader. The central research staffs of the party leaders, the financial experts on the assembly ways and means and senate finance committees, and the central staffs in such specialized offices as the bill drafting commission make the New York legislature one of the best staffed legislatures in the world.

The Growth of Internal Complexity

Growing staff has made the legislature a far more complex organization. In Congress, one of Polsby's key indicators of complexity was found in the proliferation of subcommittees and party leadership positions. In New York, there has been a similar trend with the balance tilted far more heavily in the direction of party leaders than committees. While committee work is not trivial in New York, the party leaders overawe all. The result, as former Republican Speaker Joseph Carlino once said, is that:

The Legislature is more highly organized than any other in the world—bar none. Never once in the fifteen years since I've been there have we failed to get a Republican majority for a "must" piece of legislation. We Republicans have a tradition of discipline. Any new member is immediately schooled in that tradition of Republican control.[41]

The combination of staff resources and centralized leadership is at the core of the emergence of the legislature as the coequal of the governor:

The party conferences within the legislature serve as vehicles for policy positions. The legislative staff generates information and studies to support party positions. . . . All this has allowed the legislative parties to participate in and structure policy debates within the state. . . . The legislature is now a full partner in the political process.[42]

One consequence of this new partnership is that it takes longer to get things done. The budget passed in August of 1997 was the latest in the state's history, 126 days after the constitutional deadline. The press makes much of these late budgets that have become almost chronic. What is less frequently noted is that these budget delays are "part of a larger long-term trend of longer decision processes in Albany."[43] As such they are reflective of the growing complexity of the legislature and of its growing willingness and ability to confront the governor with its own set of policy preferences.

As in Washington, the state legislature has moved irregularly but inexorably toward the creation of more and more policy-relevant titles and positions. In 1981, when Zimmerman published his textbook on New York politics, there were 30 standing committees in the assembly and 26 in the senate.[44] Today the respective numbers are 36 and 33. In the senate, this means that there are 33 committee chairmanships available to the members of the majority party, and 33 ranking minority positions on committees to be divided up among the Democrats: 66 "leadership" positions for 61 senators. In the assembly, there are "only" 72 committee leaders among the 150 members; but both houses have created a rich variety of other positions to satisfy member ambitions. Each party has a full complement of leadership titles such as assistant and deputy assistant party leaders, majority and minority whips, and a Speaker pro tempore. There are a variety of legislative commissions and task forces, joint committees, and party committees. Looking only at the standing committees, one recent study found New York second only to California in the number of committee opportunities per member.[45] Whether substantive power actually flows from these positions is another question; but the point, quite simply, is that the New York state legislature has become a large, highly differentiated, complex organization. Measured in terms of its workload, staff, facilities, and resources, the contemporary legislature would have been unrecognizable just forty years ago.

Fixed Rules and Procedures

As Polsby defines institutionalization, an important part of the process involves a shift from the personal to the routine, from discretionary procedures to fixed rules. Borrowing from the classic sociological concepts of Tonnes and Weber, Polsby looks in particular at the seniority system and the treatment of contested elections in an effort to show that established methods of allocating resources had displaced more purely personal considerations. New York's strong legislative party system makes comparison with the U.S. Congress difficult. When Joe Bruno beat Ralph Marino for the position of senate majority leader in 1995, Marino did not slip to second spot on the totem of power, he went from first to last. When the Speaker is unhappy with an assembly committee chair, she simply removes him.

The power of party leaders, while at one level intensely personal, is at another level a sign of institutional strength. Former assemblyman Arthur Kremer notes that, "In the 1960s the County Chairmen were the ones to consult when there was a tough issue, when they needed the votes."[46] Today, the bargaining takes place entirely within the institution: the rules may not be fixed, but the boundaries are. County leaders, lobbyists, and governors have to deal less with individual personalities than with representatives of the institution, that is, the elected party leaders. Instead of the highly complex rules that help give Congress its institutional identity, the New York legislature has essentially one rule: he or she who can gain and maintain control of the majority party is beholden only to his or her supporters in the legislative party caucus.

In keeping with Polsby's analysis, however, the power of party leaders in the state is institutional, not personal. That Ralph Marino went from first to last in the rankings is testimony to the fact that power inhered in his institutional role. In Congress, institutionalization is reflected in the growing complexity of norms such as the seniority system that served to isolate the institution from outside influence. In the New York legislature, the centralization of power in the party leaders performed the same essential function.

Strong Parties, Strong Committees: The Pathways of Power

The fox, an old adage says, knows many things, the porcupine only one; but the porcupine knows his very well. There is, to put it in porcupine terms, only one route to power in the New York state legislature, to know it well is to get ahead. Even in parliamentary systems, where party discipline governs political survival, there are few legislatures in the world that are more leadership oriented than New York's. Power in the New York state legislature follows a strict hierarchical ranking: at the top of the heap are the elected leaders of the majority parties, the Speaker of the assembly and the majority leader of the senate. Inner circles of their closest allies in the majority party come next followed by committee chairs. Rank-and-file Democrats in the assembly and Republicans in the senate have some legislative influence proportionate to their skills and efforts, and, in particular, to their closeness to the leadership. The leaders of the minority parties in each house are sometimes consulted, particularly in the senate. Rank-and-file minority members are almost never a factor. "If the issue is purely local," one assembly Republican told us, "that is if it only affects my district, I can sometimes get something done. And if I have a really good idea that I'm willing to let some Democrat take credit for, I can sometimes have some influence in committee. But by and large members of the minority party around here are not part of the law-making process. We just don't count."

The Speaker

Article 3, Section 9 of the state constitution provides for the election of a Speaker of the state assembly and empowers the body to establish its own rules. The Speaker is also recognized in Article 4 as fourth in line, behind the lieutenant governor and president of the senate, in the event of the death, impeachment, or resignation of the governor. These are the only two constitutional references to the office. Its powers and duties are not described. The strength of the office of the Speaker derives almost entirely from rules adopted by the assembly.

Election of the Speaker is, as a rule, the first item of business following the governor's state of the state address. Most of the time, the outcome of the vote is known in advance as party caucuses have already met to choose the Republican and Democratic party candidates. Under the "unity rule," commonly enforced by both parties, all party members are pledged to vote for the candidate receiving the most votes in the party conference. Thus the nominee of the party with the most seats is an almost sure winner. We say "almost sure" because the "unity rule" does not always work. In 1937 the Republican Party conference nominated Irving M. Ives for reelection as Speaker but could not carry the full vote of the party to the floor. Finally, with the help of a few Democrats, they were able to elect Oswald Heck as Speaker and Heck, in turn, made Ives his majority floor leader. An even more complicated situation arose in 1965 when a split in the Democratic Party produced two Democratic candidates for Speaker. For days, weeks, and even months the assembly met in unsuccessful attempts to organize. Only the intervention of Governor Rockefeller gave Anthony Travia sufficient Republican votes to put him over the top and resolve the impasse.

No legislator likes to give the governor the kind of leverage with the Speaker that Rockefeller had with Travia; and this is why the unity rule is usually invoked. Nor do members of the majority power like to let the opposition become involved in choosing a leader. Letting both the Republican governor and the Republican minority have a hand in choosing Travia as Speaker was, to assembly Democrats, like a left hook–right hook combination to a boxer. But there are times when the stakes for some members are high enough that they will risk deadlock. When an individual legislator votes for a new Speaker, he or she is doing a good deal more than electing a party leader who will set the ideological tone and strategic direction of the party. He or she is also choosing the person who will, for the foreseeable future, control his or her career, for the Speaker of the New York state assembly has the unfettered power to make all appointments.

In their study of legislative leadership in the American states, Jewell and Whicker place New York among the strong leadership states. In institutional terms, the New York legislature confronts a strong governor, but is otherwise independent and supported by strong party rules and traditions. Party leaders are independent of outside control and command highly cohesive, polarized parties. All of the important tools of leadership, from complete control over committee assignments and staffing, to access to campaign funds, are abundantly available in New York.[47]

So strong are party leaders in New York that forces, which in other states have produced a fragmentation of power, actually have worked to strengthen the hands of New York Speakers and majority leaders. In many states, for example, the professionalization of the legislature has given individual members greater independence. Alan Rosenthal argues that:

> The natural state of a legislature is fragmentation. But in a number of respects, the legislature is even more fragmented today than twenty years ago. Earlier, leaders were truly in command, and power was tightly held. Partly as a consequence of modernization and reform, legislatures have become democratized. Resources are more broadly distributed, and the gap between leaders and other legislators is broader.[48]

Increased staff, in this analysis, gives an individual legislator the tools to stake out an individual policy position, or gives a committee the resources to act on its own.

In New York, however, most of the important staff people are, in effect, agents of the party leaders. Each important committee has its own counsel, appointed by the committee chair; but it also has a counsel or program staff person appointed by the party leader. The real heavy lifting in terms of policy research on important issues is routinely conducted less by committee staff persons than by the program staff people appointed by, and responsible to, the party leaders. Committees are not trivial in New York, and there are rank-and-file members whose staff persons have considerable influence; but the pervasive source of all real power, the people who count in the crunch and whose preferences prevail in cases of conflict, are those closest to the Speaker. In New York, unlike almost every other state, in other words, the growing professionalism of the legislature has served to further centralize rather than disperse power.

Another factor cited by Jewell and Whicker as important in affecting the powers of party leaders also seems to have worked differently in New York. The decline of "the strong urban party machines that existed in many northeastern and midwestern states," they plausibly argue, "had a significant impact on state legislative institutions. . . . Some of these organizations instructed their legislators on how to vote, contributing to legislative party discipline."[49] Such instructions were not at all uncommon in New York. Instead of increasing party discipline, however, the urban (and rural) machines tended to erode it by using their voting blocs in the state assembly and senate to cut deals. Former Speaker Travia's inability to unite his Democratic colleagues was due largely to the ability of the Brooklyn machine to hold out in favor of their own candidate. Even after their election, Speakers prior to the 1950s often served less as party leaders than as brokers cutting deals between the real party leaders back in the districts. In New York it was the decline of powerful local organizations that gave the legislative party leaders their power.

One final source of leadership power derives from his or her nearly complete control over the agenda. Only the governor can issue a "message of necessity" that allows bills to be considered late in the legislative session, but in all other matters of scheduling the authority of the party leadership is complete. Technically, the assembly rules committee controls the flow of business: it decides what bills get to the floor of the assembly and when. On paper, the rules committee is a committee. In fact, it almost never meets. "Rules committee?" as one Speaker told us: "I'm the rules committee."

Other party offices in the assembly vary in importance largely as a function of the personal style and preferences of the Speaker. Generally speaking the majority leader is the only other member of the majority party whose formal position betokens real clout. Usually a close confidant of the Speaker, the majority leader is officially next in line to become Speaker in the event of a vacancy; but Stanley Fink is the only majority leader since the 1960s to have actually won the speakership. What has happened in recent years is that the Democratic majority has tended to balance New York City's lock on the office of Speaker with a corresponding tendency to award the majority leadership to upstate. Although Daniel Walsh of Franklinville, majority leader from 1979 through 1987, and James Tallon of Binghamton, who served from 1987 through 1993, were each viable candidates for Speaker, both lost and soon retired from politics. Despite these failures, both Walsh and Tallon, as well as Michael Bragman of Cicero (majority leader until he unsuccessfully challenged the Speaker in 2000), were clearly second only to the Speaker in party power. All three served as the party's official spokespersons and as floor leaders. The Speaker rarely appears on the assembly floor and the majority leader—with his or her seat on the aisle directly wired to the podium—typically conducts the day-to-day flow of assembly business.

The Senate Majority Leader

Technically, the lieutenant governor, also known in the constitution as "President of the Senate," is the presiding officer in the upper house, with the majority leader carrying the official title of "Temporary President." In fact the rules of the senate give all real power to the majority leader who as effectively controls the senate as the Speaker does the assembly. When Hugh Carey's first lieutenant governor, Mary Ann Krupsak, sought to name the person who would preside if she was not present, then majority leader Warren Anderson took her to court. He won. His explanation of why the case was brought is instructive. "I didn't care," Anderson claims, "who was actually presiding. That wasn't the point, though she thought it was. If we didn't like the ruling by Mary Ann or any other Lieutenant Governor, we could move to overrule the position of the chair. I was concerned that if she was the only person with the power to name the one to preside in her absence, she could, by not naming anybody to preside, keep the Senate from meeting or acting at all. She didn't agree, so we took her all the way to the Court of Appeals and they decided in our favor. That's why I'm the Temporary President. . . ."[50]

In a similar vein, the constitution gives the minority party two potentially enormous points of leverage that, in recent years, have applied particularly to the senate. First, budget bills require a live quorum of 60 percent: they cannot be passed, in other words, in the absence of more than 40 percent of the members of either house. Second, a variety of local bills require the consent of a two-thirds majority. Since senate Republicans have seldom held a

60 percent majority, the Democrats should seemingly be able to exert bargaining leverage either by refusing to vote for important local laws or absenting themselves from budget votes.

Our interviews yielded conflicting perspectives on the importance of these provisions. One aide to a senate leader claimed that they were an important, though often overlooked, source of minority party influence in the senate. Another veteran staffer claimed that he had never seen it used. And a former assembly leader, recalling the days when Democratic majorities were thin, called it "nonsense. The majority will always support the ruling of the chair." Former senate majority leader Ralph Marino probably put the issue in perspective when, reflecting on his relations with minority leader Manfred (Fred) Ohrenstein, said that although he could not recall a case in which Ohrenstein had threatened to invoke either provision, he was aware of them. "But those are crude instruments," Marino argued. "If Fred really wanted to pressure me he could do it far more effectively by working through the governor or the speaker."

The differences between party leaders in the senate and assembly are almost exclusively a function of size: dealing with at most thirty-five to forty followers, a senate party leader relies more on informal and face-to-face negotiations than does his or her assembly counterpart. The formal structure of the party organization is less elaborate and usually less meaningful. In particular, the role of the deputy majority leader—though he or she is clearly second in command—is not as clearly institutionalized as that of his or her counterpart, that is, the majority leader, in the assembly.

In both houses, the particular leadership style of the Speaker or senate majority leader says more about the distribution of power than any organizational chart. A table listing and describing such offices as deputy Speaker, majority whip, or conference chair could be highly misleading. These party officers sometimes do have real power and—not insignificantly—are often paid more than rank-and-file members, but the methods that party leaders use to communicate with party conferences have virtually nothing to do with organizational charts, titles, or formal rules. The official party "whips," legislators technically responsible for "whipping" party members into line, sometimes actually play that role. But as one assembly Republican told us, people who are known to be close to the leader are at least equally influential, "whether you get hit by the whip or the whap, it means the same thing."

As a group, individual senators are more important than individual assembly members. This is only in part a function of size: because there are fewer than half as many senators, it would figure that each of them would, in a certain sense, be at least twice as important. As in the U.S. Congress, however, there is also a more individualistic tradition in the senate, a tradition that extends even to the minority party. On important issues, to be sure, senate minority members are as far out of the loop as their assembly counterparts, but a tradition of reciprocity gives them a voice and vote that minority members in the assembly often envy.

Politics reinforces, and—in no small part—explains this tradition. The Democratic majority in the assembly is, arguably, as diverse as the Republican majority in the senate. But it is also larger. For two decades the assembly leadership has had a majority large enough to allow individual members to vote their districts on some issues; senate leaders have not had that luxury. In 1997, to give an illustrative example, Senate Majority Leader Joseph Bruno attempted to make the abolition of rent control a major issue. Only six of the thirty-five members of his party conference (as opposed to twenty-two out of twenty-six Democrats) were from districts where rent control was an issue, but it was an important issue for all six, and tenants' groups were mounting effective campaigns that could have threatened their reelection. Facing a unified Democratic bloc of twenty-six votes, Bruno needed at least two of the six to "fall on the sword" and cast a vote that might lose them their seats. There were, as we shall argue in Chapter 6, other forces operating on this vote, and there is little doubt that Bruno could have won in the event of a senate showdown; but the numbers are instructive. The senate is different.

Committees

Every Republican senator is either a committee chair or a party leader. Every one of them, in other words, earns a "lulu" of $5,000 or more on top of his or her base salary of $53,500. (A "lulu" is short for compensation received "in lieu of salary.") Only about 40 percent of the Democrats in the assembly are similarly blessed. Ranking minority members, that is, the senior members designated by the minority leaders in both houses to sit opposite the chairs, also receive lulus.

His or her ability to appoint all committee chairs, and indeed all committee members, is often cited as a key source of power for party leaders. It was also mentioned in most interviews as a source of considerable tension: "It was," said one leader, "the hardest thing I had to do." In order to avoid hurting colleagues or making enemies within their own parties, most party leaders have rather closely followed seniority rankings in choosing committee chairs. "There have been very few times," said one Speaker, "when the people whose seniority turn came were, in fact, passed over." Another insisted that he had "never" once violated seniority despite the fact that he had actually dismissed two chairs. "Yes," he said, "but they both got promotions." What this meant was that in both cases they were given positions of party leadership that carried bigger lulus than had their chairmanships. Their new positions, it should be pointed out, were meaningless in terms of power.

Despite the centralization of power in New York's party leaders, the standing committees of the senate and assembly play a surprisingly important role in the crafting of public policy. Many committee chairs and quite a few rank-and-file members have developed considerable degrees of expert knowledge in the areas of their committees. All of the party leaders we talked with stressed their reliance on the expert knowledge of certain committee chairs. Some, of course, are more important than others. Complaints about being bypassed or ignored by party leaders are not uncommon in conversations with committee chairs, a subject to which we shall return.

In California, and some other states, all bills referred to committees must be reported back to their parent bodies. Thus, a bill referred to the senate transportation committee, no matter how ridiculous, must be brought back to the senate floor. It comes from committee with a "do pass" or "do not pass" recommendation, and most "do not pass" bills are killed in a matter of seconds; but they do get to the floor. In the U.S. Congress, most bills referred to committees die there. A bill that cannot command a majority in committee is highly unlikely ever to be seen again. New York is somewhere in the middle of these extremes of committee power. Most referred bills, 80 to 90 percent, die in committee; but leadership has whatever tools it needs to bring them back. One former aide to a senate majority leader compared it to "a large bottle containing all the legislation. If you turn it upside down, some of it comes out, and some of it isn't going to come out. We determine what comes out."[51] But while this is true of major legislative issues, the fact of committee power on all but the most important issues is an important fact of Albany life.

The Many Systems of Local Government

More than a quarter of the New York Constitution is devoted to local governments. No state, save perhaps California, has more units and more types of units of local government than New York. New York's 1777 constitution continued the charters of local governments conferred by the King of England, and it continued the practice of granting the governor (and legislature) the power to appoint local officials. The constitutions of 1841 and 1846 granted increasing powers to local governments, but still in the context of central control. Not until 1867 did the concept of "home rule" emerge as an operative doctrine. "The meaning of home rule," as Galie rather dryly but accurately notes, "depends on the context in which it is used. Broadly conceived, it refers to the ability of local government to perform functions and activities traditionally undertaken by these governments without undue interference by the state. Home rule powers refer to the constitutional and statutory powers to enact local legislation and carry out the duties and responsibilities of the local government."[52]

Few issues proved more difficult to resolve at the 1867 convention than those arising over the issue of home rule. The tensions manifested there between proponents of home rule, on one hand, and those, on the other hand, who saw the extension of state power as a necessary antidote to municipal corruption, were to remain prominent issues well into the twentieth century.

As we noted in Chapter 2, New York's almost unique mix of local government traditions—an amalgam of Dutch and British traditions overlaid with the township provisions of the Northwest Ordinance—established a complicated grid of interdependent towns, villages, cities, counties, townships, and boroughs that few states can match. There is no standard size for any of these jurisdictions, though counties tend to be roughly proportionate in area. Cities vary in population from Sherrill (2,864) to New York City (7,322,564). The sizes and shapes of the state's towns, villages, cities, and townships has less to do with any kind of constitutional plan than with historical circumstance. Some local governments, such as those of New York and Albany, can trace their roots to colonial charters granted as early as 1686. Counties also predate the Revolution and were created to build such public facilities as courthouses and orphanages. Until the U.S. Supreme Court ruled that legislatures must be based on a system of equal representation, most counties were governed by board of supervisors consisting of one delegate from each town. Some county boards of supervisors still meet with each town supervisor casting a weighted vote, but most have gone to a system in which there is a county legislature, elected by districts of equal population, and a separately elected county executive.

Most cities in New York are governed by a mayor-council form of government, usually with what is known as a "strong" mayor (i.e., a separately elected official with clear budgetary and executive powers). The council-manager form of government—which enjoyed a wave of popularity at mid century—replaces the office of mayor with a professional city manager who serves at the pleasure of the elected council. Towns, despite the usual connotation of the name, are not necessarily small. The town of Hempstead, for example, is larger in both size and population than the cities of Buffalo, Rochester, and Syracuse. Towns are governed, as a rule, by a council elected at large (rather than by districts, as in most cities) and a town supervisor who sits on council and performs various administrative duties. In some counties, the town supervisors collectively comprise the county board of supervisors.

Villages add a more complicated level to the mix since they often overlap the jurisdictions of towns and cities. Historically, villages were formed to

perform special functions such as zoning or providing police and fire services. Governed by an elected board of trustees, they typically are limited in
their powers to the purposes for which they were created. While many villages continue to exist—and a new one was created by the legislature as
recently as 1998—their functions have largely been supplanted by a bewildering variety of special districts. In the nineteenth century, the drive to create new units of local government was based partially on demographic
changes. As previously underpopulated areas were more densely settled, the
demand for the kinds of public services provided in other areas increased.
The increasing need for centralized water and sewage systems, and for such
newly developed functions as electricity and mass transit, produced concomitant demands for the creation of local service agencies. Much of this
demand, as Nancy Burns has cogently argued, was generated by commercial
interests seeking indirect state subsidization. In many cases, as Burns writes:

> These formations are not simply technical financing maneuvers. They are
> instead implicit decisions about who pays for development in the United
> States. By and large, they have been efforts by developers to use public
> financing for development.[53]

Developers, quite obviously, can sell their houses or factories at better
prices if the government provides the roads, sewers, and water rather than
putting them in at cost. Creating a village to make such improvements provides no real savings to the homeowner; but by transferring the burden of
payment from the purchase price to the tax system it saves developers from
both the burden of financing such services and the need to add them to the
purchase price of new homes.

By the time of the Great Depression most New Yorkers lived in incorpo-
rated communities; or, to put it the other way, most inhabited areas of the
state were contained in officially organized towns, villages, or cities. Yet the
rate at which new local governments were created rose at an accelerating
rate. The reason for this new surge is found in a dramatic increase in the
number of special district formations that occurred for essentially two reasons: first, politicians—strapped for resources as tax collections slowed—
were increasingly in need of borrowed funds to provide essential services.
By the early 1930s many local governments were already at the maximum
level of borrowing allowed under the constitution. One way of evading these
limits was to create new units of local government that could tap new lines
of credit. The federal government added a second incentive for the creation
of special districts by passing a variety of laws, particularly in the areas of
soil conservation and housing, that required the creation of bond-funded

local housing authorities and soil conservation districts in order to be eligible for federal matching funds. First as governor and later as president, Franklin D. Roosevelt was a particularly enthusiastic proponent of special districts "as a way to avoid municipal defaults during the Depression; in 1934 he sent a letter to governors urging them to create public corporations that could employ revenue bonds. He urged the creation of water, sewer, and electric light and power districts. He explicitly argued that these governments should be used to circumvent debt limits and referendum requirements for the issuing of bonds. He also dispersed model enabling legislation for housing authorities and soil conservation districts."[54]

The pattern continues. While the national number of townships, counties, and municipalities has remained virtually constant since the 1940s, the number of special districts has soared from about 8,000 in the 1940s, to 18,000 in the 1960s, and nearly 30,000 in the 1980s.[55] In 1993, New York alone had 62 cities, 932 towns, 557 villages, 717 school districts, and 1,292 special units: a total of 3,560 local governments.[56] But this is only part of the story. In addition, the state had 1,522 water districts, 1,752 lighting districts, 601 drainage districts, and so on—a total of 6,525 other local government entities.[57] And this grand total of more than 10,000 does not include the literally thousands of public and interstate authorities that are governments in all but name.

One final reason for the proliferation of local governing units also deserves mention. Incorporation, not infrequently, derives from a desire to exclude certain groups and protect the privileges of others. One could argue that most suburbs were created largely to block the spread of urban areas.

> Regardless of the variations in population movement and annexation patterns, and regardless of the many different motives that give rise to separate suburban governments, suburbs are fictions, legal fictions. They are that part of the real city that chose, for whatever reasons, to stay apart and to perpetuate that apartness in the law. . . . A suburb is a parasite whose residents can enjoy the benefits of scale and specialization without sharing in all of the attendant costs.[58]

Communities, as Burns puts it, "can define their residents relatively effectively. . . . Some places, then, can have lower taxes than other places, and thus provide better business climates, as well as increase pressure on cities with poor residents."[59] Nor is this simply a conflict between cities and suburbs.

> Regardless of who wins and who loses, it should be clear that we miss much of the fight when we focus only on cities. Local government is a

collection of governments. When we discuss who has power in local politics, how much money is spent in local politics, and whether local politics
is participatory or representative, for example, we provide distorted answers if our focus is solely upon cities. While we focus upon cities, the
politics will spill into the arena of special districts, and our focus then becomes a smaller and smaller part of what is really happening in American
local government.[60]

It is also important to recognize that none of these structures are etched in
stone. Home rule notwithstanding, local governments remain the creatures
of the state: what the legislature giveth it can take away. Home rule, like
federalism, is more about politics than it is about constitutions.

The Judiciary

The constitution of 1777 created a highly decentralized court system that
relied heavily on state trial courts (known collectively as the supreme court)
and local justices of the peace. In 1821 the supreme court was divided into
trial and appellate jurisdictions. It was not until 1846 that New York created
a single court of last resort equivalent to the supreme courts of most other
states but known in New York as the Court of Appeals. The court replaced a
rather odd, House-of-Lords-like institution known as the Court for the Trial
of Impeachments and Correction of Errors, described by one journalist as an
institution "as cumbersome as its name."[61] Originally comprised of eight
elected judges, the Court of Appeals now consists of seven judges appointed
by the governor, with the consent of the state senate, to fourteen-year terms.
The chief judge—currently Judith S. Kaye of Manhattan—presides over the
court and serves as chief administrator of the state court system as a whole.
In this latter role, she is assisted by an administrative board consisting of the
four presiding justices of appellate division, and a chief administrator of the
courts, whom she appoints. Since 1977, all of New York's many state and
local courts have been administered and funded by the state.

The unified court system, as noted in Chapter 2, is a four-tier system with
the appellate division of the supreme court hearing appeals from the legal
rulings and procedures of the trial courts. The trial court system in New York
is as complicated a structure as one can find in the United States. As in most
states, it includes two levels of trial courts of general jurisdiction. At the
higher level are the county courts and the trial division of the supreme court.
Not counting those assigned to the appellate division, the supreme court consists of 323 justices elected to fourteen-year terms from each of the twelve
judicial districts of the state. Supreme court justices are paid $113,000 a year

with a bonus of $6,000 for those designated to one of the four appellate divisions. While this is considerably higher than the national average, it probably represents a substantial cut in pay for a New York lawyer considering a move from bar to bench. It is a sacrifice many appear willing to make, and the quality of the attorneys willing to forgo higher incomes for the status of a judgeship has generally been high. Quite another story prevails at the lower levels of the system. Town magistrates, who handle such low-level offenses as petty larceny, simple assault, and drunk driving, need have no legal background in order to serve. Elected by the voters largely on the basis of party affiliation and personality they are, to put it mildly, a mixed bag.

Court Reorganization

As chief administrator of the state courts, chief judge Judith Kaye has followed her predecessor, Sol Wachtler, in taking a strong interest in reorganization. She has implemented a number of small reforms. Computerization has helped reduced the backlog of criminal cases substantially, as has the creation of special drug treatment courts in Albany, Brooklyn, Buffalo, Manhattan, Rochester, and Suffolk County. Experiments with a variety of quasi-judicial panels have also proven effective in displacing formal trials with less contentious, cumbersome, and costly arbitration sessions (see Box 5.3). And a jury reform program eliminated all exemptions from jury service, raised the daily stipend and ended mandatory rules on sequestering. But the larger structural problems can only be solved by amending the constitution. "Our antiquated trial courts structure," as justice Kaye argues, "does not serve the people of New York as well as it should, and we are still committed to the creation of a system that is easy to understand and use. This year nearly 4 million cases were filed in state trial courts. Only by simplifying and restructuring the system will we be able to make maximum use of our judicial resources to efficiently handle enormous caseloads. During the 35 years since the last constitutional reform of the trial courts, there have been momentous societal changes, while the courts that serve society's most fundamental needs have remained static."[62]

Kaye's proposals would, in essence, merge a number of specialized courts into a supreme court with commercial, family, probate, and criminal divisions, and a district court system with limited jurisdiction over criminal and civil matters. Such specialized courts as the court of claims, the surrogate courts, family courts, and New York City's civil and criminal divisions would be folded into this unified system. More controversial is the proposal to create a fifth judicial department for Long Island. A similar proposal passed the 1967 convention but has never been enacted largely out of opposition from

Box 5.3

New York's Changing Court System

Judith Kaye, almost from the day she became chief judge of the Court of Appeals in 1993, has pushed a strong agenda of court reform. While her master plan for simplifying the overall structure of the system has been stalled in the legislature, she has succeeded in creating a series of "specialist" courts, some in collaboration with the independent center for court innovation. These courts include drug courts in the criminal court system, community courts for juveniles, domestic violence courts, and some very innovative drug treatment courts in the family court system. The court system is now starting to look at mental health courts.

The concept of a drug court is that the judiciary should take a more proactive role in dealing with the root problem of addiction. In drug courts, those accused of drug-related crimes are entered into treatment programs instead of prisons. The same judge continues to see each person, and, aided by a staff of addiction specialists who act as case managers, follow each case closely. The district attorney, defense attorneys, and usually the local department of mental hygiene cooperate closely using a series of "graduated sanctions" as a response to relapses. Successful completion of treatment usually means dropping the charges, while dropping out of treatment results in an immediate start of the jail sentence. It has proven a good inducement to keeping people in treatment until success is reached.

The family treatment court uses the same cooperative concept to maximize a mother's chances of successful recovery and the elimination of any neglect charges stemming from her addiction. Dropping out of treatment means an earlier availability for adoption for the baby. This concept is vastly superior to the present court practice of telling the mother to find treatment on her own, reviewing the case about nine months later, and punishing the mother if she has failed to negotiate the labyrinth of treatment facilities to find the one suitable for her. There are only fourteen family treatment courts in the country, and two of them were started in 1998 in New York state. While Judge Kaye has been unable to effect the complete overhaul of the court system that most observers agree is overdue, small innovations such as these are constantly changing the nature of the state's judicial system.

New York City where many Democrats fear they would lose judgeships to Long Island. As the Long Island caseload grows, however (and as Long Island becomes less solidly Republican), opposition to the new district has waned.

Reorganization proposals have failed in the past when they have been folded in with efforts to remove more judicial positions from the electoral process. Judge Kaye, with the support of key legislators, has insisted on decoupling the issues of court reorganization and election, and hearings held by both the senate and assembly judiciary committees in 1997 and 1998 showed widespread support for the general reorganization plan. But agreement in principle has not meant agreement in fact: tangential issues—such as legal representation for the poor in the 1998 legislative session—have prevented the issue of reorganization from moving through both houses of the legislature. Thus although it has seemed increasingly likely that the legislature will pass a proposed amendment on to the electorate sometime in the near future, the senate and assembly have been unable to agree on a mutually satisfactory plan.

The Rights of New Yorkers

Among the original thirteen states, New York was among the last to adopt a formal bill of rights; in modern times it has been a trailblazing state in both formally protecting and generally respecting individual liberties. There is, in a sense, no paradox here. As the most ethnically, religiously, and culturally diverse of the thirteen original states, New York has long been among the most tolerant. Its early constitutions were based on the premise that a government of limited powers could not and would not intrude on individual liberties. The 1777 constitution specifically guaranteed only a limited right to vote, the right to a jury trial, and religious liberty. As experience showed the need for further protections, each succeeding constitution has rather substantially expanded both the substantive and procedural rights of state citizens guaranteed in the written constitution. Even where the state constitution is silent, moreover, or where its provisions are essentially identical to those of the federal bill of rights, New York's courts have tended to be relatively liberal in deciding questions of individual liberty.

Substantive Rights

Students of constitutional law often distinguish between such "substantive rights" as freedom of speech, which pertain to what the state must allow people to do on their own; and "procedural rights" that define, in effect, how things are done by the state. With respect to the most fundamental rights of individual freedom, Article 1 of the New York Constitution differs from the national Bill of Rights in two important respects. First, it covers a substantially broader range of protected liberties, including the right to vote, to belong to a labor union, to be educated at public expense, and even the right to a decent standard of living. Long before the U.S. Supreme Court began its assault on racial segregation and Congress passed its first civil rights laws, the 1938 New York Constitution provided that, "No person shall, because of race, color, creed or religion, be subjected to any discrimination in his civil rights by an other person or by any firm, corporation, or institution, or by the state or any agency or subdivision of the state" (Article 1, Section 11). Second, New York's bill of rights, unlike the United States's, is stated largely in positive terms. Thus where the U.S. Constitution's Article 1 *prohibits* Congress from enacting laws abridging speech, freedom of religion, and so on, New York's locates these rights in the people. Section 3, on religion, for example, begins with the words "The free exercise and enjoyment of religious profession and worship, without discrimination or preference, shall forever be allowed in this state to all mankind. . . ." Contrast this with the more circumspect phrasing of the federal First Amendment: "Congress shall make no law respecting an establishment of religion, or prohibiting the free exercise thereof. . . ."

Not surprisingly, given its liberal tradition, New York state has tended toward a more liberal interpretation of questions involving individual liberties, even when the language of the state constitution is not substantially different from the federal Constitution. In the words of a New York Court of Appeals ruling:

> Freedom of expression in books, movies and the arts, generally, is one of those areas in which there is a great diversity among the states. Thus it is an area in which the Supreme Court has displayed great reluctance to expand Federal constitutional protections, holding instead that this is a matter essentially governed by community standards. . . . However, New York has a long history and tradition of fostering freedom of expression, often tolerating and supporting works which in other States would be found offensive to the community. . . . Thus the minimal national standard established by the Supreme Court for First Amendment rights cannot be considered dispositive in determining the scope of this state's constitutional guarantee of freedom of expression.[63]

Interestingly, the state's courts have not been so expansive in applying some of the constitution's more unique guarantees. The state's 1938 provision against discrimination (Section 11) was not only among the first such guarantees in the United States, but also unique in prohibiting any *private* "person . . . firm, corporation, or institution" from violating an individual's civil rights. In 1948, however, when an African-American couple was denied housing in Manhattan's Stuyvesant Town apartments, the Court of Appeals held to the very narrow argument that housing was not one of the civil rights protected in the constitution. "Since," as Galie summarizes the court's ruling in *Dorsey v. Stuyvesant Town* (1949) "there was no statute recognizing the opportunity to acquire real property as a civil right, the court concluded that the section could not apply to individuals in the appellant's situation. . . . In effect the court said the clause is not self-executing; for its prohibitions to be effective, legislation is necessary."[64]

Similarly, New York's famous Section 1 of Article 17, which seemingly establishes a state obligation to provide for the aid, care, and support of the needy has been effectively rendered meaningless by the courts' rulings that it is up to the legislature to decide who is really needy.

Procedural Rights

In the days when Earl Warren was Chief Justice of the Supreme Court of the United States (1953–69), the court substantially expanded its interpretation of the Fourteenth Amendment to make a number of federally protected rights applicable to the states. States were required, for example, to provide even the poorest defendants with the right to counsel; local police were forced to warn defendants of their rights before questioning them; and states were expected to avoid unreasonable searches and seizures. These Court rulings were, and in some cases continue to be, highly controversial. They are, however, less controversial in New York than in most other states because New York either has a similar guarantee in its constitution, or because its Court of Appeals has already inferred such rights. To put it bluntly: if you are formally accused of a crime, you have a better chance of defending yourself in New York than in almost any other state.

Although the rights of criminal defendants are better protected in New York than in most other states, and more than federal guidelines require, the differences are subtle. For most people, most of the time, it would make little difference in the 1990s whether you were arrested in New York or Mississippi. In both states, the police—following the U.S. Supreme Court's ruling in the case of *Miranda v. Arizona*—must read you your "Miranda" rights advising of your rights to remain silent and to seek the help of counsel. In both states, following federal guidelines, you have the right to counsel, to be free from unlawful detention (*habeas corpus*), to be informed of the charges against you, to not be unreasonably detained without indictment, and to confront key witnesses against you. While all of these rights pertain today in all fifty states, most of them date back in New York to the 1821 or 1846 constitutions, a time in which such guarantees were less common.

What probably accounts for New York's liberal reputation in the area of procedural rights is its weighty history of case law founded in state—as opposed to federally mandated—constitutional rights. New York's 1821 constitution, for example, is identical with the due process clause of the federal Fifth Amendment: "No person," it reads, "shall be deprived of life, liberty, or property without due process of law" (Article 1, Section 6). The federal due process clause was only recently applied to the states, and has generally been held to apply only where there is so-called state action. The state due process clause, through more than 175 years of case-law development, "has been construed to provide broader rights than the federal provision."[65] And it is arguably broader than that of most other states, particularly those whose "due process" rights derive solely from federal Court imperatives.

One of the most interesting area of procedural rights in New York—its provisions regarding search and seizure—is particularly instructive as to the "real" meaning of the constitution. Prior to 1938, the state had no constitutional guarantees against unreasonable searches. The amendment adopted then (Section 12) is almost identical in wording to the federal Fourth Amendment but it adds an interesting and progressive set of restrictions on wiretapping.

Strictly speaking, however, the New York Constitution falls short of federal practice because it does not include the so-called exclusionary rule adopted by federal courts in 1961. In fact, New York's 1938 convention explicitly rejected a proposal, "supported by Governor Lehman and others, to prohibit the use of unreasonably obtained evidence" in court.[66] What the delegates declined to do, however, the Court of Appeals went ahead and did anyway. By conflating emerging federal doctrine, a little case law, and a whole lot of its own thinking to the issue, the court essentially added the exclusionary rule to the constitution which did not originally include it. We return to our original point that the constitution of a state is not simply a text: it is a living corpus of formal parchment, statutory and court interpretations, and actual state practices.

Changing the Constitution

Although the U.S. Constitution has been formally amended twenty-seven times, most scholars agree that legislative and judicial interpretations of the basic document have been more important sources of fundamental change than written amendments to the text itself. Change of this kind, as we have seen, is not unknown in New York; but because state constitutions tend to be far more detailed and specific, the formal processes of revision and amendment loom larger at the state level. The New York Constitution adopted in 1938 has been formally amended 134 times in the intervening years.

Change through Formal Amendment

The process of amendment in New York is designed, as it is in most states, to make it considerably more difficult to change the constitution than to pass an ordinary statute. The federal Constitution requires a two-step process of amendment involving, first, passage of the proposed amendment by a two-thirds majority of both houses of the Congress, and then ratification by three-fourths of the states. Alternatively, the states may call for the convening of a constitutional convention to revise the whole document. In seventeen states, citizens may bypass the legislature by placing a proposed amendment directly on the ballot if enough registered voters sign a petition to do so. This process, known as the citizen initiative, is not allowed in New York where only the legislature can authorize a referendum. In twenty states, a majority of both houses is all that is required for the legislature to propose a constitutional amendment; about the same number require a two-thirds vote, though some of these allow simple majorities to act if they pass identical resolutions in two consecutive years. New York is one of eight states that requires a three-fifths majority in both houses.

Generally speaking, the legislature and the voters have been on the same page with regard to most amendments. Looking at the period 1967–93, Benjamin and Cusa found the voters approving 41 of the 61 amendments proposed by the legislature (67 percent).[67] As the authors note:

> No more than a quarter of the constitutional amendments passed by the legislature in the twenty-six years under study involved fundamental changes in the structure of state government. The three amendments concerning the state judiciary passed in 1977 and approved by the voters were most important. . . . Five other amendments adopted during the period, several based on ideas developed at the 1967 Constitutional Convention, were of some structural significance.[68]

The public seems most likely to reject amendments that invoke such key words as taxes and borrowing. Its record of accepting major changes in the process of governance, on the other hand, is strong.

Change through Practice and Experience

Because of its unusual specificity the New York Constitution has not changed as much through practice, statute, and judicial interpretation as has the U.S. Constitution, but a number of significant changes have occurred through such means. Most important, the rise of the legislature as a coequal of the executive in policy power has taken place without significant change in the written constitution. Many of the most important extensions of civil rights and liberties have occurred either through federal rulings that supersede those of the state or through rulings of the Court of Appeals. Historically, judicial and legislative action has been a less significant source of constitutional change at the state than the national level, but the courts have shown a growing inclination to reinterpret the basic text.

It is also true, in New York as in almost all constitutional democracies, that the living constitution is effectively amended almost every day by the acts of elected officials, bureaucrats, and even ordinary citizens. What Gross and Schneier have called "social vetoes" take place every day when a citizen exceeds the speed limit, discriminates in a hiring situation, or cheats on his or her taxes.[69] More significantly, public officials frequently defy the constitution or interpret it in light of their own policy preferences. Some of the most significant characteristics of state politics and government, moreover, are extraconstitutional. The rules of the legislature that vest extraordinary powers in the hands of the majority party leaders, for example, are based on only the vaguest of constitutional provisions.

Constitutional Conventions

The constitutional requirement that the question of whether to call a constitutional convention be put to the voters every thirty-two years adds an interesting dimension to the process of constitutional revision in New York state. When the issue came up in the 1997 elections, it was rejected by a margin of better than 3 to 2. Despite the fact that it was favored by most newspapers, former governor Cuomo, and a number of other dignitaries, incumbent politicians were sharply divided and most of the state's important labor unions came out against it. Interestingly, almost no one argued that the constitution was in no need of change. Opponents of a convention argued instead that it would be a costly waste of time, potentially dangerous, poorly representative of majority opinion, and unlikely to solve the problems of gridlock that seemed most to concern the voters.

There is no doubt that such conventions can be expensive. With each of its 198 delegates receiving the same salary as a member of the legislature ($57,500), a per diem expense account of $89, travel allowances, and a staff allocation of $15,000 for each delegate, the minimum cost of a convention would run in the neighborhood of $15 million. Assuming, however, that the convention were to operate for more than twenty-four weeks, hold public hearings around the state, and print records of its work, some estimates of a convention's real costs ran as high as $50 to $60 million. Although election night polls showed that these cost considerations troubled many voters, other arguments were equally telling. Liberals tended to oppose a convention because the method of election—founded in the Republican gerrymandered districts of the state senate—tended to favor conservatives. Some "good government" groups were opposed because the ballot access laws, deciding who could run as delegates, were highly restrictive; and because the convention process gave less time for reflection and discussion than the regular process of amendment, with its requirement that a proposal pass two sessions of the legislature before going to the voters. And the prospect that all would be in vain, that the 1999 convention, like its 1967 predecessor would have its ultimate work rejected by the voters, was probably a factor as well.

Most scholars agree that the state's constitution is unnecessarily detailed and out of date in a number of not too significant respects. The essays collected by the Temporary State Commission on Constitutional Revision offer numerous concrete, often exciting possibilities for change. With the exception of the judiciary, however, few of these proposed reforms relate to issues of basic structure: there are few advocates of a weakened legislature, fewer still of a weakened governor; while some would strengthen home rule and devolve more power to local governments, others would favor consolidation and centralization. Few, if any, suggest, that late budgets and other problems of gridlock that the public finds troublesome can be solved by structural as opposed to political change. Most agree, in the final analysis, that the "important ends of government can be declared and effectuated by statute."[70]

Conclusion

To the extent that New York differs from, say, New Jersey or Nevada, the major differences are not found in their formal constitutions. It makes a difference whether a state's constitution creates few or many electoral rivals to governor and whether it gives the office a line-item veto. It matters how much home rule is written into the constitution and whether there is a unified court system. Bills of rights are not just rhetoric. In most important respects, however, a state's living constitution may or may not coincide with the text it calls its constitution. If the social welfare provision of the New York constitution is the strongest in the nation, it does not mean that "the aid, care, and support of the needy" actually "*shall* be provided by the state" (author's emphasis) as it says in Article 17. What it means is that advocates for the poor have a somewhat stronger base for arguing their case than would their counterparts in states without such a constitutional provision. The constitution, like the federal system described in Chapter 2, the party system discussed in Chapter 3, and the pressure system described in Chapter 4, is part of the context within which the policy-making process takes place.

6

Struggles for Power, Position, and Access

In the jargon of Albany, the first step on the road to political influence is to become a "player." This circle of players shifts over time and often from one issue to another. As we saw in Chapter 4, there are few generally effective lobbyists, and even the most powerful groups tend to be issue-specific. With the exceptions of the governor and the majority party leaders of the senate and assembly, this is true of the executive and legislative branches as well. Major shifts in power tend to have long gestation periods. The most effective lobbyists, legislators, bureaucrats, and even judges have built their reputations brick by brick. Particularly in the legislature, there is a more or less continuous weighing of character and worth: whose word can be trusted, who has access to whom, who knows what. Former Speaker Stanley Fink once argued that "people gain power, particularly in the Legislature, by the accumulation of knowledge—it is, in my opinion, the single surest way that one can gain influence and power."[1] The knowledge Fink was talking about was not simply of substance but of how things work, and of whom you can rely upon for what.

It would surprise most nonpoliticians to learn how much these evaluations boil down to questions of trust. Politicians do not usually lie to each other; those that do are almost certain to pay for it. As much as they may fudge positions in public and exaggerate their records in campaigns, the only real leverage most of them have with each other is their credibility.

In the long run, credibility, knowledge, and skill are the resources that tend to separate the players from the herd. But there are short-term events—elections and their financing, indictments and scandals, most notably—that can strike like lightening to destroy the strongest leaders overnight. The 1990s have shown unusual volatility in the roster of key Albany players with Republican George Pataki ending the twenty-year Democratic string of Carey and Cuomo; Dennis Vacco becoming the first Republican attorney general in fifteen years, and then the first incumbent to lose in modern times; Carl McCall becoming the first Democratic comptroller since 1978; and Alfonse D'Amato, seemingly at the height of his powers, losing his senate seat in 1998. In the legislature, Mel Miller was forced to resign as Speaker in 1991. His successor, Saul Weprin, died in 1994. Assembly majority leader Michael Bragman's unsuccessful attempt to oust Speaker Sheldon Silver in mid-session in 2000 resulted in Bragman's immediate demotion. Ralph Marino, who replaced Warren Anderson as senate majority leader in 1989, was himself replaced by Joseph Bruno in 1995. Even that bastion of stability, the Court of Appeals, had one judge resign to work with New York City Mayor David Dinkins; another take early retirement; and, amazingly, saw its chief judge forced to resign.

Legislative Leadership

There are few more revealing events in a legislature than those revolving around changes in party leadership. Because the powers of legislative party leaders are so extensive, members who are out of favor with their leaders are generally without influence. They retain the trappings of office and whatever impact on public opinion they can exert through press releases and outside activities. Their votes on issues may be sought. But a legislator who is out of favor with the leadership is not a player.

Formally, the Speaker of the assembly and the senate majority leader are elected by the full membership of each house, though it is almost always the majority party caucus that controls the vote. When a newly elected legislature takes office every other January, choosing the new leader is the first order of business, even if it is only to reaffirm the existing power structure. Shortly after the November election returns become official, the respective party conferences gather in Albany to choose their candidates for Speaker and senate majority leader. On the first Tuesday after the first Monday in January the newly elected legislature convenes and each member responds to the roll call by stating the name of the person they support.

Party Leadership Fights in the Assembly

In the assembly, the elected Speaker is escorted to the podium by the senior majority party member and presented with the gavel symbolizing his or her formal position as presiding officer. The person with the second largest number of votes is declared minority leader, rules to govern the house are adopted—usually in a routine carryover from previous sessions—and committee chairs are named. The process of maneuvering that precedes these votes, though barely visible to the public, is one of the most fascinating in politics. Leadership is a position that is won essentially by accumulating sufficient individual commitments from party colleagues to win a majority vote in the caucus, or, roughly speaking, fifty Democrats in the assembly, twenty Republicans in the senate.

The process is not necessarily confined to the party conference. In 1964, Democrats won the majority of both houses for the first time in almost a century, but a fight between the Democratic county chairmen in New York City and then-mayor Robert Wagner spread to Albany and tied up the legislature for months. Each day the members would file into the chambers to cast their votes for Speaker in one house and for majority leader in the other; each day the clerks would announce that no one had gained the necessary majority. With no elected leaders and no committees appointed, no legislative business could be conducted. The impasse was finally broken when Republican governor Nelson Rockefeller had the Republican minorities vote for the Democrats Anthony Travia for Speaker and Joseph Zaretzki for majority leader.

The specter of that fight still haunts state legislators, putting strong pressure on the party caucus to reach some kind of consensus; but it is seldom an easy process. For individual members, there is nothing more terrifying or exhilarating than a fight over leadership succession. With county leaders less able to deliver legislative votes or protect their own members from retribution, personal friendships, regional and ideological differences, and chances for individual advancement play much stronger roles. County delegations or groups like the black and Hispanic caucuses may try to enhance their leverage by negotiating as a bloc, but in the final analysis each lawmaker is very much alone and nervous about how the outcome might change the direction of his or her legislative career.

The Rules of the Game

In the assembly, where there has been continuing Democratic control since 1975, the politics of leadership succession has divided into two scenarios: one, in which there is sufficient lead time to consider the choices, involves quiet, bloc by bloc coalition building. In a second, more frantic scenario, the actual or impending death or resignation of the Speaker dramatically compresses deliberation into a flurry of telephone conversations that is frequently over almost as fast as it begins. Here the field of potential candidates narrows, and perceptions of power and of having the necessary votes become more important.

Certain loose rules apply in both scenarios. The first is that only senior members are viable candidates. Seniority in itself is not decisive—Senate Majority Leader Joe Bruno, ranks only tenth among thirty-six Republicans, and Speaker Sheldon Silver twelfth among ninety-four Democrats—but a leadership candidate must have a record of credibility and competence that others have learned to trust, preferably as majority leader or chair of an important committee. The second rule is that the candidates are invariably members who have been looking (discreetly of course) at the job for years and quietly building up collegial relationships through small favors and political connections. The majority leader and the chair of the ways and means committee are in strong positions if only because they can do a lot of favors. They can also gather personal campaign treasuries far beyond their own re-election needs and make these funds available as campaign contributions to colleagues. It helps to be from a safe seat and confident enough of reelection to be able to spend time in Albany. Above all, it is important to be respected if not liked. Former Wisconsin Speaker Tom Loftus summarized the rules of choosing a leader as follows:

> The decision to support one colleague instead of another for a leadership post can be based on many seemingly logical reasons. These include ideology, geography, gender, race, past favors (such as helping raise money), prospects of future favors (such as committee assignments), and even whether the person is good on TV. But these reasons are not important considerations when compared with friendship. . . . That's the base.[2]

It is absolutely crucial, in other words, to begin the fight with a core of close supporters who will go to bat for you.

Coalition Building in a Multicandidate Race

In 1978, Speaker Stanley Steingut, who had led assembly Democrats to the majority in 1974, was defeated in a primary in his Brooklyn district. There was enough lead time for an orderly succession; but majority leader Stanley Fink had been Steingut's right-hand man, and although he refused to make any kind of move until after the election, he was generally regarded as a natural successor. One senior member, anticipating Steingut's impending defeat, launched an abortive campaign, but it quickly fizzled when one of his key contacts not only advised him against running but called Fink to tell him what was going on. As in the immediate turnover scenario, the battle for party leadership was over before it started.

In late May of 1986, when Fink announced that he would not run for reelection, it set off a wide open fight for the leadership. There was an up-state candidate (majority leader Dan Walsh), a Brooklyn candidate (Mel Miller), two candidates from Queens (Sal Weprin and Alan Hevesi), a candidate from Manhattan (Mark Allan Siegal), and ways and means chair Jerry Kremer (Nassau). Mel Miller, by securing a firm base in his home borough of Brooklyn, the largest county in the state, was able to use those ties and his own contacts to build a thin network of support on Long Island and upstate, just thick enough, as it turned out, to discredit enough of the other candidates to encourage them to drop out and throw their support to Miller. By the time Hevesi switched to support Kremer who—as chair of the ways and means committee had built a base rivaling Miller's—it was too late.

Speaker-elect Miller made sure that no leadership positions or committee chairmanships were announced until after the official vote in January. In a bow to upstate and the party's more conservative wing he retained Dan Walsh as majority leader, but Walsh resigned his seat to accept a higher paying job as head of the Business Council. Kremer was replaced by Weprin as chair of ways and means committee and left the legislature soon after. Within a short period of time an entirely new leadership team was in place, a transition duly noted in a body where even minor shifts of power are carefully weighed. Not one of the five once-powerful assemblymen who ran against Miller is still in the legislature.

Striking While the Iron Is Hot

In the 1990s, the rules of the game seemed to change with a series of quick Speaker successions. Mel Miller was indicted in 1991 on charges that were sufficiently ambiguous that many people dismissed them as the political ploy of an ambitious Republican prosecutor. But although few assembly members believed that Miller would actually be convicted, media coverage of the trial made the Democrats increasingly nervous about its impact on public opinion. The party caucus refused to take formal action against Miller, and majority leader Jim Tallon decided neither to campaign for the Speakership nor to allow any of his friends to campaign on his behalf, a pattern common in situations involving a sitting Speaker.

> As long as the members perceive that the leader is likely to win, they do not want to support anyone else and risk ending up on the losing side. In most states it is unusual for a presiding officer or legislative party leader to be challenged, and it is rare for them to be defeated. On occasion a leader will jump before he or she is pushed, choosing to retire in the face of growing dissatisfaction and emergence of one or more potential challengers.[3]

Ways and means chairperson Sal Weprin decided to take the risk of launching a "just in case" campaign. Although he was not directly challenging Miller, it is probable that if the Speaker had been declared not guilty, or if Weprin had lost his bid to replace Miller, he would not have remained long as chair of the ways and means committee. But Weprin was also in a much better position than Tallon to take a risk. Because his base was in Queens, which was second only to Miller's home borough of Brooklyn in the size of its assembly delegation, Weprin had more freedom of action than Tallon whose upstate base was not large, and who therefore would have needed Brooklyn to win. Weprin, moreover, was closer to retirement than Tallon and thus better prepared to take an all or nothing gamble.

Miller was convicted. Even though his conviction was later overthrown on appeal, he had to resign immediately. The contest between Jim Tallon and Sal Weprin was over after just one day of frantic phone calling made it clear that Weprin had the votes. One senior committee chair had two phones at home. One he worked on behalf of Jim Tallon, his wife answered the other. Tallon supporters were put through but he dodged calls from Weprin and his supporters. By Saturday noon he had a good count and was finally able to accept a call from Sal Weprin and pledge his support. Majority leader Jim Tallon was not replaced, but he resigned his seat a few months later to take a better paying position in the private sector. Two early Weprin supporters were appointed as part of a new leadership team. Sheldon Silver (Manhattan) became the chair of the ways and means committee, and Michael Bragman (Syracuse) became majority leader. There were no reprisals taken on the Tallon supporters, but some of them did not fare well during the 1992 legislative reapportionment.

Throwing Caution to the Wind

When Weprin died in office in 1994 it was already clear that Shelly Silver was the consensus choice for Speaker if only because he had the almost solid backing of New York City Democrats. Majority leader Mike Bragman remained as Silver's majority leader, and Herman (Denny) Farrell, a strong Silver supporter who was also the Manhattan County Democratic leader became his successor as ways and means committee chair. The choice of Bragman was viewed by many observers as more of an acknowledgment of upstate interests than of any close ties of either friendship or ideology, and as early as 1998 rumors circulated that Bragman was plotting a coup. Despite the persistence of such rumors over the next two years, most Albany observers were surprised in May of 2000 when Bragman actually attempted to unseat the incumbent Speaker (see Box 6.1).

Box 6.1

**Fending Off an Attack on the Speaker:
The Tools of Party Discipline**

As state Democrats convened in Albany in May 2000 to nominate Hillary Rodham Clinton as their candidate for the U.S. Senate, rumors began circulating about a challenge to the leadership of assembly Speaker Sheldon Silver. By the next morning, Thursday, May 18, it seemed clear that the majority leader, Assemblyman Michael Bragman of Syracuse, not only intended to challenge the Speaker but that he had the fifty or more votes he needed to win in the Democratic conference when it met the following Monday. By the time of the actual vote (on a procedural motion to bring the leadership issue to the floor), only eighteen Democrats actually stood by Bragman on the floor.

What happened between Thursday and Monday is not a matter of public record; but the decline in Bragman's support from the fifty-three pledges he thought he had on Thursday to the eighteen who actually stood with him on Monday is neatly illustrative of powers that inhere in the office of the Speaker, and explains why sitting party leaders are so seldom challenged. In a speech to his colleagues following his defeat, Bragman charged the Speaker with using the following tactics to convince people they should support him and not Bragman:

- Stripping committee chairs of their posts and telling others "they have 5 minutes to express their support to the Speaker or they would lose those Chairs";
- Saying to the child of a member who answered the phone: "Tell your father that he has 15 minutes to call the Speaker and change his position or he will lose everything he has ever cared about in this Assembly";
- Telling members that if they didn't support the Speaker "their districts would be reapportioned and they wouldn't be able to win an election again";
- Threatening those whose districts had strong party organizations that "their petitions wouldn't be circulated and primaries would be run against them";
- Threatening not to provide, or offering to provide, campaign contributions from the Democratic Assembly Campaign Committee; and
- Encouraging "specially connected lobbyists" and union leaders to lobby "the members and tell them who they ought to vote for and what the consequences would be if they didn't."*

Because two Bragman supporters lost their committee chairmanships, we know that Speaker Silver used at least some of these tactics, and it seems likely that he used them all. And the fact is that most party leaders, facing similar challenges, would have used them too.

---

*New York State Assembly, *Record of Proceedings*, May 22, 2000, pp. 26–28.

Bragman's unsuccessful challenge to Silver illustrates well why incumbents are so rarely challenged for leadership positions. Unless you have the votes locked up or have decided, as Sol Weprin did in 1991, that he was ready to risk his existing power position on the gamble that the Speaker would resign, there can be no public campaign. Coups against the leadership are more likely to begin with a series of very discreet conversations with your closest personal friends and political allies, but the point is soon reached where each widening of the circle poses greater risks of exposure. Sooner or later you will reach a member whose loyalty to the incumbent will serve as an incentive to expose your incipient candidacy. And unless this point is reached *after* you have accumulated enough commitments to win, both you and each of your supporters are susceptible to sanctions. Thus when Bragman's challenge was forced out in the open and two of his key supporters were stripped of their committee chairmanships, most of his private commitments disappeared. It is unlikely that Bragman—about as shrewd and tough an insider as one finds in Albany—would have set himself up for failure without having private commitments from something close to a majority of the ninety-six-member Democratic conference. Silver was not a popular Speaker by any means; but when the final showdown came, Bragman had only twenty announced supporters and eighteen actual votes. To better understand the logic of this dynamic, let us turn to two recent contests for control of the Republican conference in the state senate.

Power Struggles in the Senate

One April day in 1988, Governor Cuomo, Senate Majority Leader Warren Anderson, and Speaker Stanley Fink emerged from the governor's second-floor office to announce that they had reached a budget agreement. Normally, when the "three men in a room" reach their agreement, it remains only for the staff to iron out the details before an almost automatic vote of approval in both houses. But the 1988 budget was lean, and the increases in school aid it proposed did not keep up with inflation in more affluent suburban districts. A few hours after the leaders' press conference, Ralph Marino, a state senator from Long Island and normally a close ally of Anderson's, informed the majority leader that the votes were not there to get the budget through the senate. Unless school aid was substantially increased, Marino warned, every Republican senator from Long Island would vote no. Faced with a solid block of opposition in his own party conference, Anderson was forced to go back to the Speaker and governor with the embarrassing admission that he could not control his own conference. A few months later, Anderson announced his retirement from politics, and Marino—virtually without opposition—took his place as majority leader. To this day, Anderson insists that the budget debacle had nothing to do with his retirement. Marino, likewise, insists that his only motive in leading the Long Island rebellion was to get more money for schools. Many insiders remain skeptical: to challenge and embarrass the majority leader is risky business, but to do so on an issue directly linked to the needs of your constituency is to at least present a plausible rationale. Marino, in other words, could test his strength, imply that Anderson was losing touch with the rank and file, and secure his base for a campaign without directly challenging the majority leader.

Whether the 1988 fight over school funding was the opening gun of a campaign for party control, the differences between Anderson and Marino were not basically ideological. In their study of state legislative leaders, Jewell and Whicker suggest that "a tension is likely to develop between the members and those individuals who serve long tenure in leadership." And that, "One reason that some Speakers and presidents retire or run for another office is that they are sensitive to the problem of *leadership ladder gridlock.*"[4] Such gridlock is most likely to occur in a legislature, like New York's, dominated by career politicians. It is worth noting that Ralph Marino, despite twenty years in the senate, was not even second in line for the chairmanship of the key finance committee.

When Marino became majority leader, he kicked the aging John Marchi upstairs to a meaningless but high-paying position in the party leadership and installed Tarky Lombardi of Syracuse as his chair of the finance committee. Other chairmanships were shifted in ways significant enough to suggest a change in generations rather than ideology. Whether Marino had deposed a sitting party leader or merely replaced one who was planning to retire anyway, the 1988–89 transition had leadership gridlock written all over it. In 1995, Marino himself fell victim to a similar coup, but a great deal more than gridlock was involved.

Shortly after George Pataki's upset of Mario Cuomo in the 1994 election, the governor-elect, his political patron U.S. Senator Alfonse D'Amato, and the chairman of the Republican state committee William Powers decided that Marino's time had come. For Pataki, it was perhaps a question of revenge: Marino had not only opposed Pataki in his first run against an incumbent senator in 1990, but had been adamant in attempts to find a more moderate challenger to Mario Cuomo in 1994. Power and D'Amato's motives are murkier, including ideology, ambition, and a strong sense of what they felt was right for the Republican Party. But the bottom line, as Marino puts it, is that it was "three against one." Whether the governor himself made any direct contacts with former senate colleagues we may never know; but D'Amato and Powers were clearly manning the phones and there was little doubt which side Pataki was on. The question of "gridlock" was at issue: some junior members—particularly the more ideological conservatives—felt that Marino and his closest advisers were freezing them out; but what is most interesting about Bruno's ascension to the leadership is that it was not simply a question of internal politics. For the first time since Nelson Rockefeller "owned" one house of the legislature and "had a long-term lease" on the other, a governor was overtly involved in a leadership contest.

Even with such formidable allies as the governor and Senator D'Amato, Bruno could not have won without a skillful campaign. As early as mid-November at least one lobbyist warned Marino that someone was plotting his overthrow, but it was not until Thanksgiving—when one of his closer senate allies called—that the majority leader gave such rumors credibility. Marino realized that if his rivals had reached the point of calling Senator X, known to be a close friend, they must already have enough votes. Yet Marino was so unprepared that he had no staff present to help him phone, and no way on a holiday weekend of tracking down key members. Sitting by the phone in his Long Island home, it soon became apparent that it was too late to stop the coup.

Consolidating Leadership Control

Both the Speaker and the minority leader owe their positions to their respective party conferences. Running for a leadership office is part of the process of learning to be an effective leader. As Loftus puts it: "It is the campaign for the job that teaches a leader how to ask and how to distinguish a yes from a no. And it's the campaign that teaches the leader how to get a vote."[5] Despite the awesome powers of the office, all party leaders know that their continuing ability to exercise these powers derives from their continuing ability to maintain the confidence of a conference majority. In the words of one former Speaker:

> Leadership is a two-way street. I think a leader in the Legislature these days in New York would be foolish to underestimate the collective power of individual members. . . . People want to have an opportunity to be heard and take part in the process.
>
> I used to hold Democratic Conferences where all members were given an opportunity to be heard and one was cut off. . . . After . . . having the patience for them to hear me and me to hear them, and giving everybody the opportunity to be heard, I generally was well aware of the parameters of what I could or could not negotiate on behalf of this group of men and women. I never exceeded that.[6]

Generally, the most effective leaders are those who communicate most effectively with their fellow party members, though different leaders use different channels. Some meet frequently with the entire conference, others make regular use of party steering committees appointed with an eye toward the representation of all significant factions in the party. Some meet regularly with committee chairs (or the ranking minority members of key committees), and others rely primarily upon an informal network of personal allies. Most work at cultivating face to face connections through such devices "as the development of club-like atmosphere, the exchange of amenities, assistance to lawmakers in their nonpolitical problems, and the building of personal relationships based on shared experiences."[7] Sanctions are also available from refusing to move a member's bill to taking away committee chairmanships or other perquisites. Because the party leaders' ultimate powers are founded in their continuing ability to command majorities within their conferences, carrots are more frequently employed than sticks, and persuasive efforts more than both. In actual practice—as noted in the accompanying box—the distinction between rewards and sanctions is not as clear as it might seem. "The most important techniques are . . . of a political character, such as assistance to members in legislative matters (such as passing local and private bills), giving members meaningful debate assignments, granting them extra lulus or staff allotments, interceding with the executive branch on behalf of members or their constituents, and so on."[8] Most party leaders measure their own effectiveness in terms of their ability to deliver these kinds of political payoffs. As one Vermont Speaker wrote of his willingness to cater to party colleagues, "My criteria to judge how far I would go to help a member was simple and straightforward. As long as it wasn't against the law, didn't require that I go to confession, or wouldn't break up my marriage, I did it."[9]

Box 6.2

Carrots or Sticks: Member and Leader Perspectives

Most academic studies of legislative leadership emphasize its collegial, reciprocal nature. "Punishment," as Alan Rosenthal puts it, "is the exception, even when members refuse to go along with their legislative party on an issue." Every present and former party leader we talked with went out of his way, repeatedly, to make the same point. Phrases like the following appear throughout our notes of these conversations: "I never demoted anybody." "Why would I want to hurt a member of my own conference?" "Ultimately, the only real power you have is the power of persuasion."

Journalists and members often presented a very different view, emphasizing the toughness of these same leaders, and telling stories of those who had faced the Speaker's anger.

These different perspectives reflect the real world elusiveness of the concept of sanctions which, like nuclear weapons in the military theory of strategic deterrence, are most effective when they are not actually used. When Mel Miller looked Brian Murtaugh in the eye and said, "Brian, you can't do that," Murtaugh was not inclined to ask why not. Miller was no doubt convinced that he had "persuaded" Murtaugh not to act, to Murtaugh it felt like sanctions. Stanley Fink loved the give and take of the party conference; but what Fink might have seen as hard bargaining or making a tough argument could easily be perceived as threatening to one dependent on the Speaker for favors. When the speaker's counsel summons you to his office and asks why you are doing something, it is not unnatural to think that you are being asked to stop doing it.

If, in fact, formal sanctions are seldom used, this in no way negates their importance in shaping the relationships between party leaders and the rank and file. Sanctions, rewards—the whole panoply of inducements available to party leaders—are given by the members to their leaders in order to advance party goals. Members know that resources are finite and that not all of them can get what they want: what they ask of their leaders is not that they be yea-sayers but they be fair in saying yes and no. As much as every member of the senate and assembly knows and understands this fact, it still feels like a sanction when the answer you get is no.

Committee Leadership

The work of the legislature is too complex for one person to control. Leaders have no choice but to delegate many of their powers. Some rely on their personal staff, some on other party leaders, and some—particularly in the smaller conferences of the senate and the assembly minority—on the entire conference. All give considerable influence within their spheres of expert knowledge to the members and chairs of the standing committees. Interactions between party leaders and committee leaders reflect a dynamic, sometimes intensely personal process of trust building and shared perceptions. In return for the powers entrusted to them, the chairs of important committees are expected to be unusually loyal to the party leader.

Events sometimes upset established patterns as when a previously obscure issue moves to center stage as the result of a gubernatorial initiative or a change in federal policies. Generally, however, there is defined ordering of committees in which some are more important than others. Overshadowing all others are the assembly committee on ways and means and its senate counterpart, the committee on finance. Unlike Congress, which separates the legislative process of raising money from that of appropriating it, most state legislatures house all money issues in a single pair of committees. Thus any bill that spends or raises money must go through the finance committee in the senate and the ways and means committee in the assembly. Quite frequently it is "dual referenced," that is, sent both to the committee with substantive jurisdiction (such as higher education) and the money committee. Under a rule adopted in 1975 the chairman of the assembly ways and means committee can require the dual reference of any bill that he or she determines to have fiscal implications. The chair of the senate finance committee in effect has the same power. Given the jurisdictional reach of their committees, the chairs and ranking minority members of senate finance and assembly ways and means are clearly among the most powerful legislative leaders in Albany, assumed to be next in line for advancement, and—with the sometimes exception of majority leaders in the assembly—the second most powerful members of their respective parties.

The codes committee is the second most important committee in both houses, again because of dual referencing. Any legislation that imposes a criminal penalty—whether a drug bill out of the alcoholism and substance abuse committee, or a bill from the housing committee imposing fines on abusive landlords—must be dual-referenced to the codes committee, which also must deal with issues, such as the death penalty, that tap emotions in the electorate that many members would as soon avoid. A large part of the committee's work is with very tedious issues of legal reasoning. Thus there are members who, in full understanding of the power inherent in the position, would just as soon not be appointed to the codes committee. As we move down the list of preferred committees, these kinds of conflicts become increasingly important. Quite obviously a committee like agriculture—which might be enormously appealing to someone from Chautauqua County—would not be ranked nearly as high by someone from Brooklyn. Judiciary, on the other hand, has a particular appeal to lawyers and deals with issues such as crime that are visible and important. The senate judiciary committee, with the added power of screening judicial appointments, is a particularly attractive assignment. Most members of both houses are drawn to the education committee because it deals with issues of universal constituency concern and is such an important part of state policy. The health committees are increasingly attractive for the same reasons.

Party leaders try to accommodate member preferences, especially when they are important to reelection. They know, in the long run, that maintaining and building their party's electoral base is what distinguishes being in the majority from being in the minority. "Top leaders prefer to have committee chairs upon whom they can rely." And they prefer to give their committee chairs members with whom they can work effectively. "But leaders are not always free to appoint trusted allies. They have to consider some of the factors that govern the appointment of committee members: seniority, geography, other committee service, and qualifications."[10] In New York, key committees must be balanced between upstate and New York City for Democrats, and rural areas and the suburbs for Republicans. Democrats must consider ethnic balance and gender as well; and for both parties ideology is a factor. The preferences of interest groups, sometimes given weight—particularly in the case of major campaign contributors—are not likely to be controlling, as party leaders do not like involving outsiders in what they consider inside business.

Power and the Perquisites of Office

The senate and assembly formally rank leadership positions by an ascending scale of financial allowances for serving as "officers." Beyond their regular salaries, committee chairs and party leaders receive supplements ranging from a low of $6,500 for the ranking minority members of committees like tourism, consumer affairs, and mental health; to $24,500 for the chairs of the senate finance committee and assembly ways and means committee; on up to $30,000 for the Speaker and senate majority leader.[11] In Tables 6.1 and 6.2 we have used this ranking to plot the relative positions of the top majority party members in relationship to their seniority in both houses. While there is no seniority "rule" in Albany, party leaders generally claim to give considerable weight to length of service in doling out offices carrying special allowances. There is, as the tables show, little uniformity to these perquisites in large part because higher salaries do not always mean greater power, and most members are more interested in power than money. In the senate, for example, two of the eight most senior members in 1995–96, Jess

Present and Caesar Trunzo, were tied for twenty-fifth on the money list, while such junior colleagues as Guy Valella and Nicholas Spano—tied for seventeenth and twentieth in seniority—were fifth in extra compensation. Similar discrepancies can be found in the assembly where Richard Gottfried, second in seniority, ranks seventeenth in salary; Pete Grannis and Paul Harenberg, tied for seventh in seniority, tie for twenty-seventh in perks. Many members become comfortable with a particular chairmanship: having developed considerable knowledge in the field of substance abuse, for example, author Murtaugh would not have given up his chairmanship of the alcohol and substance abuse committee for a minor increment in salary and prestige. Only a major promotion to, say, the education committee or ways and means committee could tempt most long-tenured chairs to give up their special influence and connections in an established area.

Members are generally reluctant to speak ill of colleagues, and few were willing to comment specifically on the details of the rankings displayed in Tables 6.1 and 6.2; but although no one tries systematically to rank his or colleagues in terms of power and prestige, movements up and down the ladder, as well as long-standing failures to advance, are noticed. Some older members, as their stamina and ability come into question, are eased out of positions of power and into prestigious sounding, high-paying titles that carry no real responsibilities or influence. Indeed it is only as members begin to think about retirement (with pensions pegged to final salaries) that most members begin to pay serious attention to their financial supplements. When John Marchi, the dean of senate Republicans, for example, was stripped of his chairmanship of the senate finance committee, then majority leader Marino gave him a title that carried the same $24,500 allowance. But when he lost even this empty title (to sixth-ranked Owen Johnson), it suggested that Marchi was on the losing side of the majority leader Bruno's successful challenge to Ralph Marino (and it is not hard to guess which side Johnson was on).

Being on the winning side in a leadership contest is important, as is competence. Ideology also plays a role, though it tends to be folded in with the more elusive concept of party loyalty. Senator Frank Padavan of Queens is one of the more moderate Republicans in the senate: his fall from fifth to fifteenth when Bruno stripped him of his leadership title probably indicates that he, like Marchi, was late to support the revolt against Marino. But Padavan and another senior Republican from New York City, Roy Goodman, will always have trouble entering or staying in the inner circles of power because the nature of their districts forces them to be outside of the party mainstream. Party leaders are generally understanding of their members' electoral needs and usually will not ask a member to cast votes that could result in a failure to be reelected; but there are limits to how much latitude the leadership will

Table 6.1

Top Republican Senators Ranked According to Seniority, Key Titles, and Pay Rank, 1993–1994 and 1995–1996

Member	Seniority	Highest title	Pay rank	Other
Marchi				
1993–94	1	Vice President Pro Tem	2	Rules
1995–96	1	Chair, Authorities and Commissions	18	Rules
Stafford				
1993–94	2	Chair, Finance	2	Rules
1995–96	2	Chair, Finance	2	Rules
Present				
1993–94	3	Deputy Majority Leader	2	Rules
1995–96	3	Chair, Small Business	25	
Goodman				
1993–94	4	Chair, Tax and Government Operations	18	Rules
1995–96	4	Chair, Tax and Government Operations	18	Rules
Levy				
1993–94	4	Chair, Transportation	18	Rules
1995–96	4	Chair, Majority Conference	5	Rules
Johnson				
1993–94	6	Majority Whip	9	Rules
1995–96	6	Vice President	2	Rules
Padavan				
1993–94	6	Assistant Majority Leader	5	Rules
1995–96	6	Chair, Cities	18	Rules
Trunzo				
1993–94	6	Senior Assistant Majority Leader	5	Rules
1995–96	6	Chair, Civil Service	25	Rules
Volker				
1993–94	9	Vice Chairman, Majority Conference	9	Rules
1995–96	9	Chair, Codes	15	Rules
Bruno				
1993–94	10	Assistant Majority Leader	5	Rules
1995–96	10	Majority Leader	1	Rules
LaValle				
1993–94	10	Deputy Majority Whip	12	
1995–96	10	Vice Chairman, Majority Conference	9	
Farley				
1993–94	12	Secretary of the Majority Conference	9	
1995–96	12	Majority Whip	9	
Cook				
1993–94	13	Chair, Education	15	
1995–96	13	Chair, Education	15	
Lack				
1993–94	13	Chair, Majority Steering Committee	12	
1995–96	13	Deputy Majority Whip	12	

Tully				
1993–94	15	Assistant Majority Whip	14	
1995–96	15	Chair, Environmental Conservation	25	
Skelos				
1993–94	16	Chair, Aging	25	
1995–96	16	Deputy Majority Leader	2	Rules
Kuhl				
1993–94	17	Chair, Agriculture	25	
1995–96	17	Assistant Majority Leader	5	
Seward				
1993–94	17	Chair, Energy	25	
1995–96	17	Secretary, Majority Conference	9	
Valella				
1993–94	17	Chair, Insurance	25	
1995–96	17	Senior Assistant Majority Leader	5	Rules
Spano				
1993–94	20	Chair, Committee on Mental Hygiene	25	
1995–96	20	Assistant Majority Leader	5	

Source: See Table 6.3.

---

allow. One senator who voted with the Democrats against a casino gambling bill that the Republicans had vowed to pass in 1997 (see Box 3.4) was disciplined, and the majority leader was quite candid in explaining why. "Members," Bruno told the *New York Times*, "know that when they take a position that isn't reflective of the leadership, that there is a downside. [He] [the member in question] knows it might make his life less comfortable."[12]

In the assembly, conservative Democrats like Robin Schimminger, Joseph Pillitterre, and Anthony Seminerio are, by reason of ideology, almost frozen out of power positions. But Seminerio—whose Queens district would probably be Republican if he were not its representative—is, as party leaders would say, more likely to "give you a vote," that is, to go along with the party if his vote is needed. At the furthest extreme is Brooklyn Democrat Dov Hikind who is so frequently at odds with his party that despite more than fifteen years of seniority he has no chairmanships, indeed no committee assignments whatsoever. His only title is vice chair of the Democratic steering committee, a committee of, shall we say, fluctuating importance (though twenty-sixth in pay).

The party steering committees are, like the rules committees, whatever the party leaders make of them. Once, when assembly Speaker Mel Miller needed time to do a little arm twisting among his senior colleagues, he recessed the assembly in order to convene a meeting of the rules committee. It threw the members into consternation as they scurried about trying to find out who was on the committee and who wasn't. Similarly, the steering committee has sometimes played a key role as a sounding board for the leader-

Table 6.2

Top Assembly Democrats Ranked According to Seniority, Key Titles, and Pay Rank, 1993–1994 and 1995–1996

Member	Seniority	Highest title	Pay rank	Other
Eve				
1993–94	1	Deputy Speaker	4	Rules
1995–96	1	Deputy Speaker	4	Rules
Gottfried				
1993–94	2	Chair, Health	17	Rules
1995–96	2	Chair, Health	17	Rules
Barbaro				
1993–94	3	Chair, Labor	26	Rules
1995–96	3	Deputy Majority Leader	10	Rules
Connelly				
1993–94	3	Chair, Committee on Committees	7	Rules
1995–96	3	Speaker Pro Tempore	4	Rules
Griffith				
1993–94	3	Assistant Speaker	4	Rules
1995–96	3	Assistant Speaker	4	Rules
Lentol				
1993–94	3	Chair, Codes	12	Rules
1995–96	3	Chair, Codes	12	Rules
Farrell				
1993–94	7	Chair, Banks	18	Rules
1995–96	7	Chair, Ways and Means	3	Rules
Grannis				
1993–94	7	Chair, Insurance	27	Rules
1995–96	7	Chair, Insurance	27	Rules
Harenberg				
1993–94	7	Chair, Aging	27	
1995–96	7	Chair, Aging	27	
Vann				
1993–94	7	Chair, Corporations	18	Rules
1995–96	7	Chair, Corporations	18	Rules
Butler				
1993–94	11	Assistant Speaker Pro Tempore	7	Rules
1995–96	11	Assistant Speaker Pro Tempore	7	Rules
Keane				
1993–94	12	Chair, Majority Program Committee	18	
1995–96	12	Chair, Committee on Standing Committees	7	
Lafayette				
1993–94	12	Chair, Majority Steering Committee	18	Rules
1995–96	12	Chair, Majority Steering Committee	18	Rules
Schimminger				
1993–94	12	Chair, Small Business	27	
1995–96	12	Chair, Small Business	27	

Silver				
1993–94	12	Chair, Ways and Means	3	Rules
1995–96	12	Speaker	1	Rules
Sullivan				
1993–94	12	Chair, Higher Education	27	
1995–96	12	Chair, Higher Education	27	
Sanders				
1993–94	17	Chair, Mental Health	27	
1995–96	17	Chair, Education	12	Rules
Jacobs				
1993–94	18	Chair, Social Services	27	
1995–96	18	Chair, Social Services	27	
Pillitterre				
1993–94	18	Chair, Tourism	27	
1995–96	18	Chair, Tourism	27	
Seminerio				
1993–94	18	Majority Whip	12	
1995–96	18	Majority Whip	12	
Bragman				
1993–94	21	Chair, Transportation	18	Rules
1995–96	21	Majority Leader	2	Rules
Davis				
1993–94	21	Assistant Majority Whip	18	
1995–96	21	Chair, Majority Conference	16	
Dugan				
1993–94	21	Chair, Commerce	27	Rules
1995–96	21	Chair, Commerce	27	Rules
Feldman				
1993–94	21	Chair, Corrections	27	Rules
1995–96	21	Chair, Corrections	27	Rules
Green				
1993–94	21	—	0	
1995–96	21	Chair, Children and Families	· 27	
Murtaugh				
1993–94	21	Chair, Alcoholism	27	
1995–96	21	Chair, Alcoholism	27	
Weinstein				
1993–94	21	Chair, Government Employees	27	
1995–96	21	Chair, Judiciary	12	Rules
Boyland				
1993–94	29	Deputy Majority Whip	16	Rules
1995–96	29	Deputy Majority Whip	16	Rules
Greene				
1993–94	29	Chair, Consumer Affairs	27	Rules
1995–96	29	Chair, Banks	18	Rules

Source: See Table 6.3.

ship, but under Speaker Silver has fallen into virtual disuse. Despite its almost wholly symbolic status, membership on the rules committee is not trivial in a body where symbols count. Looking at Table 6.1, the fact that Senator Present not only lost a significant pay allowance but became the only one of the ten most senior members not appointed to the rules committee says a lot about his standing with majority leader Bruno. That Dean Skelos and Guy Valella, conversely, jumped seniority both to higher pay ranks and to positions on Rules, sends an important message: Skelos, indeed, is generally rumored to be the majority leader in waiting.

One recent "test" of how more senior members stood with their respective party leaders came with the 1998 appointment of conference committees to work out interhouse differences on the budget. Each house leader appointed five members each to eight issue area committees, and three members—in addition to themselves—to a general conference committee. The rankings revealed in these appointments tend generally to confirm the patterns shown in Tables 6.1 and 6.2. Thus the majority party members of the assembly general conference committee included majority leader Bragman, ways and means committee chair Farrell, and Elizabeth Connelly, the assembly's most senior woman and the person who generally presides for Speaker Silver. Senator Bruno, predictably from our rankings, included finance committee chair Stafford; and then skipped more senior members to include vice president Johnson and the up and coming Skelos.

Generally, both party leaders appointed the chairs of the relevant substantive committees to the appropriate conference committees; but both Bruno and Silver's appointments to the nine joint budget subcommittees reflected leadership preferences as well as seniority. Susan John and Roberto Ramirez—both assembly members for less than ten years—were picked ahead of members with more than twice their seniority. Because senate Republicans had more positions to fill than people to fill them, five members were asked to serve on two committees. Bruno, interestingly, gave these double assignments to the party's two freshman senators (Carl Marcellino and Raymond Meier), two in their third terms (Mary Lou Rath and James Wright), and only one to a high seniority member (thirteenth ranked James Lack, chair of the senate Judiciary committee). It is not unlikely that senator Bruno was looking toward the 1998 elections in giving junior members something to write home about.

Leadership Styles

"Rightly or wrongly," as Jones argues in his study of congressional leadership, "House leaders must attend to their majorities."[13] The interesting questions about elected leaders are questions about how they discern the wishes of these majorities, communicate with them, and maintain their trust. At the most fundamental level, a party leader must have sufficient support in his or her party conference to avoid becoming—like Ralph Marino—the target of an active opposition campaign. Particularly in the case of divided government, however, the ability of party leaders to sustain the support of their own party conferences must be balanced against the sometimes conflicting ability to negotiate effectively with other leaders, in particular the governor and the leaders of the other house. There is a non-coincidental irony to the fact that when Ralph Marino was brought down as senate majority leader, he was probably at the peak of his power vis-à-vis the governor and the Democratic leadership of the assembly. Indeed some observers believe that it was precisely because he was so effective in dealing with a Democratic governor and Speaker that he had to be deposed by his fellow Republicans when they won the governorship.

The Party Conference

Perhaps the most obvious place to look for the ways in which legislative leaders communicate with party colleagues is in the party conferences. All four conferences meet almost every day that the legislature is in session, and frequently when it is not. In their basic outline:

> Party conferences are closed-door sessions held off the floor on a regular basis for legislators only. In those sessions, members are free to make arguments about policy directions the party should take. The leadership is then generally free within those limits to negotiate with the other house and the governor over policy.[14]

How much freedom leaders take from conference instructions varies. Some conference meetings are agonizingly specific. During session, for example, the parties frequently recess to go into conference, often in the middle of debate on a bill. This is most likely to happen when party leaders sense that there is unhappiness in the ranks. On rare occasions, should it become apparent that the unhappiness is widespread, the bill will be pulled from the floor either for redrafting or to die. Sometimes, particularly at the beginning of a session, discussions in conference are wide ranging and almost philosophical in tone.

Among modern leaders, former Speaker Stanley Fink probably used his party conference the most. Fink was comfortable with the give and take of a charged debate, acting, as one member told us, "like the conductor of a symphony seeking harmony in the ranks." Participation was widespread, with discussions ranging widely and often lasting late into the night. Other party leaders have preferred a more controlled atmosphere. One assembly Republican told us that former minority leader Tom Reynolds seemed almost to be working from a script with conference discussions dominated and directed by a small circle of his most trusted party allies.

The Inner Circles

Most modern party leaders have had as their closest advisers a fairly predictable set of relatively senior colleagues. For Speakers Weprin and Miller and all recent majority leaders in the senate, formal titles have tended to coincide roughly with actual authority. Committee chairs were given considerable autonomy within their spheres of expertise, and—under Weprin and Miller—the assembly majority leaders had strong working relationships with the Speaker. The alignment of power and formal position in this pattern of leadership is clear, though seldom neat. Some committee chairs and party leaders are more important and have better access to the Speaker than others. In most cases, moreover, there are relatively junior members—often with relatively minor formal titles—who were known to be close to the leader. Assemblywoman Eileen Dugan, for example, though only in her seventh term and chair of a minor committee, was widely regarded as a pipeline to Speaker Weprin even before he confirmed her special status by designating her co-chair of the campaign committee (DACC).

More than at any time in recent history, both Senate Majority Leader Joseph Bruno and Speaker Sheldon Silver have concentrated power in their offices on the ninth floor of the legislative office building. Silver, in particular, relies heavily on his personal staff and on the party's program staff for important issues. One of the Democrats' key bills in the 1997 session, a package of proposals for improving elementary and secondary education was, for example, drafted entirely by central staff and presented to the chair of the education committee only days before it was formally introduced. Silver, as one member puts it, "plays his cards close to the vest." While he and other Democrats concede that some degree of secretiveness may be important in dealing with a Republican governor and senate, it has also caused considerable grumbling. "Damn it," one committee chairman burst out in a 1999 meeting, "if I'm supposed to be changing my stand on an issue, I'd like to know about it before the lobbyists."

It was concerns such as this that gave force to majority leader Michael Bragman's nearly successful challenge to Speaker Silver in 2000. "The leadership style must change. Members must be informed and participate in the process," Bragman argued. "This must be a member-driven Conference. This must be a member-driven House. It cannot be a Body where non-elected members of the Speaker's staff dictate the activities of lawmakers."[15]

While there is bound to be grumbling in the ranks when committee chairs feel they have been insufficiently consulted, party leaders must balance strategic calculations against such concerns. At one delicate point in negotiations with the governor and senate leadership in 1997, the Speaker's top aide sent a memo warning his staff against leaking information to the chairs of two committees whose issues were being negotiated. Many Democrats were upset with this seemingly cavalier treatment of colleagues, but there was also a strong awareness of the Speaker's need to guard against leaks. If the chair in question, for example, knew what the Speaker's bargaining points were, he or she might have been tempted to discuss them with a friendly journalist or lobbyist who, in turn, might have passed them to the governor or the senate majority leader. Silver, unlike his predecessors as Speaker, has been the lone Democrat among the big three in Albany: forced to deal with both a governor and state senate under Republican control there are sound political reasons for him to play his cards close to the vest. At the same time, Silver clearly brings a different style to the job. In Jewell and Whicker's typology of leadership styles, he is clearly a "command" as opposed to "consensus" or "coordinating" leader. He tends, according to the typology, "to suppress conflict . . . minimize participation by rank-and-file legislators, and . . . use party caucuses to disseminate information and to inform members of decisions already made. . . . They are likely to apply more pressure on members to support positions taken by the caucus. Command leaders limit access to key information."[16]

Except perhaps in the waning days of the 1994 session, when Speaker Weprin was failing in health, there have been no "consensual" leaders in modern New York history. As long as there is divided government, few legislators would be willing to trade the benefits of unity for the uncertainties of too much internal democracy. Consensus leadership, which "emphasizes debate and discussion, even at times at the expense of action,"[17] is, we suspect, seldom found in states like New York that approach the party government model. Jewell and Whicker argue that consensus leaders are not necessarily weak, but that they "can allow the governor to dominate a party agenda, especially if the governor is of the same party. They can also allow the opponent party to dominate, especially when the consensus leader represents the minority. Consensus leadership can result in continuous jockeying for power within the party and frequent challenges to leadership."[18]

This does not mean that the rank and file cannot be consulted, especially if the process and give and take is kept within the boundaries of the party conference. Summarizing recent research on legislative leadership in congress, David Rhode argues:

> If a party has sufficient common ground on issues, it may create strong leaders to act as agents in pursuing the party's legislative agenda. Such leaders do not command or control the mass of the membership (although they may seek to do so to marginal individuals who can make the difference between winning and losing). Instead the leaders use powers granted to them by the members to accomplish goals they hold in common. The members sacrifice a *limited* amount of their independence to the leaders, because the commonality of preferences ensures that most members would only rarely be pressured to take an action they do not prefer.[19]

Stanley Fink was a strong leader, yet his style, to the extent appropriate in New York could be described—in the Jewell and Whicker typology—as "coordinating," "balancing action with discussion"[20] precisely because of his working in terms of such commonalities of preference.

It is axiomatic among students of leadership that it involves strong elements of reciprocity. A leader's continuing power is a function of the trust accorded by his or her party colleagues. His or her ability to inspire such trust, however, is in part based on the ability effectively to press party positions in the outside world. Party leaders, as they deal with their counterparts, have a strong interest in presenting a united front; their fellow party members share that interest. One important function of the party conference is to develop a sense of unity or, if that is unobtainable, the image of not being divided. Combine the strong norm of party government with the persistence of divided party control, and it seems unlikely that either party will move substantially to increase rank-and file participation. It is worth noting that since the 1960s not a single candidate for leader of either house made decentralization an issue in his or her campaign for the office. The one who came closest, Mike Bragman in 2000, got his clock cleaned. (See Box 6.1 on page 193.)

Leadership Goals

A second dimension of Jewell and Whicker's leadership typology focuses on leadership goals, and here the differences—though more difficult to classify—are as pronounced in New York as they are elsewhere. Legislative leaders are classified in this schema as to whether they are motivated primarily by an orientation toward *power*, *policy*, or *process*.[21] Surprisingly few legislative leaders in New York have manifested the kinds of career ambitions that typify the power-oriented leader. Perry Duryea, who served as

Speaker from 1969 through 1974, is the only recent leader of either house who has actually run for higher office. The last one actually to move up was Irving Ives who served as Speaker in 1936 and eventually served two terms (from 1946 to 1958) in the U.S. senate. Warren Anderson tested the waters in 1978, as did Stanley Fink in 1982. Shelly Silver was widely mentioned as a candidate for governor in 1998, but although he did not discourage such speculation, neither did he actively campaign. The contemporary New York legislature is perhaps too partisan to serve as a hothouse of political ambitions: the very combative yet compromising abilities that makes a party leader effective may be just the kinds of political postures that make for weak statewide candidates.

In the assembly, the evolution from Stanley Fink to Sheldon Silver has clearly moved, in Jewell and Wicker's terms, from policy to process. Fink had a clear programmatic agenda. With his base in the liberal wing of the party, he not only put liberals in positions of power but fought his own party's governor when Cuomo began moving to the right. Although subsequent Speakers have been similarly drawn from the party's New York City wing, their ideological leanings have been more difficult to discern. Sheldon Silver, in particular, has been unusually pragmatic in his approach to issues. Rather than directly confront a conservative governor, he has attempted to counter Pataki's policy proposals with scaled-down alternatives. Expanding upon a survey research operation institutionalized by Mel Miller, Silver has used frequent public opinion polls to guide both strategic and policy decisions, and has been unusually solicitous of the needs of Democrats from marginal (and generally conservative) districts. Despite the serious misgivings of the liberal majority in his conference, Silver, in 1995, cited the polls and possible electoral setbacks in pushing assembly Democrats to accept many of Pataki's budget and tax cuts.

If trends in the senate majority, and in both houses' minority parties, are less clear, long-range developments are the same. If there was an ideological dimension to Joe Bruno's challenge to Ralph Marino, it has been muted in practice. In both houses, in both parties, frequent polling has become a hallmark of contemporary legislative leadership. The parties have confronted each other less along ideological lines than in symbolic battles over relatively trivial but powerfully resonant emotional issues such as so-called partial-birth abortions, a vividly dramatic surgical procedure that is almost never actually used.

Courting Party Leaders: Strategies of Access

Of the roughly 20,000 bills introduced every two years in the assembly and senate, few are expected to go beyond the introductory stage. When there is a serious interest in changing public policy, the locus of power shifts to a much wider road, a road that leads invariably through the tollgates of the majority party leadership. To pass either house of the New York state legislature, a bill must be acceptable to the majority party leadership; to become public policy, it must have its active support. How does one go about marshaling such support?

Party leaders are not equally accessible to all members. Clearly, they listen almost only to members of their own party. Even within their party conferences, moreover, some members do a lot better than others. Other things being equal, senior members have an advantage. Through long-standing acquaintance, they are known commodities in the eyes of party leaders, and—because of their seniority and perhaps friendship—more difficult to avoid. Most of them, moreover, have built up substantial backlogs of knowledge and connections with outside groups that make them important gatekeepers of information through the committee system.

Committees

Almost every member of the assembly and senate sits on anywhere from two to eleven committees. While seniority, party loyalty, and constituency concerns play a role in committee assignments, party leaders generally attempt to give most members what they want. Unlike Congress, however, where stability of membership is a key factor in explaining the powers of standing committees, turnover in New York is substantial. In 1997, for example, when Murtaugh's defeat led to a vacancy in the chairmanship of the committee on alcoholism and drug abuse, the committee got a new chair, a new ranking minority member, and four of ten new members. Six of the eighteen members of the committee on aging were new in 1997, only two because of retirements or electoral defeats. The assembly health committee, on the other hand, replaced Murtaugh with another Democrat, and also lost its ranking minority member in the election, but otherwise carried over its entire 1995–96 membership. On the powerful ways and means committee, only four of twenty-three Democrats and four of eleven Republicans were new to the committee in 1997.

With certain key exceptions—ways and means and senate finance committees, most obviously—members, the more junior members in particular, tend to sit lightly in their committee seats. Rapid turnover is as much a function of individual preferences as it is of the leadership's needs to put together the jigsaw puzzle of committee assignments. As in Congress, committees range from the highly desirable (ways and means or finance, health, education and—for most members—codes and judiciary; to those that vary according to where you are from (such as agriculture, housing and transportation), to those such as ethics and election law, which are more duty than privilege. Attendance at the meetings of minor committees is low, and turnover from one session to another is fairly high. It doesn't hurt, for example, to have a committee like children and families on your resume; but the reality is that the committee seldom handles an important bill, and membership on it is not highly prized. What is prized, and it is prized quite highly, is the chairmanship even of a relatively unimportant committee. As Rosenthal says of state legislative committees:

> In many respects, the chairperson *is* the committee. This is because participation by other members is often sporadic; they may have their own committees to chair or are spread thin among many assignments. Increasingly, practically all returning majority-party members have a committee . . . to call their own; that is where they focus their energies while playing a more nominal role in the affairs of other units on which they sit. The more important the committee, the likelier it is that members will be involved.[22]

Almost every Republican senator, and more than a third of the Democrats in the assembly, has either a chairmanship or regular assignment to a major committee; most other majority party members specialize in no more than two or three areas.

In 1981, Francis and Riddlesperger sent a questionnaire to the members of all ninety-nine state legislative bodies. One of their goals was to compare legislatures according to the degree that key decisions were made by party leaders, in the party conference, in committee, on the floor, and so on. Not surprisingly, committees ranked relatively low in importance in New York state where, presumably, most members would have cited the central role of party leaders and the party conference. In the Francis and Riddlesperger ranking, New York's assembly committees were thirty-ninth in their "centrality" scores, senate committees still lower at forty-seventh.[23] Committees in both houses, though more so in the assembly than the senate, do play a traffic cop role in New York exercising some control over the flow of bills through the party conferences and to the floor. Committees in New York, unlike those in most other American legislatures, have no legislatively significant subcommittees, hold relatively few public hearings, and do not "mark up" or amend bills. But if the committees as institutions are peripheral to the process of lawmaking, committee members—chairs in particular—are not.

Committee chairs have considerably more access to party leaders—on bills within their jurisdictions—than do other members; and majority party committee members, working thorough their chairs, are next in line. There are, as we shall see in Chapter 7, formal mechanisms by which members can

Table 6.3

Number and Quality of Majority Party Assembly Committee Assignments by Seniority Rank (1995–1996)

Seniority	Number	Chairs (%)	Ways and means (%)	Mean number of committees
21 years or more	10[a]	70	80	3.9
16–20 years	9	56	22	4.4
11–15 years	19	68	32	4.6
6–10 years	28	39	18	5.3
0–5 years	25	0	0	5.5

Source: Compiled by the authors from seniority rankings available from the Assembly Public Information Office and committee memberships reported in *1995–96 New York Political Almanac* (Centerville, MA: American Research Services, 1995).
[a]Not including the Speaker, majority leader, or vacant seats.

request serious committee consideration of their bills, but the reality is that committee membership is the best guarantee that your bill will be heard. Because this is true, lobbyists tend to focus their efforts on committee members (chairs especially) who deal with their issue areas. Regular interactions with these lobbyists, moreover, tends to build familiarity with the issues, and plug individual members into networks of lobbyists, bureaucrats, local officials, academics, and constituents concerned with those issues. Committee chairs are given staff allowances that permit the hiring of at least one professional staff assistant, sometimes more. With rare exceptions, moreover, the chairs have the power to block bills they do not like.

Typically, during the course of a member's legislative career, he or she will gradually narrow his focus to more limited sets of issues. As may be seen in Table 6.3, majority party members in the assembly served on an average five and a half committees each in their early years in the legislature compared with fewer than four committees after they had served more than twenty years. Senior members were considerably more likely to stay with the same set of committees from one session to the next, particularly after they had secured an important chairmanship and/or a seat on the ways and means committee.

Committee chairs seldom find it difficult to control their committees. In the final analysis, party discipline can be invoked against a dissident bloc. The more difficult problem faced by committee chairs in New York is that of maintaining control over their own turf. The first dimension for evaluating the strength of standing committees, Rosenthal suggests, "involves the extent to which the jurisdiction of committees is respected and committees are referred bills. If many bills, or the most important ones, bypass committees, then the strength of the committee system is in doubt."[24] The problem for committee chairs in New York is not at the referral stage. As in Congress and in most state legislatures most bills, including the most important ones, are properly referred to the appropriate committees.[25] The problem faced by committee chairs in New York is that of having bills taken over by the leadership either for a redrafting by central staff or by folding it into the budget. The latter problem has surfaced increasingly as a source of rank-and-file frustration in both houses. A bill is introduced and referred, let's say, to the committee on energy. Supported by the chair and a committee majority it is reported out; but before it ever gets to the floor, the Speaker or majority leader puts it up as a bargaining chip in negotiations with his counterpart and the governor. The relatively trivial problem with having your bill coopted in this manner is that you don't get full credit. As a budget item, it no longer carries your name as sponsor. More seriously, it may not emerge in exactly the form you wanted it to become a statute, yet since you got essentially what you asked for it is difficult to complain.

"To Get Along, Go Along"

This was the slogan former house Speaker Sam Rayburn passed on to every new member of the U.S. House of Representatives under his leadership. It applies with particular force in New York where a key test of a member's status as a "player" lies in his or her willingness to "go along" with the party majority, even when that vote might go against his or her conscience, constituency, or better judgment. Most of the time, members have wiggle room. With a majority as large as that which assembly Democrats have enjoyed in recent years, the Speaker is usually prepared to allow a few of his party colleagues to vote with the minority. In fact a member who might face serious reelection problems—such as a rural Democrat on a gun control bill—will sometimes be encouraged to vote against the party position. Senate Republicans have tended to have smaller majorities and therefore less freedom of action, but there are often defections in the other direction that allow most members to vote as they like most of the time. Almost every legislator, however, has at some time or another been asked to cast a vote that he or she would just as soon not. The leadership will usually try to bring the issue to vote in a form that makes most party members comfortable, but the time will come when you will be asked to "fall on your sword."

There are times when the leadership wants a show of strength, and the blood flows freely. In 1995, Shelly Silver had to push very hard to gain conference acceptance of the budget deal he had reluctantly negotiated with

Governor Pataki and the senate. Opposition to huge increases in tuition for the city and state universities, to drastic cuts in health and welfare, and to tax cuts targeted largely toward the wealthy were a bitter pill for many New York City Democrats to swallow. Discussions in conference were heated. A handful of liberals held out to the end and voted no on the floor, an act that won applause among liberals in New York City but made few friends in Albany. Those liberals who agreed, for the sake of the party, to fall on the sword and support their Speaker were particularly annoyed with what one described as "cheap grandstand votes."

Since the Speaker got the votes he needed there was no direct confrontation with the dissenting members, but these are the kinds of votes that are noted. A willingness to "go along" with the leadership is, in the long run, an important measure of how well a member will "get along" when it comes to committee assignments, help with campaign funds, reapportionment, staff allowances, and so on. It is also, in the long run, a key standard by which you are judged by your colleagues. A willingness to go along should not be confused with a member's voting record. Under normal conditions, a party leader "enforces discipline on as few of his members as possible, for there is no point in imposing further political costs once he is over the top. But he often does not know how many he can "let off the hook" until the minority members vote."[26] The way this is usually done is to hold a few votes in reserve until the final tally becomes clear. The result is often the kind of scenario once reported in the *New York Times:*

> The other night, the Republicans fell short of the votes they needed for their version of a bill. . . . Jack Haggerty, counsel to Senator Anderson, merely pointed his finger at some defecting party members, including Senator Charles D. Cook. Immediately, Mr. Cook rose and changed his vote from "nay" to "yes."
>
> After a nod from the counsel, Senator Martin S. Auer stood up to say he had just discovered $1.6 million in the bill for . . . his area, and changed his vote as well. Within moments, Mr. Haggerty had accumulated the 31 votes needed for passage.[27]

Whether these switches had been prearranged in conference, the process is not always this smooth. On a more recent assembly vote, one Democrat refused to shift his vote unless and until the majority leader went first: "If the leadership won't take a fall," he explained, "how can they ask me to?" While his logic might not have been too much appreciated at the time, it is—as a general rule of thumb—the more senior party leaders who are asked to switch first.

Tactics

Once, near the end of session, Murtaugh needed the leadership's help in encouraging senate action on one of his committee's bills. Already on the list for a formal appointment on another issue, Murtaugh decided that an "informal" encounter might suffice. When the party went into conference he carefully positioned himself on the only available aisle seat. Deftly maneuvering himself as the session broke up and ready with a carefully rehearsed speech, he positioned himself in the Speaker's only line of exit. But the Speaker, in a move worthy of a professional football halfback, managed to slide two chairs out of the way, vault the third row, and make his escape.

End of session perhaps encapsulates the problem of access for rank-and-file legislators. There is only so much money to go around, so much the party leadership can ask of the governor and the other house, so much time available. During the final weeks, everyone it seems wants to get to the Speaker, the majority leader, or the governor. If you are an assembly Democrat, you do it through the Speaker. Senate Republicans work through their majority leader; lobbyists go where they can. Minority party members, by and large, work through their party leaders' contacts in the other house. The later in the session it gets, the more difficult it becomes. Members, as indicated in our discussion of access, are "ranked," not in any formal sense, but in the sense that the Speaker or majority leader will give priority to those who have earned credibility. Such factors as seniority, committee chairmanships, and records of reliability help. In both majority party conferences, there is a particular advantage to being from a marginal district. A Democratic assembly member from a normally Republican area, for example, is far more likely to get a sympathetic hearing than one from a safe Democratic seat if only because the party and its leaders need these marginal district members to maintain their majorities.

While the kind of informal contact Murtaugh sought at the end of conference can be useful for small favors, the two most common channels for communicating with the leadership are through formal appointment and in conference discussions. Any member of the majority conference can schedule a meeting with the party leader's top aide, who seldom makes direct commitments. He or she will normally get back to the member later or schedule an appointment with the party leader. Here too it is often difficult to get a direct answer because the more important requests usually necessitate further deals: "I'll see if I can get it in the budget"; or "Well, let's move it through the assembly and I'll talk with Joe [Bruno] about it," is often about as strong a pledge of help as anyone can hope for.

In order to promote positive action from the leadership, an idea must as a rule have been pretty well fleshed out in advance, if not in the form of a bill, in terms of a concrete proposal for action. Moreover, as one former top aide puts it:

> An idea has to make sense; it has to be something that is not going to cause a problem for the other members of the Majority. There is an evaluation of individual ideas and a meshing of the different things that the members of the Conference would like to do, a placing of priorities on them.[28]

If a proposal is likely to help the party in the polls, in raising funds, or in helping a marginal member win reelection it will get a hearing; if it is good public policy, so much the better. The more easily the leadership can sell the proposal to the governor and to the other house, the better its chances. If it is a good sound bite issue that can be used to embarrass them, it is even better. Often it helps to have picked up support in the other house, or to have had it passed there in different form. It doesn't hurt for the Speaker, majority leader, or governor to hear from more than one member on the same issue, and the backing of an interest group with strong ties to the party can be a plus. For lobbyists, money talks, particularly as time runs down. During the last days of the 1998 session, according to one lobbyist, a top aide to the governor consulted a list of those who had contributed large amounts before allowing them into the room where the governor's aides were hearing last-minute pleas. Money seldom plays so blatant a role as it sometimes has with Governor Pataki, but it never hurts.

A lot of the real work in Albany, the detailed political crafting of policy proposals, takes place in the respective majority party conferences. This is where the Speaker and majority leader "listen to the members . . . , discern their positions, mesh those positions, conceptualize policies which were responsive to those distilled and reconciled positions, enunciate those policies back to the members, get their reactions, and finally modify those policies, as appropriate, based on the reactions of the members."[29] The wiser members pick their spots in conference, commenting only when they have important insights. Committee-based specialization plays a major role with committee chairs—those who are respected for doing their homework, at least—getting the most attention. At the same time, overspecialization—seeing every policy issue as one involving health, schools, substance abuse, or whatever—can turn you from being an expert to a "one-trick pony," someone whose response to every issue is predictably tied to one answer. In the assembly Democratic conference, regionalism plays a strong role with New York City Democrats tending to defer to suburban and upstate colleagues on many issues, and vice versa.

Most party conferences go fairly smoothly: as much as you may be split as a party, the bigger enemies are "out there." There are times, however, when emotions erupt or where individual members feel so strongly about particular issues that they take strong stands. The chair of the assembly higher education committee, for example, once threatened to vote against the budget if the Speaker agreed to a proposed retrenchment of one college in the New York City university system. His strong stand worked, and the Speaker went back to the governor and majority leader and reworked the CUNY budget; but as the chairman himself concedes, "you can't use that kind of tactic too often."

Governors

One of the most salient features of national politics has long been what Woodrow Wilson called "the imperious authority of the standing committees" of the Congress. Aided by the seniority system, committee and subcommittee chairs—through long periods of interaction with their counterparts in the executive branch and affected interest groups—develop close, usually friendly relations with them. The resulting "whirlpools of influence," "subgovernments," or "iron triangles," as they have been called, are remarkably resilient to challenge either by party leaders in Congress or by the White House. The autonomy of these subgovernments allows and encourages end runs around central authority. Federal agency heads who feel their programs are being slighted by the White House take their cases to their allies on the relevant congressional subcommittees. Aided by the lobbying efforts of subgovernment friends in the private sector, they frequently see their programs restored by a Congress that respects a degree of decentralization that New York's legislative leaders would not tolerate. While committee chairs in New York frequently have cordial relations with their executive branch and interest group counterparts, the tradition of central command is far stronger in Albany than in Washington. Few New York agency heads would even dream of the kinds of end runs around the governor that are commonplace in Washington and many states. Few chief executives in the other forty-nine states are as firmly in control of their executive agencies as are the governors of New York.

As in all bureaucracies, however, there are centrifugal forces. Most agencies have clients, often politically powerful groups, that take a strong and continuing interest in what the agencies are doing. Civil servants, moreover, tend to become protective of their missions: those who work for, say, the state library are trained as librarians, work as librarians, and tend to believe that what they are doing is worthwhile. A governor whose program calls for cuts or changes in the mission of a department or agency is likely to encounter resistance. Despite the relative weakness of subgovernments in New York state, the ability of state bureaucrats and their interest group allies to resist a governor, to end run his directives by appealing to the legislature, the press, or the courts, is not insubstantial. The powers of a governor are not simple powers of command.

Personal Influence

Political power involves skill as well as formal authority. Some of the factors that bolster leadership are not entirely under a governor's control. Those who face a legislature all or partially in the hands of the opposite party, as all recent governors have, operate under significant constraints. Each individual governor, nonetheless, confronts a series of choices about the use of his or her personal and political attributes that make the formal powers work. The essential problem of all chief executives, as Richard Neustadt argued in his classic study of the presidency is "how to be on top in fact as well as name."[30] Neustadt's exploration of presidential power is so brilliantly articulated that it diverts the eye from the conceptual sparseness of his analytic framework. But what Neustadt taught a generation of political scientists is that the formal powers of presidents cannot be explained simply in terms of formal roles: "outcomes are not guaranteed by his advantages."[31]

Some governors come to office with what the press and some sectors of the public perceive as significant electoral mandates. As Thad Beyle puts it:

> The premise is that the larger the margin of victory the stronger the governor will be in the view of other actors in the system. Governors with a wide margin can use that margin politically by declaring that the people overwhelmingly wanted him or her in office so that a particular goal could be achieved.[32]

Because statewide elections in New York tend to be competitive, few of the Empire State's governors have come to office with the kinds of "mandates" that command such immediate attention. Skill and circumstance can combine to turn relatively small victory margins into seemingly significant electoral mandates. Because it came in the context of a significant national shift to the right in 1994, George Pataki's razor-thin victory over Mario Cuomo was widely perceived, for example, as marking a major shift to the right in New York. In the normal course electoral "mandates" have seldom had a great deal of explanatory power in studies of New York governors, and Pataki's more substantial victory in 1998 was typically free of programmatic significance. But Pataki, in his first year at least, proved quite adept at translating press and public perceptions into a significant source of programmatic power.

Staff

Sophisticated studies of political leadership do not offer simple formulas for success. It would be impossible for a George Pataki to replicate the rhetorical skills of Mario Cuomo, and he has not been foolish enough to try. Few governors have been able to exude the personal charisma of a Nelson Rockefeller, none have had his kind of money. All of the successful ones, however, have surrounded themselves with talented aides, marshaled resources effectively, and been able to use their offices to articulate policy agendas to both the legislature and the public. New York's governors have an unusual degree of formal freedom to choose their governing teams. The law provides them with large personal staffs, generously enough paid to attract top-flight people (many earn in excess of $125,000 a year); and the power to appoint most agency and department heads. A tradition of legislative deference allows wide latitude in deciding who to appoint.

In reality, there are political constraints that encumber the power of appointment. While patronage is not nearly so controlling as in the days of the machine, there are groups and individuals with more or less legitimate claims to recognition that range from such abstract considerations as gender and ethnicity, to very concrete demands to include particular individuals or group members in important policy positions. Labor unions, for example, *expect* to be represented in a Democratic administration as the Business Council does with Republicans, not always in terms of specific individuals, but at least in general recognition of their importance in a winning electoral coalition. The sometimes pivotal role of minor parties in New York politics adds still another factor to the range of attributes governors must consider in filling the thousands of jobs exempt from civil service rules. It was almost a given in 1995 that George Pataki would consult with Conservative Party leaders and follow their recommendations in a number of key appointments.

These general constraints seldom limit effective control. There are offices with nice titles and salaries but little effective responsibility to which incompetent but politically important individuals can be appointed. In every administration, moreover, there is a sorting process that takes place in which certain individuals—regardless of formal titles—begin to emerge as key players. In the Rockefeller and Carey administrations, a single individual, William Ronan with Rockefeller, Robert Morgado with Carey—in both cases the governor's personal secretary—emerged as virtual surrogate governors. With

Cuomo and Pataki the inner circle expanded to three or four key players with one of Cuomo's key people, his son Andrew, not even occupying an official office. Because Governor Pataki spends little time in Albany and evinces little interest in the day-to-day problems of governance, power on the second floor has been more difficult to locate, though it has come increasingly to center on the secretary to the governor, Bradford Race, and former communications director Zenia Mucha who is now listed as a "senior policy advisor."

Lower ranking aides and department heads (called commissioners in most departments) drift in and out of the governor's personal orbit. The governor's cabinet—the collective body representing heads of the major departments—seldom meets and has never been an important policy-shaping body. Some department heads are considerably more important than others. When Hugh Carey became governor, he brought his personal physician, Dr. Kevin Cahill to the second floor as a one dollar a year special assistant for health care. Carey's first health commissioner was little more than an administrator; but when he and Cahill picked Dr. David Axelrod for the job, and when Cahill became less active, there was a visible shift in power. Axelrod, who continued as commissioner of health under Governor Cuomo as well, was among both governors' most influential advisers and was unusually free to run his own department and even to extend its influence into areas previously under strong local control. It is rare for a commissioner to achieve this kind of independence, even within his or her own department as a too powerful commissioner threatens the governor's chain of command.

Equally threatening are such attributes as stupidity, ethical insensitivity, and overt disloyalty. George Pataki took a lot of heat from the press in his first years in office, less from any ethical lapses of his own than from one commissioner's use of a state car to vacation in Florida, and from another's racing his horse at a track he was supposedly regulating. Both Pataki and Hugh Carey had troubles with their lieutenant governors, with both of them—Mary Ann Krupsak in the case of Carey and Betsy McCaughey Ross with Pataki—actually trying to run against their former patrons. These cases, idiosyncratic as they may be, are illustrative of a general dilemma all governors face in trying to put together governing teams. Appointments have symbolic loading. It is politically important, as a rule, to balance one's governing team in terms of gender, region, and ethnicity. When it comes to governing, however, qualities such as loyalty come to the fore and you want to have an administration that, if not in full sympathy with your program, is at least reading from the same page. An administration that is "balanced" is generally difficult to control; but this tends to be less true in New York than in most other states.

What makes New York different in this sense is that the intervening layer on the second floor—the governor's personal staff—is far larger than that of any other governor's. Whether *the governor* runs the bureaucracy in New York, *the executive office* does. Especially through the division of the budget, the executive office is large enough, professional enough, and imbued with a tradition of control that makes it virtually impossible for state officials to take significant actions without having them cleared through the second floor.

Controllers and Controllees

Although it is a problem most other governors would gladly take, the size of New York's executive office presents a challenge of a different sort. More than sixty years ago, when a special commission proposed helping the president through a major expansion of his personal staff, some of the wiser students of public administration warned against too strong a faith in what became known as "salvation by staff." The problem is twofold. On one hand, the larger the executive's staff the more time he or she must spend hiring, firing, monitoring, and motivating his own people. This leaves less time for working with others, such as legislators, journalists, commissioners, and the public. A large staff, on the other hand, is also more difficult to motivate and control and can become "institutionalized," in the worst sense of that term. Few agencies of executive power are potentially more potent than those with real budgetary authority, but as Allen Shick once wrote about the old Bureau of the Budget:

> As it became the institutionalized presidency, the Bureau became separated from the President. With a 500–man complement, the Bureau was just too large and too remote to be the President's own. . . .
>
> An institutionalized bureau could serve every President with fidelity, but it could effectively serve only a caretaker President. It could not be quick or responsive enough for an activist President who wants to keep a tight hold over program initiatives. . . . Over a period of decades, the Bureau had become a rigidified institution. . . . The routines of budgeting and legislative clearance, to mention only the two most important ones, had been solidified by years of tradition-building and practice, and were not easily changeable. It was a labyrinthian task to make even minor modifications in the procedures for budget preparation and review, and in fact, few changes were made. . . .[33]

New York's budget office is neither so large nor unwieldy, but Schick's point applies. By appointing a strong budget director, and through the power of appointment more generally, a governor can set the administration's general tone. But from the budget office down to the lowest levels of the bureaucracy, a tremendous amount of inertia is built into the system. As Martha Weinberg concluded in her excellent case study of Governor Sargent in Massachusetts, "gubernatorial intervention is limited and not even-handed for all agencies. In agencies where there is no crisis, there is often no management on the part of the governor."[34]

As much as New York's governors are empowered by large staff, control is diminished by filtering it through a second layer. Governors are not precluded from dealing directly with their commissioners—as Carey and Cuomo did with Dr. Axelrod—but they risk sending conflicting signals unless they bring their own executive office on board at the same time. On a comparative basis, no governor has more tools at his or her command for managing the executive branch; no governor has a more confusing and complicated a system to work with. Unless he or she is constantly on top of this enormous staff there is a danger of not speaking with one voice. Early in 1998, for example, Governor Pataki and Senator D'Amato jointly promised major initiatives to fight breast cancer. Months later, when the governor instructed his budget office to come up with significant cuts in the budget passed by the legislature, one of the items suggested for veto was a breast cancer initiative. When a strong public reaction brought this seeming contradiction to his attention, Pataki withdrew his veto, but the damage to his credibility remained. Because he is not a "hands on" governor, particularly by comparison with his hyperactive predecessor Mario Cuomo, the Pataki administration has frequently sent conflicting signals of this kind. Yet—again in contrast with Cuomo—the trust he puts in his staff has given it the authority to act with an intensity of purpose not seen in Albany for many years.

Credibility

In dealing with staff, governors have the ultimate sanction at their command: the ability to fire those who refuse to go along. As with most powerful weapons it is best used infrequently and with care. Whatever George Pataki gained from his 1997 announcement that McCaughey Ross would not be on his ticket in 1998, he paid a price in bad press, a perception that he was insensitive to women, and a general feeling among Albany insiders that Pataki was not really in control. Some of his 1998 budget vetoes, which, like the one involving breast cancer, were later withdrawn, have reinforced an impression, as one assemblyman put it, that "this guy's not interested in governing." All cabinet officials and appointed agency heads know that they hold their jobs at the pleasure of the governor. They don't usually need to be reminded; but a governor who gets to the stage at which firing is the only option is probably walking on thin ice.

Most of a governor's other powers are grounded less in command than in respect; even the power to fire someone is not much of a threat to someone who believes that they have less to lose from being fired. Skill is respected in Albany and is part of credibility. By the end of his eight years as governor, Hugh Carey's personal problems had made him the butt of many jokes and negative editorials, but his shortcomings, in the words of a reporter from the *New York Times* "were dwarfed by his stature as leader and the weight of his character. He brought greatness to the office."[35] The mismatch between Carey's public image and his standing among insiders led his biographer to label him "a Rolls Royce engine in a Studebaker body."[36] George Pataki, by way of contrast, does not command a great deal of personal esteem among his Albany peers, is not known for his command of the issues, and is considered by many to have little real interest in the daily problems of governing; but his willingness and ability to go to the public inspires sufficient fear among his detractors to give him a great deal of credibility.

A governor's political reputation—like a president's—is not entirely of his or her own making. If New York's economy follows a national trend into a recession, there is little a governor can do to prevent his poll ratings from following the economic indicators down. What can be controlled, however, is personal reputation: "The men he would persuade must be convinced in their own mind that he has the skill and will enough to *use* his advantages."[37] When McCaughey Ross stood throughout Governor Pataki's State of the State address it could be written off as a mistake. When she was publicly identified with feminist critiques of his budget, his tolerance of diversity could be underscored. But when she testified, at a Democrats-only hearing, criticizing the governor's education proposals, and accused his aides of wire-tapping her office, Pataki's credibility was at stake and her role as lieutenant governor was history.

Public Prestige

Few citizens cared, or even knew about, McCaughey Ross's transgressions. They were, in journalistic terms "inside baseball" issues: the kinds of concerns that fascinated a few thousand fanatic fans but were of little or no general interest. A governor has two very distinct constituencies: on one hand what we might label an "Albany" public of political insiders, including legislators, journalists, lobbyists, and other politicians; and, on the other hand, the general public. What plays with one of these constituencies may not play at all with the other. Mario Cuomo, at the peak of his power, was one of the state's most publicly popular governors, revered not just in the state but throughout the nation. In the Albany community, however, he had few friends, some grudging admirers, and numerous (silent) detractors. In our interviews with Albany insiders we found only two (both on the governor's staff) who really liked him.

Affection may or may not be related to prestige. One of the most enduring questions raised by Machiavelli in *The Prince* was whether it was more important for a leader to be feared or loved. Although Machiavelli came down largely on the side of fear (on the grounds that it is the more enduring emotion), the situation is a bit more complicated in a democracy where the ability of a governor to inspire fear (in the Albany community) may be directly related to his or her ability to engender the love of the voters. Legislators, as a general rule, hate it when a governor goes "over their heads" and appeals a policy dispute to the public; but the ability of a popular governor to get to the legislature through public opinion is enormous, particularly in the age of television. Much of George Pataki's power vis-à-vis the legislature derives from the fear most legislators have of the governor's ability to go directly to the public and make them regret opposition to his positions.

Personal Reputation

The Albany community constantly weighs and evaluates itself: influence shifts on an almost daily basis and the reputations of governors, legislators, key bureaucrats, lobbyists, journalists, and even judges are in constant flux. Given the powers that inhere in the office itself, a governor with good staff, with credibility, and with strong public support is an awesome force. By the middle of his second term, Hugh Carey's public standing was low and he was visibly tired of the routines of governing; yet Carey's firm grasp of the issues and his sensitive ability to make the most of a strong surrounding staff kept his Albany reputation in tact. Conservative gadfly Herbert London once noted that "When Hugh Carey was governor, I disagreed with him much of the time." But, London continued, "Carey did *run* this state."[38] It is perhaps the ultimate compliment.

Dealing with the Legislature

Nothing of consequence has changed since the 1950s in the formal powers of the governor. And it would be difficult to make a case that a Thomas Dewey or Nelson Rockefeller was smarter, more skillful or had better staff than Hugh Carey or Mario Cuomo. Yet if you look at New York politics in the time of Dewey and Rockefeller, or further back to the administrations of Al Smith, Franklin Roosevelt, and Herbert Lehman, it is clear that *their* powers, relative to those of legislature, were overwhelming. Even Averill Harriman, a relatively weak governor in terms of skills and popularity, pretty much got what he wanted from the legislature. The rise of the legislature as a coequal part of the process has revolutionized the nature of New York politics. With Rockefeller, as Norman Adler—political scientist, lobbyist, and gubernatorial aide—has put it, it was "like the Harlem Globetrotters playing against the Saugerties Little League. They were giants with enormous resources. . . . That's simply not true anymore."[39]

Symbolic Politics

It would be misleading and wrong to portray the contest between legislatures and executives as one in which the growing power of one comes simply at the expense of the other. In New York, as in national politics, both executive and legislative powers have grown as governments in general have become more important in the lives of the people. Many issues, once resolved privately or at the local level, have been politicized particularly in the years since Franklin Roosevelt became president in 1933. Astonishingly enough, it is still within the memory of living Americans when the governments of neither the United States nor the state of New York had any significant role whatsoever in such key areas as health, welfare, and environmental conservation. In many areas, a general expansion of government power has resulted in increased powers for both the legislature and the governor.

A good deal of the seeming conflict between governors and legislators, moreover, is more symbolic than substantive. Particularly in a state like New York where both executive and legislative powers are centralized, certain kinds of "conflicts" have taken on an almost ritualistic character. Throughout the Carey and Cuomo years, for example, both governors made it abundantly clear that they would veto any bill proposing capital punishment, and there was always a large enough block of antideath penalty assembly members to sustain the veto. Thus although there was usually a majority in both houses for capital punishment, there was no way its proponents could ever marshal the two-thirds majority they would have needed to override a veto. Every year, however, the senate, sometimes joined by an assembly majority, would pass some form of death penalty bill and send it to the governor for his ritualistic veto. Both sides, of course, would issue numerous press releases, with the Republican's point being to embarrass a Democratic governor and assembly majority on what they saw as a "hot button" issue with voters. To underscore the point, they would usually package their proposal around the most heinous crimes imaginable—what one assemblyman called "the lurid crime of the month bill"—providing capital punishment for such crimes as planting a bomb on an airplane (after the bombing of a PanAm jet carrying many New York state residents), or for the torture-murder of a senior citizen.

Governors frequently propose programs they know will not pass. Mario Cuomo's annual state of the state message was filled with an ambitious agenda of policy initiatives, many of which he himself failed to include in his own budget message. In 1989 the *New York Times* counted almost 150 new program proposals in Cuomo's state of the state address. As Rosenthal points out:

> With so many initiatives it was virtually impossible for the governor to build much legislative support. Nor did Cuomo really try; his style was not that of courting and cajoling. From a legislative point of view, his political leadership was wanting. Cuomo laid out an agenda and then abandoned it.[40]

When governors propose bills they have no intention of pushing, they are not necessarily playing games. Cuomo's eloquent speeches, it could be argued, though not intended as blueprints for that year's public policy, were politically sincere and significant statements of aspiration. In academic terms, he was, arguably, trying to set the policy agenda, using his visibility as a means of initiating a dialogue about new priorities. It is, in Polsby's terms, "the politics of inventing, winnowing , and finding and gaining adherents for policy alternatives before they are made part of a 'program,' and likewise the politics of moving alternatives from the unlikely to possible or probable candidates for inclusion on an agenda for enactment."[41] There are times, to be sure, when a governor's motives are more suspect, when the intent is less to initiate policy change than to reap partisan advantage from emotional appeals to the voters. But whatever his or her motives, no player in New York politics is better situated than the governor to play an agenda-setting role.

The governor is aided in these efforts by being the ceremonial leader of the state. He or she gains and maintains visibility by opening county fairs and new highways, appearing in ads touting the state's tourist attractions, welcoming presidents and foreign dignitaries to the state, and so on. The ceremonial governor is also able to use this nonpartisan role as a means of giving a subtle push to certain kinds of issues, as when he or she marches (or chooses not to) in a gay rights parade, to give a speech (or not give a speech) at the annual dinner of the American Civil Liberties Union, or to visit a newly opened wildlife refuge. The governor, moreover, however much he or she chooses to play a leadership role, is the preeminent member of his or her party in state.

Party Leadership

How serious various governors have been in attempts to change the policy agenda is not always clear. There are times when it is charged, not without justification, that attractive policy proposals are put forward less to move them to an agenda for enactment than to get good ratings from the public. Policy proposals, particularly those contained in the governor's budget message to the legislature, can also be strategic in intent, that is, a governor will propose something he knows the legislature will not accept in order to later trade it for something else. School funding has almost always been such an issue. Every recent governor has sent the legislature a budget that, if enacted, would result in cuts in state aid to many local school districts. The governor knows that the legislature will restore the cuts, but hopes to get something back in exchange.

Whatever its purpose, the usual focus of symbolic politics is the public. Republicans pushed the death penalty in the 1970s and 1980s to make Cuomo, Carey, and Democrats in general appear out of step with public opinion. In 1998, Governor Pataki outflanked assembly Democrats in his push for "Jenna's law" by using a crime victim's family in an emotional series of television appeals. In the ideal party government, the purpose of these symbolic battles is to underscore, for the benefit of the electorate, the philosophical differences between the parties. Purists might argue that most of these appeals are demagogic, but there is little doubt that they can be effective in forcing legislative action.

The governor is, in theory at least, the leader of his or her political party. In the responsible party model, governors and their fellow party members in the legislature present a program to the public, attempt to enact it, and run for reelection on their records in office. That model has never worked particularly well in New York. Governors Dewey and Rockefeller, to be sure, dominated the Republican Party. For two decades, they were able to control both the executive mansion and the Republican contingents in both houses of the legislature. Through adroit uses of patronage and centralized campaign fundraising, they were able to overwhelm even the stronger county organizations. Unfortunately for the advocates of responsible parties, the Democrats were seldom able to provide a cohesive opposition. On the rare occasions when they were able to gain legislative majorities, squabbling between county leaders and between regional factions was intense. After Rockefeller, moreover, the Republican Party also began to fragment, not so much along regional lines as between the assembly, senatorial, and gubernatorial wings of the state party. The sudden absence of Rockefeller's money, as former majority leader Warren Anderson has suggested, forced senate and assembly Republican leaders to develop their own campaign organizations or risk having control to slide back to the county organizations.[42]

Since 1994, state Republicans have, as noted in Chapter 4, increased the coordination of both their campaign and research operations, but it is un-

Box 6.3

The Speaker Blinks

On rare occasions an individual member can force the legislative leadership to change positions on controversial issues. Assemblywoman Nettie Mayersohn did just that with what came to be known as the "Baby AIDS Bill."

Hospitals in New York routinely perform blood tests on most newborn babies in order to provide a public health base on certain diseases. In the early years of the AIDS epidemic, many activists were opposed to the disclosure of the results of these tests to the mothers of HIV-positive babies, on the grounds that the knowledge that they were going to be tested and informed might drive many HIV sufferers underground.

Arguing that "any mother would want to know," Assemblywoman Mayersohn was horrified by the idea that someone could know a baby had tested positive for AIDS and not tell the mother. She introduced legislation early in the 1990s to unmask the test and inform the mother.

Both AIDS activists and many feminists reacted strongly against the bill as an invasion of the mother's right to privacy (since it was her blood that had to be tested in order to evaluate the baby's). Assembly Health Committee Chairman Dick Gottfried agreed with that position, as did a majority of the Democrats on the committee where it was routinely held for session after session.

The longer the bill was held, the angrier Mayersohn—a smallish grandmother from Queens who herself was on the health committee—became. She went to war. Through a barrage of press releases and meetings with the editorial boards of media across the state, she started obtaining editorials calling upon Speaker Silver to get the bill out of committee and onto the floor where it had the votes to pass. Many Republicans jumped on the bandwagon effectively repeating Mayersohn's line that "any mother would want to know." Letters began to trickle into members' offices. The Speaker finally decided the issue was getting too big to contain and decided to push the bill through.

Since Gottfried was still opposed on policy grounds, the Speaker reached into the committee to get the vote switches he needed to get the bill reported. One progressive woman from New York City was willing to switch, but facing pressures from women and AIDS activists in her district, did not want to cast the deciding vote. As the committee began its session, one known "no" voter after another was called from the room to talk on the phone with the Speaker's chief counsel Fred Jacobs who explained the problem and asked for help.

The Speaker found the extra vote and the bill passed; but those members who said no, including Murtaugh, were not so warmly welcomed in the chief counsel's office for a while. There were no retaliations, but you were hesitant to ask for any favors. Nettie had won.

likely that Pataki or any future governor will achieve the kind of unified operation characteristic of the Dewey and Rockefeller years. Not only do the senate and assembly parties have their own fundraising capability, but individual members have developed financial constituencies of their own. As former Speaker and assembly minority leader Perry Duryea notes, the more independent the assembly party became from the governor's, "the more the individual candidate raised his own money, the more he became separated from the political organization."[43] While members understand the value of party unity *within* the legislature, there are few career incentives for the kind of party unity that cuts across institutional boundaries. Governor Pataki and Senate Majority Leader Joseph Bruno frequently agree on the issues, and Bruno would probably not be where he is without Pataki's help; but Republican senators have both the ability and the motive to maintain a certain level of autonomy. Mario Cuomo almost took pride in *not* becoming involved in legislative campaigns.

The picture we are drawing—essentially one of six distinct party systems, gubernatorial, assembly, and senate for both Republicans and Democrats—while not inaccurate, may underplay the role of the governor as party leader. While governors no longer control the career fortunes of legislators, their ability to set party agendas, or define party issues in their terms (rather than those of legislative majorities) is more extraordinary than ever. Because Governors Carey and Cuomo opposed the death penalty, most voters assumed that assembly and senate Democrats were anticapital punishment as well. While it is true that the crucial one-third of the votes to uphold a veto came almost entirely from Democratic ranks, the issue lost much of its partisan loading when Pataki was elected and the death penalty sailed through both legislative bodies.

The Power of Provision

Some sources of power—particularly those based on reputation and credibility—can be incubated and multiplied; others are scarce, once used they are gone. A governor can dangle a possible appointment to the Court of Appeals before four attorneys, and perhaps hold some of them in his thrall, but once the appointment is made, he has created, as an old saying has it, three enemies and one ingrate. When resources are declining, as they were in Cuomo's last years as governor, his failure to provide continuing or growing levels of support for various constituency groups produced an almost perceptible erosion of power. When resources are relatively abundant, power, used effectively, builds power. Judiciously used, patronage is a potent resource; so is money, especially when people believe you have it to distribute.

New York, in a tradition little changed from the days of boss rule, has given its elected officials an abundant array of goodies to distribute. While civil service reform took most of the operating bureaucracy outside party control, the number and variety of patronage positions remains substantial. There are literally dozens of obscure boards and commissions, some of which almost never meet, that pay decent salaries and provide pension credits for the politically connected. The government is a major customer of everything from prison food and pencils, to iron bars and printing presses. Construction jobs and supply contracts are awarded through competitive bidding, but there are ways of writing specifications or reviewing capabilities that can clearly tilt a job to a politically favored company. In addition, state budgets have traditionally provided both the governor and the legislature with large discretionary accounts. Depending on party, seniority, electoral needs, and clout, an individual legislator may be able to distribute as much as half a million dollars in the assembly and a million in the senate in virtually unrestricted grants to local groups. The press enjoys poking fun at the legislature's so-called member items, special pockets of money cleared through legislative party leaders for special local purposes such as providing computers for Baruch College, promoting Long Island seafood, or supporting a farm museum in Queens. Member items are also subject to attack from partisan politicians. The *New York Times Magazine* once quoted an upstate Republican assemblyman, John Faso, on the uses of these funds for essentially political purposes: "Say with a senior citizens' center in New York City. Those centers become almost local political clubs for the member who got the money," Faso charged. The *Times* went on to note that Faso himself had recently distributed a newsletter in which—under the heading, "John Faso: He Listens and Leads"—the assemblyman boasted of the $22,000 grant he had been "instrumental in securing" for a senior citizen's center in Ravena.[44]

Assemblyman Faso no doubt thought his senior citizens different from those he was criticizing, just as New York City journalists are likely to be more critical of upstate items, and so on; but for all the attention given to these relatively small pockets of money available to individual legislators, it is surprising how little attention is focused on the really large discretionary accounts available to the governor. These come in four primary forms. First, the budget almost invariably puts a bit of wiggle room into the funding for most agencies. These discretionary accounts are expected to be used primarily for unexpected changes in mission as, for example, when an unusually hard winter forces the highway department to spend more than planned on snow removal. In many cases, such as heavy snows, these expenditures are event driven; but they are—whatever the nature of events—discretionary accounts, and the governor, in the final analysis controls them. Thus, in 1998, when Pataki was under heavy fire for vetoing a successful and popular item in the community college budget, he simply restored it by shifting discretionary funds. The governor did not need to specify what programs he was cutting. He didn't know, and probably no one else would, at least until the spring semester when other accounts began to come up short after the discretionary funds were gone.

A second large pocket of money that has not been earmarked is available to the governor in certain parts of the capital budget. In 1996, for example, the voters approved a large environmental bond act that allowed the state to borrow money for projects ranging from land purchases to preserve open spaces, to river dredgings, and landfill closings. Although the act outlined the general terms of how the money would be spent, and the legislature and governor skirmished over some details in subsequent years, the governor basically allocated the funds. While few capital projects are quite as open-ended as those authorized in the environmental bond act, the governor's ability to move capital projects around the state is not inconsiderable. Closely related is a third form of gubernatorial power: his or her ability to move existing jobs from one part of the state to another. Just as Democrats Hugh Carey and Mario Cuomo moved jobs to Harlem and the Bronx (in largely black and Hispanic neighborhoods) so did George Pataki move them out of Albany and New York City into the lower Hudson Valley. In both cases, supporters of the moves cited motives of efficiency and community development. Critics pointed to the tendency for the Bronx and Harlem to be heavily Democratic, and the Hudson Valley Republican.

Finally, governors and legislative leaders have frequently set aside special slush funds of their own, particularly in election years. Although member items in the senate and assembly must be cleared through the leadership—and party leaders take their own district-oriented shares—most budget agreements provide them with additional discretionary funds. The 1998 agreement went further than most in this regard, allowing Governor Pataki, Majority Leader Bruno, and Speaker Silver to divide nearly $1.5 *billion* (roughly 2 percent of the total budget) for unspecified purposes. As the election approached each of these officials managed to find good uses for their shares of this substantial resource.

The Judiciary

Scholars have paid considerable attention to swings of power between the legislative and executive branches, but substantially less to the role of the judiciary. Perhaps taking a cue from Alexander Hamilton's description of the courts as "the least dangerous branch," there has been a widespread, though diminishing, disinclination to look at the judiciary from the perspective of politics. The image of justice as a blindfolded woman is designed to suggest a blindness to bias, and a sense of being above the rough and tumble of politics. In reality:

> Although some judges deny it, courts occupy a significant position in the policy-making process by ratifying choices made by legislatures and governors, by interpreting their policies (and thus adding or subtracting to their substance), and by vetoing policies when the courts declare them unconstitutional. Moreover, they routinely exercise discretion as they impose the norms specified by statutes and administrative regulations while ruling on the disputes brought before them. Thus judges are very much the kinds of officials who might be held responsive to the electorate.[45]

Selecting Judges

The question of whether judges should be elected or appointed has been debated throughout the history of the state. Opponents of the electoral system argue that some of the best qualified attorneys are the kinds of people least likely to subject themselves to the rough-and-tumble of a political campaign, and that some of those best able to run are least likely to have judicial temperaments. While "judicial temperament" is difficult to measure, most studies of state courts do not show that judges elected in partisan elections differ much from those selected through gubernatorial appointments or nonpartisan elections.[46] A study of the 324 state supreme court justices appointed in the fifty states between 1980 and 1981 found that states with merit appointments had significantly fewer Catholics and Jews but more blacks than states with elected justices, but that there were no significant differences in their legal backgrounds or experiences.[47] If elected judges are not exactly mirrors of their communities, neither are their appointed counterparts.

A more telling argument against the election of judges is that it is unseemly. The ethical codes of the bar association prohibit campaigns based on issues, and candidates usually avoid indicating how they might rule on specific cases. Interest groups, however, are under no such constraints: the $7 million California campaign against chief justice Rose Byrd and two other justices in 1986, based on the issue of the death penalty, stands out as a particularly ugly case that demeaned both the court and the process. Besides, regardless of how a campaign is run, it requires money. Jacob Fuchsberg's 1973 campaign for a seat on the New York state Court of Appeals cost the then shocking sum of more than half a million dollars, and his extensive use of emotional television commercials narrowly skirted bar association rules on issue advocacy. Although Fuchsberg turned out to be a better judge than expected, his campaign so alienated many people that the constitution was amended to give the governor power to appoint judges of the Court of Appeals from a list of candidates selected by a state commission on judicial nomination, with the approval of the senate.

Various attempts to amend the constitution and make other judgeships appointive have failed, although, ironically, the argument for depoliticization may well be strongest at the lower levels of the system. Perhaps the outstanding example of deficiencies that inhere in the system of electing judges is found in New York City's system of surrogate judges. The county surrogate's job is essentially that of probating wills, normally a routine task. When someone dies without a will, however, it is up to the county surrogate to appoint a lawyer to handle the estate. Since the lawyer in question can be paid as much as one-third of the total inheritance plus fees for his or her services, the business can be quite lucrative. Under the provisions of the Code of Judicial Conduct, a judicial candidate is forbidden to know the names of campaign contributors, but there is no way to enforce this rule. Surrogate campaigns in New York City are financed almost exclusively by lawyers who specialize in probate; these lawyers, in turn, receive almost all of the probate assignments.

The nexus between campaign support and judicial decision making is seldom so clear, though there is little doubt that—throughout the system—the major contributors to judicial campaigns are lawyers. There is, on the other hand, a strong argument to be made for local electoral control of the judiciary. As the most democratic system of selection it provides some assurance that the judiciary will be reflective of local community norms and changes in social values. The system, whatever its defects, has worked quite well producing a history of fairness, efficiency, and even distinction. If party hacks, mountebanks, and charlatans occasionally slip past the voters, there is no guarantee that appointed judges—appointed, in the final analysis, by party politicians—will be any better.

The records of the parties in choosing judicial candidates vary enormously. In New York City's borough of Manhattan, where the Democratic nominee is virtually sure of election, the reform Democratic clubs have long insisted on a prescreening of candidates by a panel of supposedly nonpolitical lawyers. Since these reform clubs took control of the county organization in the 1970s, the caliber of judicial candidates has increased and the quality of the bench has been higher in Manhattan than in the outer boroughs. Politics is still very much a part of the process, deals are made, and the voters seldom have a real choice on election day; but very few really bad judges have slipped through the screening process. As one recent study of the screening panel system concluded, "merit selection produces a younger, more representative, better educated, highly qualified and more politically diverse judiciary."[48]

Critics of the Manhattan screening panels argue that the system serves simply to change the nominating elite by transferring real power to the bar associations and elite lawyers who comprise the screening panels. Party leaders may no longer be in control, but neither is the electorate. Much the same thing happens in many upstate counties where the party organizations frequently cut deals to cross endorse a "bipartisan" slate of judges. Each party agrees to nominate only its negotiated "share" of potential judgeships (say, one of the three seats up that year). As in areas where one party dominates, the effect of such deals is to take control away from the electorate and lodge it in the hands of party leaders. While it may be true that the electorate serves as an ultimate check on the worst of these insider deals, the fact is that judges are seldom actually chosen in competitive elections: the system is essentially a fraud.

Even in competitive districts there is some question as to whether any system of election brings forth the best judges. Describing his own campaign for the Court of Appeals, former chief judge Sol Wachtler concedes that he and his Republican running mates "weren't exactly picked for our judicial talent. I was picked because I was a downstate Jew who could get votes. Gabrielli was picked because he was an upstate Italian who could get votes. Hugh Jones had never been a judge. He had been president of the state bar association."[49] Nor did a screening panel take politics out of the equation. Wachtler had at first been rated "unqualified" by the Nassau County Bar Association. "Only after the matter went before the association's board of directors, which was conveniently packed with Rockefeller's friends, was Wachtler declared 'qualified.'"[50] That Wachtler, by most accounts, became an outstanding jurist does not exonerate the system; most legal scholars are more comfortable with the present system of an appointed Court of Appeals. Whether the system can be changed at the lower levels is another question entirely. Attempts to make fewer judgeships elective have been popular neither with legislators (some of whom aspire some day to run for the bench), lawyers (ditto) nor with ordinary voters.

Politics and the Courts

An appointed judiciary can be every bit as much political as one that is elected. Indeed a case can be made that almost everything judges do is in some sense political. What our system of justice tries to sustain is a courtroom environment in which decisions are made according to the participants' perceptions of the facts of the case and the relevant laws. If this process were as automatic as it sounds, few cases would come to trial, far fewer than the 3,322,045 cases filed in New York in 1993.[51]

The United States is one of the most litigious societies in the world, and New York has more lawyers per capita than any American state. The reach of the courts into crime, business, housing, family relations, health, and almost all aspects of daily life is enormous and growing. But as much as the role of the courts is expanding, their proportionate share of government power has been in steady decline. New York, like all of the fifty states save Louisiana, is, technically speaking, a common law state. Judicial rulings are based on a long series of precedents running back through prerevolutionary colonial courts to those of seventeenth-century England. The history of law in New York, however, is one of growing codification. More and more, courtroom procedures, rules of evidence, criminal sentences, and the definitions of criminal behavior are determined by statute rather than litigation. At the time of the revolution most crimes were so-called common law crimes, that is, the meaning of such offenses as assault, rape, manslaughter, and murder was derived through the principle of *stare decisis* from a long string of precedent cases. By the end of the nineteenth century, virtually all of these rulings had been embodied in or superseded by statutory definitions, that is, by laws enacted by the legislature and signed by the governor defining—often in considerable detail—the various shades of meaning of offenses like murder, voluntary and involuntary manslaughter, reckless endangerment, depraved indifference to human life, and so on. The penal code of 1891 actually abolished the concept of common law crime. No act, it read, "shall be deemed criminal or punishable, except as prescribed or authorized by this Code, or by some statute of this state."[52]

Codification of the civil law was a bit slower in reaching the legislature, and common law traditions continue to play a somewhat stronger role in civil as opposed to criminal cases; but what has happened in both arenas is clear: the power to define what the law is has moved steadily if not decisively from the courts to the legislature. This move won the day, in part because it coincided with two complementary aspects of modernization: the professionalization of the legal system, on one hand, and the depersonalization of the legal process on the other. In colonial days, most trials truly involved juries (and judges) of one's peers: they were community events involving people who usually knew each other well. Questions of guilt, damage, and liability were decided both by considering the legal issues and the people involved. An upstanding citizen could almost always get away with more than the village ne'er do well, and strangers and outsiders were likely to be treated very harshly indeed. In many larger communities, "less than half of all felony defendants went to trial . . . in others they were 'tried,' but in slapdash and routine ways, in trials that lasted a few hours or a few minutes at best. And most were convicted."[53] The move toward codification and away from common law crimes was fueled, in Friedman's words, "by that pervasive feature in American legal culture, horror of uncontrolled power. Lawmakers believed that courts should be guided—ruled—by the words of objective law, enacted by the people's representatives; nothing else should be a crime."[54]

New York, under the leadership of the jurist David Dudley Field (1805–1894), was at the forefront of the move toward codification, and for many years the statutory reforms he proposed and that were adopted in New York and other states were known as the Field Code. Field's argument in support of statute-based law has been well summarized as follows:

1. Judges should not be lawmakers, as they are under case law.
2. Codification will make the law "cognoscible" to laymen, who cannot understand case law.
3. Codification will make the law systematic and clear, so that prediction will be more reliable.
4. The code will permit flexibility and interpretation and will not be a straight-jacket.
5. Even an imperfect code is better than none, no nation that has once adopted a code has ever gone back to uncodified law.
6. The code can be amended as imperfections develop.[55]

The argument against Field, as articulated by members of a bar association committee chaired by the prominent attorney James Coolidge Carpenter, was, as Patterson summarizes:

Judges will continue to make law after the code is adopted, because they will be unable to apply the code to novel situations without resorting to the case law that preceded it. Furthermore judges will torture the language of the code to mean what they think it should mean.[56]

The code, Carpenter's committee continued, would be no more accessible to laymen, nor more predictable or easier to master. If "phrased in very specific terms," it would prove "arbitrary and unjust for new cases, and the judges will have to distort the language to cover them"; yet if left more open-ended, "A code will impede the growth of law since amendments can come only after the mischief has been done; a code overgrown by amendments will be an incoherent mass."[57] Although Field's arguments won the day, the legal system's preference for judicial interpretation has continued to be an important part of the common law tradition. As Patterson says, "Carpenter's assertion that the judges would resort to the case law which preceded the code was confirmed by the New York decisions interpreting Field's code of procedure, which for half a century after its enactment in 1848 was rendered partly ineffective by historic interpretations."[58] There are many ways in which this is true even today.

Almost all major modifications of the statutory code are made at the appellate level because these are the courts that focus on interpretive rather than factual questions. Indeed a case can, as rule, reach an appellate court only when the losing party in a trial alleges that the judge has either misinterpreted or misapplied the law. How much latitude the judges should have in ruling on these questions has been the source of many arguments, with those surrounding recent nominations to the U.S. Supreme Court often becoming quite heated. There are important issues at stake.

Judicial Power

Statutes passed by the legislature, signed by the governor, and codified in *McKinney's Laws of New York State*[59] form the backbone of both the criminal and civil laws. They create the entitlements, crimes, prohibitions, and penalties that give rise to legal disputes. Those disputes that cannot be negotiated are brought to the courts, which must interpret the ways in which the laws in the code apply to the particular case. Sometimes, governors and members of the legislature are not pleased with these interpretations and a whole new round of lawmaking takes place in which they try to restate their "true" intentions. This new statute becomes what is known as a "pocket insert" in *McKinney's* (it is literally a page or pamphlet inserted in a pocket in the back of the relevant volume to update the law between editions of the full volume), and it becomes the starting point for future legal disputes.

Reaching and Self-Restraint

A judge who wishes to change the direction of the law must operate within the constraints of a system of separated powers. He or she must recognize the importance of balancing legislative and judicial policies: courts that reach too far in revising statute law are likely to be effectively "overruled" by subsequent statutes. Mindful of the ability of the governor and the legislature to revise the code, and even to alter the structure of the courts themselves, even the most activist judges tend to practice some form of what scholars call "judicial self-restraint." With regard to the supreme court of the United States, most scholars would agree with William Lasser's argument that "the modern Court has achieved its power and influence by distancing itself from precisely those issues capable of creating full-scale crises and thereby revealing the limits of its political strength."[60]

In a similar manner, New York's Court of Appeals has largely avoided an activist role in policy areas that might most threaten its relations with the governor and legislature. As noted in Chapter 5, for example, the court has refused to give teeth to the state constitution's seemingly clear guarantee of the "aid, care, and support of the needy," holding instead that it is up to the legislature to decide who is needy. They have similarly steered clear of the fight over equity in educational funding, defining it again as a largely political question to be left to the other branches. In playing its activist role primarily in the areas of criminal procedure and civil rights, while leaving economic issues largely to the governor and legislature, New York's courts have essentially followed the national pattern once described by Justice Lewis Powell as follows:

> The irreplaceable value of [judicial review] lies in the protection it has afforded citizens and minority groups against oppressive or discriminatory government action. It is this role, not some amorphous general supervision of the operations of government, that has maintained public esteem for the federal courts and permitted the peaceful coexistence of the counter-majoritarian implications of judicial review and the democratic principles upon which our Federal Government in the final analysis rests.[61]

Judge Wachtler expressed much the same kind of thinking, though expressing it in a more positive vein, when he argued that, "There is a place for judicial restraint. But the protection of such things as individual and privacy freedoms is a uniquely judicial obligation and responsibility. Judicial restraint should not be confused with judicial abdication."[62]

Building a Record

Most judges, however strong their personal feelings, operate in an atmosphere of enormous restraint. They fear not only the possibility of arousing the sleeping giants of legislative, gubernatorial, and public disapproval, but also the judgments of their judicial peers. Most judges don't like to be reversed by higher courts. Most of the time, moreover, the cases that confront judges—even at the appellate level—do not raise profound policy issues. Indeed it is a rare case that matters much to anyone but the people in the courtroom. Taken individually, few court cases involve anything more than dispute resolution; only in the aggregate, over time, do they produce important changes in public policy. Even trial courts, in the long run, make policy. Indeed one of the ironies of judicial policy making is that its most profound impacts may come in areas attracting the least public attention. Tarr cites the shift in child custody cases as an example of such change. From an automatic assumption that the best interests of the child could be served only by awarding custody to the mother, divorce cases have increasingly weighed a number of other variables in the decision and given fathers an increasingly important role.

> In sum, then, cumulative policymaking occurs when the courts, by deciding a series of essentially similar cases, in effect define policy in a given area. Although legislation or rulings by appellate may circumscribe the range of judicial choice, trial judges often retain considerable leeway in deciding individual cases. In exercising this discretion, judges rarely announce broad policy standards. Indeed, they may give little consideration to the broader policy their decisions are creating. Nonetheless, the results of their decisions constitute the state's policy.[63]

When courts do strike out into new areas, the savvy jurist recognizes the importance of what might be called the doctrine of seeming restraint. The more dramatic your decision—and this is a rule that applies to legislators and governors as well as lawyers and judges—the more important it is to be sure of your facts and be meticulous in marshaling them. In his halcyon days on the Court of Appeals, Sol Wachtler was, in the words of his biographer, "a consummate coalition builder . . . . willing to compromise for the sake of presenting an image that the court was cohesive, even when it wasn't."[64] Criticizing his predecessor as chief judge, Lawrence Cooke, for his failure to compromise, Wachtler once argued that "when you go into new areas of law, it is important that the imprint be a strong one. The perception out there when you had a 4–3 decision is . . . that the decision was tentative and could be overturned in a couple of years. I thought it very, very important that . . . the new court come out as unanimously as possible."[65]

The Who of Policy Making

Judge Wachtler's emphasis on consensus reinforces a theme that has persisted throughout this chapter. Power in politics derives largely from the ability to build enduring coalitions, to convince other people in politics to make the necessary deals to get at least part of what they want. People skills are a very important part of political leadership which is, in no small part, the ability to bring people together.

Political power is also a function of knowledge. Cases are often won in court because one lawyer presents a better argument than the other. Court decisions are more likely to stand when they are well argued. Our discussion of power in this chapter has focused largely on the more manipulative aspects of the power struggle in Albany and around the state. It should not obscure the fact that many legislators, governors, and judges gain power through rectitude: they succeed because other people believe that what they are doing is right.

Politicians and government officials, judges not excluded, seek power. Few people run for public office for the money. Some do it for prestige; most do it because they want to change the way things work, they want to be "players" rather than spectators. The road to being a player—whether as lawmaker or bureaucrat, judge or governor—involves, perhaps more than anything else an ability to sense where you and your goals fit in with your environment. It is also essential to know the rules of the game, the "how" as well as the who, what, and why of the game.

7

Making Public Policy

The legislative process in Albany flows, like a deep river, on two levels. Below the surface there is a steady stream of relatively "trivial" legislative activity: laws are crafted to bring New York into compliance with new federal guidelines, to allow two local governments to merge, to take account of a new medical procedure, or to change the tax laws to account for the increasing popularity of equipment leasing. These laws are "trivial" only in the sense that they seldom attract the attention of the mainstream media, the general public, or even most members of the legislature. They are important, in the cases cited, to those who live in the affected communities, or need the new medical procedure or lease properties. A lot of what happens in Albany, in Washington, or in most state capitals is this kind of ordinary, everyday, routine business.

Closer to the surface of the legislative river are the bigger, more controversial issues that may even be covered on the nightly news: fights over the budget, welfare reform, rent control, or abortion. This stream of legislation in New York concerns a broader public and evokes a different kind of legislative politics, a flow that is far more centralized, usually more visible, and frequently more partisan than that which runs at the lower depths.

What has happened in Albany over the past few decades, and at an accelerating rate in the Pataki years, is that the strong currents of partisanship and centralization have deepened, cutting increasingly into the normal flow and markedly centralizing the process. With more and more items brought to the surface, logjams and delays have become increasingly commonplace. The "policy space," to use a concept developed by the late Aaron Wildavsky, has become more crowded and policies keep bumping into each other. Party leaders link policies together, not because they have any tangible relationship to one another, but to secure bargaining points. Thus, in recent years, budgets have been held up long after the major actors have agreed in principle on the major money issues. These budget agreements have, in effect, been held political hostage to such seemingly unrelated issues as workmen's compensation reform (in 1996) and the extension of New York City's rent control laws (in 1997).

This chapter divides the policy-making process into a series of stages that move from agenda-setting through decisionmaking, implementation, and enforcement. As useful as these signposts are, it is important to remember that the actual process is less sequential than continuous. Today's decision often becomes tomorrow's agenda. One legislative aide described to us a transportation bill she helped draft in 1988. In consultation with various interest groups, local officials, and experts in the department of transportation, the bill went through three or four drafts before passing both houses of the legislature and being signed by the governor. In drawing up the detailed regulations (the "regs," as they are commonly called in Albany) needed to implement the law, officials in the Department of Transportation (DOT) discovered technical flaws which were corrected in a new law, passed by the legislature and signed by the governor in 1989. By 1992, with both enforcement officials and the affected groups agreeing that the law was not accomplishing all that had been intended, it was revised again. By 1997, a somewhat different constellation of affected groups was back before the legislature arguing for still further changes in the law which, when enacted, produced yet another set of revised DOT regulations.

If an issue such as this were controversial enough, it might further feed back not just into demands for new policies but for new political configurations as well. A distinction between politics and policy making can be as misleading as the attempt to divide the process into artificial stages: contests over leadership positions are seldom without policy implications, and vice versa.

Transportation groups, if they were upset enough about the policy in question might try to change the people by making appropriate campaign contributions, lobbying for leadership changes, or seeking to change the Department of Transportation's powers or personnel. They might also try to shift the battlefield away from the legislature and into the courts by bringing various kinds of lawsuits challenging aspects of the program.

The Normal Legislative Process

The governor's annual budget bills go directly to the legislature from the second floor. All other bills must be sponsored by legislators. Even a "governor's program bill," which may embody a major policy of the administration, must be introduced by a state senator and a member of the assembly, usually by the chairs of the appropriate committees. There is no requirement that such bills be introduced at all, and some are not. In 1985, for example, 18 of the 105 program bills proposed by Governor Cuomo were not introduced.[1]

Once introduced, legislation follows a fairly predictable track. Most legislation goes nowhere, or rather is "held" in committee, where it is said to have "died." To become law, a bill must not only get out of committee, but do so in both the senate and assembly, be passed in both houses in the exact same form, and be signed by the governor. In recent years, members of the senate and assembly have typically introduced more than twice as many bills as are introduced in the next most prolific state, Massachusetts. Many of these bills are redundant; indeed some are exact copies of each other. On average, about a thousand bills are favorably reported by assembly committees, slightly fewer in the senate, and almost all reported bills pass their respective houses. A quarter of these bills will pass only one house of the divided legislature. Somewhere between 700 and 800 bills will pass both houses in the same form and be sent to the governor, who will veto about 10 percent. Thus in 1996, a total of 15,639 bills were introduced, 813 were sent to the governor, he vetoed 95, and the legislature (in a rare move) overrode one of his vetoes. The year before, 777 laws were enacted, of which 67 were vetoed. For the statistically inclined, a bill introduced in New York state has about one chance in twenty of becoming law.[2]

The Origins of Legislative Issues

Members' motives for sponsoring legislation vary, as do member attitudes toward legislative activity. Some members—minority party members in particular, but also those who Barber classifies as "spectators"—focus primarily on constituent services and are relatively inactive in this phase of legislative politics.[3] For others, as one assembly aide put it, "Constituent service and all that is important; but legislators like to score points, and you score more points with legislation." Many bills are introduced with no real legislative intent. A bill can be, as one member put it, "a great way to get people off your back." Even if doomed to failure in this session, a bill serves as a publicity device aimed at future legislators, or as a statement of principles designed to contrast with other bills. In 1985, a fairly typical session, the average number of assembly bills introduced was fifty-six per Democrat and thirty-two per Republican, with higher seniority members, committee chairs, and party leaders the most active.[4] A handful of Republican bills, essentially those dealing with local issues, had a realistic chance of passing the assembly; most were introduced to make a point. In 1985, the mean number of bills to survive the committee process to a formal vote on the assembly floor was 12.5 for the Democrats and 2.3 for the Republicans. Figures for the senate, with the opposite political loading, were about the same.

A bill that does not pass in one session must be reintroduced in the next or it will be dropped. A large proportion of those that fail will show up again: old bills, it seems, never die. One of the first functions of a legislator's staff at the beginning of session is to dust off last year's bills for reintroduction. This process is often so routine that one member, upon being asked about a bill he had introduced every year for twelve years, promptly sent a note to the chair of the committee to which it had been referred asking that it be withdrawn: "Oh my god," he said in our interview, "is that turkey still around?" Sometimes members copy bills from one another. One freshman assembly member, who had narrowly defeated an incumbent in the Democratic primary, instructed his staff simply to reintroduce all of his predecessor's bills.

Fortunately for this member as for most, the laws of copyright do not apply to legislation. Frequently the copying flows across state lines with the result that:

> Statutory precedent grows as case-precedent grows. . . . Legal science call this the doctrine of *stare decisis*. The legislative process is similar. For example . . . Connecticut adopted a statute relieving the operator of a motor vehicle from liability to a guest except for "wilful or wanton conduct." Twenty three states followed that lead. Described in juristic language, the legislatures have followed the rules of precedent, the statute has been copied. The result is the same.[5]

The proportion of bills borrowed from other states (Horack uses the phrase *stare de statute* to describe the process) has increased in recent years, in no small part because of the proliferation of national associations of state legislators connected both by annual meetings and the Internet. Interest groups and the press can also play a role in bringing bills from one state to another. Businesses that operate across state lines have a strong interest in statutory uniformity; and the national meetings of environmental groups, unions, and so on are a fertile source of legislative cross fertilization.

But legislators need not look to other states for ideas when they can find them closer to home. In Schneier's study of the bills in the state assembly, 11 percent of the bills considered were borrowed, received, or simply stolen from other members; and another 6 percent came from the senate.[6] Only one of the bills transmitted from one assembly member to another came as a gift, in this case from a committee chair to a freshman Democrat from a marginal district. Muggings were far more common. Indeed bill theft has the status of a fine art in some offices. One majority party member who shared a media market with a legislatively active minority party member developed a source in the printing office who would provide advance warning of his rival's legislative initiatives. Taking advantage of a little-used rule that allows a member to "reserve" certain bill numbers, he was able not only to steal his bills, but to give them a lower number and thus give the impression that he was the victim of theft rather than the mugger.

Agenda Setting and Initiation

Tracing the true paternity of a bill is tricky enterprise because participants in the process often lie. Staff persons and lobbyists often try to hide their true roles even as politicians generally exaggerate theirs. A more serious research problem is that the path of innovation is frequently complex. In the mid-1980s, for example, the breakup of Bell Telephone's near-monopoly on phone service had a substantial impact on the property tax base of many New York communities whose elected officials came to Albany seeking relief. Although the legislature took these requests seriously, no one felt sufficiently competent to develop a legislative solution to a very complicated technical issue. With the administration offering little help, the legislature created a commission to study the problem. Its report served as the basis of a bill, endorsed by the governor and introduced by the chairs of the appropriate senate and assembly committees. This is a bill with parents, godparents, foster parents, and guardians, many of whom might claim true paternity or maternity. What we tried to do, in classifying the origins of complex bills such as this, was narrow the list of key participants to the original source of agitation and the actual initiator of legislative action. In the present case, the sources—those who first identified the problem as one which might have a governmental solution—were the local officials who came to the legislature seeking help. And the legislative initiators—those who devised the particular form a legislative remedy might take—were the members of a government commission. The distinction here is similar to that made by Anderson and other students of public policy between "agenda setting," which establishes the general parameters of policy problems, and "initiation," which is the "development of appropriate and acceptable proposals for ameliorating" these agenda issues.[7]

In many instances, the distinction between agenda setting and initiation is moot. In 1985, for example, a member of the assembly—ordered by his physician to reduce his salt intake—was frustrated to discover that few food labels provided the necessary information. Acting as both initiator and agenda setter he introduced a bill requiring sodium labeling. Even in a seemingly simple case such as this, others were involved. By his account, the assemblyman used an existing law requiring sugar labeling as a model and drafted his bill by simply substituting the word salt for sugar every time it appeared. Clearly a twofold scheme overlooks the role of other important forces that

Table 7.1

Source and Legislative Parent of 100 Legislative Proposals in the New York State Assembly, 1985–1986

Legislative parent	Original source of the idea for legislation						
	Member	Staff	Lobby	State	Local	Other	Total
Member	16	3	5	3	15	10	52
Legislative staff	0	2	1	3	3	0	9
Lobbyist	0	0	11	1	0	0	12
Governor or state agency	1	0	0	5	5	0	11
Local official or constituent	0	0	0	2	9	2	13
Other	0	0	0	0	1	2	3

Source: Edward Schneier, "On the Origins of State Legislative Issues: The New York State Assembly, 1985–86," paper delivered at the 1987 Annual Meeting of the Southwestern Political Science Association, Dallas, Texas, March 18–21, 1987, p. 15.

are sometimes involved in the development of legislative issues. But since all bills have a starting point—the point at which someone says "there ought to be a law"—and a point at which they become concrete proposals, these are the points analyzed in Table 7.1.

What this table shows most strikingly is the extent to which members of the assembly are themselves policy entrepreneurs. They think in terms of making laws. In the 1985–86 session 17 percent of the ideas for new legislation came from members themselves, and more than half of the legislative solutions crafted to meet these problems and others were devised by legislators. The second most common source of legislative issues was local government officials, a finding which—given the nature of state-local relations—is not surprising. Every time a local government wishes to change its boundaries or tax rate the only recourse of local officials is the legislative process. If there are surprises in Table 7.1 they arise in connection with the limited roles of interest groups on one hand and the executive branch on the other.

Low levels of interest group activity in initiating legislation fly in the face of traditional observations. Writing in 1979, one scholar went so far as to say that, "Although a problem may achieve agenda status in a variety of ways, the primary and most frequent sponsor is the formal interest group."[8] Groups are an important source of ideas for legislation; but even allowing for the reluctance of either legislators or lobbyists to acknowledge their true roles, failure to find more than one bill in five originating with lobbyists points up the essentially defensive nature of most lobbying. Business groups in particular are more concerned about staving off government action than encouraging it. Many groups, moreover, recognizing that close identification with a special interest can be a kiss of death, prefer to work with agendas devised by others.

The Role of the Governor

More striking than the relatively small role of interest groups (sources of only twelve of the 100 bills) was the surprisingly small role played by the governor and executive agencies in initiating legislation. Fourteen bills had their sources in executive actions; but in half of these cases the bills were designed to overturn executive actions rather than to fulfill program requests. These figures are misleading in that the sample did not include budget bills where governors have tended—with increasing frequency—to place many of their key programs. But the fact is that neither the governor's office nor the bureaucracy has been a major source of policy innovation. Governors, like presidents tend to be involved "at the margins" of legislative gestation, and even those who have appeared dominant "were actually facilitators rather than directors of change."[9] Most governors come into office, particularly in their first terms, with agendas based on promises made during their campaigns: Pataki's promise to reinstitute the death penalty, for example, made capital punishment an issue in the 1995 session; but even a change-oriented governor like Pataki did not overwhelm the legislature with a complex package of ambitious legislative proposals. Mario Cuomo, who frequently did produce large portfolios of program bills, seldom pushed his own agenda, tending to use his legislative agenda more as a political symbol.

Ideas for legislation are seldom in any real sense "innovations"; most changes in public policy involve incremental shifts in existing law.[10] Frequently the ideas for such changes come from those most affected by existing policies: constituents and local government officials in particular. Bureaucrats tend to be more cautious, preferring to work around laws that are working badly than to propose new laws. Most people with ideas for changes in policy, moreover, tend to take their problems right to the legislature which is itself the source of more than half of the actual bills proposed in Schneier's study, and, we suspect, in most legislative sessions. Most legislators not only like to introduce new bills, they do so frequently.

The Art of Drafting

Each lawmaker is assigned a legislative bill drafter to put legislative concepts into the proper bill form. The bill drafting offices of the two parties in each house are staffed by highly valued professionals whose skill can avoid considerable legal problems if bills become law. Some bill drafters gain expertise in certain types of legislation, and getting the services of a competent specialist in drafting legislation is one of the favors legislative leaders can grant to junior members. At the same time, bill drafters work for the leadership: unlike the house and senate offices of legislative counsel in Washington they are not bipartisan. Even if they do not always put the leadership's spin on issues, they can be slow to draft bills that go against party policy, and they may keep the Speaker or majority leader up-to-date on bills that might cause problems.

Tensions between bill drafters and politicians are common. As one bill-drafter wrote:

> Our drafting conference proceeded smoothly as long as the discussion centered on the broad objectives to be accomplished by the new legislation. But, as always, there were subordinate policy issues of which the committee had not thought until the draftsman raised them and requested the committee's instructions. Which of two administrative bodies should be entrusted with enforcement of the statute, or should an entirely new authority be created to carry the policy into execution? How severe should the sanctions be, and what procedural rights would be guaranteed to persons affected by the statute without interfering too much with its administration?[11]

These tensions do not normally arise when a bill is introduced for symbolic reasons; and the fact is that many bills are introduced with little prospect of becoming law. Even when a member is simply trying to float an idea for discussion, the relationships between central staff and individual legislators reflect party control. One junior legislator worked with a lobbyist to develop a new approach to school funding. His assigned bill drafter arrived with five other central staff people who kept pointing up the complexities of the issue. For months the proposal languished in bill drafting until quite suddenly a leadership bill, only slightly different in its approach, appeared. The junior member stopped pushing for his own bill. Had he been more senior and secure in his relationship with the Speaker, he might have been offered something in return for going along—leadership, as noted in Chapter 6, is a two-way process—but the essential fact is that bill drafting, as much as any part of the legislative process in Albany, flows through party leaders.

The Asking Price

For the legislator proposing a policy initiative, there are a number of strategic questions that must be addressed. First among these is what Schneier and Gross call the asking price:

When a person thinks of selling a car, three figures usually come to mind: the price one would like, the price one expects; and, finally, the asking price. If sellers ask too much, they run the risk of frightening off would-be purchasers. If they ask too little, there is no room for bargaining. Framers of a bill face the same problem. In the case of appropriation bills . . . the considerations are identical. Like those selling cars, 'Agencies do not usually request all the money they feel they could profitably use.' At the same time, it is important not to ask too little. If you don't do some 'padding' or leave room for bargaining, you find, in the colorful words of one official, that 'you get cut and you'll soon find that you are up to your ass in alligators.'[12]

The problem does not apply only to money bills. Many of those most active in the right-to-life movement—those from the Catholic Church in particular—would prefer a ban on all abortions and contraception as well. But although some states once had laws of this kind, New York was not among them and would be highly unlikely to ban contraceptives today. Nor is it likely that the public would support a ban on all abortions, or that the courts would accept it. Rather than fight battles they know they will lose, the movement has therefore focused on issues that (a) have some prospect of becoming law, and (b) dramatize their central concerns. Thus the movement has targeted issues like late-term (so-called partial birth) abortions and parental consent. By seeking more limited objectives, the movement has both a better chance of legislative success and the ability to use these more popular proposals as levers for raising the public's conscience.

Packaging

The state legislature is allowed to have multisection, nonfiscal bills. That means the you can amend a lot of laws in one overall bill, which is sometimes called an "omnibus bill." Care is usually given as to which section of the existing law is amended first as that could determine which committee of jurisdiction could receive the bill. More important, since the governor's line-item veto extends only to bills increasing state expenditures, it is possible for a clever bill drafter to "hide" controversial changes in larger packages of popular proposals. The advantage of a narrowly drafted bill is that it focuses attention on the issue in question and limits the list of potential groups whose opposition might be aroused by a broader measure. The more limited the scope of a proposal, in other words, the less the chance of its being dragged down by peripheral issues. If, on the other hand, your goal is to push something controversial, it is sometimes best to surround it with a package of more popular items in an omnibus bill. This strategy is often used to please both sides in a difficult bargaining situation: in 1997, for example, the governor's proposal to cut local school taxes was not popular with assembly Democrats who objected to its caps on school spending; the governor was not pleased with Democratic attempts to extend prekindergarten classes and reduce class sizes. Since neither side quite trusted the other, the solution was to put both the tax cut and the smaller classes in the same omnibus bill.

The packaging of bills is more important in New York than in Congress or in most other state legislatures. This is because the New York state assembly and senate have a long tradition of not amending bills, neither in committee nor on the floor. Provisions buried in an omnibus bill must be accepted or rejected as part of the package. This is true as well of budget bills and is one of the reasons party leaders have tended to load more legislative language into the budget.

Whatever the package it comes in, the sponsor of legislation must also decide how specific to be in detailing what actions will be covered, who will enforce the policy, and so on. Leaving it to the administration to develop the specific rules (the "regs"), is fine if you trust the administrators. Vagueness can also make it easier to get a bill through the legislature. The less you say about how, when, and where, the easier it often is to get agreement in principle. More serious problems arise when trust breaks down. Both Warren Anderson and Ralph Marino frequently skirmished with Mario Cuomo, but they generally trusted him—once an agreement was reached—to follow through. Assembly Speaker Silver has not, by most accounts, developed that kind of trust in Governor Pataki. Some of the problems Silver, Pataki, and Majority Leader Bruno have had in reaching agreements on budget issues have derived from the assembly leader's insistence on crossing the ts and dotting the is either in the budget bills themselves or in side memorandums specifying how funds will be allocated.

Relation to Existing Legislation

Another key decision a legislative draftsperson must make is whether to create a new statutory title or amend existing language. The problem is confounded by the fact that many existing statutes have been substantially modified by subsequent regulations and court rulings. In some fields of policy, the revised statutes and regulations are so dense that it is almost impossible to add to them without repealing some old rules and revising others.

Every bill must be accompanied by a memorandum explaining the bill's general provisions and, if necessary, including a "repealer" section showing just which existing laws will be eliminated. There is, however, no legal requirement that these memos be true, or, in fact, that bills themselves be clearly written; sometimes, in fact, they are quite misleading. While most of these errors are probably unintentional, deliberate deception is not unheard of. A classic case of deceptive bill drafting was once perpetrated by the late Robert Moses. The story, as told by Robert Caro, is as follows: in 1924, Moses, as head of the Long Island Park Commission, drafted a bill defining the commission's powers. Buried in the bill was a clause empowering the commission to acquire land by condemnation and appropriation "in the manner provided by section fifty-nine of the conservation law." To most legislators, the word appropriation meant simply "an allocation of funds by the legislature," and none of them thought there might be anything worth checking in the 1884 laws. But Moses knew, as Caro writes, "that in that section 'appropriation' had quite a different meaning. Worried in 1883 about incursions by lumbering companies into the Adirondack forests, the legislature empowered the Conservation Commission to condemn the forests to preserve them. But during that year, between the start of condemnation proceedings and the actual transfer of title, the lumbermen stripped the parcels of their trees. In 1884, therefore, the legislature passed an act—section fifty-nine of the conservation law—empowering the state to 'appropriate' the forest lands and defining 'appropriation' as a procedure in which a state official could take possession of the land by simply walking on it and telling the owner he no longer owned it.[13]

The growth of legislative staff makes it far less likely that a contemporary Robert Moses could pull so blatant a power grab, and some forms of deceptive bill drafting are prohibited by the constitution and legislative rules. But the growing complexity of policy issues increases the likelihood that new statutes will impact on old in ways that even their sponsors may not have predicted. New York's Court of Appeals has established an office to deal with legislative relations, and both the governor and the attorney general have shown growing interest in the question, but many areas of law have become so complicated that confusion is built into the process.

Sponsorship

The first big decision after you know what you want is who should be the lead sponsor. The lead or prime sponsor is the person who "carries" the bill and who will be the lead debater if the bill reaches the floor. Sponsorship is critical. Most legislation, other than home rule legislation (bills dealing with purely local issues at the formal request of local governments), should be introduced by a majority party member if it is to have a serious chance of passage. Under divided government this can be tricky since it requires finding a Republican in the senate and a Democrat in the assembly. It is even better, in both houses, to have the appropriate committee chair as your prime sponsor.

The question of cosponsorship then becomes important. Cosponsorship of difficult legislation is a sign of political support which can be used to convince the legislative leadership to allow a controversial bill on the floor for a vote. In New York, there are two forms of cosponsorship. Any cosponsor, accepted as such by the bill's prime sponsor, can claim part of the credit for the bill, should it pass. Being listed as a coprime sponsor is a step up that can allow you not only to claim partial credit, but also to be given a "pen certificate" for mounting on your "trophy wall" should the governor sign it into law. (Governors use a lot of pens at bill signing ceremonies). Sometimes the coprimes are the more important sponsors, whose work is essential to getting the bill passed. Many senior committee chairs will give routine "departmental bills" (that is, bills—usually technical in character—drafted by state agencies) to junior members of that committee to "carry" as the prime sponsor. The junior member is the lead debater on the bill if it is debated, and gets the "chapter," as successful legislation passed into law is sometimes called. (Most legislation is introduced as a chapter amendment to existing laws). The committee chair will then become a coprime sponsor, just to send a signal, and to be able to join in the floor debate if opposition appears. In some cases, a member can gain a measure of immortality through his or her role as a prime sponsor. While few modern state-supported co-op owners know anything about former assemblyman Alfred Lama or Senator MacNeil Mitchell; they know that they live in what everyone calls "Mitchell-Lama housing."

When Murtaugh first became an assemblyman in 1980, it was common to cast a wide net in seeking cosponsors. A bipartisan list of cosponsors—sometimes even including coprimes—was considered an asset in the assembly and, more important, in gaining senate cooperation. This is seldom true today. Indeed it is unusual for an assembly Democrat or senate Republican even to send a "Dear Colleague" letter to members of the minority party. Within party ranks, you are faced with the choice of making specific requests to strategic members asking for active support or just sending out a description of the bill with an opportunity for members to sign up as supporters. While there is certainly strength in numbers, the more the merrier, it can sometimes hurt to dilute the credit-claiming possibilities available to key players if you limit your search for sponsors. And in the perverse logic of politics, a long and strong list of cosponsors is sometimes viewed as an indicator of weakness rather than strength: if you have the support of both the committee chair and party leadership, why do you need coprimes?

The Wind Tunnel

Former assemblyman Jerry Nadler (now a congressman) describes the Albany legislative process as "a big wind tunnel where you can see legislation go in at the front, but you sometimes don't see what happens to it inside that wind tunnel until it is too late. You just know that it is not coming out the other end. There are a lot of places inside that wind tunnel where your bill can stick and your job is to track its progress as closely as you can." Congressman Nadler tells of one piece of legislation that he was trying to pass on behalf of some statewide women's groups. Former state senator Mary Goodhue was the senate sponsor, and there was considerable concern over the bill's chances in the state senate where the issue was more controversial. The women's groups therefore concentrated their lobbying on Senator Goodhue and her colleagues. They were so successful that Senator Goodhue's strong support of what was really a Nadler bill persuaded the senate leadership to put the bill high on its "trade list" with the assembly at the end of session. The assembly top staff negotiators saw this concern and held the Goodhue bill hostage for a bill the assembly had on their trade list. This was a miscalculation. The senate would not do the assembly bill, and by the time assemblyman Nadler found out it was too late to get the bill to the assembly floor in time to be passed that year. It passed the next session, but unexpected problems like that one can sometimes be fatal.

In examining legislation before the assembly, former chief counsel to the Speaker, Ken Shapiro, liked to ask three basic questions: "Who is for it? Who is against it? How much does it cost?" The answers to these questions, and assessments of their political weights, can give a rough idea of your bill's chances. Even when the forces are with you, however—when support is strong, opposition weak, and resources abundant—there are no sure things in politics. The extreme fighting bill, discussed in Chapter 4, shows how quickly the winds can change.

The wind tunnel in Albany, as Congressman Nadler now concedes, is far less mysterious and complex than that in the Congress. In Albany, success depends essentially on convincing your party's leadership that the bill is worthwhile, and upon the party leaders, in turn, convincing the governor and the leadership of the other house that the bill should go forward. Although there are in Albany—as in Washington—many places in the legislative wind tunnel where a bill can mysteriously or perversely become stuck, the general rule is essentially the same: it takes only one negative decision to kill a bill, it takes many positive steps to make it into law.

Moving a Bill

Having drafted a bill and whatever cosponsors seem useful, one hopes that the leadership will accept your suggestion for committee referral. A friendly committee chair can be very helpful. The bill must receive a sponsor's request for committee consideration (called a "99 request" after the form that is used in the assembly, or a "form 63" in the senate). Many times, when a bill will not be passing the committee, a majority party sponsor will receive a phone call from the chair's office, asking that the bill be "held at sponsor's request." This saves the chair from having to give the committee a negative recommendation, saves the sponsor's colleagues on the committee from choosing between him and the chair, and saves the sponsor from the embarrassment of losing in committee. Even when they have the votes to win, most sponsors withdraw such bills because they know that inventive chairs can find other ways to kill bills further down the road.[14]

The most visible legislative proposals tend to be governor's program bills or those sponsored by the legislative leadership. Program bills are usually taken seriously but are likely to pass only when they have leadership support. Generally speaking, program bills from a Republican governor will not be taken up in the Democratic assembly until after they have passed the senate (and vice versa). Bills that list the speaker or senate majority leader as lead sponsor are generally considered sure things in their chambers, but have no particular standing in the other body. "Departmental bills," though not of the same status as governor's program bills, are also given serious attention at the committee level. Indeed departmental bills are usually carried by the chair of the committee of jurisdiction or someone he or she has designated for the honor. Such sponsorship does not mean that the committee chair necessarily supports the legislation. Sometimes a committee chair will sponsor the bill to control or even kill it. A bill sponsor cannot guarantee whether a bill can pass, but he or she generally *can* control its not passing, and will be consulted about revisions. No bill moves unless the lead sponsor approves, or unless the leadership folds it into negotiations on the budget. Sponsor control even applies to sending a bill to the governor after it passes both houses. The house that passes the bill first controls its submission to the governor, and the sponsor will play a key role in timing the process. Sometimes bills can be sent to the governor's desk and pulled back before the ten working days limit for the governor to veto. This also is part of bill negotiations, where the governor's office may need more time. Twice in the history of the legislature, bills that were passed by both houses never were officially submitted to the governor. Although there is no legal justification for such withholding—senate and assembly rules clearly mandate transmittal—it may be politically convenient to ignore the rules. It is unlikely that a lawsuit would be sufficiently timely to produce action, or that the courts would not rule the issue essentially political and let the bill die.

Dual Committee Reference

There are three committees in each house that have "dual reference" power. These are the codes committees, the ways and means committee in the assembly and finance committee in the senate, and the rules committees. The codes committee can only demand jurisdiction (called a "flag" for the mark that is put next to the bill on its cover page), if the bill affects the criminal code. The ways and means and finance committees can only "flag" bills that have fiscal implications. In theory, the committees should only consider the bill's criminal code or fiscal implications, and not the particular merits of the bill. The reality may be that you will have to fight for the bill on the merits all over again in each committee as if they were committees of jurisdiction. The ways and means committee in particular is known as the Bermuda Triangle, as there are bills that go in and are forever lost. What is particularly difficult about this committee is that it rarely schedules public debate. The committee staff can make a negative recommendation, the chair will report that recommendation, and the bill is dead.

Bills that are introduced early in the legislative session and are reported out of the standing committees reach the floor each week and are put on the legislative calendar that is published each Monday. Starting in about mid-April the number of bills reaching the floor increases to a point to where the rules committees take jurisdiction. Thereafter, only bills that are reported by the committees go to the floor. Although the rules committees of the assembly and senate differ in some respects (see Box 7.1), they are both essentially agents of the majority party leadership. Thus the end of session flow of legislation is regulated almost entirely by the Speaker and senate majority leader, a source of considerable power. One sure sign that the legislature is nearing adjournment is the line of sometimes quite senior members queued up outside the speaker's chief counsel's office, looking to get their bill either reported to the floor, or put on the assembly trade list. Much the same happens in the senate.

When a bill is sent to the floor from a committee it is given its first "reading" and printed on the senate or assembly calendar of bills. The next day that the calendar is printed, the bill is on second reading. Not until it appears on the official "Order of Third Report" can it come to a vote. The rules committee can make special exceptions, saving a day in the process, by reporting bills to the "Order of Special Report." And the governor has the power to compress the process into a single day by issuing what is known as an "order of necessity." These fast-tracking devices are usually important only in the hectic days either of putting the budget together or during the end-of-session rush. They are important in New York because of its tradition

Box 7.1

The Rules Committees

Both houses have rules committees, but there are significant differences in how they work in each house and under different leaders. In the senate, the committee has tended to hold regular public meetings. Often, in fact, lobbyists have been known to attend senate rules committee meetings to see what bills will be appearing on the senate calendar. The assembly rules committee is similarly comprised largely of senior members and is only supposed to serve the largely routine function of routing and pacing the legislative flow of traffic. This limitation on the power of the assembly rules committee was a reform that the Democratic study group—a caucus of liberal, more junior members—negotiated in the mid-1970s to open the flow of legislation to the floor. Although the argument was made that these limitations did not challenge the power of the Speaker, since he already had the ability to influence what came out of the standing committees in the first place, few Speakers have been comfortable with the reform, and the assembly rules committee has seldom actually met. "The rules committee." as one committee chairman puts it, "meets in the Speaker's hat." Generally its role is to function as a front for the Speaker's staff deciding in what order bills will reach the floor during the end-of-session rush. This is essentially true of the senate rules committee as well, though some majority leaders have also used the committee as a sort of party executive committee communicating between the party leadership and the other members of the party conference.

Knowing that there would be a court challenge to the reapportionment bill, Speaker Weprin formally convened the committee in 1992 to make sure that every technical requirement was being met. The meeting was announced off the assembly floor to take place in the Speaker's conference room while the legislature was in session. At the announcement members looked at one another and asked, "Who is on rules? Am I on the rules committee?"

of not amending bills. Thus if the assembly will only agree to a senate bill if it contains a particular clause not in the original senate bill, the only way to amend the senate bill is to report a new draft out of committee which would otherwise have to "age" three days before coming to a vote.

Almost as quickly as bills move to the floor they can be moved back off, usually through a process known as "starring." The sponsor of a bill may at any time request that a star be placed on his or her bill on the calendar. In the senate, stars may also be placed on bills by the majority leader, a power relinquished by the Speaker in the Democratic study group reforms of the 1970s. A star may only be removed by the sponsor or, in the senate, by the majority leader. In practice, of course, stars are almost always leadership devices as it would be folly for an individual legislator to try to pass a bill that the leadership opposes. As a general rule, stars are used to provide bargaining time, to give party leaders and concerned lobbyists the time to work out deals with the governor and the other house of the legislature.

Voting

Bill sponsors having live bills on third reading should be prepared to debate them when they are called by the clerk. Typically, the clerk will call the bills on third report in the order listed and votes will be taken without debate on those that are not controversial. A special consent calendar allows these routine matters—mostly dealing with local issues—to move quickly unless there is dissent. When all of the noncontroversial bills are disposed of, debate on the controversial bills begins. Although the majority party is always in firm control and almost never loses a vote, debate can be surprisingly vigorous and, from time to time, influential. Even the usually irrelevant minority party can be important if it uncovers real substantive problems in a bill. Minority party arguments, moreover, may portend the kinds of problems a bill may encounter in the other house. On major bills, if significant arguments emerge, the leadership will usually recess to the party conference room for a candid, intra-party strategy session. If the really unexpected has happened, a bill at this point may be starred pending preparation of a new bill. Generally, however, mid-session party conferences are used to count heads, make sure there are enough votes to pass the bill, and discover how many members, if any, will be voting with the opposition.

Almost no decisions in the New York state legislature are made by voice vote or show of hands. Virtually every significant issue is decided by an electronically recorded, roll call which becomes a matter of public record. There are three kinds of roll calls. Most common are the so-called fast roll calls that were designed to expedite consideration of less controversial bills. In a fast roll call, the clerk calls the names of the first and last persons in the alphabet, and the majority and minority leaders ("Abbate, Wright, Bragman, and Faso" in the 1999 assembly). Every member who has activated his or her electronic device is then recorded as having voted in the affirmative *whether they are actually present and voting or not.* Those who wish to vote no must push the no button and have their names specifically recorded. Similar to fast roll calls are "party votes." Here the party leaders agree to record all of their respective members as voting in opposition to one another: exceptions, as in fast roll calls, can be made, but unless a legislator specifically requests otherwise all Republicans will be recorded as voting no, let's say, and all Democrats yes. It is a rare day that individual members make such requests.

Slow roll calls are the most fun to watch. Although you know that the majority party is rarely going to lose—the leadership would not have allowed the bill to come to a vote if they hadn't counted a winning margin in advance—there are frequently unpredictable votes. Most interesting are those occasional votes in which the parties do not take positions.

As in Congress and in most states, a variety of organizations rate the members of the legislature on the basis of their roll call voting records. Thus the AFL-CIO evaluates members in terms of their prolabor records, the American Civil Liberties Union in terms of their support for civil liberties, and the Farm Bureau in terms of the percentage of agricultural issues on which individual legislators voted a "profarm" position. General "liberalism" scores are calculated by Americans for Democratic Action, with a "conservatism" index from CHANGE-NY serving as its mirror opposite.

The End of Session

It is hard to describe exactly the "end of session rush" in the last few weeks of the legislative year. This "crunch" time has to be witnessed to be fully appreciated. Legislative sessions invariably end with a flurry of activity marked by two to three weeks of intensive work, usually capped by a weekend, and an all night session that can last well past dawn. In almost all legislatures, the flow of business follows the same pattern: early in the session there is a flood of initiation with dozens, even hundreds of new bills coming from the printer every day. This flood of proposals slows to a trickle as the session winds down, but the pace of enactment flows in the opposite direction. In the early months, while the leadership's attention is focused on the budget, committees are getting organized, and bills are being circulated for cosponsorship, almost nothing happens on the floor. A tourist, venturing into the senate or assembly chamber on a cold Tuesday in February might see the legislature convene, spend an hour or so welcoming various visiting groups, engage in perfunctory debate on one or two bills (already defeated in the other house the year before), vote, and adjourn. That same tourist, arriving in the heat of late June would see bills debated in a matter of minutes, witness twenty or thirty "fast" roll calls an hour, and a legislature sometimes in session (or in party conference) for upwards of twenty hours a day.

The 1999 session was somewhat atypical in that continuing arguments over the budget kept both bodies in session for a few extra weeks in July and August. But the rhythm of the session was typical. The senate passed 21 bills in January, 53 in February, 154 in March, and 135 in April—a total of 463 in the first four months. In June it passed 789, with almost 500 of these passing just before adjournment on June 14 through June 17. The pattern in the assembly was much the same. In typical fashion more than half of the bills enacted in both houses passed in the last month, with 497 of the session's 1,580 bills passing one or both houses in the last four days alone.

There are a number of institutional reasons that dictate this end-of-session rush. First, it naturally takes time for bills to work their way through the legislature, especially if they are "compromise bills" which feature a lot of negotiations. Second, a lot of tough bills could be negotiated forever if there were not a deliberate feeling of "do it now, or the train will leave the station." This is a concept which forces reluctant negotiators to make some very tough decisions and reach a bottom line that—without a deadline—they might never accept. Third, it is not uncommon, particularly in divided government, for one bill to be linked to another in such a way that, for example, senate acceptance of an assembly mass transit package becomes contingent upon assembly acceptance of a highway bill. The last reason is that many bills are linked politically in passage with other bills that may not be related in substance. All of these bills will be done together. Unfortunately, that can make for some sloppy bill drafting done by exhausted staff members who basically haven't slept much in the last week. The bills are then voted upon by equally tired lawmakers. At the end, this process takes on a life of its own, and nobody really controls the situation. Exhausted lawmakers will be at their desks at 5:00 A.M. waiting for revised bills to be delivered from the printer. The session continues until the bitter end because people are afraid that agreements will become unraveled if too much time lapses after agreement is reached.

Resolving Differences between the Senate and Assembly

In order to be sent to the governor, a bill must be passed in identical form by both the senate and assembly. A bill that has passed one house is treated as a new bill in the other house and referred to the appropriate committee. If the committee chooses to send it to the floor unchanged it is called a "unibill" and, if passed, can be referred directly to the governor. If, on the other hand, the committee chooses to pass its own bill—even if it differs in only the tiniest detail—it cannot become law without further action by the other house. On routine policy issues, when the assembly and senate pass different versions of the same essential bill, the committee chairs or their staffs will meet to see if a compromise can be reached. The assembly or senate may then agree to pass the other body's bill, or entirely new bills—embodying whatever compromises have been reached—in both houses. When relations between committee chairs are not cordial, lobbyists frequently act as go-betweens in these negotiations. On larger issues, and when negotiations fail, they are kicked up to the leadership. In some cases, where both sides generally want to act but have been unable to reach common ground on the details, high ranking staff assistants may attempt—in consultation with their respective committee chairs—to work out a deal. In many cases no action is taken because nobody really wants an agreement. The overwhelming majority of bills passed by both the assembly and senate are, in fact if not by design, one-house bills passed for ideological reasons or as bills to please individual members or lobbyists.

When one house or the other is serious about a bill rejected in the other body it goes on a list of items to be negotiated by the party leaders either as part of the overall budget deal or during the end of session rush. For individual assembly and senate members, committee chairs in particular, and for lobbyists, a key test of their influence lies in their ability to get party leaders to put their bills on the "trade list." This in itself is not easy, but still not enough. Even if the bill is passed by both houses it must still go to the governor before it goes into the books. In Congress and in all but two other state legislatures, differences between the two houses are often worked out in conference committees drawn from the appropriate standing committees of each house.[15] New York has recently begun to experiment with such committees, particularly as we shall see in Chapter 8, in putting together the 1998–2000 budgets; but it is too early to judge them a significant part of the legislative process in Albany. Whether the party leaders of either house would ever surrender their control over interhouse negotiations is problematic at best.

The Governor Votes

If the governor fails to take action on a bill within ten days it becomes law automatically, as it does if he signs it into law. One peculiar feature of New York politics, however, is the relatively high frequency of gubernatorial vetoes. What makes this aspect even more curious is the fact that vetoes in New York are almost never overridden. In analyzing the history of the veto, Zimmerman described the power as "nearly absolute," and the term still applies.[16]

When a bill is sent to the governor, he has ten days in which to veto it or sign it, or thirty days after the legislature has adjourned. Technically, the governor can also "pocket veto" a bill by simply not acting on it after the legislature has adjourned. By custom, New York governors have not used this device, and in recent years could not have since the legislature has not formally adjourned. Stung by various governor's use of the period following adjournment to make unpopular "interim" appointments to the courts and various agencies, the senate and assembly have adopted the practice of "recessing" instead of adjourning when regular business is done. To meet the technical requirements of the constitution, a senator and an assemblyman from the Albany area actually go to the capital every weekday to convene a "session" that lasts just long enough for a quick prayer from the chaplain and a banging of the gavel. In order to give the governor time to consider the enormous flow of bills coming out of the end of session rush, the legislature has adopted the process of also using these mock sessions to spread the flow of bills to the governor. Thus a bill actually passed in June may not formally be "sent" to the governor until September, and it is only then that the ten-day clock begins to tick.

When a bill is sent to the governor, a "bill jacket" is created and the public invited to submit comments. Most affected interested groups, and a surprisingly large number of ordinary citizens, submit statements or letters that are available for examination in the capitol library. Less formally, the governor's counsel has the job of consulting with the top officials of those agencies most affected by a potential new law, and—if there are fiscal implications—with the budget office. Most vetoes are not surprising; many are anticipated and even welcomed.

> Sometimes, as Governor Rockefeller once explained, legislators went along with bills to please individual members as a courtesy on local matters only because they were confident there would be a gubernatorial veto. "I'll be the guy who vetoes the bill," the governor said. This is all part of the act.[17]

Sometimes legislators are surprised when the governor fails to veto a bill. This is apparently what happened in 1994 when Governor Cuomo refused to take the heat and instead signed a bill he was "supposed" to veto giving Staten Island the right to consider seceding from New York City.

Particularly through their line-by-line ability to veto increases in budget items, New York governors have made the veto power a significant source of political influence. They can both block programs and expenditures that they don't like, and use the threat of a veto to secure support for things they want. "Both the item veto and the simple veto," as Muir writes of California, "could be used to break an individual legislator's resistance."[18] Threats of vetoes are also an extraordinarily useful tool in dealing with the Speaker and majority leader during budget negotiations. Although, as we shall see in Chapter 8, there are methods by which the legislature can protect itself from certain kinds of budget vetoes, there is no doubt, as Rosenthal concludes, that the governor's veto is "a source of considerable power . . . [that] allows him or her to negotiate from a position of strength both with legislative leaders and with individual members."[19] What makes it a particularly potent weapon in New York is the persistence of divided government, which makes it virtually certain that one house or the other will be embarrassing its party leader if it votes to override a gubernatorial veto.

The Governor and the Legislative Process

Beyond the veto power, the governor is involved in the legislative process both informally in negotiating with party leaders and formally through budget and program bills, by the exercise of certain procedural powers, and through the issuance of executive orders that carry the force of law. The governor, as we have noted, cannot introduce a nonbudgetary bill without having a member of the legislature as its sponsor. His or her role as the initiator of legislative issues has been limited in terms of the percentage of bills in the assembly and senate that can be traced to the second floor; but the governor's agenda-setting powers are enormous when defined in terms of his or her ability to move issues to active status. Bills that have been languishing in Albany for years—as one-house bills or going-nowhere-at-all bills—achieve new status when they are endorsed in the governor's state of the state address, introduced as program bills, or folded into the governor's budget. Except for their first terms, when there are campaign promises to fulfill, governors are seldom policy entrepreneurs. Whatever new directions they take are usually borrowed from someone else; but no other actor in the system can so quickly and surely make issues viable: when the governor gets serious about an issue, others get serious as well.

Once an issue is in the policy stream, the dynamic shifts again. In many ways, even with regard to program bills, the governor is just another lobbyist. Although he or she can frequently call in the chips with his or her own party members, divided government requires negotiation. Thus in the "normal" legislative process the modern (post-Rockefeller) state legislature has played an increasingly important role rising to a coequal and sometimes preeminent position. But the legislature has never, as we shall see in Chapter 8, been able fully to assert its independence in crafting the budget; and the more that the flow of budgetary politics overlays the stream of other business, the more the governor is again the dominant player. It is also significant, as we shall see with particular force in our discussion of the budget, that the governor gets to go last. Through regular and line-item vetoes, he or she has the last say in the bargaining process. Although it can only be done at some risk to their long-term credibility, governors may even use their veto powers to void deals they had previously agreed to with legislative leaders.

Running on Two Tracks: The Budget and Other Business

The "end of session rush" was made considerably more difficult in the last few years when the budget adoption was so late that it virtually became the end of the session. Traditionally, the year in Albany—or half year as it usually played out—was divided into three segments. The first period, extending roughly from the opening in the first week of January until the first of March, was one of organization, introduction, and preparation. Perhaps the most serious legislative business at this stage was at the staff level in the offices of the party leaders, ways and means, and finance, in preparation for negotiations over the budget. Legislators introduced bills, the governor introduced the budget, committees began to process bills, and party conferences increasingly focused on the budget. Relatively little of substance happened on the floor of either house.

In early to mid-March, the budget takes over almost entirely. Typically, the legislative schedule shifts at this point into a higher gear. Where members had been arriving in Albany on Monday and heading home early on Wednesday afternoon, five-day sessions become the norm. Then when the budget is passed, the pace recedes for a few weeks before rebuilding to the end of session rush. The third phase of the process, historically extending from the budget deadline of April 1 through late May or early June, was the time for home rule bills, revisions in the criminal and civil codes, and most of the major (and minor) proposals for nonbudgetary changes in policy. In 1988 the state's very poor fiscal situation exacerbated tensions between Governor Cuomo and the legislature, and the budget was not adopted until early May. In 1990 it was June. Indeed since 1988 the budgetary process has been finalized in April only three times. This means that stage three of the "normal" process has been compressed, and, to an increasing degree, folded in with the budget.

Since most important budget issues are negotiated by the previously described "three men in a room"—the governor, speaker, and senate majority leader—the last few weeks of the session have taken on an increasingly surreal quality. Prevented by the absence of a budget from moving on to other issues, yet largely peripheral to the main battles, legislators hold perfunctory sessions waiting to be consulted and briefed by their leaders in party conferences. Stuck in Albany in the hopes that there will be breakthroughs in the negotiations, they sit in their offices swapping rumors with lobbyists and with each other waiting for something to break. The legislature's 1998 experiment with conference committees, appointed to work out differences between the houses, made the process more public and involved more members, but the jury is still out on whether they really made any difference.

With characteristic bluntness, former Speaker Mel Miller says, "politics is the budget. Everything else is crap." There are issues that transcend Miller's epithet; but both in temporal and political terms, there is little doubt that the budget has become the 2,000–pound gorilla of legislative politics, crowding or scaring almost everything else out of the arena. It is the subject of Chapter 8. Meanwhile, it is worth noting that the process of policy making neither begins nor ends with the legislature. Governors and bureaucrats make policy; so do the courts.

Administering and Executing the Laws

On the Thomas E. Dewey Thruway between New York and Albany, the posted speed limit varies between 55 and 65 miles per hour. That is the law. Or is it? Both authors can attest from experience that you can go 65 in the 55–mile zones with no fear of being arrested. Generally you can "get away" with 67 or 68; but pass a radar gun at 70 and you almost certainly see flashing lights in your mirror (yes, even if you have "Member of the Assembly" license plates). Since the 65–mile-an-hour sections are relatively new, the rules are less clear: the low 70s are acceptable, but over 75 puts you at risk. What is the "real" speed limit? Is it the 55 and 65 miles per hour enacted by the legislature, or is it the 67–68, 74–75 actually enforced?

Bureaucratic Discretion

While an occasional academic or political reformer rails against the evils of bureaucratic discretion,[20] most students of politics agree that a certain amount of flexibility is not only necessary but desirable. The early twentieth century ideal of dispassionate civil servants neutrally enforcing clearly defined laws has been dismissed as unrealistic. "Without administrative discretion," it is generally agreed, "effective government would be impossible in the infinitely varied and rapidly changing environment of twentieth century society."[21] Nor would most citizens be happy with laws—like speed limits—that were *too* rigidly enforced. A recurring complaint about bureaucracy, as Charles Goodsell perceptively notes, is that in too many instances:

> Individual clients with individual problems are treated as a "case." "A person is far too complex to be effectively processed by a bureaucracy," it has been argued. From the client's standpoint this is certainly so. He or she wants to be treated as an individual because he or she *is* an individual.[22]

There are policy arenas in which the issue of how much autonomy should be granted the bureaucracy is largely technical. The legislature, for example, can set standards for road construction that specify in considerable detail the kinds of materials, thicknesses, gradients, and widths to be used in building new highways; but the particular mix of concrete to be poured in a particular location under varying weather conditions is best left to the people more expert in road building than most legislators. As the early civil service reformers used to argue, there isn't a Republican or Democratic way to build a road. Where that road goes, however, is another question. While few citizens or their legislative representatives care very much whether a road is paved in asphalt or concrete, they do tend to care if it is routed through their homes or someone else's. If decisions such as these are to be made by bureaucrats, we want to make sure that the administrative experts designing the highway are subject to citizen control.

Just what does citizen control mean? In practice it means those most closely affected by the policy, and this is where the problems begin. For many students of politics, the problem with citizen control is that the "citizens" in question are seldom a cross section of the public. In this view, "what public bureaucrats mostly want to do is use the discretionary powers they confer on themselves to advance the interests of the very private actors—mostly the stockholders and managers of counterpart industries—who the bureaucrats were originally appointed to regulate."[23] In its extreme form, this view posits a set of "subgovernments" or "iron triangles" of specialized bureaucrats, interest groups and the relevant subcommittees of Congress (at the national level) operating with virtual independence from the president and Congress.

Empirical evidence supporting the subgovernment theory is spotty, and students of politics have begun to use looser terms like "interest networks" and "advocacy coalitions" to account for the weaknesses of the iron triangles.[24] There remains a sense, however, that "governmental bureaucracies are not controlled by any superior. . . . They have some accountability to Congress and the president, but it is not final."[25] This is less true in New York than nationally. The centralization of legislative and executive powers in New York has seriously undermined the attempts of special interests to construct the kinds of issue networks that can lead to the development of iron triangles. In New York, the budget process gives both the governor and the legislative parties a strong weapon for micromanaging agency decisions. The weakness of the committee system in the legislature, moreover, by weakening a key leg in the structure of iron triangles, makes it more difficult to capture the lower levels of the administration.

This does not mean that the laws are administered without bias. Civil rights groups have long charged, with considerable evidence, that the state police are far more likely to stop and search cars driven by young, African-American males. And many environmentalists are convinced that the Department of Environmental Conservation has been unusually lenient toward General Electric in efforts to remove PCBs from the Hudson River. The suspicion that major corporations and privileged individuals sometimes get special treatment is widespread. At the same time, many business leaders feel that government agencies are too meddlesome, too arbitrary in their decisions to make the economy work well. It is an article of faith among conservatives that through "rigid regulations that escalate the price of doing business, small firms are told directly and indirectly that they aren't welcome in New York state."[26] Larger firms sometimes argue that they are especially singled out by overzealous regulators, and there is often justification for this complaint. State law, for example, prohibits a form of deceptive advertising which features only the low-end price. If a week in Paris costs $899 to $1,999, the ad must include both prices in the same size type. With thousands of products advertised every day, the consumer affairs division of the department of law tends to enforce these regulations only on the largest offenders. Thus a small travel agency can probably get away with an ad that American Express cannot.

A certain amount of unevenness in the enforcement of the laws is virtually inevitable. It would be prohibitively expensive and virtually impossible for the attorney general to monitor every travel advertisement in every newspaper and magazine. Similarly, there is no way that the state's department of environmental conservation could monitor all disposals of hazardous waste. Its policy objective is thus "defined in terms of managing most of the waste, not most of the generators." The technical difficulties of its enforcement job are made manageable by the fact that "fewer than 150 companies produce nearly three-quarter of all the state's hazardous waste."[27] While the burden of law invariably falls more heavily on some shoulders than others, the state of New York has taken a number of historical steps to guard against favoritism and corruption in applying the laws. A few weeks after the federal government passed the Pendleton Act in 1883, New York Governor Grover Cleveland signed a bill establishing a similar state civil service system that provided that all vacancies in the executive branch would be filled by those scoring highest on objective exams, that promotions would be based on merit, and that civil servants could neither be active in politics nor forced to contribute to campaigns. It is also required local governments to implement comparable reforms.

"The New York State civil service system has a reputation as one of the best systems in the nation."[28] Since its establishment, charges of corruption, gross incompetence, and political bias have seldom been heard. One of the key goals of civil service reform was to limit the inclination of government officials to award contracts to other government officials on the basis of politics rather than merit, and in that respect it has been generally successful. Increasingly, moreover, more subtle forms of favoritism have been curtailed by requiring civil servants to implement the laws based on formal rules rather than considerations of the individual case.

Rule Making

In early New York, and even today in some small towns, governments and citizens interacted on a face-to-face basis. Laws were administered by people who were known to their clients, and town officials exercised considerable discretion in deciding how they would apply. Increasingly, however, we have become a society of formal rules. Indeed this shift from interpersonal relations to interrelations based on laws is a hallmark of modernization, and it is also a part of the democratic creed which takes pride in providing what John Adams's original draft of the Massachusetts Constitution proclaimed "a government of laws and not of men." If civil service reform was designed to take politics out of administration, rule making is designed to wash out other forms of discrimination and thus neutralize the bureaucracy.

Administrative fairness comes at a price. The more elaborate and carefully designed the rules, the less flexibility bureaucrats are given, and the more likely it is that citizens will complain of bureaucratic insensitivity. And the clearer the rules, the more complicated they become. As Kaufman puts it:

> Were we a less differentiated society, the blizzard of official paper might be less severe and labyrinths of official processes less tortuous. Had we more trust in one another and our public officials and employees, we would not feel impelled to limit discretion by means of lengthy, minutely detailed directives and prescriptions or to subject public and private actions to check after check. If our policy were less democratic, imperfect though our democracy may be, the government would not respond as readily to the innumerable claims upon it for protection and assistance. Diversity, distrust, and democracy thus cause the profusion of constraints and the unwieldiness of the procedures that afflict us.[29]

What we sometimes rail against as red tape is, in other words, a check on arbitrary action, a means of assuring objectivity and preventing corruption.

Given the complexity of the problems confronting the state, how can such objectivity be assured? Surely we cannot expect a legislature comprised largely of lawyers, teachers, and businesspeople to develop detailed rules governing all aspects of public policy. They can provide general guidelines for Medicare, but it would be absurd to expect the senate and assembly to set reimbursement limits for treating strep throats, removing tonsils, or putting casts on broken ankles. They can set general rules for highway safety but have neither the time nor the training to decide at what point on Route 22 in Hoosick the speed limit should go from 55 to 45 (or should it be 30?). While it is inevitable that bureaucrats must be given some discretionary powers, there must be limits as well, limits that sustain the rule of law. One of the key arguments that Lowi and others have made against delegations of power is that they turn public policy into a series of private deals. If you give administrators too much flexibility, Lowi argues, the citizen cannot know what rules he or she needs to follow: is it safe to go 75 miles an hour in the 65–mile-per-hour zones? Is this a matter of fixed practice, which we can all understand, or of negotiations with a state trooper? The answer, increasingly, has been to delegate powers to the bureaucracy not in the form of individual discretion but through the administrative process of rule making.

> Rules are products of the bureaucratic institutions to which we entrust the implementation, management, and administration of our law and public policy. . . . The rules issued by departments, agencies, or commissions are law; they carry the same weight as congressional legislation, presidential executive orders, and judicial decisions. . . . Rulemaking occurs when agencies use the legislative authority granted them by Congress.[30]

Rule making is a form of delegated power that stands between statutory law on one hand and bureaucratic discretion on the other.

Rule-making power is generally limited by the agency's defined role of authority in general and its specific statutory authority. The law that created, say, the Department of Agriculture and Markets lays out the broad areas of administrative authority that the agency can exercise. Various statutes—a law, for instance, to encourage organic farming—specifies the particular authority to be exercised. At both the national and state levels a number of procedural safeguards have also been built into the process. The federal Administrative Procedures Act of 1946 "was written by Congress to bring regulatory and predictability to the decision-making processes of government agencies,"[31] and in general outline has been copied by many states, including New York in 1975.

Although New York was slow to develop legislative guidelines for rule making, a substantial body of case law had been developed in the courts based on Article 4 Section 8 of the state constitution that requires all rules and regulations to be published and filed with the Department of State. Under the 1975 act, new rules may not go into effect within thirty days of such publication, and until the public has had an opportunity to comment. Amendments to the state administrative procedures act further require each agency to file a statement examining the proposed rule with respect to its:

1. Statutory authority
2. Compliance with legislative intent
3. Impact on the economy and on the government operations of the state and its local governments
4. Impact on affected parties.[32]

A 1978 act created the Administrative Regulations Review Commission (ARRC), comprised of three members of each house of the legislature, to which all new rules must be submitted.

In practice, the rule-making process in New York typically begins with the statute itself and the guidelines it sets for the agency. Before the new regulations are filed with the secretary of state they are cleared through the second floor, particularly if they have budgetary implications. A good lobbyist or well-connected legislator will usually have a pretty good idea at this point of the general outlines of the new regs. While the governor's office often suggests modifications at this point, legislators and lobbyists will usually wait until the public comment period to make their case. Where administrators and legislative committee chairs have good working relationships, preliminary conversations regarding the intent of the statute may have already taken place. In the formal commentary stage, interest groups, local governments, and individual legislators all will be heard from. In about one of every ten instances, the ARRC will contact the agency with objections to a proposed rule. Whether these suggestions come from the ARRC or from individual legislators, "Agencies put a high priority on being responsive to legislators because they wish to foster and maintain positive relationships. When legislators express concern over a particular rule of regulation, agencies consider their comments seriously."[33] If an agency persists, there is always the possibility that the legislature will pass a new law, but the threat of legislation can achieve the same end. The Board of Regents, for example, has long tried to require all students to meet the same standards for achieving degrees; but the legislature has been considerably more sensitive to the special needs of students with disabilities. Thus when the board attempted to set uniform rules, and persisted throughout the review process, a bill was introduced in the legislature to change the statute on which the new regulations were based. The regents withdrew the rule.[34]

At both the federal and state levels, administrative procedure acts have made it difficult for bureaucrats to issue regulations that clearly subvert legislative intent, but some bending of the guidelines is not unusual and may even be encouraged. Those interest groups and legislators that are attentive at the rule-making stage are not always representative of those who were first involved in passing a bill. While all legislators, for example, participate in passing an insurance bill, and while a number of lobbyists may be involved in the legislative process surrounding it, the audience for the rule-making stage is likely to be comprised largely of legislators on the insurance committees and lobbyists representing the industry. "It is clear," says Kerwin, "that the opportunities to participate, which have grown and diversified during the past several decades, have created a rulemaking process in which interest groups are major forces."[35] Rule making thus meets only part of the objection that critics like Theodore Lowi bring to delegations of legislative power: it limits the discretionary powers of those enforcing the laws; but it does not eliminate—and may even promote—the fragmentation of the policy process into a series of deals negotiated by private interests. Kerwin's conclusions apply to Albany as well as to Washington. Rule making, he argues, "is essential."

> It frees Congress to attend to many more problems than it would otherwise have time to deal with. It relieves Congress of the burden of maintaining and managing enormous staffs who possess the expertise essential to refining the operating standards and procedures for a myriad of programs. Finally, it is the best means yet found to break legislative deadlocks and to avoid difficult political decisions. On the other hand, as an indispensable surrogate to the legislative process, rulemaking has a fundamental flaw that violates basic democratic principles. Those who write the law embodied in rules are not elected; they are accountable to the American people only through indirect and less-than-foolproof means.[36]

Rule Enforcement

In most agencies, rule making is separated from implementation. The legislature sets the speed limit, the Department of Transportation decides where the speed limit will go from 55 to 30; but it is the job of a state trooper or local police officer to decide whether going 63 or 70 in a 55–mile-an-hour zone is "speeding." Compounding the problem of rule enforcement in New York is its decentralized system of governance. More than most states, New York places the problem of implementation in the hands of local officials. Thus rule making is separated from enforcement not only by being in a different office but at a different level as well. In the Medicaid program, for example, when the legislature (in 1991) enacted a mandatory program of managed care, it left it to each local service district to develop a specific plan for its patients. Each local plan is subject to state review and must conform to certain basic guidelines, but each plan is separate and distinct from each other; there is, in other words, no state implementation of the rule.[37]

Similarly, the Board of Regents sets the basic standards of educational quality for the state, but actual implementation is in the hands of hundreds of elected and appointed school boards. Local control of education means that the board can mandate various standards of testing, teacher training, and class size, but will need constantly to struggle to see that these minimal levels are actually sustained. The Board of Regents, like most state agencies, spends a good deal of its efforts enforcing both statute laws and its own regulations on local districts. The comptroller's office is also heavily involved in the process of enforcing state rules on local governments. Finally, the courts play an important role in making sure that local governments meet state standards in enforcing the law.

"Contracting out" has not been as popular in New York as in other states, but a number of services are administered by private corporations and nonprofits. Whether it is a private carting firm that collects the trash in Buffalo, or a church's drug treatment center, implementation is removed still another step from hierarchical control. There are strong arguments for privatization and local control, but the price of both is an elaborate structure of audit and control. The more policies are administered by persons who are not directly responsible to agency supervisors, the greater the need for monitoring their actions and assuring equity. Vice President Gore recently estimated that one-third of the federal government's civilian employees were engaged in the job of managing, controlling, and auditing the others.[38] The proportion in New York is even higher.

Corruption and Red Tape

In William Riordan's delightful evocation of Tammany Hall, the party boss, George Washington Plunkitt, carefully distinguishes between "honest" and "dishonest" graft. Taking a bribe, Plunkitt argued, would be dishonest; but seeing one's opportunities and taking them is quite another:

> Suppos[e] it's a new bridge they're going to build. I get tipped off and I buy as much property as I can that has to be taken for the approaches. I sell at my own price later on and drop some more money in the bank. Wouldn't you? It's just like lookin' ahead in Wall Street or in the coffee or cotton market. It's honest graft and I'm lookin' for it every day of the year.[39]

Americans are probably more obsessed with official corruption than are the citizens of most other societies: the laws of both Albany and Washington are larded with checks on graft, whether "honest" or "dishonest" in Plunkitt's terms. As Plunkitt implies, the kinds of self-serving maneuvers we applaud in the world of commerce are frowned upon in government.

There are, in essence, five techniques for limiting corruption: *insulation, competitive bidding, audit, disclosure,* and *the limiting of discretion.* The civil service was created, essentially, to *insulate* the bureaucracy from politics. Because they are not dependent upon politicians for their jobs, civil servants are in theory less likely to be pressured by certain individuals, interests, or communities in making decisions. And just to make sure that they are not getting delayed payoffs, government employees in New York are not allowed to work for private sector employees in their fields for two years after they leave the civil service. There is no doubt that civil service reforms largely freed the civil service from the most overt pressures of political favoritism, but just to make sure that individual bureaucrats do not cut deals of their own, a variety of auxiliary precautions have been built into the system. *Competitive bidding* generally requires all major purchases and service contracts to be advertised in advance and given to the low bidder. Thus if an agency is buying new computers it must solicit bids from at least three companies and buy from the one submitting the lowest bid. To provide still a further check on possible corruption, a third set of controls—involving *audits, disclosures,* and other forms of investigation and exposure—are also required in many areas. Most of the larger agencies have their own divisions of financial audit and control that, together with the office of the state comptroller, regularly audit the books. Government employees are routinely required to disclose aspects of their private lives: many agencies, for example, require periodic reports listing any sources of outside income; most require annual performance reviews; and some require periodic medical exams and drug tests. Special investigations of various agencies and individuals are not uncommon, and of course the press is always interested in stories involving official malfeasance. Even private firms and individuals who work for the state or local agencies are fair game for secret investigations of their finances and aspects of their private lives. Finally, corruption can be controlled by *limiting discretion,* by erecting elaborate systems of rules and regulations that prescribe exactly how decisions must be handled.

While there is no doubt that these checks have reduced the most blatant forms of corruption in state politics, and sharply limited its appearance in local government, the pursuit of integrity comes at a price. While no one has systematically tallied the direct costs of testing civil servants, auditing agencies and contracts, investigating both public servants and suppliers, administering drug tests, processing the forms designed to limit conflicts of interest, and so on, there is no doubt that the direct costs of corruption control are

Box 7.2

Special Prosecutors

Prosecuting corruption has always been good politics for ambitious district attorneys (DAs). Thomas Dewey was propelled into the governorship in the 1940s largely on the basis of his exposure of the connections between various Tammany leaders and the mob in New York City. Perhaps because of the Watergate investigation, which led to the resignation of President Richard Nixon in 1974, federal law enforcement agencies have become increasingly active in investigating and prosecuting corruption by state and local public officials; but there are circumstances under which even these overlapping layers of regular investigation and prosecution do not work.

In 1970, a series of articles in the *New York Times* uncovered pervasive patterns of bribery and extortion in the operations of the New York City Police Department. A commission to investigate allegations of corruption in the city of New York, popularly known as the Knapp Commission, was appointed by the mayor. It found not only that the accusations were true, but that in many cases known instances of corruption had not been prosecuted either by the department's internal affairs divisions or by the city's district attorneys. Because the DAs were, as the commission put it, such "close allies" of the police department, only a special anticorruption prosecutor could be counted on to do the job. In authorizing the state attorney general to create the Office of the Special Prosecutor of Corruption, Governor Rockefeller similarly reasoned that, "only an independent agency . . . can break through the natural resistance of government agencies to investigate themselves or their close allies, can overcome the force of inertia, and can finally deal a decisive blow to narcotics, crime and corruption in New York City."

The special prosecutor of corruption's office continued to function until 1980 when Governor Cuomo concluded that it had done its job. Since then, numerous special prosecutors have, with varying degrees of success, investigated a wide variety of agencies and individuals to the point at which they have become almost a constant force in government. While corruption has by no means been abolished, looming prosecutors have become almost a routine part of the public service.

Source: Frank Anechiarco and James B. Jacobs, *The Pursuit of Absolute Integrity: How Corruption Control Makes Government Ineffective* (Chicago: University of Chicago Press, 1996), Chapter 7.

substantial and growing. There are numerous indirect costs as well. If the copy machine breaks down in a government office, you do not simply go to the store and buy another one, as you might in the private sector; nor can you call a temporary agency to replace a key worker who has been ill. The requirements of competitive bidding and merit hiring that generally guide such acts in government often make it difficult to cope with emergencies of this kind. The number of steps that need to be taken before a purchase order can be processed is extraordinary: in the colleges of the City University of New York (CUNY) it can take months to replace the ink supply of a computer printer. And it takes so many weeks for most suppliers to be paid that many businesses simply refuse to take orders from branches of the CUNY system. In New York, and probably in state and local governments more generally, "The public contracting system is in need of major surgery. It is mired in red tape and multiple levels of oversight."[40] A system of competitive bidding, auditing, and investigation requires those contracting with government agencies to jump through so many hoops that many refuse even to try. A vicious cycle has been created in which:

> The perception that greedy, dishonest contractors are poised to exploit any opportunity to defraud the city has led to more monitoring, double-checks, stringent contract terms, slow payments, and lately the screening of contractors for integrity. In turn, this leads to increased cynicism among contractors who feel that they are being treated like quasi-criminals, and it provides them with a rationalization for further dubious practices. This, in turn, is likely to spawn more safeguards and greater suspicion.[41]

Civil servants are caught in the same trap. Knowing that they might not be able to replace a piece of equipment when it breaks down, they order a new one in advance. Unable to find a contractor willing to work under the conditions specified by law, they rewrite the request for proposals. Lacking authorization to buy a badly needed ink cartridge for the printer they list it as stationary and conspire with a supplier to submit a phony bill. Auditors, in order to combat these evasions of the rules, tighten the rules still further. The cycle continues in no small part because no government agency wants to be caught in a conflict of interest. In the words of one former director of the federal budget office:

> The public servant soon learns that successes rarely rate a headline, but governmental blunders are front-page news. This recognition encourages the development of procedures designed less to achieve success than to avoid blunders. Let it be discovered that the Army is buying widgets from

private suppliers while the Navy is disposing of excess widgets at a lower price; the reporter will win a Pulitzer prize and the Army and Navy will establish procedures for liaison, review, and clearance which will prevent a recurrence and also introduce new delays and higher costs into the process of buying or selling anything. It may cost a hundred times more to prevent the occurrence of occasional widget episodes, but no one will complain.[42]

In a similar manner, government rules designed to protect the environment, encourage minorities, decrease substance abuse, prevent injuries, and guarantee due process—all laudable goals—serve also to increase the cost of government, decrease its efficiency, and tie up the bureaucracy in more red tape. Citizens and politicians often complain about bureaucratic inefficiency, and bureaucrats, as a group, tend to be cautious; but much of what we call red tape is the product of very real, very important concerns about good government. As Kaufman puts it, "the more values the government tries to advance, the more red tape it inevitably generates."[43]

The Legal Process

Structurally, as noted in Chapter 5, the court system in New York is as complicated as that of any two other states combined. Differences between New York City and the rest of the state, between county, municipal, and town courts, and between a bewildering complexity of specialized benches—such as surrogate's courts, family courts, traffic courts, trial courts, and the various courts of the appellate division—make it almost impossible to chart a typical case. Most legal issues in New York, nonetheless, tend to travel one of two well-worn paths. Civil cases, usually involving disputes between private parties, enter the process through civil courts of general jurisdiction and such specialized benches as housing, small claims, and family court. Criminal cases, in which the government is the prosecutor, enter through a trial court system with a separate set of rules and procedures. The systems merge as they move upward, culminating in a single state Court of Appeals.

The Rules of the Game

In both civil and criminal courts, the rules of the game evolve out of a mix of the common law, statute law (which includes agency-drafted regulations), and the rather vague concept known as equity. New York's courts, like those of all but one other state,[44] have their roots in the common law tradition of Great Britain and the principle of *stare decisis*, a Latin phrase that means "let the decision stand." There are still some legal rules in New York that can be traced to a decision reached centuries ago in an English court, but New York has long tended toward a more rigid system of legislated rules and executive decrees. Lacking access to the large case law libraries needed to sustain a common law system, and confronted with cases unique to a new environment, New York and the other colonies began both to develop their own common law tradition and to write their laws into statutory codes. Without access to printed records, "Case law—court decisions—did not easily pass from colony to colony. . . . To borrow statutes (even whole codes) was easier to do."[45] As early as 1664, the Duke's Laws—copied largely from existing codes adopted in Massachusetts and Virginia—were adopted as the prevailing rules in New York, Delaware, and Pennsylvania. Modified by state constitutions, legislative statutes, and the rulings of administrative agencies this basic corpus of statutory law largely supplanted the British common law tradition in governing the operations of the courts.

Just as the U.S. Congress publishes federal laws in constantly revised series of volumes known as the *United States Code*, the collected statutes of New York state can be found in *McKinney's Consolidated Laws of New York*, and *McKinney's Session Laws of New York* which provides annual updates. The many volumes of *McKinney's*—organized by topics such as "Cities," "Real Property," "Assault," and "Evidence,"—have become the guiding text for lawyers and judges in New York. Section 2, line 675 of the New York penal code, enacted in 1881, provided that "no act . . . shall be deemed criminal or punishable, except as prescribed or authorized by this Code, or by some statute of this state," language that would seemingly eliminate judge-made, precedent-based law. But statute law, like the common law, evolves through judicial interpretation: it is illegal under the code to tap your neighbor's phone wire, but does that make it illegal to listen in on his or her cellular phone? The zoning laws permit a town to prohibit the construction of outbuildings. Does that mean that you cannot have a birdhouse on your property? Well, just how big a birdhouse are we talking about? *McKinney's* doesn't cover that question, but case law does. Civil law, even more than criminal, continues to give considerable latitude to judges in cases such as these.

From time to time judges are faced with cases they cannot decide fairly by application of any statute or precedent. Family courts in particular run into cases where punishment of one party or the other would only make things worse. In such cases, judges sometimes apply their equity power, a right to decide according to principles of fairness. Obviously, one judge's vision of fairness may not be another's, just as one's citing of precedent or the controlling statute may not agree with another's. It is in cases such as these that the appellate courts come into play, and their decisions in turn become part of the common law tradition that will guide lawyers and judges in future cases.

Box 7.3

The Agony of Judicial Choice

Cases that actually come to trial are usually difficult ones: if they weren't, they would probably have been resolved by plea bargains or agreements between the litigants. Every judge has had cases on which they would have liked to vote "yes and no," or "maybe," or perhaps "guilty but . . . ." Decisions are often second guessed by the media in ways—frequently ill-informed—that make judges look silly. And the losers in both civil and criminal cases sometimes hold the judge personally responsible: one town justice in the small town of Hillsdale told us she still gets threatening, late-night phone calls from a woman she ruled against years ago in a domestic dispute.

Perhaps the worst nightmare of a judge is that he or she will make a judgment that will come back to haunt. Death penalty cases frequently involve that kind of risk, and there are many judges who would prefer not to take them. But even a seemingly simple case can inspire regret. A few years ago, a family court judge in Albany made a routine decision in a custody case. A father, who had won custody of his two children, was having trouble caring for them and wanted to turn them over to the mother. The mother agreed and so did the judge. The mother had an extensive history of mental illness which was well known to the state office of mental health, but this information was not available to the judge. Six weeks after receiving custody, the woman drowned the children. That decision will haunt him for a long time.

Criminal and Civil Procedure

There are, essentially, four ways that you can find yourself in court. The most pleasant way is to go as a tourist or student to get a sense of how the system works. Alternatively, you can go as a juror, and the chances are very good in New York that someday you will. Using voter registration lists, utility billing records, and tax rolls, persons eligible for jury duty—and this includes almost all citizens—are chosen randomly by court clerks or jury commissioners to appear in the appropriate courthouse for anywhere from a few days to as long as it takes to conduct a trial. A far less pleasant way to get into court is to be arrested. And finally, you can find yourself in court either as the plaintiff or defendant in some kind of civil suit.

Criminal Cases

A criminal case usually begins with an arrest at which time the accused must be informed of his or her basic rights. These include—as anyone who has ever watched a police show on television knows—the right to remain silent, to consult with a lawyer, and to have a lawyer provided to them if they cannot afford one. The police cannot keep a person in custody without going before a judge to determine whether there is probable cause to believe that a crime has been committed. If the answer is no, the case is dismissed. If the answer is yes, the defendant will be indicted and scheduled to appear again. Usually, he or she will be released on bail, a deposit of money that must be forfeited if one fails to appear. A first offender, with a stable home and job will often be released on his or her own "recognizance," that is, a promise to show up at the appointed time. A repeat offender with a high probability of leaving town may be given high bail or denied bail entirely. At this point, responsibility for prosecution shifts from the police to the offices of the district attorney who decides what charges to bring. The defendant is then brought back into court for arraignment and asked to plead either guilty, not guilty, or guilty by reason of insanity. An admission of guilt at this point is equal to conviction and constitutes a waiver of one's right to a trial. All that is left is for the judge to impose a sentence. Most criminal cases end at this point through a process known as plea bargaining, which allows the accused to avoid trial by pleading guilty to a lesser offense. Let's say that A has had a few too many at a wedding reception and is stopped by the police for driving while intoxicated (DWI). In New York, intoxication is defined largely by a blood test in which an alcohol level higher than .01 constitutes DWI and can result in a prison term, a fine, and the loss of one's driving license. Driving while alcohol impaired (DWAI)—showing a level between .005 and .01—is less serious, punishable by a fine and perhaps mandatory counseling. Unless A was in an accident or far above the .01 level, he or she will usually be allowed to "cop a plea." That is, A's attorney will reach an agreement with the district attorney (DA) that her client will plead guilty to the offense of driving while impaired in exchange for dropping the DWI charge. If the judge agrees, a fine is paid, A avoids jail, the DA gets a conviction, and the state is saved the costs of a trial.

When the defendant and prosecutor are unable to reach agreement, or the defendant pleads not guilty, it is up to the judge—or, in the case of serious crimes, a grand jury—to decide whether to bring the case to trial. As much as it saves time and money, plea bargaining is controversial. Conservatives often argue that it allows too many dangerous felons to avoid significant punishment. Civil libertarians argue that the real effect is often to inflate charges, to encourage DAs to seek stiffer penalties than the facts might justify. Ideology aside, plea bargaining has become an accustomed, almost essential part of the process. The statutes that provide uniformity and, in theory, equal justice, cannot distinguish individual cases as the process of plea bargaining often does.

In many jurisdictions, smaller ones in particular, plea bargaining takes place between prosecutors, defense attorneys, and judges who have dealt with each other frequently in disposing of similar cases. A sort of common law of pleas develops in which the outcomes of similar cases in the past set the standards for what is happening now. In some jurisdictions, prosecutors, judges, and defense attorneys have been working with each other for so long that they seem more in cahoots than adversarial. One author goes so far as to describe the criminal court system as a bureaucracy and "the practice of law as a confidence game."[46] While this may be too strong a term to apply to most major cases, the day to day operations of most criminal courts are more bureaucratic than judicial. Traffic courts, which account for about half of the cases brought in most jurisdictions, seldom do more than affirm the recommendations of the arresting officer, and have earned the label "cafeteria courts" for their ability to process their patrons quickly to the cash register. Many trial courts operate in much the same way. It is their business, as Stumpf and Culver write, "to process large numbers of cases quickly and with an element of bureaucratic efficiency. . . . [M]uch of the work occurs in private—meetings between opposing counsel, conferences with the judges in chambers, and so on."[47] In civil court cases, a New York Bar Association study estimated that fewer than 4 percent of the poor in New York had adequate legal assistance; and although the Legal Aid Society and court appointed attorneys provide a minimal level of representation in criminal cases, it is, in most cases, truly minimal. With fewer than 10 percent of New York's lawyers enrolled in pro bono programs, and Legal Aid's case loads often running to dozens of cases a day, most clients' days in court are begun and finished in a matter of minutes.[48]

Assuming that the defendant does not "cop a plea," or that the prosecutor refuses to accept it, or that the judge voids an agreement between the prosecution and the defense, the case goes to trial. At this stage, under our adversarial system of justice, it is up to both sides to make their best case, advancing whatever evidence is in the best interests of their side. They can bring in expert witnesses, introduce physical evidence, and coerce testimony—through the issuance of subpoenas—to persons unwilling to come forth on their own. Because the state has the resources of the police on its side, the defense is given certain accommodating advantages: the state may not, for example, introduce a defendant's prior arrest records into evidence, compel him or her to testify, or resort to evidence gained by illegal means (such as coerced confessions).

Every person charged with a felony in New York has the right to a trial by jury,[49] though that right is often waived by the defendant in favor of a trial before a judge, known as a bench trial. Jury trials begin with the selection of a jury of twelve citizens drawn from lists of voters, taxpayers, and those on the records of various utility companies in the county. Each attorney is allowed to ask the judge to dismiss an unlimited number of jurors for cause, that is because they are obviously prejudiced, and a limited number without specific reason. "Although considerable efforts sometimes go into attempts to fathom how jurors may react to testimony, few attorneys leave a jury trial with the confidence they have at the end of a bench trial or plea negotiations."[50]

Typically, the prosecution begins its case with testimony from the arresting and investigating police officers. As experienced witnesses, the police seldom surprise either the prosecution or the defense, and they are seldom tripped up on cross examination. Yet there is frequently an extended session of technical sparring at this stage as the prosecution tries to show both that the evidence is compelling and that it was properly obtained. In the widely reported California case against O. J. Simpson the defense won acquittal on charges of murder largely by creating the suspicion that the police investigation was both biased and incompetent. Even if the defense cannot sway the jury by impeaching police testimony, the fact that it may lay the groundwork for a future appeal makes this stage of the trial an important one. When other witnesses take the stand, predictability declines enormously. "Ordinary people," as Jacobs observes, "feel great stress on the witness stand, may respond in quirky ways to cross examination, and may display mannerisms that belie their testimony."[51]

The highly publicized Simpson trial left many observers with serious doubts about the ability of juries to deal with emotionally volatile cases. The most thorough investigation of the issue compared more than 7,500 criminal and civil jury trials with the verdicts that the trial judges would have rendered: judge and jury agreed in three-quarters and disagreed in their reading of the evidence in some others, but in only 9 percent of the cases did the judges believe the jury had substantially erred in its legal reasoning.[52] Lawyers and judges divide sharply in their views of the general competence of juries, though most would agree that they are difficult to predict. Both lawyers and judges tend to agree moreover, that the process of jury selection is tediously time consuming. A New York City judge once estimated that he spent "one third of his time . . . in jury selection, one-third in hearing pre-trial motions, and only one-third in actually trying cases."[53] Perhaps reflecting this perspective, the proportion of jury trials in criminal cases has been declining slowly and has become far less frequent in civil cases.[54]

Once the judge or jury has decided the question of guilt, judges impose sentences of more than a year in about 28 percent of the cases resulting in conviction, and prison sentences of less than a year in another 28 percent. The remaining proportion of those convicted were sentenced to time served (because they could not raise bail), placed on probation, given suspended sentences, fined, or required to perform community service.[55] A felon on probation must report periodically to a probation officer and stay out of trouble or face arrest. Those serving suspended sentences can have their jail times reinstated if they are arrested again. Typically, suspended sentences and probation are given to first offenders while those arrested again are likely to do time. While the legislature has refused to back a so-called "three strikes and you're out" law, in which Governor Pataki proposed mandatory life sentences for third-time violent felons, repeat offenders tend to draw maximum sentences. Overall in New York state, the proportion of convicted felons doing time is slightly higher than the national average with between 58 and 64 percent of those convicted between 1989 and 1993 facing incarceration.[56] Because of these high rates and the tendency to impose longer sentences, the number of individuals incarcerated in New York has grown rapidly from just over 45,000 in 1982 to nearly 100,000 in 1993.[57]

Civil Justice

Civil cases arise from the failure of participants to resolve disputes. The plaintiffs in civil cases are usually asking the court to compel other parties to give them something to which they believe they are legally entitled, such as money, a divorce, bankruptcy, damages, custody of children, maintenance of an apartment, an inheritance, or whatever. Law schools tend to divide civil practice into four main areas: torts, which are disputes about alleged injuries; contracts, involving disagreements about the meaning of previous agreements; property; and domestic relations. In New York State, roughly 600,000 civil cases pending are in family courts and involve such diverse issues as foster care, custody, adoption, chronic delinquency, and spousal abuse. More than a quarter of the million other civil cases pending in a typical year involve disputes between landlords and tenants, and about 10 percent involve small claims cases seeking judgments of less than $1,000.[58] Whatever the category, civil cases arise when people have grievances that they feel have been unjustly afflicted upon them by another party. Not all grievances become cases: if you fall down your own front steps, you may be injured, but unless the steps were improperly installed you have no one to blame but yourself. If you fall down the stairs of a hotel, however, you may have a case.

The United States generally is considered the most litigious society in the world, a reputation that is not entirely deserved. Although Japan has a dramatically lower rate of litigation than the United States, other countries—including Australia, Denmark, England, and Israel—are roughly comparable.[59] Among the American states New York is a leader. New Yorkers who fall down hotel stairs, in other words, are less likely to blame themselves and more likely to call a lawyer. In tort cases such as this, lawyers are likely to work for contingency fees, payments contingent upon reaching a settlement with the hotel, in which case they may pocket up to one-third of the total award. In many other civil actions, and for the hotel in cases such as these, the cost of hiring a lawyer provides a strong incentive to settle out of court. The ordinary citizen is likely to have as his or her attorney a general practitioner with limited experience in a particular area such as liability or malpractice. His or her opponents, conversely are likely to be experienced "repeat players" who "have the equivalent of the home field advantage of a sports team. They know the peculiarities of the courtroom setting and are familiar with the courtroom personnel."[60]

In its pretrial phase a civil case typically goes through four steps after the filing of a complaint. A case begins with a pleading in which a complaint is filed explaining the basis of the suit, the law being invoked, and the damages or other relief being sought. If a defendant fails to reply, the court may order a default judgment in which the plaintiff automatically wins. In the discovery phase each side is entitled—by subpoena if necessary—to all relevant information bearing on the case. Although such requests are generally quite limited, the discovery phase can be long, expensive, and embarrassing. In the first five years of the federal government's antitrust case against International Business Machines (IBM), the discovery process involved 64,000,000 pages of records and documents.[61] Some clients are so reluctant to disclose certain facts that they settle rather than go to discovery. A philandering husband, for example, may prefer paying alimony to having his ex-wife's attorneys interviewing every woman he knows. Attorneys are not above using discovery to fish for whatever embarrassing facts might turn up and perhaps "convince the opposing party it will be less expensive and burdensome to settle the case than to comply with the requests."[62]

During and following discovery, attorneys for both sides may file motions seeking further information, expanding the charges, or asking summary judgment. Frequently, a series of motions from both parties points the way toward resolution of a case. The best estimate is that about a quarter of all civil cases are settled by the judge at this point in the process.[63] Even when cases actually come to trial, it is not uncommon for the case to be settled in the judges chambers before all the witnesses are heard. Many civil cases come to trial only because the parties have become so antagonistic toward one another that only a trial can force them to agreement. This is all too often true in divorce cases where it is sometimes said the only winners are the lawyers. In the 1970s, New York took a series of steps in its matrimonial laws to ease this process and consequently reduce the number of cases coming to actual trial. For many years the only grounds for divorce in New York were adultery and extreme physical cruelty. As much as many couples wanted divorces, few men or women were comfortable stipulating before a judge that they had cheated on or beaten their spouses. So-called no-fault divorce laws in which couples may simply agree to separate have both increased the actual number of divorces and decreased the proportion of such cases coming to trial.

Reducing the Caseload of the Courts

No-fault divorce laws show that there is a connection between statute law and the incidence of litigation. Despite various attempts to make it easier to settle disputes without going to court, however, litigation continues to rise. Between 1984 and 1990 the number of civil filings in New York increased by 73 percent, the largest increase in any of the states examined in one study.[64] A variety of reforms have been proposed to reduce the workload of the courts and bring greater logic to their organization. In the area of criminal justice, for example, the so-called Rockefeller drug laws—which mandate up to life imprisonment for dealers—put an enormous burden on the criminal justice system and have not proven effective in controlling the drug trade. By some estimates, as many as 80 percent of the state's convicts are incarcerated on charges related to drugs. The creation of special drug courts, emphasizing treatment rather than punishment, has eased the burden somewhat but they are still largely experimental. And the high penalties left over from the Rockefeller era make it a virtual certainty that many drug cases will come to trial.

In the area of civil justice, Governor Pataki succeeded in making it more difficult for injured workers to sue large corporations, but other attempts to curb litigation in the area of liability law have proven unsuccessful. The Business Council has long argued that the state's liability codes allow plaintiff's too much latitude in the form of what are called "punitive damages" and encourage litigation by allowing plaintiffs to go after what are sometimes known as the "deep pockets" in a case. To deal first with the former, the idea behind the concept of punitive damages is to deter individuals and corporations from irresponsible behavior by allowing the victims of such behavior to sue not just for the cost of the actual injuries sustained but for added dollars designed to punish the company for its irresponsibility. Under the "deep pockets" rule a plaintiff may sue many people—the car dealer, let's say, and the mechanic who worked on the car and really caused the problem—and get most of his or her money not from the person most responsible (the mechanic) but from the one best able to pay (the auto company).

We could go on with a variety of reform proposals that have more or less possibility of being enacted. Tort law reform, many business interests charge, is blocked by the political power of the Trial Lawyer's Association. Drug law reform, many argue, is made politically impossible by the voters' simplistic equation of tougher laws with reduced crime. These "legal" issues, in other words, are intensely political. Former justice Richard Neely of the West Virginia Supreme Court has written a wonderfully refreshing book in which he points out that there are groups who actually have an interest in maintaining legal inefficiencies, and that many of the problems we blame on the courts result from a political failure to decide what we really want them to do:

> For example, when courts work efficiently in civil litigation, the net result is that plaintiffs as a class prosper to the detriment of defendants as a class. Silly as it may sound, the world as a whole breaks down into groups like injured workers, who are usually plaintiffs in civil cases, and groups like insurance companies, which are usually defendants. In cases between working people on one hand and insurance companies, employers, or business people on the other, it is fair to say that courts are in the business of redistributing the wealth. When the machinery breaks down, no wealth is redistributed; this is obviously an advantage to insurance, slum landlords, and fly-by-night businesses.[65]

The Appellate Process

Losers in trial courts sometimes have the option of appeal. In order to achieve what judges call "standing" at the appellate level, the loser in a criminal or civil case must show that there has been some error of law or procedure in the precedent legal process. A good deal of legal sparring one observes in a court case has its origins in the attempts of one attorney or the other to score sufficient points to appeal his or her case. Fewer than 10 percent of state trial court cases are appealed, and most appeals are rejected, but most good lawyers have it in their minds throughout the process what points they might later appeal. It is this long shadow of appellate proceedings, more even than actual cases heard and decided, that gives the appellate division its legal clout.

Through its interpretation of the rules, the appellate division is the real arbiter of what the laws mean. The seven-member Court of Appeals, standing at the top of the appellate division as New York's highest court, has the final word in this process unless there is conflict with a federal standard. There are whole categories of cases, particularly in the area of civil law, in which the rulings of the Court of Appeals are final. As a general rule, the court's rulings are grounded in interpretations of statutes, though the court does have the power of judicial review, that is, the power to rule a statute unconstitutional. It seldom does so. In fact one study of the court's 1990 term found that constitutional issues were involved in only 20 percent of the cases decided.[66] Still less common are cases in which the constitutionality of a statute is challenged. From 1981 through 1985, for example, a total of just 80 cases were brought before the Court of Appeals challenging the constitutionality of laws passed by the legislature. In only twenty was the law ruled unconstitutional.[67]

Deciding What to Decide

In cases involving the death penalty, the right of appeal is automatic. In all other cases, attorneys for the losers must file briefs in the appellate division explaining why their cases were improperly decided. Most of these motions are denied and the decisions of the trial courts stand. The number of cases reaching the Court of Appeals is very small, particularly in the area of criminal law. A few publicized cases have led some politicians to attempt to create an impression of the court as "a soft-on-crime bench fairly racing to let dangerous felons off the hook."[68] In fact the court in recent years had displayed a decided bend toward the prosecution. In its 1994–95 term, for example, 3,036 defendants applied for hearings before the Court of Appeals; 74 received permission; and 34—just over 1 percent—were granted new trials. In the same year, prosecutors were granted 11.7 percent of their motions for appeal.[69]

The Court of Appeals must hear cases in which the lower appellate division courts have disagreed, or where there has been a significant modification of the original opinion. While these cases often raise important issues, most judges and legal scholars would probably agree with Chief Judge Stanley Fuld who wrote in 1967 that:

> Innumerable appeals are brought to the Court as a matter of right, at the option of the litigants, not because they are of any moment or merit but merely because there has been some disagreement, no matter how trivial, either between the Appellate Division and the lower court, or within the Appellate Division itself, as to the proper final disposition of the case.[70]

Other cases are heard only by permission and tend to involve significant legal or constitutional issues. Unlike the U.S. Supreme Court, the New York Court of Appeals can issue advisory opinions and it need not have an actual "case or controversy" before it in order to hear a case. The Court of Appeals, moreover, has its appellate jurisdiction firmly established in the constitution and the legislature cannot change it by ordinary law. Thus although the court has exercised a degree of self-restraint in taking on the other branches of government, it is considerably less constrained in its formal jurisdiction than is the federal Supreme Court.

In the Court of Appeals motions for appeal are randomly assigned to each of the seven judges for preliminary screening. After examining the papers filed by opposing attorneys, and any friend of the court briefs filed by other interested parties, the judge in question summarizes the case for his or her colleagues and makes a recommendation. By tradition, the court will grant a hearing if two judges agree that the case is one that should be reviewed.

New York's highest court is a highly collegial body. It meets each morning in the library to consider each justice's memorandums on assigned cases. These discussions are frank, learned, and sometimes heated: "almost all of the judges admit that they are have felt one way about a case going into a conference but completely changed their minds before the conference was over."[71] After a short lunch, the court convenes in its chambers at 2:00 P.M. to hear oral arguments on cases already granted review. After another session in the library, the judges traditionally dine together downtown before going back to chambers to prepare the next morning's memorandums.

The public face of the court is tellingly revealed during oral argument. Each attorney is given fifteen minutes (half an hour in some cases) to defend his or her written briefs. For all but the most hardened veterans it is an intimidating experience as it soon becomes clear that the justices have done their homework and are quick to find and explore the weakest points. As the short period allocated to oral argument indicates, the bulk of the courts' work in appellate cases comes from the careful reading and comparison of opposing written briefs, but most judges will concede there have been cases in which something said during oral argument has changed the direction of their thinking about a case.

After oral arguments, the judges return to the conference room—sometimes called the "tea" room—where they draw from a deck of index cards containing the names of each case. Known as a "hot bench," because the judges do not know during oral argument who will be assigned what case, the one who draws its card becomes the reporting judge on that case. In conference, discussion begins with the reporting judge who presents the case. The others comment in reverse seniority order and then, as a rule a preliminary vote is taken.

Cases are primarily decided in conference, but the decisions are not final-ized until draft opinions have circulated. Typically, if the reporting judge holds the majority, he or she will write for the court. Otherwise the junior judge in the majority will write the main opinion. If a dissent must be written, usually the first one to raise an objection—frequently a more jun-ior jurist since the case is conferenced in reverse order of seniority—gets the chore.[72]

Although it is rare for a judge to switch his or her vote on the basis of the written opinions, the case is not finally decided until both the majority and minority opinions have been studied by all the judges. In a long and firm tradition, the votes of the court in conference, the probable outcomes of cases being argued, and the nature of the arguments within the Court have never been leaked. Not until the final vote is taken and opinions have been printed will the litigants or the public know who won or lost. A simple majority is all it takes to win, though 4–3 opinions are uncommon.

Some decisions of the Court of Appeals, if they involve substantial fed-eral questions, can be taken for further review at the national level. Most do not. It is also possible for the legislature and the governor to enact a law that effectively overrules a decision of the court. This is also a rare occurrence. And there are times when the decisions of the court are not fully enforced: when the police violate rules of procedure established for criminal cases; when the governor and legislature fail to provide sufficient funding to carry out a court order; or when lower courts gradually reinterpret the court's rul-ing in applying it to new cases. The primary role of the courts remains that of resolving disputes, of deciding individual cases; but the courts are very much a part of the policy-making process in New York. As important as this role is, the courts in the American states will generally remain—as Alexander Hamilton described the Supreme Court of the United States—the "least dan-gerous branch," least dangerous, in large part, because they play at best a tangential role in directing the flow of economic resources.

8

Taxing, Spending, and Public Policy Priorities

Former New York City mayor Ed Koch once conceded that his eyes glazed over when he had to read a budget. Yet Koch probably recognized, as do most political leaders, that a budget "is a representation in monetary terms of governmental activity. . . . If one asks, 'Who gets what the government has to give?' then the answers for a moment in time will be recorded in the budget."[1]

The Budget as a Guide to Policy

In theory, a budget serves as a map of resource allocation. In fact, it is a map that few can follow and one that is frequently out of date before it is printed. If it fails to provide a clear guide as to what actually happens in terms of taxing and spending, it is a manifestly important statement of what the governor and the legislature would like to have happen in the coming year. While understanding state budgets is thus essential to understanding state government, there are two particular reasons why they can be misleading, and why politicians do not always know what they are doing when they create their budgets.

Predicting the Future

The first problem in budgeting is a problem of timing. The state's fiscal year begins on April 1, so when the legislature passes a budget in, for instance, the spring of 2000, the money it allocates will actually be raised and spent over the *next* twelve months. The budget proposal the governor submits in January is an attempt to predict what will happen four to sixteen months later; and when agencies submit their program requests to the governor's budget office (usually the previous September), they are looking ahead an additional four months. The highway department, for example, must try to

291

predict in September 2001 how much to allocate for snow removal in the winter of 2002–03. The corrections department must try to predict how many prisoners will finish their terms and how many new convicts will arrive as much as a year and a half in the future.

In order to balance the budget, moreover, the governor's office must try to guess how much revenue the state will capture. It must predict the employment and inflation rates, how the stock market will do, what retail sales levels will yield in terms of the sales tax, and so on. When the governor submits his or her budget to the legislature these estimates will be among the first items of contention. Each house of the legislature hires its own consultants to compare their projections with those of the governor and the comptroller, who generally does still another set of revenue estimates.

Not surprising, these estimates of how much the government will take in and spend are seldom precise. There is no surefire way to forecast how much snow will fall on the highways or what the unemployment rate will be next year; and the problem of prediction is compounded by its political loading. A politician who favors a tax cut or increase in spending has a short-term interest in overestimating revenues. Budgets passed in election years tend to be particularly optimistic. But politics aside, any attempt to estimate future economic activity, to predict the inflation rate in health care, or the weather in winter is tricky business at best. "By its nature," as one former budget director advised future governors:

> Budgeting is an error-prone activity, and those errors do not necessarily reflect a lack of technical capability or a failure of effort on the part of your budget staff. Forecasts are simply wrong, and from time to time your budget officer will bring you news of those errors.[2]

Interpreting the Numbers

The second important thing to understand about the budget of the state of New York is that it is large and complicated, too big and complex for a single individual—even the state's full-time budget director—really to understand. There are just too many units of government doing too many things. Budgets, generally, are high-level abstractions that sometimes relate only tenuously to programmatic realities. Here is an indicator from just one small part of state government that we know rather well, the Department of Political Science of the City College of the City University of New York (CUNY). What does it cost to offer roughly twenty-five courses in political science to approximately 550 students a semester? The most expensive item is the million or so dollars we pay each year for the combined salaries and fringe benefits of thirteen full-time faculty members. Some of our faculty, however, teach one or more of their courses at the graduate center, in the international relations program, ethnic studies, urban legal studies, or at our center for worker education. Others have college appointments as administrators. The department is "compensated" for some (but not all) of these faculty members' contributions to other programs with funds to hire part-time replacements. When it comes to things like stationery, photocopying, telephones, and secretarial help, the department is given an annual allocation of money. For less direct services—such as campus security, or the services provided by college advisers, electricians, and librarians—the general college administration makes the allocations. In some systems of budgeting, the department would be charged its "share" for some of these college-wide services, in others they would go down as general overhead. Before your eyes glaze over, there is no really right or wrong way to make these allocations, and City College doesn't really try. No one at the college could really tell you how much it costs us to teach those twenty-five classes, or how much is spent on political science education, as opposed to biology or history. Only in times of serious economic crisis is there any attempt seriously to examine these overall allocations of resources. Most years we simply do pretty much what we did last year.

No one in the governor's office or the legislature has any idea how the department is spending its money. "Budget data," in this sense, "are like a fog bank. The current system gives one a feel for a tier of numbers, one or more times removed from the actuals."[3] What the city university system essentially does (reality is a bit more complex) is allocate each college in the system a certain number of full-time faculty lines based on overall enrollments which, in budget jargon, are calculated as "FTEs." (An "FTE" is a full-time equivalent, meaning one student taking a full-time program of 15 credits, or five students taking 3 credits each). Every other budget line— from deans to desktops and to part-time teachers—is some proportion of this number. The number itself does not tell anyone very much about how the college is educating its students or how much it costs, but it serves as a crucial indicator of how it stands in relation to others. If FTE costs are higher at City College than at Queens College or John Jay, the CUNY board of higher education is concerned. If FTE costs this year are significantly higher than last year, everyone is concerned. When the budget gets to Albany, figures from the CUNY system are compared with FTE numbers in the State University of New York (SUNY) system, and another round of judging begins.

Looking at their enrollment, comparing the department of political science with, say, biology; comparing City College with other public colleges;

comparing this year with last, Albany has a set of very rough indicators of how much is being spent to educate how many students. Beyond that, budget numbers tell them little. This is true not just for City College, but for almost every bureau and commission in the state. Budgets tell us how many correction agents oversee how many inmates at the Greenhaven penitentiary, but not how many are in Cell Block E at midnight or how they are interacting with the prisoners. We can count the number of patients treated in the emergency room of a hospital and compare it with the amount spent on doctors and nurses; but the result provides at best a rough estimate of how efficiently the hospital is run.

Conflicting Perspectives

It is generally assumed that agencies will defend their programs and that budget people will challenge them. Bureaucrats are expected to believe that their programs are important. In most organizations, workers resent the "insensitivity" of budget people and use names like "number crunchers" to imply that they have little awareness of real world problems. Actual allocations of resources often emerge from a dynamic series of interactions between the numbers people and various agencies. At City College, to continue our example, the dean of social science will sometimes allow a small course to float if the chairman can make the case that the course is required for graduating seniors, or that it is particularly important pedagogically. The dean can allow such exemptions, but knows that she can get only so many of them past the provost, who knows in turn that he cannot allow more than a certain number of small classes to float without attracting the notice of the budget people at CUNY or in Albany where a class with "only" nine students stands out like a sore thumb. While the dreaded letters "FTE" are seldom uttered at this stage, every department chair and dean knows that certain guidelines must ultimately be met. No one ever says that a class *must* have a certain minimum number of students, but certain target numbers do come down from the office of the vice president for finance and management. The vice president also looks at the budget projections from the state and central CUNY and lets each dean know whether he or she will have more money, less money, or about the same as last year.

Tensions between agencies and budget officials grow as different agencies and programs are compared. When the dean of social science at City College makes his or her case to the provost, the provost is—implicitly at least—comparing the case for an underenrolled political science course with a comparable case being made by the dean of humanities for a philosophy course; or for a course in the school of engineering; all in the context of the overall FTE numbers. At the central office of the university, similar comparisons are made between City College and other CUNY colleges. And in Albany, the numbers from CUNY are matched with SUNY and, ultimately, with other agencies and programs in the budget. Most professors would bristle at the suggestion that they are competing with other departments or colleges, much less with the office of aging or the corrections department. Yet in a sense, every nickel spent by every agency is coming out of someone else's budget. The decision to float a small course or to put an extra guard in a prison is a decision with implications for others. As Wildavsky puts it:

> In the most general definition, budgeting is concerned with the translation of financial resources into human purposes. A budget, therefore, may be characterized as a series of goals with price tags attached. Since funds are limited and have to be divided one way or another, the budget becomes a mechanism for making choices among alternative expenditures.[4]

Strategic Budgeting

Individuals and families confront these same problems: money spent on movies cannot pay the rent. Corporations must also allocate resources and personnel. Governments differ from families in that many more people and problems are involved; they differ from corporations in that services are more difficult to compare. How does one decide how much collective welfare is gained by allocating money to prisons as opposed to colleges, health care as opposed to parks, or highways versus subways? In families, resource allocations depend on the decisions of so small a number of people that everyone knows what they are getting. In the private sector, resource allocations are decided—in theory at least—by which divisions are most profitable. Government services, by their very nature, are neither simple nor measurable in strict economic terms. Murtaugh, when he was chair of the assembly alcohol and substance abuse committee, could make a case that treatment was—in the long run—cheaper than incarceration for low level drug-addicted dealers; but his case was soft by comparison with that of a corporate advocate showing that his or her product was more profitable than that of another division's.

Wildavsky's argument that all government budgeting is essentially incremental has dominated most studies of the process. Governments, he argued, are on one hand too large and complex to understand without simplifying shortcuts: "No human being," as a former chairman of the house appropriations committee once put it, "regardless of his position and . . . capacity could possibly be completely familiar with all the items of appropriations contained in this defense bill."[5] Even if, on the other hand, one could really understand one agency's program:

> There remains the imposing problem of making comparisons among different programs that have different values for different people. This involves deciding such questions as how much highways are worth as compared to recreation facilities, national defense, schools, and so on down the range of government functions. No common denominator among these functions has been developed. No matter how hard they try, therefore, officials in places like the Bureau of the Budget discover that they cannot find any objective method of judging priorities among programs.[6]

Budget officials, Wildavsky argues, make these complex calculations through a set of simplifying assumptions, the most important of which is "incrementalism":

> The beginning of wisdom about an agency budget is that it is almost never actively reviewed as a whole every year in the sense of reconsidering the value of all existing programs as compared to all possible alternatives. Instead, it is based on last year's budget with special attention given to a narrow range of increases or decreases. Thus the men who make the budget are concerned with relatively small increments to an existing base. Their attention is focused on a small number of items over which the budgetary battle is fought.[7]

In New York, as one assemblyman says, "we fight over maybe two to three percent of the budget. No matter how far apart the governor, the senate, and the assembly may seem, what is really quite remarkable is that we all take a base of about 70 billion for granted while we scream and shout about the other two."

Wildavsky's concept of incrementalism has been criticized for failing to encompass major upheavals such as that produced by the Proposition 13 tax-cutting initiative in California or the New York elections in 1994. From the perspective of those who might be called *decrementalists*:

> The fundamental concepts of incremental budgeting are completely inverted by retrenchment. For example, although the incremental budgeting process is decentralized, decremental budgeting inherently requires centralization. Similarly, the substantive decisions of incremental budgeting are made in a fragmented manner, but decremental budgeting requires a comprehensive package.[8]

Such periods of retrenchment are not trivial, but they are episodic. Even when a governor with a whole different set of priorities comes into office, as did Pataki in 1995, he or she is likely to focus major attention on at best four or five areas. Higher education took a very hard shot in Pataki's first budget, as did mental health; but subsequent changes in this areas were essentially incremental until 1999, when again the election was behind him.

Even when the process is not incremental, two of Wildavsky's analytic methods of dealing with complexity are likely to be used by most participants. These are what he calls an agency's "fair share" and "base." "The base is the general expectation among the participants that programs will be carried on at close to the going level of expenditures but it does not necessarily include all activities."[9] The budget of the city university, for example, may go up or down a few percentage points, but no college is likely to be closed, no major program terminated. The assumption is that the process of decision making that led to the creation of a college or program in the first place took into account the major arguments for and against. If the arguments were good then, why bother reviewing them now. "No one was born yesterday; past experience with these programs is so great that total reconsideration would be superfluous unless there is a special demand in regard to a specific activity on the part of one or more strategically placed Congressmen, a new Administration, interest groups, or the agency itself."[10]

"Fair share" is a more elusive concept. It means, "not only the base an agency has established but also the expectation that it will receive some proportion of funds, if any, which are to be increased over or decreased below the base of various governmental agencies."[11] A new administration—as with Pataki in 1995—can change these calculations dramatically; and priorities may shift over time in such a way as to redefine the concept of fair shares. Over the past decade, for example, the state has gone from spending three times as much for higher education than corrections, to budgets in which more money goes to prisons than to colleges; but even these changes, on a year-to-year basis, have been largely incremental.

Program advocates seek to protect their bases and maintain or expand their fair shares. A favorite agency device is to protect its revenue stream in the form of a "locked box," a tax or fee that can be used only for a specific purpose. (In New York, for example, license fees for fishing must go into fishery management funds, thruway tolls are controlled by the thruway authority, and so on). Different kinds of accounting procedures can be adjusted to alter perceptions of program effectiveness, and a variety of decision procedures can be used to circumvent budgetary guidelines. Meyers depicts a key part of the budgetary process as a "dynamic competition" between what he calls "controllers" and "spending advocates" to structure the budget pro-

cess. A series of shifting coalitions struggle not only to influence actual allocations of money, but to change the process itself. The struggle is continuous.[12]

The Budgetary Process

The division of the budget, or DOB, plays a critical role in shaping the direction of this struggle in New York. In Meyers's terms it is the key "controller"
in the system. Although its director and a half dozen top employees serve at
the pleasure of the governor, the division is comprised largely of civil servants and takes pride in its political neutrality. The division is organized by
units to which various clusters of agencies are assigned. The health and social development unit, for example, is responsible for the departments of
social services, health, and labor, the division for youth, the office for the
aging, the council on children and families, and the division of human rights.[13]
Each of these units monitors its respective agencies both in terms of program
evaluation and budget development. Their annual reviews of agency requests
serve as a base for the process of developing the overall budget plan presented by the governor.

Preparing the Budget

Preparation of the executive budget typically begins in June when each agency
begins to compile its annual estimates for the following year. These requests
are reviewed by budget analysts, who look for major changes, indications of
padding, inaccuracies, and consistency with the programs of the governor.
Meanwhile, the fiscal planning division of the DOB is beginning—in consultation with the governor—to develop estimates of revenues and overall
levels of expenditure. When these numbers are fed back to the budget units,
they are translated into preliminary projections for the next fiscal year's spending levels. Each unit then sends its agency's budget guidelines in the form of
a "call letter," calling upon them to submit budget and program proposals
that conform with the projected fiscal estimates and the governor's program
priorities.

   Once each agency submits its plan to the DOB, budget examiners meet
informally with the fiscal officers and top officials of each agency to hear
requests for changes. Larger departments and some with unique problems
may be able to schedule formal hearings.

> At these hearings, the commissioners make presentations to the Office . . .
> as well as the secretary and chair and staff personnel of the two legislative
> fiscal committees. Both major political parties are represented. During the

past two decades these formal hearings have come to provide mainly an informal overview. One budget examiner described them as "marketing sessions."[13]

What the commissioners are trying to market at these sessions is some notion either that their programs are being cut at the base and denied their fair shares, or that there is some unique set of circumstances that justifies special consideration. Whether this case is made in formal hearings or informal discussions with budget examiners, it is made in the context of the resources available in the governor's overall fiscal plan. In order to persuade a budget examiner to make a case at the higher levels for modifications, a program advocate must be able effectively to answer the following questions:

- Is there really a need for the proposed new program?
- If so, would it best be handled in that particular department or in another one?
- Is the suggested organizational structure the best option?
- Are the workload indicators (estimating the amount of staff needed) realistic?
- Are the stated goals likely to be reached?[14]

When the budget examiners finish their program reviews (typically in late November) they present their recommendations to their unit heads in closed-door sessions that are, in many ways, at the heart of the budget preparation stage. Typically, the budget examiner's presentation is rooted in a construct known as a *spending baseline*, an important concept which represents "the level of agency or program services at next year's prices for labor and materials."[15] For most agencies this is a fairly straightforward process. Salaries, for example, are adjusted upward (or downward) to account for collective bargaining increases, retirements, and other changes in wages and personnel. Supply costs are adjusted for inflation, and so on. This process of projecting spending levels, known as annualization, is not always straightforward. If tougher sentencing laws, for example, make it likely that the prison population will increase, the spending baseline for the corrections department would seemingly be due for an increase, but the calculation of just how much of an increase is a much trickier process than with something like the increase in the price of paperclips. In presenting his or her budget, moreover, a governor may have an interest in fudging baseline numbers in order to obscure painful cuts or make program comparisons difficult. In his 1999–2000 budget message, for example, Governor Pataki did not use baseline numbers in presenting his CUNY and SUNY proposals. By ignoring increased costs (including a 4 percent salary increase) he could argue that what were really substantial net cuts was a budget "equal to the comparable 1998–99 academic year funding."[16]

While controversy abounds in areas such as this, the baseline concept has been widely accepted by budget makers at the local, state, and national levels. It provides what most participants regard as a realistic picture of what each departmental program is most likely to cost in current dollars. As Forsythe says:

> From a broad political perspective, the idea of "current services" mirrors the last adopted budget and therefore uses the prior year's legislative agreement as a starting point. From the perspective of an agency manager, the upward adjustments made in the baseline budget means that the agency at least starts even in its budget battles and does not have to fight for funds simply to pay for inflation or collective-bargaining adjustments, neither of which are under the agency manager's control. For the budget office, the baseline "exercise," as they often call it . . . provides for budget-making a starting point that is more or less consistent from program to program and agency to agency.[17]

Once the examiner's reports and projections are completed, the process of comparing programs and adjusting them to the overall numbers begins at the higher levels of DOB and in the office of the governor. In December as the outlines of the budget begin to emerge, a final round of communication with the agencies takes place. At this stage in Maryland, a state similar to New York in the extent to which party leaders dominate the legislature:

> Legislative leaders meet with the governor and express individual and collective priorities that run the gamut from local matters to executive departments and agencies to statewide policies. Governors usually try to accommodate these requests so the legislative leaders feel ownership and will push the budget through.[18]

This seldom happens in New York. While committee chairs and legislative party leaders are sometimes consulted and informally advised of where things are headed, the process of preparing the budget in New York is strictly in the provenance of the second floor. Indeed the precise contours of the governor's budget are generally shrouded in considerable mystery until the day in late January when he or she officially delivers them to the legislature.

As they prepare their budget messages for delivery in January, governors would try, one would think, to impart the stamp of their own policy preferences. In theory, they would adjust the baseline figures of each agency to fit the overall fiscal plan in a way that reflected their policy priorities. "This rational approach," as Forsythe puts it, "would create a spending plan that most accurately reflects the governor's own programmatic and political priorities, but the result would be a significant redistribution of state spending . . . likely to increase political conflict and make passage of the budget by the legislature more difficult."[19] An alternative is simply to roll with the punch using baseline figures to keep things pretty much as they were the year before. And there are also important tactical considerations to take into account. A governor who wants, for example, to increase spending for a program that is not popular in one house of the legislature may propose drastic cuts in a more popular program, not because she actually wants the cuts, but because he wants to have something to trade. To read the governor's budget, then, as a statement of his or her real priorities will not do. New York's constitution gives the governor thirty days to revise his or her original budget presentation. Whatever shifts are made—and they are usually trivial— the governor comes to the legislature in a remarkably strong strategic position. Among the states, few governors are better positioned to get what they want from the legislature.

The governor's strength is rooted in part in his or her control over the executive branch and the consequent inability of most agencies to use subgovernment networks to end run the governor. As one study of the process notes:

> When the Governor's budget has been submitted to the Legislature, agencies are expected to fall in line and support the document. Even if some of their requests were slashed, appeals to the Legislature at this stage can be interpreted as treasonous. "After all, we're all in the Executive Branch together," stated one manager.[20]

Even in the absence of such togetherness, agency managers know that the governor is still likely to have the last word since the line-item veto applies to any increases the legislature may propose. Thus, by low balling items popular with legislators, the governor enters the process with a large stack of bargaining chips. Almost all legislators—senators and assembly members, Republicans and Democrats—are strongly inclined, for example, to maintain school funding levels and those parts of the budget that support local governments. Almost invariably, governors submit budgets proposing very low levels of expenditure in these areas. For the legislature to satisfy its local constituents and maintain state school aid levels, it must give the governor something he or she wants, such as—in the case of Governor Pataki—tax cuts and increases in prison expenditures.

Enacting the Budget

When governors present their budgets to the legislature, they are referred to the fiscal committees that quickly put their staffs to work on detailed analysis. Formal hearings are scheduled, giving interest groups an opportunity to be heard and agencies a last chance cautiously to appeal cuts. Meanwhile, party leaders, in consultation with the staffs of the ways and means committee in the assembly and the finance committee in the senate, and with the chairs of key committees, begin to prepare their own counters to the governor's budget. Some of the early maneuvering in the legislature, through press releases and informal negotiations, may produce relatively minor changes in the governor's budget; until they are presented, and until the fiscal committees have completed their analyses, there is little significant movement toward compromise (see Box 8.1). In January and early February, the fiscal committees schedule a series of hearings on different parts of the budget. Although these hearings seldom develop any new insights or surprises, they are well attended by members, staff aides, and lobbyists who find in them what one staff aide describes as "both a useful review of the numbers and a series of insights into the political nuances. If you listen carefully," he continued, "to the kinds of questions asked and the ways in which people shade their answers you can learn a lot about how strongly various people feel about different parts of the package."

Not until late February do the first real negotiations begin. These early sessions, typically, are rather large and formal, including both the majority and minority leaders of both houses, the governor, and numerous staff persons. As the process moves toward deadline, the number of participants decreases to the ultimate "three men in a room": the governor, the majority leader, and the Speaker, plus a handful of top staff persons.

For many years, conventional wisdom held that "one and one makes three," meaning that if any two of the key negotiators cut a firm deal the third would go along. The rule seems to have worked in the Rockefeller and Carey years, and when Mario Cuomo's friend and neighbor Sol Weprin was Speaker; but the process has become less predictable. Divided government partly accounts for this shift, and there are even times when it seems advantageous to be the odd man out, particularly as politics becomes more oriented toward the media. Assembly Democrats, who were quick to capitulate in the immediate wake of Pataki's 1994 election, have proven less willing to go along with the governor's subsequent budgets and have tried to hold out as defenders of popular programs against the conservative onslaught. But although this line of cleavage has tended to be the main stumbling block in budget negotia-

---

Box 8.1

Preparing for the Worst (or at least making it look as if you are . . .)

One way in which many families and governments avoid the risk of debt is by creating a contingency fund, otherwise known as saving for a rainy day. Thus the 2000–01 budget adopted by the legislature in June 2000 provided for a seemingly prudent reserve of more than $4 billion in funds set aside for unanticipated emergencies, downturns in the stock market, or faulty economic projections. As recalculated by the state comptroller, however, the real rainy day funds in the budget had a projected balance of only $550 million.

What the governor and the state legislature did in order to create a prettier picture was to place and sustain a number of programs in places where they were seemingly funded by sources outside of the main budget. On closer scrutiny, however, these "outside sources" turned out to be the rainy day accounts. They also counted as "reserve" funds more than $600 million allocated to increased salaries for state workers. Since the largest civil service union had already negotiated its contract, these numbers could easily have been folded into the budget. It is like a family who knew that their rent was going up by $100 a month, but instead of budgeting an extra $1,200 for twelve months of rent claimed to be "saving" that $1,200 for a rainy day!

The state's tax receipts were unusually strong in 1999. Even if they were to remain strong throughout the 2000–01 fiscal year, tax cuts passed in 1998 that go into effect in 2001 make it more important than ever to have a strong reserve. Instead, the governor and the legislature chose, as many families do, to live for today and hope that tomorrow takes care of itself. As the comptroller points out, New York's actual "rainy day reserve represents a mere 1.5 percent of General Fund receipts; whereas, the national average for states is about 4 percent."* By the comptroller's calculations, this will leave the state with a projected shortfall of $3 billion in 2001–02 and nearly $5 billion in 2002–03.

---

*H. Carl McCall, *2000–01 Budget Analysis: Review of the Enacted Budget* (Albany: Office of the State Comptroller, 2000).

---

tions, the lines of alliance are fluid. Twice since 1995, senate and assembly leaders have agreed on the essential numbers only to have the governor dig in. Forsythe suggests:

> Other factors besides party allegiance can create a competitive relationship between a governor and a legislative leader. Deference to the chief

executive is not necessarily a value that helps a leader win election in a legislature. Indeed, a newly elected legislative leader may find it necessary to do battle with a governor of the same party, as a demonstration of independence.[21]

As close as Sol Weprin was to Governor Cuomo, for example, it can be argued that assembly Democrats had elected Mel Miller because they believed he would not be.

Generalization in this area is, however, difficult. Ken Shapiro, who served as chief counsel to three Speakers, argues that although people "tend to remember the isolated instances" when the patterns were clear, in most sessions it would be impossible to "make determinations for the session and say 'This week we're going to be Warren Anderson's partner,' or 'This year we're going to be Mario Cuomo's partner.' I think the issues and events during a given year determine who your partner will be."[22] There are patterns that persist. Both legislative parties, for example, try to protect their politically marginal members who tend to come from the same kinds of districts in the suburbs and small cities where school aid and general aid to localities issues have particular importance. Almost every year, and particularly in years when the cupboard is bare, therefore, legislative leaders tend quickly to coalesce in opposing cuts to these programs; but Shapiro's point that alliances are unpredictable and issue-specific is beyond refutation.

Bargaining Postures

At the core of the Speaker and majority leaders' ability to negotiate with the governor is the question of trust. Their negotiating postures are firmly rooted in their abilities to retain the trust of their respective party conferences. Whatever deals they negotiate with each other and with the governor must pass muster in both their party conferences and in the negotiating room. Any compromises they agree to with the governor and each other are valid only insofar as they can win approval in both houses of the legislature. From the very start of serious budget negotiations, then, talks among the three key actors are frequently punctuated with pauses in which the Speaker and majority leader return to their party conferences for consultation and advice. The ability of legislative leaders to take a hard line in negotiations is a function of their ability to negotiate with solid party conferences behind them.

The Legislature and the Governor

Trust is also important in defining the relationships between party leaders and the governor. Until a final agreement is in place, there is a sense in which everything is always on the table. An agreement reached on the budget for, say, highway spending may suddenly come unglued when one of the key players compares it with a later agreement on something else. Most American legislatures decentralize these bargaining points. In congress, for example, once the overall budget guidelines are set, substantive committees and appropriations subcommittees fill in most of the actual numbers and negotiate them with the other house. Despite New York's 1998 experiment with conference committees, the bargaining process in Albany continues to focus on the "three men in a room." No matter how much they are acting as agents of their party conferences and other forces, the fact that most deals must ultimately be cut this way significantly impacts the process and differentiates it from practice in other states.

With some very recent exceptions, preliminary negotiations are broken down into "tables," groups of staff people who focus on particular issues with representatives from each of the three negotiating groups. Certain tables are almost always kept open until the final days with each side holding open those issues that another cared about strongly. When the assembly, for example, cared a lot about welfare and the senate about elementary and secondary education, these tended to be the last tables to close. More recently because prison cells have been high priority issues for the senate and the governor, and mental health for the assembly, these tables have been kept open to give each side bargaining leverage. Although the budget is technically divided into separate chapters, and some tables conclude their work with little controversy, in practice the governor and both houses of the legislature must agree to the budget as a total package. Even when a table is seemingly closed, the process, in the immortal words of Yogi Berra, "ain't over until it's over."

One of the interesting paradoxes of the budget process is the extent to which, as the key players move toward closure, the weak become strong. The rule of one plus one equaling three not only goes out the door at this point but it gets stood on its head. One top budget aide for Governor Cuomo suggests that some of Cuomo's most difficult negotiations with the state senate occurred in the years when he was closest to the assembly leadership. Acting on the widespread perception that the governor and Speaker Weprin were "joined at the hip," the senate leadership made it increasingly expensive to "buy the final agreement." By "buy the agreement" you mean that you have to find the funds to support the particular programs that the senate was pushing in order to reach a final deal. Many times, in the Cuomo years, the senate majority leader would come to a tentative agreement and then return to the next session and report that he could not sell it to his conference. Anderson, according to Forsythe, "used to storm out of meetings every year" just as negotiations seemed to be close. The walkout, for Anderson "signaled the start of the final round of horse-trading not a breakdown in talks."[23] In recent years, assembly leader Sheldon Silver has tried—with limited success—to play the same game with Governor Pataki and majority leader Bruno, but the rules of the contest have changed.

Since he took office in 1995, the player most likely to play the end-game role has been Governor Pataki. In legal terms New York's governors—because they can still veto any items the legislature increases—are well positioned to take a tough negotiating stance. When relations between the governor and the legislative leaders are at their best, the process of bargaining is relatively straightforward: the governor yields to the senate and assembly on some increases in education and aid to localities; the assembly and the governor give the senate more for highways; the governor and the senate force assembly acceptance of cuts in mental health in exchange for a few extra dollars in mass transit; and so on. But a governor serious about cutting funds that both houses of the legislature want—education is a good example—has enormous advantages.

As a governor plainly uncomfortable with the details of policy issues and the politics of bargaining, George Pataki has sought and encouraged alternatives to the traditional budgetary process. Some of these attempts—such as negotiating with legislative leaders in public sessions—were immediate failures not likely to be repeated. Others, such as a tendency to insert statutory language in budgetary proposals may not pass constitutional muster. Pataki's rather heavy-handed use of his veto and resource allocation powers are not new, and they carry political risks that make them unlikely to endure. Combined, however, with a willingness to simply walk away from the table, stay out of Albany, and leave the legislative leaders to stew, he has added a new wrinkle to the traditional process. Conventional wisdom had long suggested that it was the governor who had most to lose from late budgets. By absenting himself, however, Governor Pataki has somehow managed to transfer the onus of blame to the legislature. Indeed the harder legislative leaders work to reach a compromise that will bring the governor back to the table, the more the press and the public have tended to focus on them rather than the absent governor as the source of the problem. Whether future governors will be able to play similar roles is not clear. Pataki has nonetheless shown how the formal powers of the governor can be used to tilt the dynamic in his favor and away from a tripartite process of bargaining among equals. Whether in response to these changes, or because of forces internal to the legislature, a recent movement toward the establishment and use of conference committees may have also changed the dynamic.

Conference Committees

In New York, as we have noted, bills are not amended in the legislature. The usual way in which the two houses reconcile differences is by passing new bills. Unlike Congress, or the legislatures in most states, the New York legislature has almost never used conference committees to negotiate differences between the houses. In 1995, a new joint rule was passed authorizing such interhouse committees; but although the bill increasing the state speed limit to 65 mph was negotiated in a conference committee later that year, most legislation has continued to follow the traditional path. In 1998, in a dramatic departure from this tradition, the assembly and senate leaders appointed conference committees to negotiate the budget. The device worked well enough to have been used again in both 1999 and 2000.

Appointed by the party leaders, there were nine subcommittees appointed to deal with particular chapters: taxes and economic development; transportation, the environment, and housing; higher education; education; public protection; health; general government and local assistance; mental health; and human services. Each subcommittee consisted of ten members, five each from the assembly and senate with four of the five appointed by the majority, one by the minority. A general budget conference committee met first to set spending targets for each subcommittee and later approve the final packages. This committee included the top leaders of both houses including the Speaker, the majority and minority leaders, and the chairs of the finance committees.

The Speaker and majority leader (in consultation with their respective party conferences) were clearly in control at almost every step in the conference proceedings. Especially in the early stages when basic resources were allocated—so much for education, public protection, human services, and so on—the majority party leaders were clearly calling the shots ("two men in a room," as one journalist quipped). One could argue, as some journalists did, that once these decisions were made the work of the subcommittees was largely that of rearranging the deck chairs on a liner whose direction was already clear. At the other extreme were those who suggested that "the process puts to the lie the notion that . . . rank-and-file members were somehow incapable of participation."[24] At least for those on the committees there was a strong sense of involvement, and it seems clear that within the overall fiscal context set by the leaders, details of the budget were worked out directly by the rank and file.

As the process has matured, party leaders and their staff assistants have asserted more control. In 1998, and to a lesser degree in 1999, there was a subtle but not insignificant shift in power to the more senior members serving on the conference committees and away from the central staff people who traditionally had bargained over the details left after the party leaders had reached their agreement on the overall numbers. This does not seem to have been the case in 2000. According to former majority leader Michael Bragman, "When one of the members of the General Conference Committee dared to suggest that they wanted to question one of the [staff] reports, a staff person, *a staff person*, dared to tell them that they could not do that."[25]

Seemingly the big loser in the reformed process, should the reforms become more meaningful, would be the governor, who not only is frozen out of negotiations over details but forced—in their final negotiations on the bottom line—to face a majority leader and Speaker whose differences have already been negotiated. Pataki, however, has been able to use the new process to his advantage. In 1998 he began by insisting that he would veto those parts of the legislative budget which brought total spending over the approximately $74 billion cap he had set. With that condition met, the governor and the legislative leaders called a press conference smilingly to announce the first nearly on-time budget agreement in more than a decade. Unsuspectingly, the Speaker and majority leader turned to other business and the legislature moved toward early adjournment. But the governor was not finished. In apparent violation of his agreement with the legislature, Pataki used his line-item veto on more than 1,300 budget items, many in the areas of education and aid to localities most sacred to legislators. With senate Republicans and Democrats in both houses outraged by the governor's seeming breach of faith, the stage seemed set for a rare legislative override of gubernatorial vetoes. Out of the west, however, came the rag-tag cavalry of assembly Republicans—usually a cipher in the power game—with a quiet pledge to vote as a bloc to uphold each and every veto. The governor had clearly won the battle. Whether he won the war is far less clear as the legislature refused in both 1999 and 2000 to send the governor a budget without prior agreement on vetoes. The 1999 battle showed that the legislature was not without budget weapons of its own, but the price—from the perspective of rank-and-file legislators—seems to have been a return to backroom bargaining in which the roles of the conference committees have become increasingly cosmetic.

The "Take-It or Leave-It" Budget

Normally, when the economy is sound and state coffers are full, the process runs smoothly. This should have been the case in 1999 when a hyperactive stock market and a recovering economy began the fiscal year with a budget surplus of several billion dollars. There were two troubling clouds. First, the

1997 and 1998 budgets had backloaded substantial tax cuts and spending increases into the future. Some of these delayed items were so large that a number of informed observers (Comptroller Carl McCall in particular) were already warning of severe fiscal problems in the year 2000 and beyond. Second, the governor's 1998 vetoes had put a serious strain on his relations with the legislature. Not feeling that they could trust Pataki to keep his word, legislative leaders had been devising ways to force the governor to keep his part of the agreement when a final budget was passed.

The legislature usually takes some steps to, in effect, keep the governor honest. It can, as one former staff director of the ways and means committee put it, "set a series of time bombs" in the budget bills.[26] Typically the budget is put together in eight separate bills. Four of these are appropriations bills that deal largely with numbers, and four are "language" bills that detail how the dollar amounts in the appropriation bills will actually be sent. One way in which the legislature can time bomb the governor is by passing two bills at a time, sending the governor the bills that include education, for example, ten legislative days before sending him the bill that includes corrections. In this way, the governor knows that the items he vetoes in the first bill may haunt him in trying to get what he wants in the second. The language bills can also be used to reduce the threat of veto either by conflating budget items in such a way that the line-item veto does not work, or by linking budget lines the legislature wants to those on the governor's list of priorities.

Perhaps anticipating this kind of battle, the governor took the unprecedented step of submitting his 1999 budget in the form of one bill instead of the traditional eight. By folding all his "language" into an appropriation bill (which the legislature cannot change), and by sending everything in one package (which had to be passed or rejected all at once), the governor gave the legislature almost no negotiating power. His aides, speaking candidly but off the record, described "the packaging of the budget as a masterstroke that hobbles the Legislature and greatly increases the Governor's power."[27] Substantively, the governor's budget did not include the funds he agreed to in 1997 for decreasing class sizes in grades one through three, increases he had specifically agreed upon in a deal with the assembly to pass his 1997 plan for cutting school taxes. But the governor had the legislature in the difficult position of having to take his budget essentially as submitted or craft a new one of its own. What enabled the legislature to reassert itself at this stage was the ability of the senate and assembly leadership to present a united front to the governor insisting on its own priorities. This tactic essentially worked, and the 2000 budget was submitted in a more traditional eleven chapters rather than one. The final agreement on an overall package—an agreement which included a pledge of limits on what kinds of vetoes the governor might exercise—was negotiated by the traditional triumvirate of the governor, Speaker, and majority leader. The result was the longest budget standoff in the history of the state.

If conference committees and take-it-or-leave-it budgets become the norm—and it is not clear as we write that they will—the days of three men in a room would seemingly be over and the process in New York will closely resemble that of other strong-party states. What seems more likely is that the three men will pop up in some other location or stage in process. Assembly Democrats have challenged the governor in the courts, and a new governor may prefer the face to face bargaining characteristic of the old system; but the more likely prospect is evolution toward more confrontational politics: budgets, like other issues, will be negotiated by press releases and oriented more toward symbols than substance. The process has always involved, as a staff member once described, "the annual dance of the budget flamingoes . . . where the birds bow and then strut around flapping their wings" before getting down to serious negotiations.[28] The danger with the new process is that it will be all flapping and strutting.

Administering the Budget

Once the budget has been approved, money must actually be allotted to each agency or local government. The legislature, when it passes the final draft of the budget, compiles its detailed summary of the agreements it has reached with the governor into a document known as *The Green Book*, which—although it does not have the legal status of the actual appropriations bills—is so much more user friendly that it tends to serve as the document used by most legislators and bureaucrats trying to figure out what the numbers mean. Within weeks of the budget agreement each agency is required to submit a spending plan to the DOB that explains how it plans to operate within the budget and when it will need each allocation of funds. Before it can actually write any checks, an agency's spending plans must be approved by the DOB and cleared by the comptroller. While these clearances are normally routine, it is understood that as needs and circumstances change, adjustments must be made. When the highway department, for example, confronts a particularly stormy winter, the DOB will not usually challenge its need to exceed its budget authority for snow removal, though it may require it to find the money through savings in some other part of the departmental budget.

DOB approval of an agency's spending plans comes in the form of a certificate of approval confirming the availability of funds: absent such a certificate, the comptroller may not issue any checks. In good times, an agency with a record of reliability and relatively predictable spending needs can get a certificate of approval for its entire budget. When funds are tight, or when an agency lacks the confidence of the governor and the budget office, money may be allocated a quarter or even a month at a time.

Adding and Cutting Appropriated Funds

Theoretically, no agency can spend more or less than the amount of money budgeted for a specific function. Budget categories are usually broad enough to allow minor adjustments, and the rules are seldom so rigidly enforced that key programs are delayed or impaired. When an agency really faces a crisis, however, it must return to the legislature for what is called a deficiency appropriation. While the governor and the legislature will normally respond to such requests when really essential, "they are not designed to provide another opportunity for the agencies to make a pitch for more money. One DOB examiner stated that, on occasion, agencies have come to the Division just a few months after the budget was passed, looking for substantial deficiency appropriations. 'There is a difference between a legitimate need for a deficiency appropriation, and a fundamental lack of respect for the laws, the Legislature, and the Governor.'"[29]

Agencies, on the other hand, can be cut. While the governor of New York is not authorized by the constitution to impound (or refuse to spend) appropriated funds, impoundments have become almost routine. They are restricted in three significant ways.

First, the governor may not touch the budgets of either the courts or the legislature. Second, debt payments and capital projects currently under construction cannot be stopped. Third, and most important, local assistance appropriations cannot be impounded or reduced. Once the state aid formulas for health care, schools, and general aid to localities have been signed into law, the Court of Appeals has ruled, they cannot be changed.[30]

When projected revenues are coming up short, these restrictions put a heavy burden on state agencies. Because the accounts that cannot be cut—aid to localities most importantly—comprise more than 60 percent of total state spending, the impact of even a small deficit on the remaining agencies can be quite significant. If it appears in November, for example, that state tax collections are running a billion dollars behind the amount projected in the budget, an across-the-board cut would reduce spending by less than 2 percent, *if* it was truly across the board. Most agencies can find ways to cut spending by 1 or 2 percent; but with so many budgets protected by law, the reality of a $1 billion cut for the nonexempt agencies is cuts in the range of 5 percent or more. And since the year is half over, and something like half of the originally planned dollars have already been spent, the impact in the last half of the year may be double that.

Funds that are withheld or impounded to meet a looming fiscal crisis seldom provoke great controversy unless there is a perception that the governor has unfairly concentrated on a few programs. In 1983–84, when Governor Cuomo impounded funds that had specifically been added to his budget by the legislature, it very nearly provoked a constitutional crisis. Although the governor had agreed to restore some of the funds his budget had cut from the offices of mental health and mental retardation, and the state and city Universities, he persisted in imposing staff cuts on these agencies in seeming defiance of his agreement with the legislature. The immediate crisis was resolved when the governor agreed to "very specific language requiring him to report on the deviations from the staffing levels that had been agreed to."[31] In every budget since then, the legislature has written into its *Green Book* language that is very specific not just as to dollar amounts but also as to minimum, maximum, and average staffing levels; and it has added very specific reporting requirements to the appropriation language bills.

One DOB examiner cited in a 1988 study of budgeting argued that the practice of impounding funds had become less common. As the study explained:

> The Legislature and DOB have to work together each year in the budget process. If Budget were routinely to allocate less than the amount appropriated, this would create unnecessary tensions between it and the Legislature, making everyone's job more difficult. The flexibility that results from the power to allocate less than the full appropriation enables the Division to keep the books balanced even in instances where revenue projections were too high. The basic purpose of the full appropriation must be achieved, however.[32]

It follows that most governors would be reluctant to risk antagonizing the legislature by stretching their impoundment powers. Governor Pataki, however, has been even more willing than his predecessors to impound appropriated funds for programs that he simply does not like.

What does an administrator do when confronted with such an impoundment? In 1995 when the governor announced that he was cutting the city university's budget for the spring semester the chancellor acceded. Cries of outrage from some faculty, student groups, and legislators were of little avail as long as the chancellor herself was not prepared to spend the money. Although she was widely criticized for not taking a more aggressive stance, no administrator heading into a new budget year wants to begin by picking a public fight with the governor. One high official in the state insurance department told us that the only realistic option he would have in a similar circumstance was to "go to the second floor and beg."

Where the Money Comes From

Most of the time when journalists and politicians talk about "the budget" they are referring to the $70 billion or so included as "all funds" spending in the governor's budget. Of this amount, only about $50 billion is actually state money; the rest comes, essentially, from the federal government; and only about $40 billion is "general fund" spending.[33] It does not include funds borrowed for the capital projects of authorities and special programs nor the fees collected by independent authorities to support their operations. One recent study by the U.S. Census Bureau estimated that the state actually raised more than $87 billion in 1999.[34] More important, New York, as we noted in Chapter 2, is unusually reliant on its localities—and on local taxes— to support major services. Thus, although its combined state and local tax burden amply justifies its reputation as a high tax state, the state itself is below the national midpoint in taxes it directly imposes on its citizens. The formal state budget, to put it another way, is deceptively small and tells only a part of the story of how funds are raised and spent. The state and its local entities collected roughly $140 billion in 1997–98. The state's share of this total amount, which is our focus for the next few pages, was—not including federal funds—a little more than half of the total.

State Taxes, Transfers, and Fees

In 1998–99 the state took in roughly $38.5 billion in taxes, $9.5 billion in miscellaneous receipts, and $22.5 billion in federal grants. By far the most important source of tax revenue is the personal income tax, which generates more than half ($23 billion in 1998–99) of all tax receipts. So-called user taxes (mainly the sales tax) and fees (such as motor vehicle registration charges) are second in importance, generating $7 to $8 billion a year. Corporate taxes account for about $4.5 billion. As we have noted, however, these numbers tell only part of the story.

When we add in the capital budget, only part of which shows up in the budget adopted by the legislature, the $12 billion or so in money borrowed by various public authorities, or other so-called off-budget accounts administered by state agencies, and the taxes and fees imposed by local governments, the most significant long-term trend in New York's pattern of raising revenue is a continuing decline in the proportion of dollars captured by taxes on individual and corporate income. The state income tax has been reduced at both ends to the point where it is virtually a flat tax. At the close of the Rockefeller era, New York had one of the country's most sharply progressive personal income tax systems, with the very poor paying nothing and the very rich paying as much as 15 percent on their highest earnings. Gradually the legislature worked with governors Carey, Cuomo, and Pataki to cut the top rate and increase the low end at which people begin paying taxes. In 1998, the top rate was reduced to 6.85 percent, a rate paid not just by millionaires but on any income over $47,500 for a single person with no deductions. Under this system, no one pays taxes on their first $7,500. A single person earning $20,000 pays nothing on the first $7,500, 4.3 percent on the balance. At $47,500, the first $7,500 is still exempt, but every extra dollar earned pays the maximum 6.85 percent. From there up, taxes are no longer adjusted for income.

Despite these cuts in corporate taxes and the new policy of taxing the rich at the same maximum rate as the middle class, the state was able in part to keep itself afloat through economic growth. In years when private sector income grew more rapidly than government spending, the state could afford tax cuts without significant cuts in services. Those years were few and far between through most of the Carey-Cuomo era. The Pataki administration has benefited from an unusually long and strong period of sustained economic growth combined with record profits on Wall Street and a major decline in the number of people in need of social services. By cutting taxes still further and maintaining spending, however, it too has been unable to effectively balance the budget. As in the Cuomo years, Pataki's administration has essentially disguised and made up the shortfall by a variety of gimmicks, devolutions, and devices. Four are particularly important.

First, the state continues to resort to a variety of fiscal gimmicks that provide cosmetic rather than real solutions to the state's fiscal problems. The 2000–01 budget adopted by the legislature in June 2000, for example, seemingly included a reasonably prudent $4 billion in reserve and "rainy day funds," or funds set aside for unanticipated emergencies, downturns in the stock market, or faulty economic projections. As recalculated by the state comptroller, however, the only real rainy day fund in the budget had a projected balance of only $550 million. What the governor and legislature did to present a prettier picture was create and sustain a number of programs seemingly funded outside of the main budget, and count as "reserve" funds more than $600 million allocated to fund increased salaries for state workers. By setting aside as contingency funds money for the raises already negotiated by the Civil Service Employee's Association and being negotiated by other unions, the "budget" was thus made to look $600 million smaller than everyone knew it actually would be. The "rainy day reserve," therefore, turned out to be more fog than rain, totaling just over one percent of total receipts.[35] (See Box 8.1, p. 303)

Second, New York continues to devolve an unusually high proportion of its tax burden to local governments. Between 1986 and 1993, according to one study, local property taxes jumped from 37 percent of total nonfederal funds to 41 percent. During the same period, the revenue from personal income and corporate taxes fell from 36 percent of state and local funds to 31 percent.[36] Third, it has shifted the focus of its revenue collections from broad-based corporate and personal income taxes to a wide variety of more targeted taxes and fees including the lottery (which nets about $1.6 billion a year). Governor Cuomo made up for some of the revenue lost in corporate and personal income tax cuts by sharply increasing so-called "sin" taxes on beer, liquor, cigarettes, and pari-mutuel betting. And Governor Pataki, at the same time that he was cutting the top end of the income tax rate schedule, sharply increased tuition at the state's public universities and the fees charged for the use of public facilities such as campgrounds. Local governments have followed much the same path. "In 1990, 22.5 percent of state general revenue from its own resources (not including federal aid) came from this source. For local governments, the percentage was 25.6."[37] The fourth way in which the state has made up for the revenues lost to tax cuts—particularly in bad years—has been by borrowing; and, by ways of manipulating the accounts that make borrowing look as if it is really something else.

Debt and Deception

When it resorted to borrowing to begin the Erie Canal in 1817, New York pioneered a new strategy of economic development that was soon imitated throughout the United States. A century later, Robert Moses expanded upon and refined this development strategy through the creation of a network of debt-funded public authorities. Local governments, with state encouragement, were soon to follow. Government borrowing generally takes three forms: short-term borrowing, general obligation bonds, and long-term revenue bonds. Short-term borrowing is used largely to meet cash-flow problems and cover emergencies. The idea behind long-term debt is that some expenditures, particularly those for capital projects like school buildings, highways, and fire trucks, because they benefit future taxpayers as well need not be paid for all at once.

Capital Budgeting

Under the state constitution, long-term borrowing plans must be passed by the legislature and submitted to public referendums. If the electorate approves, the state—or one of its local governments—issues bonds, which it promises to pay off over a stipulated number of years. These bonds, called "general obligation bonds," are backed by what is known as the "full faith and credit" of the state, which means, in essence, that the bondholders have first claim to the state's future revenues. Because of the security this commitment affords, and because the interest earned on government bonds is tax free, they can be sold at relatively low interest rates. The state, to put it another way, by providing a safe investment can borrow money at a lower rate than a corporation or private citizen would have to pay.

Bonds, like other investment tools, are sold in a competitive market. Thus a bank or individual considering an investment in New York bonds will compare them with bonds from Kansas, New Jersey, other state and local governments, corporations, and the federal government. Some of these investments are rated safer than others. Although it might seem unlikely that a state as wealthy as New York would not be able to pay its debts, defaults of this kind are not unheard of. On April 14, 1975, for example, the city of New York ran out of money and no bank could be found to extend the loans that would allow it to pay its bills. This was, moreover, the third time in its history that the city had gone broke.[38] Many state and local governments—particularly in times like the Great Depression of the 1930s—have weathered similar crises. Obviously, an investor seeking security will be reluctant to loan his or her money to a city or state with a poor payment record. And while the chances are fairly remote that a state's bondholders will not get their money back, a state that has borrowed too much is also likely to get a low rating from potential investors. Governments with poor histories of debt management can also have problems with the voters. Although New Yorkers are generally supportive of public education, a 1997 school bond issue was defeated by the voters in what appears to be a growing tendency to reject new borrowing plans. The government, however, has other ways of borrowing money.

Revenue Bonds

Unlike general obligation bonds, so-called revenue bonds are not backed by the full faith and credit of the state, rather money from an identified revenue stream is pledged as a safeguard for investments. Bonds issued by the state dormitory authority, for example, are backed by the promise of future rentals to college students; state thruway bonds by future tolls, and so on. Although the state itself cannot issue revenue bonds without the approval of the electorate (and neither can its municipalities), public authorities need only the approval of the legislature to float new bonds. It is this ability to avoid the electorate and not add to "official" (general obligation) debt that has led to the creation of so many public authorities in New York and other states.

Strictly speaking, funds borrowed through revenue bonds are supposed to be used to build facilities that will generate revenues. Some public authorities, however, have been allowed to bend the rules. City College's main classroom building, for example, was built by the state dormitory authority, though nobody has ever paid to sleep there. Increasingly, moreover, the state has allowed its public authorities to issue moral obligation bonds. Although there are limits on how much such paper can be issued, the line between revenue and general obligation bonds has been blurred beyond recognition. A relatively new device for avoiding the referendums required for general obligation bonds or the revenues backing revenue bonds is so-called "lease-purchasing." The Albany South Mall and office buildings in Binghamton and Utica, for example, were built with local revenue bonds, which were guaranteed by the promise of future rental of the facilities by the state. More recently, one state agency "sold" the Attica prison to another agency, which paid for it with borrowed money and then leased it back.

The financial crisis faced by New York City in the 1970s was founded in a cumulative reliance on fiscal gimmicks such as these. Rather than raise taxes or cut services, the city continued to project unrealistic levels of economic growth. In good years, higher tax collections and more state and federal aid allowed the city to muddle through; in bad years it resorted to borrowing to the point, in 1974, where New York accounted for nearly 40 percent of all municipal debt in the United States![39] Some of these borrowed funds—such as a "transit fare stabilization fund"—did not even pretend to be for capital purposes. The governor and legislature authorized these gimmicks rather than face demands for more state money; eventually the city's short-term debt exceeded a full year's worth of revenues. The financial control mechanisms installed in bailing out New York City have banned some of these practices and strongly regulated others, but if the distinction between various kinds of debts was never precise, it is even murkier now.

Short-term Borrowing and Fiscal Reality

As long as a government's credit is good, the advantages of long-term borrowing are clear. It both spreads payments over a longer time span, and generally comes at lower interest rates. But there are times when more expensive forms of debt must be incurred. In New York for many years the state annually engaged in an expensive ritual known as spring borrowing. The problem was that even when the budget was in balance by the end of the year, the state usually had a stream of receipts at odds with the flow of disbursements.

While most of the money disbursed to local governments and school districts went out in the first quarter (April through June), most taxes were collected in the fourth (January through March). Thus in 1985–86 the state was forced to borrow $4.3 billion and pay nearly $250 million in interest just to cover this gap. Between 1959–60 and 1988–89, the aggregate costs of spring borrowing in terms of interest paid was $2.8 billion, money that could have been spent on tax cuts or improved state services.[40] The practice of spring borrowing has been replaced by changes in the flow of certain revenues and disbursements, and by converting some forms of short-term debt into bonds; but both the state and its local governments must sometimes borrow to meet emergencies.

Short-turn borrowing always occurs when a downturn in the economy results in lower than expected revenues, or when expenses are unusually high. But while such miscalculations are likely to occur from time to time, the frequency with which they have arisen in New York suggests that they are almost endemic to the budget-making process. Indeed the governor and the legislature sometimes pass budgets that they know are unrealistic in the hope that they can make up the difference next year. As Raymond Keating says:

> These shady debt practices . . . were perfected during Governor Rockefeller's tenure. Voter approval of long-term debt presented a serious drag on his plans for expanding state government, so Rockefeller stepped around the voters through the use of public authorities as well as debt arrangements with localities.
>
> New York state-only debt has skyrocketed in recent decades. For example, according to the most recent U.S. Department of Commerce numbers, total per capita state-only debt in New York was more than double the U.S. state average in 1994. Since the mid-1960s, inflation-adjusted per capita state debt had leaped by better than 230 percent. Over the same period, real per capita interest paid on state debt jumped by almost 500 percent. Combined state *and* local per capita debt in New York tops the U.S. average by 70 percent (1993 is the most recent data available).[41]

Governor Pataki and the legislature have expressed considerable concern with the debt problem. The key business service organizations, like Moody's, that rate the investment value of government and corporate bonds now rate New York's among the lowest in the nation. This means that in order to borrow money New York must offer a higher rate of interest. Since interest on old debt already accounts for more than 5 percent (or $3.8 billion in 1998) of the "all funds" budget, there have been serious discussions about using the surpluses generated in 1998–99 and 1999–2000 to begin paying off some of the principal. But while the legislature passed a debt retirement initiative proposed by the governor as part of his 1998–99 budget, most of the real debt payments it provides for are projected for future years. In actual fact, the state contracted more debt in 1998–99 and in 1999–2000 than it paid off. Despite their noble sounding plans, the governor and the legislature have continued to borrow money for the environmental projects approved by the voters in 1997 and to consider new bond issues for such important state needs as school construction. Borrowing by authorities and local governments, meanwhile, continues and is difficult to contain as long as state aid lags behind inflation-adjusted needs. Focused on tax cuts and the maintenance of existing services with a rate of economic growth that is too slow to pay for both at once, politicians at the state and local level find:

> Circumvention is cheaper than change, even though its outcomes may well be far from ideal. The complexity of the system increases over time: when new circumventory mechanisms are created, the mechanisms of the past are retained rather than eliminated.[42]

Who Pays?

Recent cuts in the state income tax—in particular those initiated by Governor Cuomo in 1987 and by Governor Pataki in 1995—have been directed almost entirely toward the top brackets. As a result, the income tax, which accounted for nearly a third of state and local revenue in the 1980s, will provide less than a quarter of the funds raised by the state and its localities in 1999. In the normal order of things, economists rate the "progressivity" of a tax system according to the degree to which it taxes the rich at a higher rate than the poor. By the conventional rule of thumb, sales and property taxes are considered regressive in the sense that they impose the same burden on everyone regardless of ability to pay; income taxes, because the rates typically rise with earnings, are progressive.

In New York, ironically, conventional wisdom doesn't work. The very poor, those earning less than $15,000 to $20,000 a year, pay very little income tax. Middle-class families and individuals, on the other hand, pay income taxes at the same rates as those who are more affluent. Because they are less likely to itemize deductions, middle-class families sometimes even pay higher effective rates than their wealthier neighbors. User fees, similarly, hit low- and middle-class families harder than the more affluent: in New York you pay the same to register a 1989 Chevrolet as a 1999 Rolls Royce; the millionaire pays the same for his or her fishing license as the pauper. The sales tax in New York, conversely, is not as regressive as it is in many other states because it excludes such items as food and medicine that form a large share of a low income family's budget (see Box 8.2).

Box 8.2

The Complexities of the Tax Code

The late Russell Long of Louisiana, for many years chairman of the U.S. Senate Committee on Finance, neatly summarized most citizens' attitudes about taxes in the phrase, "Don't tax me, don't tax she, tax that man behind the tree!" The trick for most politicians is to find the man behind the tree. In some ways the complexities of the tax laws are part of a deliberate attempt to keep their true nature hidden: taxes that are buried in the prices of phone bills, real estate transactions, hotel rooms, and bets on horse races are—like the man behind the tree—popular with politicians because they are invisible to most people. The complexities of the tax code, however, are also the product of a series of difficult and contentious political struggles. If the tax code is most fundamentally the revenue plan of the state, it is also a profoundly political document and a window into a system's most basic values.

Reflecting the state's progressive tradition, many aspects of New York's tax code are designed to protect less affluent residents from taxes on such necessities as food. What foods are necessary? Here it gets a little tricky. Working from the premise that eating out is a luxury, restaurant food is taxed. This means that the same glass of milk you drink tax free at home is taxed in a cafeteria. Candy is taxed; cake is not. There is no sales tax on pure fruit juice (it must be 100 percent), but there is on juice drinks. You can buy a cold medicine to treat your runny nose without paying a sales tax, but if it doesn't work you will be taxed on the tissues to blow your nose.

Politics are also important in the tax equation. Lobbyists for retail stores won a major victory in 1999 when they persuaded the governor and the legislature to exempt most items of clothing from the sales tax. The stock markets have long been able to avoid increases in taxes on stock transfers by threatening to move to New Jersey if such tax increases are planned. The income tax laws are filled with exemptions for some kinds of income (such as pensions) and deductions for such expenses as business lunches and entertainment. Even the property tax is, in most cases, lower for senior citizens and not charged at all on the lands and buildings of various religious and charitable institutions.

Every now and again, some good government group calls for a "simplification" of the tax code. While some of these efforts are sincere, in most cases their real purpose is to shift the burden of payment from "he," "she," and "me" to that good old guy behind the tree. There is, in the final analysis, no tax reform plan that doesn't require some people to pay more and lets others pay less.

Generally, the property tax is America's most hated tax.

> Unlike other taxes, it usually has to be paid in one large, painfully visible
> lump sum. It doesn't go down when personal income and the ability to pay
> it go down. Its assessments are uneven: People who own similar properties
> may pay widely divergent taxes. And in many communities the weight of
> the tax is tilted to ease the burden of business so a heavier load falls on
> homeowners.[43]

Because it relies on its local governments to fund so many key programs, and because property taxes form the backbone of our system of local government finance, the property tax plays an unusually significant role in New York and, as we shall see, accounts for substantial inequities, especially when it comes to school finance.

Gimmicks

"There are," Forsythe warns, "no simple definitions of 'budget success'. . . . A successful budget is one that delivers on a governor's programmatic objectives, and does so within financial constraints that help achieve or maintain structural budget balance."[44] Throughout his intriguing memos to a hypothetical governor, Forsythe makes the sometimes explicit assumption that a key role of any governor is to keep a wild-spending legislature from giving away the store. It is true that legislators, without regard to party or ideology, are more generous with the taxpayers' money for certain kinds of spending programs. Because legislators' political risks are more localized they tend to be more solicitous of local interests, and thus are frequently at odds with governors in fighting reductions in school aid and general state aid to local governments. But for all their seeming frugality when it comes to issues such as these, all of the state's recent governors have shared a love of tax cuts, prisons, and economic development initiatives that often far outweigh the costs of all the spending increases proposed by the most spendthrift legislators.

How is it possible to cut taxes, increase school aid and transportation funding, build more prisons, and not make substantial cuts in vital areas such as health? The most desirable way is through the kind of economic growth that, by producing increased tax collections and lower costs for social welfare programs, is the rising tide that lifts all ships. Like the tide, however, it is something over which the state has little direct control. What the governor and legislative leaders can control are their perceptions and projections of economic growth. In bad times, and especially in election years, there is a strong temptation for all sides to agree to raise their estimates in a triumph of hope over intelligence. If the budget ends up out of balance by a billion or so, we can worry about that next year when the time comes.

Similar fudging can be achieved by introducing programs in stages, hoping that by the time the last payments are due there will have been enough economic growth to pay them. Governor Pataki's tax-cut plan, for example, was heavily backloaded, providing only $1.4 billion in cuts in its first year but rising to $11.3 billion in 2000–01. Before the state changed its accounting rules in the 1980s a favorite device for hiding deficits was to postpone expenditures, or, in effect, pay the bills late. If, for example, a payment to the civil service pension fund due in the last quarter of one fiscal year is not actually paid until the beginning of the next year the money has apparently been "saved." (Do not try this at home.) Devices such as this, or the example given earlier of one state agency "selling" an asset to another and then leasing it back, are known as "one shots" since they only work once. They have been frequently deplored, but just as frequently used to make budget agreements less painful. Longer run "solutions," such as those which involve "backdoor" borrowing (backdoor in the sense that they are neither approved by the voters nor dedicated to revenue-producing capital projects), or that transfer the costs of state programs to local governments, are equally common. In the words of former state comptroller Ned Regan:

> The way Albany works is very clear: it's gain here, pain there. It's gain in Albany and pain in Yonkers or New York City. . . . It's gain here and the pain is fifteen years later when you're paying the debt service for all those borrowings made to balance the budget. It's always the same pattern, shift responsibility to another government, shift from the operating budgets to the capital budget. You shift the gain this year for the ribbon cutting ceremonies and the rebuilding effort and spread the pain out over time.[45]

New York is not unique in its resort to such gimmicks. There is, at the same time, some consensus that the game is played more recklessly and persistently in New York than in most other jurisdictions. One explanation, frequently offered, is that budget gimmicks are more common in New York because the state is so uncommonly generous in catering to special interests and the poor. Before we examine the overall dynamic of policy politics in New York, let us turn to the issue of how the state allocates its resources.

Where the Money Goes

It costs about $3 billion a year just to keep the government going. State courts alone account for more than $1 billion, the legislature for almost $200 million, and the offices associated with the governor just under $100 million. It costs $250 million just to raise the taxes to pay for everything else. About $4 billion a year pays the interest on old debts, and another $4 billion pays the pensions of retired state employees. Not counting local governments and authorities, in other words, the state spends more than $10 billion a year without educating a single child, repairing a road, or treating a gallon of sewage. Roughly one dollar in every seven of general fund disbursements supports the operations of past and present governments. Of the remaining six dollars, more than four are transferred to local governments. Only 19 percent of all general fund spending falls in the category of what are called "state operations."

If you strip the state budget to its naked essence, it amounts to this: pensions, debt services, and general government operations aside, about 40 percent of the state's money goes to health, 30 percent to education, and 30 to everything else. Much of this money is channeled through and frequently augmented by varying levels of local expenditure, but even at the local level, health and education comprise the big ticket items on the government bill. Let us put this very explicitly: *if you really want to cut public spending in New York, you are talking about health or schools; there just isn't much else to cut.*

Health

New York's public health care system is largely driven, as are those of most states, by the federal Medicaid program, but it is unique among state health care systems in both size and complexity. Long before the federal government became involved, New York governments played a huge role in the area of health. New York City in 1960 through 1964, for example, spent a higher percentage of its budget on health than it did after Medicaid was adopted. While most states found Medicaid's cost-sharing requirements a drain on their treasuries, New York took the 1965 establishment of the federal program as an opportunity to use federal funds for services it was already providing, and to augment and expand existing state efforts. Despite attempts to cut back, New York's system of health care delivery remains the largest, most closely regulated, and most complex in the United States. In 1998, it maintained 265 hospitals with more than 68,000 beds, and 684 nursing homes with nearly 140,000 beds. Medicaid costs alone comprised $28.4 billion—or 39 percent—of the state's "all funds" budget; and New York continued "to be number one in total spending, spending per capita, program cost per recipient, rates paid to providers, and in almost every Medicaid spending category."[46]

Although health systems throughout the state are administered by the state department of health, New York City's Health and Hospitals Corporation (HHC) actually has a larger payroll, and local governments throughout the state play an unusually large role both in managing and financing health policies. In few areas of public policy, and in few areas of the United States, is the term "marble cake" federalism (See Chapter 2) a more appropriate descriptive term.

Medicare and Medicaid

Although the federal government had been involved in caring for veterans and providing some funds for hospital construction and medical education, the policy dynamic changed completely with the passage of Medicare and Medicaid in 1965. While many liberals had long been pushing for a program of national health along European lines, Medicare emerged as a compromise proposal designed to focus on the particularly acute needs of senior citizens. Almost as an afterthought, Medicaid was added on to help the nonelderly poor. Medicare, as an add-on to Social Security, is essentially a two-part program of health insurance on one hand, and hospital insurance on the other, paid for by federal taxes and individual payments. Except as regarding payment schedules and fees, the program has relatively little direct impact on state finances. Medicaid, conversely, because it is a program of matching funds, has a very substantial and direct impact on the state and its localities.

The line between Medicare and Medicaid is not as clear as it once seemed. As seniors require long-term care, Medicare runs out and they are forced into Medicaid. A very substantial proportion of the funds spent on Medicaid is spent on the long-term nursing home care of senior citizens who were not poor enough to qualify when they first became ill. Cumulatively, the numbers are staggering:

> In 1989, about 80 percent of New York State's 104,000 nursing home beds were paid for by Medicaid, only three percent by Medicare. About half (51 percent) of the Medicaid eligible elderly also receive Supplemental Security Income (SSI), income assistance from the federal government. The other 49 percent are the elderly of higher income levels who have "spent down" their financial assets and are then eligible to have their health care costs paid by Medicaid. . . . While those over 65 were only 13 percent of New York State's eligible Medicaid population, their care consumed 41 percent of New York's Medicaid budget. Almost 30 percent of Medicaid went to pay for nursing home costs.[47]

The welfare reform measures initiated at the federal level in the 1990s will put still greater pressure on the state health system by forcing Medicaid to make up for losses in SSI coverage.

Medicaid is operated by the states according to federal guidelines. In New York, the federal government covers roughly half the overall costs and the state about one-third, with local governments (counties outside of New York City) responsible for the balance. New York also pays for its own (nonfederally covered) Medicaid, which is operated within the national system with half state and half local funding. Until recently, Medicaid funds were channeled through a broad array of local care providers including hospitals, clinics, nursing homes, physicians, dentists, and pharmacists. In this "fee for service" system the provider billed Medicare according to a schedule of fees set by the state with federal approval. As the state attempted to save money by periodically cutting fees to lower levels, a growing number of private providers dropped out of the system leaving much of it in the hands of government-run clinics and hospitals. The private-practice doctors willing to accept the set rate of $11 per office visit were usually found in what became known as "Medicaid mills," privately run clinics in which the level of service was cursory at best. Medicaid mills could be highly profitable by processing patients very rapidly and by engaging in such practices as "ping-ponging" patients from one specialist to another. This approach is being changed under the terms of a law passed in 1996 and accepted by the federal government in 1997 allowing the state to implement a statewide mandatory managed care program. Although managed care is often criticized by both physicians and advocacy groups, it has proven enormously cost effective in delivering at least minimal services to target populations.

Balancing Cost Containment with Public Health and Safety

Most Americans (56 percent)—and most New Yorkers (52 percent)—receive health coverage through their jobs. With its high poverty rate, New York is slightly above the national average in the percentage of those eligible for Medicaid (14 percent) and those with no health coverage at all (17 percent). Despite attempts by the state to increase Medicaid coverage to include the children of families above the poverty line, a substantial reduction in private coverage has resulted in a rapid increase in the ranks of the uninsured. The low income working poor, recent immigrants in particular, are most disadvantaged with 46 percent uninsured. New York City has a particularly large proportion of this population, with 28 percent uninsured as compared with 13 percent in the rest of the state.[48]

New York City's HHC, with an operating budget of more than $3 billion, is bigger by far than any other hospital system in the United States. While many of their patients are privately insured or reimbursed through Medicaid, HHC hospitals serve enormous numbers of indigent, uninsured patients. While this would be a significant financial burden under normal circumstances, the higher incidence of tuberculosis and AIDS in New York City (in 1991, 23 percent of all AIDS cases nationwide were in New York[49]), and its higher rates of homelessness, alcoholism, and drug abuse compound the problem. To understand the dynamics of health care politics in New York, these differences between New York City and the rest of the state must be kept in mind.

The Politics of Health

Throughout the United States the cost of providing health care has climbed at a rate far higher than inflation. Per capita health expenditures in 1990 were more than two-and-a-half times what they were in 1980, and more than doubled again in 2000. At all levels of government, cost containment has become the name of the game. By moving Medicaid patients into mandatory managed care programs, the state expects to realize significant savings through increased primary care use, lower emergency room use, and fewer inpatient days. Other attempts to cut spending on health care, however, have been strongly resisted by the legislature in general and the assembly's Democratic majority in particular. The legislature's general reluctance to cut the health care budget derives from three key political facts. First—and this applies to governors as well as legislators—health care is popular with voters, senior citizens and their children in particular. Nursing home care in New York is expensive but it is also good, better in most cases than in other states. And its hospitals and doctors are among the finest in the world with more prestigious teaching hospitals than anywhere else. Second, people do not like to see hospitals closed. Although many hospitals are inefficient or duplicate the services of nearby facilities, closing a hospital is a tough sell with voters. Third, the health care lobby is large and diversified. It spends a lot of money, employs some of Albany's most skillful legislative representatives, and cuts across the political spectrum. It includes both the Republican-leaning state medical society and two large labor unions representing hospital workers that have close ties to the Democrats. It also includes several large insurance companies, the Greater New York Hospital Association, and the Healthcare Association of New York. Five of these organizations were among the top spenders in the lobbying commission's 2000 annual report.[50]

Democrats in the assembly are particularly protective of health care, partly because of these pressures, largely because they believe the government should provide basic health care for all, and very significantly because even relatively small cuts in the state's health expenditures are magnified in the city. The eleven hospitals and numerous clinics operated by the HHC receive more than five million ambulatory care visits a year at an annual cost of more than $3 billion. The bulk of its patients are poor and without private health insurance. The state adds a surcharge to all hospital care transactions to help finance a charity pool that reimburses both public and private hospitals for the cost of treating persons unable to pay their bills, but this fund typically covers less than half of the hospitals' actual costs.

For years hospitals absorbed the medically indigent by charging insured patients more. This practice, long attacked by the insurance industry, has become almost impossible under a managed care system of health. The problem for municipal hospitals is particularly acute. The more Medicare rules are tightened, the less their revenue. In order to keep the city hospital system afloat, therefore, legislators from New York City must fight to keep Medicaid dollars flowing. Although the city must put up fifteen cents of every Medicaid dollar, it is the eighty-five cents in state and federal funds that keeps public hospitals running. There is, then, a paradox: cuts in Medicaid, instead of saving the city money, force it to dig deeper into its own resources to keep marginal hospitals afloat. From a fiscal and political perspective, in other words, neither New York City nor its representatives in Albany can afford substantial cuts in state health funds.

Education

New York state's public schools enroll more than 2.5 million students at an average cost of more than $9,000 per student.[51] As we noted in Chapter 1, a high percentage of New York's graduates were among those commended by the National Merit Scholars Program, writing advanced placement exams, and winning prestigious prizes. But while graduates of New York's public and private schools were averaging ten points higher than the rest of the nation on combined college board subject tests, SAT scores of New York students ranked forty-second in the country. And the state ranked a dismal forty-third in terms of estimated public high school graduation rates.

Funding the Public Schools

These extremes of excellence and failure are closely related to the extremes of poverty and wealth that characterize New York. Poor children and those from families with substandard educations tend to do poorly in school. Higher income families not only tend to provide home environments more conducive to learning, but they tend to live in communities where other families also value education. These differences are further exaggerated by a system of school financing that tends to provide better schools to the better-off students and very poor schools to the very poorest pupils.

Although most of the rules and regulations governing educational policy are state rules, local control of the schools is one of the most sacred cows of American federalism. Local school boards continue to play a minor role in setting policy, deciding, for example, whether to fund a football team, or whether to require school uniforms; but their primary role is budgetary, and what local control really means is that each school district in the state is the ultimate arbitrator of how much will be spent on education in each community.

New York's richest school district—comprising a handful of year-round residents on the Fire Island seashore—has a pupil-to-teacher ratio of four to one and spends more than $30,000 a year on each student. To compare this with a school in New York City or in the northern Adirondacks, where per pupil expenditures may run as low as $6,000 to $7,000 per year, is to ignore too many complicating variables to be meaningful. The most widely accepted measure of equity in school funding compares the first school in the top 10 percent in terms of per pupil expenditures with the highest cost school in the bottom 10 percent. By this test, in 1994–95 "the district at the 90th percentile of expenditure per pupil spent 76.9 percent more than the district at the 10th percentile ($12,949 versus $7,320 per pupil).[52] Although state law is designed to give more help to students with the greatest needs, school districts in high poverty areas often lack the resources to keep up. Inner city districts do poorly, particularly in areas like Buffalo, where the tax base has been eroded both by suburbanization and a long period of economic recession; but the poor rural areas are also at the low end of the per pupil expenditure scale.

The gap between rich and poor school districts has been growing to the point at which New York ranks fifth among forty-nine states (Hawaii is excluded because it does not have separate school districts) on a scale measuring equity in per pupil funding. These differences are, by and large, less the product of deliberate policy than of two important demographic facts: First, income disparities in the state are not only growing at a dramatic rate but they are becoming more geographically based with wealthy communities and poor ones growing apart at an accelerating rate. Second, some of the highest growth areas in terms of students are in the poorest areas economically, and state aid formulas are slow to adjust to population growth. But although demographic variables are at the root of the equity problem, state policies supposedly designed to minimize the effects of these differences on the schools have not been doing the job. As in most areas of retrenchment, budget cuts have tended to have their most severe impact at the lower levels. To understand why this is so, one must look less at economic variables than at politics.

The Politics of Education

The basic system of school funding in essence gives each school district a per-pupil allocation from the state. In order to equalize opportunity, this basic allocation is adjusted to give more state aid to districts with fewer resources, measured largely by property values. The basic idea is that the poorer the district, the less able it is to raise money from local property taxes, the more state aid it will get. In reality, the system of school funding is more complex.

The problem begins with the process of putting the budget together. Except in the rare case of an election year in which the state is awash with money (as in 1996), governors almost invariably propose cuts in baseline funds for education. They do so knowing that there has not been a governor's education budget in recent history that the legislature did not augment. By low-balling their school budgets, governors are able to offer a "balanced" budget overall that also includes room for later bargaining. Because legislators—suburban legislators in particular—fight hard for their education dollars, when it comes time to cut money from, say, parks, the governor can say, "Look, I've given you this money for schools, now help me balance the budget." In the final analysis, no one can accuse the governor of hurting school children, who get their money; park supporters and others who are cut blame the legislature for cutting the governor's original numbers, and the governor has pretty much the kind of balanced budget he originally wanted.

Problem two for the poorer school districts derives from the way in which the legislature has gone about restoring these gubernatorial "cuts." Within days of the governor's budget presentation, the state education department fleshes out the raw numbers with computer printouts describing precisely how the numbers will impact each and every school district not among the Big 5 (Buffalo, New York City, Rochester, Syracuse, and Yonkers). Local newspapers in every corner of the state will report exactly how much each community will lose, and they will usually speculate on the kinds of school programs that will have to be cut or the kinds of property tax increases that will need to be enacted. Every legislator from outside of the Big Five districts will know exactly what each of the school districts in his or her constituency will be getting from the state if the governor's budget goes through unchanged; and he or she will likely be inundated with letters and phone calls from unhappy voters in the towns threatened by cuts. To isolate themselves from such pressures, rural and suburban legislators have built a variety of protections into the aid formula. Without going into the technical details, the most important of these are the so-called "save harmless" formulas that make sure that no district loses state money while others gain. By constructing this kind of floor under the amount of aid that goes to the wealthier districts, the legislature typically leaves little money for the upgrading of schools in the poorer districts.

Why, you might ask, do the representatives of the poorer districts put up with this? Why don't the Republicans representing the poor rural districts team up with Big Five Democrats to equalize educational opportunities for their constituents? There are, of course, political problems in forging such an alliance, and it is also true that poor people are both less likely to vote and less likely to be attentive to school budget issues than those from more affluent areas. More important, schools are just not the dominating issue in rural and urban districts as they are in the suburbs. The reality of the assembly's Democratic conference on school funding issues is that of a world in which the tail often wags the dog. The core of the party is liberal, largely urban, and—to a growing degree—black and Hispanic. About half of the 90–plus Democrats in the assembly are from New York City. Another 15, typically, are from the four other big cities. Like their counterparts from the Big Apple, most of them have little or no trouble beating their Republican opponents in the general election. Altogether these urban Democrats dominate the Democratic conference by a margin of almost two-to-one. But with 60 to 65 seats, they are nowhere near controlling a majority of the 150 seats in the lower house as a whole. Their continuing ability to elect a Speaker, to dominate committees, politics, and policy, depends on their continuing ability to elect Democrats from outside the cities, particularly in the suburbs.

How does a suburban Democrat get reelected? Not by cutting school aid, that's for sure. So if party leaders want to save the seats of marginal members they must give Democrats from affluent communities the ability to go back to their districts with the good news of a "save-harmless" deal on the school budget. And city Democrats go along because they understand that if they lose their party majority in the assembly they will lose their influence in education, mass transit, housing, health, and other areas. And they go along because they also know that nobody back home has those nasty printouts: if urban schools deteriorate you can blame the mayor—"we gave him the money, he just didn't spend it on schools."

Meanwhile in the senate there is a similar, though slightly more subtle political dynamic. Here the marginal seats also are largely suburban. If the Democrats were ever to regain control of the senate, they would do so by winning seats in the suburbs, particularly in the areas surrounding New York City. Large numbers of people living in the bedroom communities of Long Island, Westchester, and Rockland County moved there and put up with long commutes in no small part because of the schools. Driven by the concerns of state senators representing these areas, the Republican conference has almost always been friendly to increased spending for schools in general, and to save-harmless formulas in particular. The 1988 overthrow of then majority leader Warren Anderson, as we have seen, originated largely in his failure to understand the importance of the school issue to the suburban members of the Republican conference.

There is one last wrinkle in the process that sometimes leads to underfunding poor schools. In the Big Five districts, per-pupil aid does not go directly to local school boards. Instead, each city gets a lump-sum payment into its general account. When municipal finances are shaky, it is possible for city governments to divert increases in school aid to other uses. From time to time the legislature has tried to block these diversions through so-called "maintenance of effort" laws that require the Big Five to use increased education funds on education. In 1996, however, when both houses of the legislature passed maintenance of effort bills, the bill was held on the majority leader's desk instead of being sent to the governor, an extraordinarily unusual procedure that kept the bill from becoming law. While there was some speculation that New York City Mayor Rudolph Giuliani, faced with serious budget shortfalls, had gotten to his fellow Republicans, it seems equally likely that Democrats on the New York City council had worked through the assembly Speaker to have the bill put aside so that they could divert part of the increased aid to a threatened summer youth program. Maintenance of effort may thus have lost in 1996 not because New York City Democrats don't care about schools, but because they have so many other "good programs" to fund that education just becomes part of the mix. In New York City:

> Members must concern themselves with a variety of noneducational state support programs for such purposes as public assistance, Medicaid, public health, and public housing, which usually provide less benefits to the higher income areas outside New York City. City legislators are more likely to focus on those concerns that they perceive to be of greater importance to their constituents. On the other hand, many legislators representing independent school districts focus on state aid to education.
>
> In many cases, members from rural areas and small towns upstate are more like Democrats from the City than their suburban Republican colleagues. Faced with such poverty-related issues as Medicaid, and burdened too with enormous road maintenance bills and the unique concerns of agriculture they don't have the luxury of fixating on the issue of school funding.[53]

Education groups, such as the United Federation of Teachers and the school boards association are, as indicated elsewhere in this volume, high on the list of well-financed and effective lobbies. As such, they make an important contribution to this political dynamic. While they all support higher levels of spending on schools, none of them have any abiding interest in issues of equity since their members come from both rich districts and poor districts.

CUNY, SUNY, and Other Claimants

Neither education nor health care becomes cheaper over time. New technologies in both fields, and the labor intensive nature of the delivery systems, militate against cost cutting. No one wants to have hospitals with bigger caseloads and ancient X-ray machines, or schools with larger class sizes and no computers. The strong desire of state legislators to sustain these programs puts intense pressure on other parts of the budget when times are difficult. Because school funds and health funds are virtually untouchable, and because they jointly absorb nearly two-thirds of the operating budget, there is little room left to maneuver in other areas. Only the most essential and/or politically powerful programs can avoid taking the brunt of whatever cuts hard times, tax decreases, or other political dynamics dictate.

The city and state university systems have become increasingly vulnerable to cuts. Unlike elementary and secondary school taxes, which show up directly on annual property tax bills, the costs of college education are borne more directly by the state. Because tuition costs are still a bargain by comparison with most private colleges, parents are unlikely to be too upset by modest increases in tuition and fees. College students, moreover, do not vote in large numbers and neither they nor the faculties are strongly represented in Albany. Most important, perhaps, New York does not really have a tradition of public higher education. Although the City College of New York (CUNY) was established in 1848 as the first public, free-tuition institution of higher learning in the country, New York state did not participate in creating land-grant state colleges, and—a handful of teacher's colleges excepted—did not get into the business of higher education until after World War II." In the words of one observer:

> There was a vacuum, an abdication of responsibility for higher education which prevented any significant policy proposals or master plans. . . . There was no system at all; there was merely a weak and undistinguished group of public institutions lumped together in a State University on the one hand, and a diverse group of private institutions on the other.[54]

All this was to change when Nelson Rockefeller effectively "created" the SUNY and CUNY systems in 1959; but public education in New York— particularly when compared with systems in other states—continues to play the role of ugly stepchild to the private colleges.

Because the legislature has so much trouble cutting health and education spending, programs such as higher education, as we have noted, take unusually hard hits when times are bad. Even if revenues are off by as little as 1 or 2 percent, fixed cost programs like debt service, and politically safe programs like elementary and secondary education, force legislators to look for extra large savings from other areas. Thus colleges, mental health agencies, parks, the council on the arts, and programs for the poor and the disabled tend to fluctuate dramatically from one year to the next, and to lurch, as it were, from crisis to crisis in making financial plans. The exceptions to this rule are those programs that either perform highly popular functions in the context of the times, or that are politically connected to the politically powerful. Perhaps the best example of the former, in recent years, has been correctional institutions, which—fueled by tough anticrime measures and the "war" on drugs—have been a growth industry (see Box 8.2, page 320).

Some other programs have survived in hard times and grown in good because of their positions either as the favorites of powerful interests or because they are politically situated to maximize their basic clout. The state's transportation budget in many ways epitomizes the importance of politics in program preservation. Voters in New York City, where fewer than half the adults even have licenses to drive, have little or no interest in highways or commuter rail lines. Rural voters are almost entirely dependant upon their cars, trucks, and the highway systems as part of their everyday lives. Suburbanites worry about commuter lines and to a lesser degree about highways and other forms of mass transit. These complementary concerns set the stage for a continuing log roll: senate Republicans are left by assembly Democrats to write their own ticket with regard to highways in exchange for mass transit; suburban legislators in both parties broker the deal and cut their own share for commuter lines. The pieces are in place, in other words, for a compromise achieved not by splitting the difference but by letting each side write its own ticket. Once they agree on how much to allocate to each function, it is up to city residents to decide how mass transit money will be spent, to rural and suburban interests to allocate highway funds, and to suburbanites to write the ticket for commuter lines.

Less fluidly, the assembly and senate bargain urban housing and social welfare programs for upstate agricultural issues, and so on. But although the legislature through logrolling can avoid protracted fights over many of these issues, the programs are not as firmly entrenched politically to survive the ups and downs of the economy or the will of a governor determined to change spending priorities. Unlike schools and most health programs, then, transportation and other issues are not highly predictable.

The Ongoing Woes of Local Government

The so-called devolution revolution, as noted in Chapter 2, may or may not have returned control over many programs to local governments, but it has transferred the burden of paying for many services from both the federal and state levels to localities. General fund aid to localities in New York went from roughly $1 billion in 1960 to $4 billion in 1970. It doubled to roughly $8 billion from 1970 to 1980, and again to almost $16 billion in 1990. The figure projected for 2000 is $25 billion, a slowing in state aid that coincides with comparable cutbacks in federal funds. As both state and federal funds decline as a share of local expenditures, the "fiscal health" of most munici-palities—a measure of the balance between a community's effective expen-diture needs and its revenue-raising capacity—has declined significantly since 1980. One study of big city politics between 1982 and 1988 placed both Buffalo and New York City in the top quartile of cities whose fiscal health had declined.[55] Their situation has not significantly improved in the inter-vening years. This study also found that there was a tendency for larger cit-ies to suffer more from resource problems than smaller ones.

Cities, some analysts have charged, have tried to do too much. By at-tempting to sustain major social problems and cater to the demands of count-less special interests, their reach has increasingly exceeded their grasp. Problems rooted in bad policies, this argument continues, have been com-pounded in cities like Buffalo and New York by problems rooted in bloated bureaucracies and government inefficiency. But, as Helen Ladd points out in comparing Philadelphia and New York:

> Although the financial difficulties in these cities may be exacerbated by politics or management practices, the fact that both cities were among the 10 least healthy cities in 1988 suggests that their financial problems prima-rily reflect underlying structural problems that are largely outside the con-trol of city officials. Stated differently, one explanation for the political difficulties that these cities face in balancing their budgets may simply be that their options are all unpleasant; poor fiscal health implies that a city must choose between severe cuts in public services and tax hikes.[56]

As agriculture continues to decline, small towns and cities outside New York City's suburban fringe are falling on hard times. Upstate New York as a whole has simply not participated in the economic boom of the 1990s that has eased the financial woes of New York City and its surrounding metro-politan area. New York City has dodged the bullet of disaster it faced in the 1970s largely through the cash windfall that has flown into the city's coffers by virtue of the sustained bull market on Wall Street. Absent economic growth in this sector, the city economy has essentially been in decline for two decades, and despite expanding tax revenues, the city still projects budget shortfalls in excess of $1.5 billion in 2001 and 2002. Absent Wall Street, many upstate cities have literally been mired in a twenty year slump. The sustained nature of this recession has put many communities in a situation where borrowing is no longer an option, where the tax base is already severely stretched, and basic city services are already underfunded. Almost one-quarter of the 1999 budget of the city of Syracuse—to use an extreme but increasingly typical case—will be used to pay for the interest on past debts. Troy has only recently emerged from a three-year period when it was, in effect, operating under the bankruptcy direction of the state comptroller's office.

Big City Governments, Politics, and Fiscal Constraints

The declining ability of local governments to maintain fiscal soundness has been—to revert to the models introduced earlier in this chapter—both incremental and episodic. Mayors, and local governments generally, have an impact on expenditures but very little control over income. Intergovernmental aid, or money that comes to New York City directly from the state or federal government, has declined significantly from the halcyon days of the 1970s. A process of slow erosion in the long-run has been punctuated by dramatic cutbacks during times such as the early Reagan years in Washington, or the 1994–95 period when New York's local governments confronted both a newly elected governor, Pataki, and a Republican Congress in Washington bent on reducing the size of government. In contrast with the 1970s, when federal programs like general revenue sharing simply gave federal funds to local governments, and when the state aid to localities program was a major budget item, virtually all of the state and federal funds that are transferred to local governments today are earmarked for such purposes as Medicaid, transportation, housing, or education. One tabulation, by the state comptroller, after excluding aid for these specific functions, put the proportion of the state's budget allocated to "support for local governments" at a measly 3.2 percent.[57]

The Big Five cities in New York have, in theory at least, more flexibility in allocating resources than do the state's other localities. The mayors and councils of Buffalo, New York, Rochester, Syracuse, and Yonkers have fewer obvious rivals for power in setting their budgets. School aid, in particular, flows into their general budgets instead of to the independent school boards that control school budgets in the rest of the state. New York City, moreover, shares neither functions nor funds with county governments.[58] But the plethora of independent authorities that blanket the state loom even larger in urban areas, particularly in New York City. Such agencies as the Metropolitan Transit Authority, the Port Authority of New York and New Jersey, and the City University of New York are largely independent of local political control.

Politically too, the fiscal constraints on local governments loom large. In most towns and cities, major chunks of the budget are virtually untouchable. The amounts that local governments spend on health and social welfare are set by state regulations and the number of persons needing assistance in any given year. These numbers are basically out of the control of local governments—worse, they tend to go up in years when revenues are going down. (When the economy is bad, tax revenues decrease at the same time that more people tend to fall below the poverty line making them eligible for safety net programs). Many other services, while they are technically subject to budget controls, are virtually uncontrollable in the real world. It is almost impossible, for example, to make serious cuts in expenditures for law enforcement or to close a firehouse. Even more than at the state level, therefore, political actors in local politics are often faced with the prospect of making enormous cuts in programs with weak political constituencies and/or low public priority. (The logic of this problem is as follows: if revenues are down 5 percent, but half of the budget cannot be cut, all other items must be slashed 10 percent in order to balance the ledgers. When fixed items total 75 percent, cuts can reach 20 percent for the remaining programs, and so on). Little wonder that local governments are even more inclined than the state to resort to fiscal gimmicks and borrowing, particularly when nonincremental cuts in state or federal aid hit home.

Despite the constraints within which local governing officials operate, some mayors have been able to change the direction of spending in significant ways. City-funded spending in New York City, for example, increased by an average of 7.4 percent per year between 1982 and 1990, by 4.7 percent between 1991 and 1995, but only by a projected 2.1 percent between 1996 and 2000.[59] Under the leadership of Mayor Rudolph Giuliani there has also been an unusually significant shifting of priorities away from social services and education to public safety. In his drive to reduce taxes, cut spending, and shift government priorities, the mayor has had a lot of help from changes in state and federal policies as well as the windfall from Wall Street. Welfare reform and a variety of cost-cutting mandates relating to both Medicare and Medicaid have saved New York City literally billions of dollars.

It would be misleading to suggest that municipal governments lack the power or will to effect substantial changes in policy. Between March 1995 and March 1998, to use figures provided in the mayor's fiscal year 2000 executive budget, the welfare caseload in New York City declined by 40 percent, a rate far in excess of the national average. The booming city economy contributed to some of this decline, and Mayor Giuliani achieved further savings by persuading the city council to pass local laws strongly enforcing the new federal guidelines. He was also helped by state implementation laws that, for example, made it virtually impossible for welfare recipients to attend four-year colleges. Giuliani also used his executive powers to cut the welfare roles by ordering his social services administrators to slow the processing of applications, force recipients to meet the absolute letter of the law, deny benefits to those who failed accurately to complete increasingly complex application forms, and refuse emergency assistance to most applicants. These efforts are being challenged in court and by the federal government and are likely to be ruled illegal. Many of the most needy cases, moreover, wind up costing the city in other parts of its budget by seeking refuge in shelters for the homeless, in hospitals, and even in jail; but there is little doubt that in the short run at least, the mayor has substantially reduced the social services budget and substantially reduced the public assistance caseload.

New York City and Rochester: A Tale of Two Cities

As important as what students of urban politics call "the permanent government" is in constraining urban policy options, Giuliani's first six years as mayor serve as a reminder of the potential powers that inhere in the office of mayor. Despite revisions in the city charter that give the city council significantly more power, the council's overwhelmingly Democratic majority has by and large accepted the mayor's restructuring of fiscal priorities, and the mayor was able to promise tax cuts totaling nearly 3 percent of total revenues by the year 2000. His administrative orders to make it difficult even for the most needy to qualify for welfare illustrate the important part that controlling the bureaucracy plays in setting policy priorities.

One way of demonstrating both the potential and limitations of politics in urban policy is by comparing the budgetary priorities of two diverse cities, New York and Rochester. Rochester has far fewer extremes of wealth and poverty than New York, is a far smaller (some would say "more manageable") city, and shares taxing and governing authority with surrounding Monroe County. But although it is another world entirely from New York City both in the way it raises money and spends it, in the final analysis the two cities' bottom lines are quite similar.

Rochester gets almost 40 percent of its revenue from taxes on real property, New York City a little more than half that proportion, or 21 percent. New York City, at the same time, has an income tax, which Rochester does not, and that tax accounts for roughly an eighth of the city's budget. Another eighth of New York City's budget comes from federal grants, compared with only 2 percent for Rochester. Most of this money, however, is for Medicare and Medicaid, which in Rochester is paid for by the county: 19 percent of county revenues are from the federal grants. Rochester relies far more heavily than New York on the sales tax (27 percent as opposed to 9 percent), and receives an extra rebate on Monroe County's share of sales tax receipts; but New York City more than makes up for this difference through an astonishingly high array of miscellaneous taxes and fees ranging from a stock transfer tax to taxes on hotel rooms and flights from the city's airports, and fees for everything from vendor's licenses to building permits. Almost 30 percent of New York City's revenues come from such taxes and fees as opposed to only 16 percent of Rochester's. The most important difference, a legacy perhaps of New York City's more liberal political past, is the 10 percent of its revenues it raises through taxes on banks and corporations, taxes that are relatively trivial in Rochester and Monroe County, and which have declined in New York City as well.[60]

In terms of expenditures, the most striking differences between New York City and Rochester are found in the area of elementary and secondary education. The city of Rochester spends roughly 20 percent more per pupil than does New York City, despite the fact that it has far less "wealth" to tax.[61] The differences between Rochester and its surrounding suburbs, moreover, are not nearly so striking as they are in the New York City metropolitan area. Thus the poorest school district in Monroe County, in the town of Brockport, spent $6,771 per student in 1994, while the wealthiest district, in suburban Brighton, spent $10,008. Per-pupil spending in Rochester was $9,659. In the counties adjoining New York City there are only two school districts that spend less per student than the city average of $7,921; but there are suburban districts in communities like Elmsford ($20,603), Great Neck ($16,281), Jericho ($15,843), and Pocantico Hills ($23,858) that spend two or even three times as much.[62]

New York City's schools are shortchanged in part, as we have noted, by state aid formulas that do not provide the equalization funds promised in the basic aid law. Unlike Rochester, moreover, which gets help from its surrounding suburbs through Monroe County, New York City is on its own. Except for a relatively small income tax on commuters (which the legislature and governor voted to abolish in 1999) and the nickels and dimes they contribute in taxes on lunches and theater tickets, New York's suburban neighbors contribute nothing to the city's budget. The city also has more competing demands on its resources. In 1975, New York City's *short-term* debt (not capital debt, which is still larger) had risen to equal a full year's tax revenue, and the predicted shortfall for 1976 was almost 17 percent of total spending.

By creating the municipal assistance program, the state helped New York City convert much of this burden into longer-term obligations that it is still paying off. In the city's 1999 budget, for example, $3.5 billion of a projected $36 billion budget was marked for debt service and budget stabilization. Even in the prosperous 1990s, the city continued to spend more than it took in, adding to its future debt. Rochester and Monroe County, though they never fell to the depths of New York City in 1975 and have balanced their most recent budgets, must still allocate nearly 6 percent of their combined budgets to debt service.

Along with debt service, New York City's budget can be explained essentially in terms of three large operating budget categories: education (25 percent); health and social services (26 percent); and police, fire, corrections, and sanitation (14 percent). These are also the primary spending categories in Rochester and Monroe County, though the proportion allocated to education is considerably higher and the allocations to the uniformed services lower. In both New York City and Rochester, the bottom line is roughly the same: beyond debt service, schools, social services, and protection—functions mandated either by the state or political necessity—less than a quarter of the municipal budget goes for everything else.

There are important differences between New York City and Rochester, differences that have sharpened since Rudy Giuliani moved into Gracie Mansion, the official home of the New York City mayor, in 1994. Rochester and New York differ from Syracuse, Hudson, Brockport, and Yonkers as well. Most strikingly, New York City continues to raise a significant (though diminishing) share of its revenues from taxes on personal income and corporations. Compared with their upstate and suburban neighbors, middle-class homeowners—particularly those in single-family homes in the outer boroughs—pay trivial property taxes. In effect, the city subsidizes the housing of long-time residents by keeping taxes low on older homes and by imposing rent control on older apartments. In Rochester and in most suburban and upstate communities, by way of contrast, property taxes—whether paid directly by homeowners or indirectly through rent—are higher for many residents than all other taxes combined. Rochester, though it has a reasonably good network of city buses, has nothing to compare with New York's subways and commuter railroads. It does, on the other hand, spend a good deal more on highway maintenance.

Government at the Grassroots

Mayors and other local officials operate in a world of strong constraints. State mandates, funded, unfunded, and partially funded, determine where most of their tax dollars will go. History, geography, and demographics also impose significant constraints. Even if he wanted to, Mayor Giuliani could not abolish the city tax on corporations without the unlikely consent of the state legislature. Today's mayors in New York, Syracuse, and Troy must pay off the debts incurred by previous administrations. Neither Rochester nor Monroe County can realistically avoid paying more per capita for snow removal than cities in the southern part of the state. New York has more citizens of school age and more below the poverty line than most other municipalities: its budgets for schools, for Medicaid, and Medicare invariably reflect that reality.

Elected officials are able to order some priorities at the local level. For the ordinary citizen of New York state it makes a difference where you live and who your public officials are. Monroe County and the city of Rochester have made a financial commitment to public education that manifests itself in better schools than one finds in New York City or any of the Big Five cities. If you move from New York to one of its more affluent suburbs, you will trade a small income tax and a lot of nuisance taxes on such things as parking for a much higher property tax. You will almost certainly have better funded (and probably better quality) schools. In the grand scheme of things, however, your quality of life in New York is set more by what happens in Albany than in New York's City Hall, in Monroe County, the city of Rochester, or the East Greenbush Town Hall. One of the continuing ironies of New York politics is that most of its citizens know and care more about local governments which affect them less than the state system to which they pay little heed.

Conclusion: New York's Changing Fiscal Priorities

New York remains in many ways one of the more progressive of the states in the ways in which it raises and spends money. By exempting food, for example, its sales tax is less of a burden on the poor and middle class than it is in most other states. New York City and Yonkers, by keeping property taxes low on one- and two-family homes, and by imposing rent controls on many larger apartment buildings, help make housing affordable for millions of people in one of the world's most expensive real estate markets. And by relying heavily on income taxes to raise revenues for the state and its largest city, New York—in theory at least—retains one of the nation's more progressive tax systems.

In its spending priorities, New York has a long tradition of providing for the less fortunate, with many of its social welfare programs serving as prototypes for others. It continues to have some of the most generous Medicare and Medicaid programs in the country. Its public park system is among the most extensive in the nation, as is its system of mass transportation (particularly in the New York metropolitan area). In countless small ways as well, New York continues to develop innovative and progressive social policies, pioneering in equal rights laws, in regulating and improving the environment, in treating victims of AIDs, and in providing homemaker and other in-house services to senior citizens.

Clearly, however, the focus is shifting, overtly in the Pataki administration, more quietly but no less decisively during the Carey/Cuomo years. The fiscal crisis of the 1970s, which first erupted in New York City's brush with bankruptcy and spread to state agencies such as the dormitory authority that were overburdened with debt, forced Governor Carey and the legislature to tighten up both its own borrowing and spending policies and those of local governments and state authorities. As part of the price of this overhaul, Carey began a policy of cutting taxes and expenditures that has continued to this day. On the tax side of the ledger, the most significant cuts have been from the higher brackets, giving all but the very poorest citizens what amounts to a flat tax in which the working poor, the middle class, and the very rich all pay the same essential rate. Corporate taxes have also been cut substantially. The state has saved money by effectively ending general aid to localities and by cutting back on its share of targeted local aid accounts, thus forcing local governments outside of New York City to rely more on regressive property taxes. In the city and in other local jurisdictions, governments have turned increasingly to fees for everything from garbage disposal, and water and sewer hook-ups, to library cards and tire disposal fees to capture lost revenues. Most of these fees, together with higher tuition costs at CUNY and SUNY, and sharply increased taxes on cigarettes, beer, and gambling have also had regressive impacts.

In terms of spending, local governments have been increasingly squeezed by cutbacks in federal and state funding for education, and, more recently health care. The economic boom of the 1990s has helped both the state and its municipalities avert the kinds of fiscal crises that hit in the 1970s, but it has also obscured some very deep structural problems lurking in the budgets of the state and many local entities. Further borrowing as a means of rebuilding the state's crumbling infrastructure is an increasingly less viable action; and although the state can maintain most social services in good years, its ability to sustain programs for the poor when revenues are short, or to expand them when the coffers are full, is practically nonexistent. With ever-longer prison sentences filling the jails, moreover, the corrections system increasingly swallows up whatever discretionary funds might be left in a good year's budget. Thus although New Yorkers may still be less inclined than the citizens of some other states to let the poor fend for themselves, the prospects for redistributive policies are not good. Even if the will were there to equalize educational opportunities, to bring the state and city university systems back to the level of other states, to broaden the economic safety net for the poor, or to rebuild decaying highways and rail systems, the effort would require tax increases and financial reforms that few have been willing to espouse.

Epilogue

It has been a quarter of a century since Governor Hugh Carey solemnly told the people of New York that their days of wine and roses were over, and that the new watchwords of politics in the state would be fiscal caution and restraint. With some exceptions, that has pretty much been the case. Prisons aside, governors Carey, Cuomo, and—it seems safe to predict—Pataki, will leave no legacies comparable to DeWitt Clinton's canals, Teddy Roosevelt's parks, Al Smith's social welfare programs, or Nelson Rockefeller's state university system. The later governors' collective twenty-eight years in office will end in January of 2003 with the state spending less per capita (adjusted for inflation) on most basic services than it did when Carey took office in 1975. There is a widespread perception, moreover, that the quality of most of these services has declined.

What Ails New York?

As indicated in Chapter 1, New Yorkers are less inclined than some to blame the political system for these perceived ills; and we are considerably more inclined, in evaluating the state of the state, to see the glass as half full rather than half empty. Our parents, who came of age in the first third of this century grew up in a different New York than we did. Our children, maturing in the last third, will see a still different New York, in many ways a better one. New York's schools, although much maligned, are sending twice as many graduates to college than they did just three decades ago. The health care system, badly flawed to be sure, reaches far more people far more effectively than ever before. Air and water quality continues to improve. Crime rates are down.

There are, from our avowedly liberal perspective, some troubling signs as well. The state, more than ever in recent history, is splitting in two, not so much along the old lines of upstate-downstate as between rich and poor. Whether the state can or should act aggressively to redistribute income is a question we will leave for other times and places. What troubles us is the growing disparity of opportunity, particularly access to education, basic nutrition, employment opportunities, addiction services, and health care that seem more manifest, yet less at issue in state politics. Instead of investing in human and physical resources, we seem to be hoping that if we ignore the poor they will just go away. Still more troubling is the state of state politics: the system is failing, in our view, to confront important issues or to present meaningful alternatives to the electorate. The electorate, not surprisingly, is turning away from politics and turning off on governance. Three problems, in particular, will confront New York with increasing urgency in the twenty-first century: (1) lack of government responsibility, (2) rigid bureaucracy, and (3) lack of citizen involvement.

The Passed Buck

As president, Harry Truman had a sign on his desk that said, "the buck stops here." In New York, the buck has yet to stop: not since the restructuring of New York City's debt in 1975 has anyone stepped up to say the buck stops here. Passing the buck takes two forms, analogous to the lateral and the forward pass in football. In the lateral, one group of politicians simply passes the costs of vital programs sideways to other politicians, from the federal government to the states, from states to localities, or from state agencies to "off-budget" authorities. In the forward pass, costs of current programs are passed to succeeding generations, largely in the form of bonds, but more subtly through tax cuts and spending programs that phase in over a period of time and usually place the bulk of the fiscal burden in the year immediately following the next election.

How do politicians cut taxes, increase spending, and still balance the budget? One way, as Governor Pataki and the legislature showed us in 1998, is to throw themselves or their successors a forward pass and hope that if you look good enough throwing it no one will notice too much whether or not it gets caught. In crafting the budget that election year, the governor and the legislature made a deal: in exchange for billions of dollars in tax cuts pushed largely by the governor, assembly Democrats received a commitment to cut class sizes in the first three grades of school and to fund a statewide system of pre-kindergarten instruction. The beauty of this wonderful deal is that it didn't cost the taxpayers a penny (at least not in 1998–99). The governor, his budget rightfully balanced, could boast of the billions in dollars in income tax savings soon to be realized. His office sent out official notices advising homeowners how to register for the property tax savings they would realize under the just-approved STAR program. Democrats, meanwhile, a balanced budget behind them, could similarly trumpet the soon to be realized improvements in education, and the tax cuts as well.

The governor's 1999 effort to welsh on his part of this deal by leaving the education funds out of the budget put the Democrats in a bad position since it would have been extremely difficult for them to retaliate by rescinding the tax cuts already officially promised to voters. But that is beside the point here. What is of primary concern is the glib willingness of both parties to claim political credit for economic commitments they both knew they probably could not meet. Despite the continuing strength of the economy, the most optimistic estimates of the budget gap in 2001 if the tax cuts and educational spending plans both were to take effect, ran from 4 to 6 billion dollars.

Add to this shortfall the amount borrowed—with voter approval—under the environmental bond act, the amounts borrowed through revenue bonds, authority bonds, local bonds, and so on, and the picture that emerges is one of a government funding its present operations and cutting taxes for this generation in order to present the bill to its successors. Excessive borrowing has short-term consequences too. New York bonds are among the lowest rated in the country, meaning that both present-day residents as well as future generations will pay high interest rates on the outstanding balances. The bonds of two of New York's largest counties, Erie and Nassau, currently are rated as risky for investors as corporate junk bonds.

In his eight years as president, many observers now argue, Ronald Reagan lost his battle to dismantle the domestic programs of the New Deal and Great Society; but when he saddled the nation with its hugest debt he won the war against liberalism by guaranteeing that Washington would lack the resources ever in the foreseeable future to resurrect a liberal agenda. Whether deliberately or not, New York's most recent governors may have accomplished the same objective for the Empire State.

The Bureaucracy Problem

New York has too many public officials, patronage employees, and civil servants, not so much in Albany as throughout the state, in an indefensible mess of overlapping local governments, special districts, and public authorities. In 1995, the Brookings Institution published a book by Paul Light called *Thickening Government* in which he described what he called the "thickening" of the federal bureaucracy:

> New agencies and units widened the government's base, while new management layers increased its height. Together these two tightly related events

pushed the hierarchy upward and outward, expanding the president's scope beyond any hint of scientific control.[1]

Although government organizations are not immortal, either in New York or in Washington, they can live far beyond the life spans of many organisms. Instead of coming under the general jurisdiction of the state highway department, for example, most of the state's major highway bridges are controlled by separate boards and authorities that meet on an irregular basis at best. Although the bonds that were originally used to create these authorities have long been paid off, the organizations that run them continue to function. In the governor's office in Albany there are three separate agencies dealing with general economic development. At the local level, a snarl of overlapping towns, villages, counties, authorities, and special districts diffuse accountability and frustrate cost-saving efforts.

As in Light's study of the federal bureaucracy, the thickening of government in New York takes a variety of forms. At the highest levels of the state, the total number of senior executives and gubernatorial appointees continues to grow in a pattern that Light describes as "vertical" thickening. As in Washington, there appears to have been considerable growth in the number of layers of management found in most executive departments, and an explosion of titles makes it difficult to profile the hierarchy accurately. But a seat of the pants look at one large department (in this case health) shows at least thirteen senior management levels below the commissioner. As of 1997, there were the following:

- — 1 executive deputy commissioner
- — 1 first deputy commissioner
- — 2 deputy commissioners
- — 1 general counsel
- — 9 directors
- — 2 executive directors
- — 2 executive deputy directors
- — 1 associate director
- — 3 assistant directors
- — 27 untitled heads of regional and special function offices

As in Light's study, "It is important to note that these . . . layers do not stack neatly one on top of the other to compose a unified chain of command."[2] Nor can one learn much about one department by looking at another. In the department of insurance, for example, the offices of the first deputy superintendent and general counsel are combined, though there is a "special counsel" as well. There are also a number of titles reflecting the special mission of the agency that one does not find in health such as "supervising attorney" and "assistant chief examiner." While it is again difficult to discern exactly how many senior levels there are in the superintendent's office, some twenty distinct senior management job titles are listed.

"Horizontal" thickening, to again borrow Light's terminology, involves the proliferation of government agencies. The state constitution, as we saw in Chapter 5, limits New York to twenty executive departments, but a quick perusal of the state *Red Book*[3] shows some fifty-five offices in the executive branch that report directly to the second floor and thus have at least quasi-departmental status. Franklin Roosevelt liked to create administrative overlap on the premise that competing agencies would keep him informed of each others' failings.[4] But Roosevelt's Washington of the 1930s was nowhere near as complicated, redundant, and large as today's bureaucracy in Albany, where all too often one hand does not know what the other is doing. Every year, City College submits a wish list of capital improvement projects to the state. A few years ago, the college sought funds to renovate the interior and fix the leaky roof of a badly deteriorating building. The proposal had to be split and sent to two different offices where the interior renovations were approved but the roof job put off. By the time the roof work was finally approved, the completed renovations of the interior had been literally washed away.

A third form of thickening occurs both within agencies and around them. Within the major executive departments, there has been a proliferation of monitoring and control offices with such titles as auditor and inspector general; of outreach agencies including divisions of public affairs, communications, and legislative affairs; and internal support divisions for such tasks as data management, planning, and information systems. Light quotes from a study group headed by Vice President Al Gore which found:

> Counting all personal, budget, procurement, accounting, auditing and head-quarters staff, plus supervisory personnel in field offices, there are roughly 700,000 federal employees whose job it is to manage, control, check up on or audit others. *This is one third of all federal civilian employees.*[5]

It is probably even a higher proportion in New York, where the idea that somewhere someone may be getting away with something has—as we showed in Chapter 7—created a huge apparatus of corruption control mechanisms that inflate the cost of governing and cripple innovation.

Finally, the thickening of government is vividly evident at the local level where the inefficiencies of small units are compounded by a crazy-quilt pattern of overlapping jurisdictions and authority. A small but telling example comes from the rural community of Copake where the popularity of taking an evening walk has grown to the point where the town council was thinking it might be a good idea to install streetlights and walkways along the most popular trail. There are already three existing street lights on the route, which were installed more than fifty years ago to help dairy farmers load their morning milk for predawn pickups. The lights were installed by a local lighting authority controlled by the town's dairy farmers. The farmers created the original authority that floated the bonds to pay for the lights, which only the farmers needed. It would hardly make sense for the town to ignore the existing lights, which the lighting authority still owns, but to hook into the existing system would cause an accounting nightmare. To abolish the lighting authority, on the other hand, would require both a vote and approval by the state legislature. The lighting plan has been put on a back shelf.

The hopelessly complex structure of New York is probably inefficient in some direct sense. Journalists and politicians enjoy conveying "the notion that bureaucrats get in the way, that they impose needless rules to justify their existence, that they are doing jobs not really worth doing."[6] Whether significant savings can be achieved by streamlining the bureaucracy is not as clear as it seems on the surface. Some rules are in place for good reasons, and civil servants in New York are not paid enough to make a huge difference in the overall budget. But if the notion that major savings could be achieved by simplifying the government is simplistic, it does not mean that it is not worth the effort for other reasons. One of the worst problems with complex institutions is a tendency to become rule bound. As the chain of command becomes more difficult to trace, more monitoring agencies and rules are developed to guard against empire building, delinquency, and deviance. Because it is not always clear, in other words, who reports to whom, compliance is increasingly secured by rules that limit individual discretion, and by monitoring agencies (like auditors, inspectors general, personnel directors, and internal affairs units) that enforce these rules and require piles of reports. Not only is the government incapable of acting, but it inspires a great deal of mistrust from a public that literally does not know where to turn or who to blame. Government officials themselves often do not know whom you have to see in order to get something done.

The Eroding Base of Citizen Support

The most fundamental premise of a democratic polity is that the citizen has the power to "throw the rascals out." You may not know if the people you are voting for will actually do any better, but the retrospective ability to fire the people whose performance you do not like is fundamental. A public that doesn't know who to blame is denied this basic right. By confusing lines of responsibility, New York confuses its voters and muddies its politics.

We have no empirical evidence that New York's abysmally low rates of voter turnout are connected with citizen confusion or disgust. As we saw in Chapter 3, a variety of demographic variables including large numbers of immigrants and persons of low income and education that are correlated with nonvoting, are present in New York. New York's arcane election laws and gerrymanders that reduce competition are also important factors. But even when these variables are taken into account, voter turnout rates in New York are strikingly low: in races for governor between 1989 and 1994, for example, only five states had rates lower than New York's percentage voting of 33.4.[7]

There is, as we have noted, a circular relationship between turnout and public policy: the young and the poor whose nonvoting is based in part on their perception that politics is irrelevant to their lives are ignored by politicians in search of votes, thereby fulfilling the expectations of those who feel ignored. The gap between rich and poor in New York is thus both economic and political and widening along both dimensions. Theorists since Aristotle, and modern empirical studies as well, have traced a strong connection between the existence of a viable middle class and the persistence of stable democracy. To this extent, New York is a troubled state and getting worse.

On the Decline of Representative Democracy

A competitive party system can function as a democratizing force. Greedy for votes, competitive parties reach out to all comers, offering programs designed for mass appeal and proving—through effective governance—that they can deliver. Electoral competition, because it is a process of mobilizing large numbers of people, has, in theory at least, the capacity to marginalize the role of special interests by forcing politicians to focus on large blocks of the public. In the responsible parties model, "popular control over government . . . can best be established by the popular choice between and control over alternate responsible political parties; for only such parties can provide the coherent, unified set of rulers who will assume collective responsibility to the people for the manner in which government is carried on."[8]

An alternative model of representation stresses the dynamic role of interest groups engaged in a pluralistic battle for political influence in which politicians are forced to balance and weigh the competing claims of a rich variety of self-interested champions of particular interests.

In New York, the trappings of party responsibility remain carefully draped on the body politic, but they serve only to hide a system that is dying in its ability to serve as an effective vehicle either of representation or governance. Similarly, the pressure system pulsates with vim and vigor, yet its representative nature is questionable both in terms of its scope and quality. Too few groups are effectively represented in Albany, and those that are do not always represent the long-term best interests of their members.

The Miasma of Responsible Parties

Parties in New York are not lacking in cohesion. The old days when the county leaders called the shots for their delegations in Albany, or when the governor owned one house and had a lease on the other are over. The legislature is ruled, as the responsible party model suggests, by cohesive parties that, when they achieve internal consensus, can and do put their programs forth. The role of the minority in each house is essentially that of a critic who hopes that exposing the flaws in majority programs will force reconsideration, and that by posing overall alternatives to the majority party agenda to defeat it in the next election. The financing of competitive campaigns, and even the nominating process in the case of open legislative seats, has become increasingly centralized.

For three reasons, however, the strong party system has not worked either to define real alternatives to the voters or to encourage responsible governance. The first of these problems, endemic to American politics in the past few decades, may be exacerbated by strong parties.

> Politicians have become increasingly sophisticated in their ability to anticipate how the news media will report their words and deeds, and how the public will respond to these reports. They have developed increasingly effective strategies for managing or circumventing the news, shaping the images, and channeling public perceptions. . . . The result is a democracy of the uninformed, one that is ever more vulnerable to the wispiest breezes of public expediency.[9]

Individual politicians who are more interested in making news than in making policy are tolerable to a point. Playing what is often called the "outsider" role, these politicians can help revise the political agenda, bring new questions to the fore, or question the prevailing orthodoxy. But when party leaders use their weekly public opinion polls to play on the latest popular events, they are neither innovating nor questioning. By trying to one-up each other in exploiting the latest fads, they tend, in divided government, to lock themselves into positions that make compromise virtually impossible. Passing press releases and one-house bills is not the same as passing laws, though there are times when it seems as if contemporary leaders are more interested in seeing their work in the evening news than in *McKinney's*.[10]

A second problem with party government, as it works in New York, is that it keeps much of the process hidden from public view. We do not believe that sunshine laws need apply to all political meetings: sometimes meaningful compromise can be achieved best behind closed doors, especially when the result of deliberations is more important for us to know than who traded what for what. The free swinging, give and take of the party conferences often works to keep the leaders in touch with the rank and file only when it is carried out in private. Increasingly in New York, however, it is not just the public that is being kept out of the meeting rooms, but major players as well. Governors who seldom consult their commissioners, party leaders who by-pass committee chairs in drafting new policies are both wasting talent and stifling the deliberative process.

Finally, New York's disciplined parties are not responsible in providing the public with a coherent set of alternatives. Instead of Republican and Democratic parties each with defined sets of policy goals, we have three Republican parties and three Democratic parties that only coincidentally read from the same page. Advocates for responsible parties have cited the role that party discipline can—and, in their mind, should—play in overcoming the deadlock and inertia that often characterizes politics in a system of separated powers. A popular governor, in theory, should be able to sweep his or her fellow party members into the legislature where they can put the party's campaign platform into policy. Three decades of partisan reapportionment, the rise of campaign finance committees controlled by the legislative parties, and the generous staff and mailing allowances that make most incumbents unbeatable, have combined to increase rather than minimize the gaps between the parties of the gubernatorial, senatorial, and assembly parties. Party cohesion in a legislature that seems permanently divided between the two parties may be a recipe, in the media age, for deadlock and demagogy rather than responsibility.

Perverted Pluralism

Where party systems are weak, there is a tendency for interest groups to be strong, providing, in effect, a supplementary system of representation known as pluralism. Strong interest groups coexist with strong parties in New York, often working in strong partnerships, particularly in the area of campaign finance. As in national politics and in the other state capitals, pluralism in New York is not representative of a broad spectrum of the state's population: the universe of organized interests underrepresents the poor and such broadly diverse groups as consumers. Although unions are bigger and more organized in New York than in most states, the business community, as we saw in

Chapter 4, is the voice that speaks loudest in terms of money and effective representation in Albany.

What most distinguishes the pressure system in New York is the nature and extent of the accommodation it has achieved with the entrenched party system. In Chapter 4, we described many groups in New York as being "power-tropic," tilting as plants toward the sun in the direction of those best able to serve their short-term interests. Divided government makes it easy for those groups whose goal is the preservation of the status quo cheaply to defend their core interests. Since a bill can be blocked in either house of the legislature, groups strongly identified with the Democratic Party count on the Democratic assembly to protect their interests. Republican groups count on the senate. The net result for the people of New York is that it is extraordinarily difficult to get anything done that affects the well being of an entrenched group. Examples abound on both sides of the aisle. Some seemingly simple environmental measures have been blocked because they would be expensive to a corporation or industry with strong ties to senate Republicans. On the other side, the state's Wick's law—which requires most construction jobs to be broken down into jobs for small contractors—is opposed by almost everyone. Yet repeal of the law continues to die in the assembly largely, it seems safe to guess, because of the strong ties between the building trades unions and the Democratic Party.

A number of groups, just to be safe, play both sides of the aisle. This is particularly true of groups like the teachers' and public employees' unions that may need both houses of the legislature to fend off budgetary attacks from the governor. Although the Public Employee's Federation, the United Federation of Teachers, and the Civil Service Association typically take stands on a variety of legislative issues, and tend—on most of these issues—to side with the Democrats, most of their real efforts are directed toward organization maintenance and the narrow interests of their members.

The bottom line, quite simply, is that the political system in New York frustrates change. A limited suffrage, an inattentive electorate, and an ossified party and pressure system combine to make sure that this year's policies will look pretty much like last year's. Even the seeming mandate George Pataki brought to the governorship in 1994 has, in the long run, resulted in nothing much new. His conservatism, like Mario Cuomo's liberalism, has proven to be more poetry than prose.

The Potential for Change

One of the enduring ironies of American politics, one that continues to keep democracy alive despite evidence to the contrary, is that many of its seemingly most unchangeable realities are not that unchangeable at all. A strong, programmatic governor could on his or her own do much to trim and reorganize the bureaucracy. The patchwork of local governments will prove more resilient; but perhaps a serious, strong, and independent commission could make a cogent enough case to the legislature to at least begin a move toward consolidation. A regional effort of this kind in the capitol district has enjoyed some success in identifying areas of possible reform in the Albany area, but its limited ability to inspire real change also shows how deeply entrenched many local forces are.

For New York to get a grip on state and local debt offers a stronger prospect. Liberals got the message a long time ago about social programs that cost money. Although the state has many pressing needs in the areas, such as health and education, that scream for attention and have strong public support, there are few politicians in New York or anywhere else who want to campaign as big spenders. And the public, it seems, has begun to see through the "tax cuts" scam that closes the library on Tuesdays, increases school class sizes, raises college tuition, and saves the average taxpayer eighty-seven cents a week. The defeat of the 1998 school bond issue, and the narrow victory of an environmental bond act the year before, shows considerable concern for the overall issue of public debt. If another wake up call was needed, the 1999 downgrading of Nassau County bonds—one of the wealthiest counties in the country—may have been it.

There is an obvious need for campaign finance reform, recognized by every recent governor, by both houses of the legislature, and by virtually every newspaper in the state. As in Washington, however, rhetoric and reality seldom meet when it comes to this issue. Most reform proposals are politically loaded with some having strong partisan implications, others impacting incumbents as opposed to challengers, and so on. The last time the legislature was able to agree on a significant package of reform it was vetoed by then-governor Cuomo whose own fundraising efforts would, to be candid, have been impacted more by the law than would those of most legislators. But by picking on a few pieces of a complex bill, the governor made the legislature look like it was passing a self-serving piece of garbage in the name of reform. Editorial opinion throughout the state echoed the governor's rhetoric and proved highly embarrassing to then-speaker Mel Miller and majority leader Ralph Marino who—whatever the faults of the bill—felt they had made a sincere effort at real change. Subsequent party leaders (and governors as well) have been extremely reluctant to fall into the same trap and have resorted instead to a stream of one-house bills and/or press releases that, in the name of reform, are really party-serving attacks on the core financial constituencies of their opponents. The 1999 session was typical: the assembly passed a bill which would have reformed the system largely in terms of loopholes that particularly advantage corporations and wealthy individuals, key groups for Republicans; the senate went for proposals aimed largely at labor unions, which give most to Democrats. The governor weighed in with a slightly more balanced proposal, but didn't offer it until almost the last day of the legislative session when he could be fairly certain it would go nowhere.

The fight for campaign finance reform is not really a fight over policy issues at all. Few of those already in office, having done rather nicely by the existing rules, are sincerely enthusiastic about changing those rules, especially in ways that might weaken advantages for incumbents. The various proposals floated in recent years have been glorified press releases, designed to embarrass other parties rather than serve as blueprints for law.

A public fed too many such hollow press releases will become increasingly cynical about politics and politicians. There was a refreshing sort of honesty in Mario Cuomo's admission that the aspiratory "poetry" of his state of the state addresses to the legislature was not to be confused with the more realistic "prose" of his budgets. But there was also something horribly cynical about thus teasing the public with a vision of policies he had no intention of implementing. George Pataki seriously pushed a promised program of anticrime legislation, tax cuts, and substantial cuts in state spending on education and social services in 1995. Pursuing what was widely perceived as a conservative mandate when he first took office, Pataki marshaled the conservative wing of his party in the state senate and rolled over the frightened assembly Democrats to get much of what he wanted. In the classic tradition of the responsible parties model, the voters were given a clear choice. Within two years, however, whatever had been clear in stands on issues had become murky at best. Pataki to this day seems at best disinterested in governing, and neither the assembly Democrats nor the senate Republicans have tried to stake out distinctive policy agendas. Victories in Albany are increasingly measured in column inches and sound bites rather than chapter codes of law.

Government by press release is bad government. It will end, in the final analysis, only when attentive publics in the state focus more on substance than rhetoric, when politicians are rewarded more for what they do than what they say, when the press begins to pay serious attention to what happens in Albany, when the rank and file of the labor movement and other associations insist on real representation, and when average citizens begin to realize how important the government in Albany is to their lives.

Box 9.1

The 2000 Elections

Hillary Clinton was elected in November 2000 as the state's first female senator in one of the country's most expensive, most widely watched, and most contentious campaigns. The former first lady was first expected to face New York City Mayor Rudolph Giuliani; but a series of personal crises forced the mayor to drop out in favor of Long Island congressman Rick Lazio.

The Clinton-Lazio race brought 6.3 million voters to the polls, a little more than half of those eligible to vote, in what otherwise was a predictably unremarkable election. Early in the campaign, the Republicans all but conceded the state's thirty-one electoral votes to Vice President Al Gore, and neither party mounted a meaningful campaign in the state. In races for the House of Representatives, Republicans and Democrats traded seats on Long Island, with the Democrats winning Representative Lazio's old district and the Democrats losing a seat in Suffolk County. But, otherwise, all incumbents won easily. Democrats recaptured an assembly seat in Niagara Falls from the Republican who had defeated an incumbent two years before, but no other seats changed hands. Despite state senator Guy Valella's indictment a week before the election, both he and all but one of his incumbent colleagues in the state senate won re-election, though it took a court decision to secure a victory for Manhattan Republican Roy Goodman.

As the first first lady ever to run for office, Mrs. Clinton brought both high visibility and a lot of her husband's baggage to the campaign. Though a far less visible figure than Mayor Giuliani, Representative Lazio had little trouble raising campaign money from Clinton-haters across the country; but the first lady was more than able to match him. Because the race had appeared close in most polls taken throughout the campaign, Clinton's 12 percent margin of victory surprised most observers. She ran very strongly among black voters who, according to the *New York Times*, made up 11 percent of the electorate as compared with 9 percent in 1998, and far less strongly among Jews. Perhaps the most interesting aspect of the 2000 race was the continuing slide of many upstate areas from Republican to Democratic. Mrs. Clinton carried ten upstate counties and lost the areas north of Westchester and Rockland counties by less than 3 percent, and Vice President Gore actually won upstate by a margin of more than 100,000 votes.

That the Democrats' strong upstate showing at the top of the ticket did not percolate down to races for the legislature is powerful testimony to the rigidity of the state's electoral system. Unlike the Democrats' landslide victories in 1964 and 1974, which permeated down to the levels of both the state senate and assembly, Gore's 60 percent to 35 percent margin—while it may have helped Mrs. Clinton—did nothing to upset the state's legislative status quo.

Appendix A

A Citizen's Guide to the 2001–2002 New York State Legislature

Note: When the legislature is in session—typically from January through June—members are usually in their Albany offices Monday through Wednesday and in their district offices the rest of the week. To write, all members can be addressed at The State Assembly (or The State Senate), Legislative Office Building, Albany, New York 12248. All Assembly and Senate phone numbers are in the 518 area code and begin with the prefix 455-.

The state assembly

Member	District	Town or borough	Party	November 2000 election %	District phone # and Albany ext.
Peter J. Abbate, Jr.	49	Brooklyn	D	75	718–236–1764. 3053
Patricia Acampora	1	Riverhead	R	72	631–727–1363. 5294
Thomas W. Alfano	22	Franklin Square	R	59	631–437–5577. 4627
Carmen E. Arroyo	74	Bronx	D	96	718–292–2901. 5402
Jefferson L. Aubry	35	Queens	D	Unopposed	718–457–3615. 4561
James G. Bacalles	130	Corning	R	63	607–776–9691. 5791
Robert D. Barra	21	Lynbrook	R	58	516–593–3980. 4656
Thomas F. Barraga	7	West Islip	R	61	631–422–1321. 4611
William F. Boyland	55	Brooklyn	D	98	718–498–8681. 4466
Philip M. Boyle	8	Bayshore	R	63	516–665–0125. 5021
Michael J. Bragman	118	North Syracuse	D	Unopposed	315–452–1044. 4567
James F. Brennan	44	Brooklyn	D	84	718–940–0641. 5377
Richard L. Brodsky	86	Scarsdale	D	68	914–472–0319. 5753
Harold C. Brown, Jr.	121	Camillus	R	62	315–487–3011. 4505
Daniel J. Burling	147	Warsaw	R	74	716–786–0180. 5314
Marc W. Butler	113	Herkimer	R	Unopposed	315–866–1632. 5393
Kevin A. Cahill	101	Kingston	D	66	914–338–9610. 4436
Nancy Calhoun	94	New Windsor	R	61	914–564–1330. 5441
Ronald J. Canestrari	106	Troy	D	77	518–274–8395. 4474
Ann Margaret Carrozza	26	Bayside	D	Unopposed	718–321–1525. 5425
Pat M. Casale	108	Mechanicsville	R	89	518–664–1043. 5777

Member	District	Town or borough	Party	November 2000 election %	District phone # and Albany ext.
Joan K. Christensen	119	Syracuse	D	66	315–449–9536. 5383
Barbara M. Clark	33	Queens Village	D	89	718–479–2333. 4711
Adele Cohen	46	Brooklyn	D	93	718–648–6663. 4811
Michael Cohen	28	Forest Hills	D	72	718–263–5595. 4926
Samuel Colman	93	Pearl River	D	89	914–624–4601. 5118
William Colton	47	Brooklyn	D	71	718–236–1598. 5828
James D. Conte	10	Huntington Station	R	61	516–271–8025. 5732
Vivian E. Cook	32	South Ozone Park	D	Unopposed	718–322–3975. 4203
Clifford W. Crouch	122	Sidney	R	Unopposed	607–563–7981. 5741
Lena Cymbrowitz	45	Brooklyn	D	77	718–743–4078. 5214
Robert A. D'Andrea	100	Saratoga Springs	R	71	518–587–5151. 5404
Gloria Davis	79	Bronx	D	95	718–588–3119. 5272
Francine DelMonte	138	Niagara Falls	D	58	716–282–6062. 5284
Roann M. Destito	116	Utica	D	89	315–732–1055. 5454
Ruben Diaz, Jr.	75	Bronx	D	96	718–893–0202. 5514
Jay J. Dinga	123	Johnson City	R	Unopposed	607–777–9437. 5526
Jeffrey Dinowitz	81	Bronx	D	83	718–796–3545. 5965
Thomas P. DiNapoli	16	Great Neck	D	70	516–482–6966. 5192
Patricia A. Eddington	3	Patchogue	D	50	431–447–5393. 4901
Steven C. Englebright	4	Setauket	D	65	631–751–3082. 4804
Adriano Espaillat	72	Manhattan	D	91	212–544–2278. 5807
Joe Errigo	136	Rochester	R	52	716–359–1440. 5662
Arthur O. Eve	141	Buffalo	D	78	716–895–2464. 5005
Herman D. Farrell, Jr.	71	Manhattan	D	87	212–234–1430. 5491
John J. Faso	102	West Coxsackie	R	92	518–731–1093. 5314
Donna Ferrara	15	Westbury	R	62	516–338–2693. 4684
Gary Finch	126	Auburn	R	Unopposed	315–255–3045. 5878
John Flanagan, Jr.	9	Northport	R	66	631–261–4151. 5952
Sandra R. Galef	90	Ossining	D	60	914–941–1111. 5348
David F. Gantt	133	Rochester	D	71	716–328–7280. 5606
Michael N. Gianaris	36	Long Island City	D	69	718–932–4052. 5014
Deborah J. Glick	66	Manhattan	D	83	212–674–5153. 4841
Diane Gordon	40	Brooklyn	D	89	Not available. 5912
Richard N. Gottfried	64	Manhattan	D	Unopposed	212–807–7900. 4941
Alexander (Pete) Grannis	65	Manhattan	D	74	212–996–4906. 5676
Roger L. Green	57	Brooklyn	D	91	718–596–0100. 5325
Aurelia Greene	77	Bronx	D	97	718–538–2000. 5671
Alexander Gromack	92	New City	D	95	914–634–9791. 5735
Jacob B. Gunther, III	98	Monticello	D	69	914–794–5807. 5355
James P. Hayes	142	Williamsville	R	53	716–634–1895. 4618
Carl E. Heastie	83	Bronx	D	93	718–324–0664. 4800
Marc Herbst	14	Hicksville	R	63	516–938–3168. 5411
Brian M. Higgins	145	Buffalo	D	65	716–825–6080. 4691
Dov Hikind	48	Brooklyn	D	93	718–853–9616. 5721
Earlene Hill Hooper	18	Hempstead	D	80	516–489–6610. 5861
Sam Hoyt	144	Buffalo	D	75	716–852–2795. 4886
Rhoda S. Jacobs	42	Brooklyn	D	82	718–434–0446. 5385
Susan V. John	131	Rochester	D	59	716–244–5255. 4527
Stephen B. Kaufman	82	Bronx	D	80	718–829–7452. 5296
Thomas J. Kirwan	96	Newburgh	R	56	914–562–0888. 5762
Jeffery Klein	80	Bronx	D	80	718–409–0109. 5844
Brian M. Kolb	129	Geneva	R	57	315–781–2030. 5772
David R. Koon	135	Fairport	D	58	716–223–9130. 5784
Steven L. Labriola	12	Massapequa	R	69	516–844–0635. 5305
Ivan C. Lafayette	34	Jackson Heights	D	85	718–457–0384. 4545
John W. LaVelle	59	Staten Island	D	54	718–494–3200. 4677

Member	District	Town or borough	Party	November 2000 election %	District phone # and Albany ext.
Joseph R. Lentol	50	Brooklyn	D	83	718–383–7474. 4477
Steve Levy	5	Oakdale	D	74	516–589–8685. 5937
Elizabeth O'C. Little	109	Glens Falls	R	Unopposed	518–792–4546. 5565
Vito J. Lopez	53	Brooklyn	D	99	718–452–1112. 5537
Martin A. Luster	125	Ithaca	D	Unopposed	607–277–8030. 5444
William Magee	111	Oneida	D	69	315–361–4125. 4807
William B. Magnarelli	120	Syracuse	R	53	315–428–9651. 4826
Patrick R. Manning	99	Hopewell Junction	R	72	914–221–3400. 5177
Margaret M. Markey	30	Elmhurst	D	Unopposed	718–651–3185. 4755
Naomi C. Matusow	89	Mt. Kisco	D	59	914–241–2649. 5397
Nettie Mayersohn	27	Flushing	D	Unopposed	718–463–1942. 4404
Joel M. Miller	97	Poughkeepsie	R	56	914–463–1635. 5725
Joan Millman	52	Brooklyn	D	75	718–246–4889. 5426
Howard D. Mills	95	Goshen	R	62	914–291–3631. 5991
Joseph D. Morelle	132	Rochester	D	70	716–467–0410. 5373
Kathleen P. Murray	19	Levittown	R	54	631–731–8830. 4633
John J. McEneny	104	Albany	D	77	518–455–4178. 4178
Brian M. McLaughlin	25	Flushing	D	Unopposed	718–762–6575. 5172
Charles H. Nesbitt	137	Brockport	R	Unopposed	716–637–0090. 5363
Catherine T. Nolan	37	Ridgewood	D	84	718–456–9492. 4851
Clarence Norman, Jr.	43	Brooklyn	D	97	718–756–1776. 5262
Robert H. Nortz	114	Watertown	R	59	315–786–0284. 5545
Robert C. Oaks	128	Lyons	R	Unopposed	315–946–5166. 4633
Maureen O'Connell	17	Westbury	R	61	516–222–0007. 5341
Felix W. Ortiz	51	Brooklyn	D	90	718–492–6334. 3821
Chris Ortloff	110	Plattsburgh	R	66	518–562–1986. 5943
William L. Parment	150	Jamestown	D	64	716–664–7773. 4511
Amy R. Paulin	88	Scarsdale	D	60	914–723–1115. 5585
Nick N. Perry	58	Brooklyn	D	Unopposed	718–385–3336. 4166
Audrey I. Pheffer	23	Rockaway Beach	D	72	718–945–9550. 4292
Adam Clayton Powell, III	68	Manhattan	D	92	212–828–1058. 4781
Robert G. Prentiss	107	Ballston Lake	R	52	518–877–7113. 5931
James G. Pretlow	84	Mt. Vernon	D	93	914–667–0127. 5291
John A. Ravitz	73	Manhattan	R	54	212–861–9061. 4794
Pauline Rhodd-Cummings	31	Far Rockaway	D	96	718–327–1845. 5668
Jose Rivera	78	Bronx	D	95	718–933–2204. 5414
Peter M. Rivera	76	Bronx	D	90	718–931–2620. 5102
Joseph E. Robach	134	Rochester	D	78	716–225–4190. 4664
Steven Sanders	63	Manhattan	D	84	212–979–9696. 5506
William Scarborough	29	St. Albans	D	98	718–949–5216. 4451
Dierdre K. Scozzafava	112	Gouverneur	R	95	315–287–2384. 5797
Robin Schimminger	140	Kenmore	D	77	716–873–2540. 4767
David E. Seaman	139	Lockport	R	71	716–433–5838. 5511
Frank R. Seddio	39	Brooklyn	D	76	718–968–2770. 5211
Anthony S. Seminerio	38	Richmond Hill	D	76	718–847–0770. 4621
David S. Sidikman	13	Plainview	D	65	516–822–5590. 5456
Sheldon Silver	62	Manhattan	D	85	212–312–1420. 3791
Richard A. Smith	146	Blasdell	D	65	716–826–1878. 4462
Michael J. Spano	87	Yonkers	R	92	914–779–8805. 3662
Will Stephens, Jr.	91	Carmel	R	Unopposed	914–225–5098. 5783
Robert A. Straniere	61	Staten Island	R	73	718–667–0314. 6062
Scott M. Stringer	67	Manhattan	D	84	212–873–6368. 5802
Edward C. Sullivan	69	Manhattan	D	88	212–866–3970. 5603
Frances T. Sullivan	117	Fulton	R	61	315–598–5185. 5841
Robert K. Sweeney	11	Lindenhurst	D	90	516–957–2087. 5787
James N. Tedisco	103	Schenectady	R	73	518–370–2812. 5811

Member	District	Town or borough	Party	November 2000 election %	District phone # and Albany ext.
Fred Thiele, Jr.	2	Bridgehampton	R	59	631–537–2584. 5997
Ronald C. Tocci	85	New Rochelle	D	96	914–235–7900. 4897
Paul A. Tokasz	143	Buffalo	D	78	716–852–2791. 5921
Paul D. Tonko	105	Amsterdam	D	71	518–843–0227. 5197
Darryl C. Towns	54	Brooklyn	D	94	718–235–5627. 5821
David R. Townsend, Jr.	115	Oriskany	R	Unopposed	315–736–8823. 5334
Albert Vann	56	Brooklyn	D	95	718–919–0740. 5474
Eric N. Vitalliano	60	Staten Island	D	70	718–761–5083. 5716
Robert J. Warner	124	Binghamton	R	93	607–723–9047. 5431
Helene E. Weinstein	41	Brooklyn	D	97	718–648–4700. 5462
Harvey Weisenberg	20	Long Beach	D	72	516–431–0500. 3028
Mark Weprin	24	Bayside	D	72	718–428–7900. 5806
Robert G. Wertz	6	Smithtown	R	66	631–724–2929. 5185
Georg H. Winner, Jr.	127	Elmira	R	85	607–734–8580. 4538
Sandra Lee Wirth	148	West Seneca	R	60	716–675–7170. 4601
Keith L. T. Wright	70	Manhattan	D	Unopposed	212–866–5809. 4793
Catherine M. Young	149	Olean	R	74	716–373–7103. 5241

The state senate

Member	District	Town or borough	Party	November 2000 Election %	District Phone # and Albany ext.
James S. Alesi	55	Fairport	R	74	716–223–1800. 2015
Michael A. L. Balboni	7	Mineola	R	54	516–873–0736. 2471
John J. Bonacic	40	New Paltz	R	95	914–255–9656. 3181
Neil D. Breslin	42	Albany	D	72	518–455–2225. 2225
Joseph L. Bruno	43	Saratoga Springs	R	Unopposed	518–583–1001. 3191
Martin Connor	25	Brooklyn	D	92	212–298–5565. 2701
John A. DeFancisco	49	Syracuse	R	97	315–428–7632. 3511
Thomas K. Duane	27	Manhattan	D	82	212–414–0200. 2451
Pedro Espada	32	Bronx	D	90	718–991–8132. 2510
Hugh T. Farley	44	Schenectady	R	54	518–455–2181. 2181
Charles J. Fuschillo	8	Freeport	R	58	516–546–4100. 3341
Vincent J. Gentile	23	Brooklyn	D	61	718–491–2350. 3137
Efrain Gonzalez	31	Bronx	D	94	718–299–7905. 3395
Kemp Hannon	6	Westbury	R	52	516–222–0068. 2200
Daniel Hevesi	13	Forest Hills	D	96	718–544–9750. 3431
Nancy Larraine Hoffman	48	Syracuse	R	60	315–478–0072. 2655
Owen H. Johnson	4	Babylon	R	91	631–669–9200. 3411
Roy M. Goodman	26	Manhattan	R	50	212–417–5563. 2211
Carl Kruger	21	Brooklyn	D	95	718–743–8610. 2460
John R. Kuhl	52	Bath	R	Unopposed	607–776–4111. 2091
Seymour P. Lachman	22	Brooklyn	D	78	718–449–1443. 2437
James J. Lack	2	Hauppauge	R	61	631–360–0490. 2071
William J. Larkin	39	New Windsor	R	95	914–567–1270. 2770
Kenneth P. LaValle	1	Selden	R	65	631–696–6900. 3121
Vincent J. Leibell	37	Brewster	R	95	914–279–3773. 3111
Thomas W. Libous	51	Binghamton	R	76	607–773–8771. 2677
Serphin R. Maltese	15	Glendale	R	95	718–497–1800. 3281
Carl L. Marcellino	5	Oyster Bay	R	54	516–922–1011. 2390
John J. Marchi	24	Staten Island	R	96	718–447–1723. 3215

Member	District	Town or borough	Party	November 2000 election %	District phone # and Albany ext.
Marty Markowitz	20	Brooklyn	D	92	718–284–4700. 2431
George D. Maziarz	61	Lockport	R	Unopposed	716–438–0665. 2024
Patricia K McGee	56	Olean	R	66	716–372–4901. 3563
Raymond A, Meier	47	Utica	R	Unopposed	315–793–2360. 3334
Olga A. Mendez	28	Manhattan	D	96	212–860–0893. 3361
Vilmanette Montgomery	18	Brooklyn	D	93	718–643–6140. 3451
Thomas P. Morahan	38	Nanuet	R	56	914–425–1818. 3261
Michael F. Nozzolio	53	Seneca Falls	R	Unopposed	315–568–9816. 2366
George Onorato	14	Long Island City	D	76	718–545–9706. 3486
Suzi Oppenheimer	36	Port Chester	D	96	914–934–5250. 2031
Frank Padavan	11	Bellerose	R	62	718–343–0255. 3381
David A. Patterson	29	Manhattan	D	29	212–222–7315. 2441
Mary Lou Rath	60	Williamsville	R	72	716–633–0331. 3161
Stephen M. Saland	41	Poughkeepsie	R	70	914–463–0840. 2411
Nellie Santiago	17	Brooklyn	D	99	718–827–5743. 2177
Eric T. Schneiderman	30	Manhattan	D	83	212–397–5913. 2041
James L. Seward	50	Oneonta	R	91	607–432–5524. 3131
Dean G. Skelos	9	Sayville Center	R	60	516–766–8383. 3171
Ada L. Smith	12	Jamaica	D	Unopposed	718–322–2537. 3531
Malcolm A. Smith	10	St. Albans	D	93	718–291–9097. 2195
Nicholas A. Spano	35	Yonkers	R	52	914–969–5194. 2231
William T. Stachowski	58	Buffalo	D	75	716–826–3344. 2426
Ronald B. Stafford	45	Plattsburgh	R	Unopposed	518–561–2430. 2811
Toby Ann Stavisky	16	Flushing	D	98	718–445–0004. 3461
Ruth H. Thompson	33	Bronx	D	94	718–547–8854. 2061
Ceasar Trunzo	3	Hauppauge	R	61	631–360–3236. 2111
Guy J. Valella	34	Bronx	D	54	718–792–7180. 3264
Dale M. Volker	58	Depew	R	75	716–656–8544. 3471
James W. Wright	46	Watertown	R	95	315–785–2430. 2346

Sources: Election returns, all unofficial, are those reported by the *New York Times,* CNN, the Albany *Times Union,* and the offices of several candidates on November 9, 2000 (two days after the election). Addresses and phone numbers were those provided, respectively, by the Assembly and Senate offices of public affairs. They are accessible at www.nys.assembly.gov and www.nys.senate.gov.

Appendix B

Maps

Source for all maps that follow: New York State Legislative Task Force on Demographic Research and Reapportionment, "1992 New York State Congressional and Legislative Districts: State Senate and State Assembly" (New York: State Legislative Task Force, 1994), pp. S1–3 (senate) and A1–3 (assembly).

364

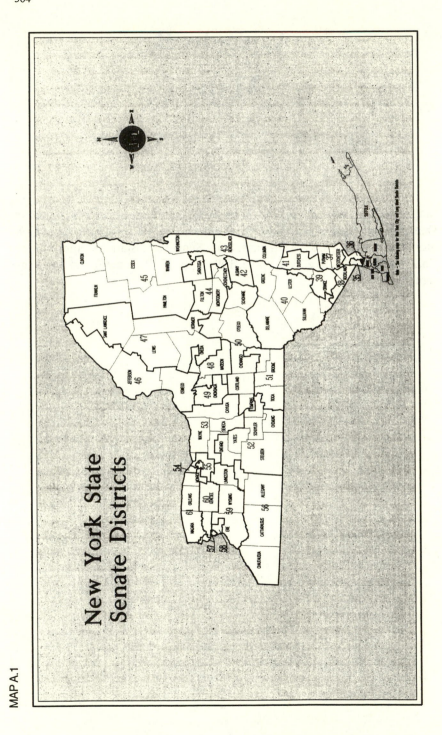

MAP A.1

New York State
Senate Districts

MAP A.2

City Of New York
Senate Districts

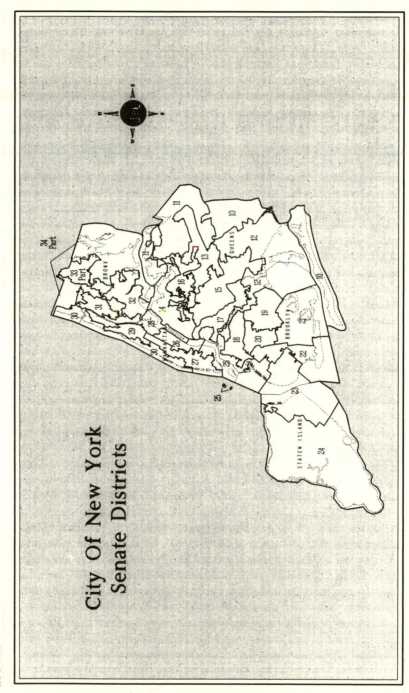

MAP A.3

Long Island Senate Districts

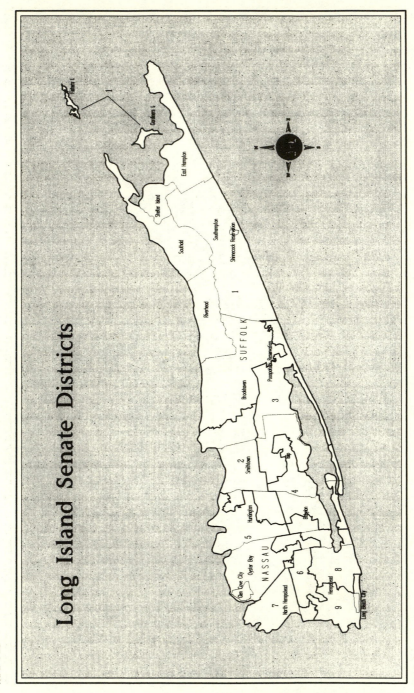

MAP A.4

New York State
Assembly Districts

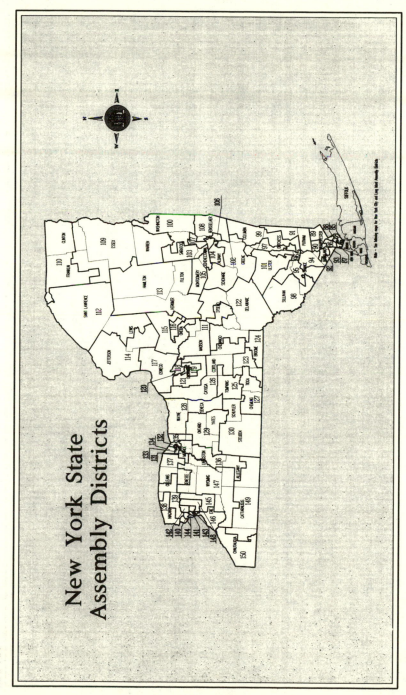

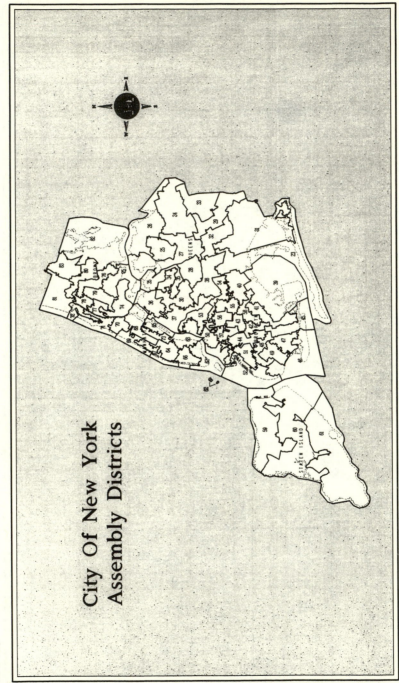

MAP A.5

City Of New York
Assembly Districts

MAP A.6

Long Island Assembly Districts

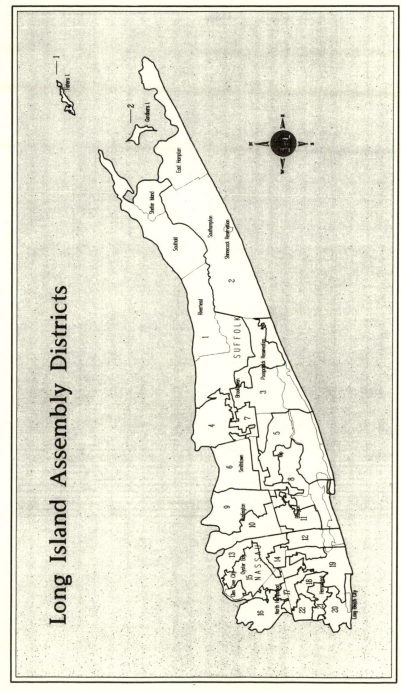

Notes

Notes to Introduction

1. Most of these figures are gleaned from the Council of State Governments, *The Book of the States, 1996–97* (Lexington, KY: Council of State Governments, 1996) and from the endlessly fascinating book by Victoria Van Son, *CQ State Fact Finder: Rankings Across America* (Washington, DC: CQ Press, 1993).

2. Michael Barone and Grant Ujifusa, *The Almanac of American Politics 1994* (Washington, DC: National Journal 1993), p. 885.

Notes to Chapter 1

1. Mark Twain, *Life on the Mississippi* (London: Chatto and Windus, 1883), p. 9.

2. William Cronin, *Changes in the Land: Indians, Colonists, and the Ecology of New England* (New York: Hill and Wang, 1983), p. 12.

3. Milton M. Klein, "New York in the American Colonies: A New Look," reprinted in Klein, *The Politics of Diversity* (Port Washington, NY: Kennikat Press, 1974), p. 189.

4. Joyce D. Goodfriend, *Before the Melting Pot: Society and Culture in Colonial New York City, 1664–1730* (Princeton, NJ: Princeton University Press, 1992), p. 5.

5. David M. Ellis, James A. Frost, Harold C. Syrett, and Harry T. Carman, *A Short History of New York State* (Ithaca, NY: Cornell University Press, 1957), p. 118.

6. Shays' Rebellion, often cited as a key incident in provoking landholders to seek a strong federal Constitution, took place largely in Massachusetts; but it had important conections with New York. The rebels' ability to slide across the Berkshire hills and thus evade Massachusetts' State authority pointed up what many thought to be a fatal flaw in the Articles of Confederation. Shays had many sympathizers in the adjacent Livingston manor (now Columbia County and part of Dutchess) and throughout the Hudson Valley.

7. Ellis, et al., *Short History*, p. 163.

8. Ibid., p. 264.

9. Ibid., p. 281.

10. Chris McNickle, *To Be Mayor of New York: Ethnic Politics in the City* (New York: Columbia University Press, 1993), p. 5.

11. This engraving, by the then-twenty-four-year-old Homer, is reprinted in Eric Homberger, *Scenes from the Life of a City: Corruption and Conscience in Old New York* (New Haven: Yale University Press), 1994), p. 22.

12. Ellis, et al., *Short History*, p. 472.

13. David M. Ellis, *New York: State and City* (Ithaca: Cornell University Press, 1979), p. 140.

14. Ibid., p. 134.

15. Ellis, et al., *Short History*, p. 403.

16. Like many large companies, Xerox and Kodak—Rochester's largest employees—laid off thousands of industrial and managerial employees in the 1980s and 1990s. Both companies, however, because they are strongly unionized and have long prided themselves on their responsibility to the Rochester community, made a particular effort to downsize through generous early retirement programs and retraining options. The community impact of these retrenchments, though substantial, has not been of the same magnitude as the complete closing of steel plants in Buffalo and Lackawanna or the General Motors plant in Tarrytown. In the 1990 census, Monroe County continued to rank among the five New York counties highest in percentage of workforce (27.7 percent) engaged in manufacturing. Kodak's latest rounds of downsizing, in 1996 and 1997 will probably change that picture substantially in the 2000 Census.

17. John Hull Mollenkopf, *A Phoenix in the Ashes: The Rise and Fall of the Koch Coalition in New York City Politics* (Princeton, NJ: Princeton University Press, 1992), p. 47.

18. Herbert London and Edwin S. Rubenstein, *From the Empire State to the Vampire State* (Lanham, MD: University Press of America, 1994), p. ix.

19. R. Scott Fosler, William Alonso, Jack A. Meyer, and Rosemary Kern, *Demographic Change and the American Future* (Pittsburgh, PA: University of Pittsburgh Press, 1990), p. 24. Unless specifically noted, the population statistics presented in this section are taken from various years and publications of the United States Bureau of the Census.

20. Ibid.

21. Nathan Glazer, "The New New Yorkers," in ed. Peter D. Salins, *New York Unbound: The City and the Politics of the Future* (New York: Basil Blackwell, 1988), p. 65.

22. These frequently cited figures are derived largely from studies by the Congressional Budget Office, the Citizens for Tax Justice, and the Bureau of the Census. A good overview of these and other studies can be found in Paul Krugman, "The Right, the Rich, and the Facts," *The American Prospect*, Fall 1992, pp.11–14.

23. Center on Budget and Policy Priorities, *Where Have All the Dollars Gone? A State-by-State Analysis of Income Disparities Over the 1980's* (Washington, DC: Center on Budget and Policy Priorities), August 1992.

24. Fiscal Policy Institute, *The Right Choice for New York 1995* (Albany: Fiscal Policy Institute, 1995), p. 20.

25. Center on Budget and Policy Priorities, *Pulling Apart: A State-by-State Analysis of Income Trends* as cited in "Common Cents," the January 1998 newsletter of the New Yorkers for Fiscal Fairness, p. 4.

26. New York State Education Department, *New York: The State of Learning, Statistical Profiles of Public School Districts* (Albany: The University of the State of New York, 1995), pp. 125, 126.

27. Glazer, "The New New Yorkers," pp. 68–69.

28. Herbert Bienstock, as quoted in Andres Torres, *Between Melting Pot and Mosaic: African Americans and Puerto Ricans in the New York Political Economy* (Philadelphia: Temple University Press, 1995), p. 87.

29. Mollenkopf, *A Phoenix in the Ashes*, p. 47.

30. Glazer, "The New New Yorkers," p. 72.

31. Torres, *Between Melting Pot and Mosaic*, p.127.

32. Ibid.

33. Ibid.

34. William L. Riordan, *Plunkitt of Tammany Hall* (New York: Alfred A. Knopf, 1948), p. 86.

35. Moffat interview in Gerald Benjamin and Robert T. Nakamura, editors, *The Modern New York State Legislature: Redressing the Balance* (Albany: Rockefeller Institute, 1991), p. 4.

36. New York is larger than many of its residents realize. A major league baseball fan in Jamestown, by way of illustration, lives closer to the home fields of *nine* teams— the Baltimore Orioles, Cleveland Indians, Chicago Cubs and White Sox, Detroit Tigers, Montreal Expos, Philadelphia Phillies, Pittsburgh Pirates and Toronto Blue Jays— than to the New York Mets or Yankees.

37. Lee Benson, *The Concept of Jacksonian Democracy: New York as a Test Case* (Princeton, NJ: Princeton University Press, 1961), p. 165.

38. McNickle, *To Be Mayor*, pp. 1–2.

39. Ellis, et al., *Short History*, p. 119. The other important early leader in New York politics who was decidedly not of aristocratic heritage, Alexander Hamilton, never held elective office. The seminal work on New York's aristocracy is the recently reprinted doctoral dissertation of Gabriel A. Almond, *Plutocracy and Politics in New York City* (Boulder, CO: Westview Press, 1998).

40. Robert A. Dahl, *Who Governs? Democracy and Power in an American City* (New Haven, CT: Yale University Press, 1961), p. 12.

41. Leonard Ruchelman, *Political Careers: Recruitment through the Legislature* (Rutherford, NJ: Fairleigh Dickenson University Press, 1970), p. 164.

42. Benjamin and Nakamura, eds., *The Modern New York State Legislature: Redressing the Balance*.

43. Alan Ehrenhart, *The United States of Ambition* (New York: Times Books, 1991), p. 16.

44. Torres, p. 64.

45. Daniel J, Elazar, *American Federalism: A View from the States* (New York: Harper and Row, 3rd edition, 1984).

46. See, for example, Ira Sharkansky, "The Utility of Elazar's Political Culture: A Research Note," in eds. Daniel Elazar and Joseph Zikund, II, *The American Cultural Matrix* (New York: Thomas Y. Crowell, 1975), pp. 262–84; and Jody L. Fitzpatrick and Rodney E. Hero, "Political Culture and Political Charactersistics of the American States: A Consideration of Some Old and New Questions," *Western Political Quarterly* 41 (June 1988): 145–53. A University of Nebraska Press series of books that plans eventually to cover all fifty states uses the Elazar construct as its principal organizing theme. The New York volume, edited by Sarah Liebschutz, does not make a big deal of the concept.

47. Robert S. Erikson, Gerald C. Wright, and John P. McIver, *Statehouse Democracy: Public Opinion and Policy in the American States* (New York: Cambridge University Press, 1993).

48. Frank Lynn of the *New York Times* as quoted in John Kenneth White, "New York's Selective Majority," in ed. Maureen Moakley, *Party Realignment and State Politics* (Columbus: Ohio State University Press, 1992), p. 218.

49. Ibid., p. 221.
50. Ibid., p. 224.

Notes to Chapter 2

1. Morton Grodzins, "Centralization and Decentralization in the American Federal System," in ed. Robert A. Goldwin, *A Nation of States* (Chicago: Rand McNally, 1963), pp. 3–4.

2. Alexander Hamilton, John Jay, and James Madison, *The Federalist*, Number 39.

3. Ibid.

4. Three times during Congressional consideration of the Bill of Rights advocates of state power tried to add the word "expressly" to the sentence referring to powers delegated to the national government. Three times they lost. Although this would seem to indicate an expansive view of federal power, some advocates of states' rights—including, most notably, Chief Justice William Rehnquist—continue to construe the text as if federal powers were limited to those "expressly" delegated.

5. *McCulloch v. Maryland*, 4 Wheaton 316 (1819) 322.

6. *Gibbons v. Ogden*, 9 Wheaton 1 (1824) 3.

7. Russell L. Hanson, "Intergovernmental Relations," in eds. Virginia Gray and Herbert Jacob *Politics in the American States: A Comparative Analysis*, 6th ed. (Washington, DC: CQ Press, 1996), p. 45.

8. David B. Walker, "The Evolving Federal Role in Program Administration," in eds. Robert E. Cleary, Nicholas Henry, and Associates, *Managing Public Programs: Balancing Politics, Administration, and Needs* (San Francisco: Jossey-Bass, 1989), p. 39.

9. Richard Snelling, as quoted in Hanson, "Intergovernmental Relations," in Gray and Jacob, *Politics in the American States*, p. 48.

10. Terry Sanford, *Storm Over the States* (New York: McGraw-Hill, 1967).

11. Deil S. Wright, *Understanding Intergovernmental Relations*, 3rd ed. (Pacific Grove, CA: Brooks-Cole, 1988), p. 23.

12. Lawrence D. Brown, "The Politics of Devolution in Nixon's New Federalism," in eds. Lawrence D. Brown, James W. Fossett, and Kenneth T. Palmer, *The Changing Politics of Federal Grants* (Washington, DC: The Brookings Institution, 1984). Background material for much of this section is drawn from this excellent collection of essays.

13. Daniel Elazar, *American Federalism: A View from the States* (New York: Harper and Row, 1984), p. 42.

14. Richard P. Nathan, "The 'Devolution Revolution:' An Overview," in ed. Michael Malbin, *Rockefeller Institute Bulletin* (Albany: Nelson A. Rockefeller Institute of Government, 1996), p. 11.

15. Quoted in Theodore J. Lowi, "Ronald Reagan—Revolutionary?" in eds. L. Salamon and S. Lund, *The Reagan Presidency and the Governing of America* (Washington, DC: Urban Institute Press, 1984), p. 96.

16. Quoted in Malbin, *Rockefeller Institute Bulletin*, p. 29.

17. Ibid., pp. 29–30.

18. Advisory Commission on Intergovernmental Relations, *Significant Features of Fiscal Federalism* (Washington, DC: Advisory Commission, 1994).

19. Ibid., p. 36.

20. Sarah F. Liebschutz, "Political Conflict and Intergovernmental Relations: The Federal-State Dimension," in eds. Jeffrey M. Stonecash, John Kenneth White, and Peter W. Colby, *Governing New York State*, 3rd ed. (Albany: State University of New York Press, 1994), p. 58.

21. Monica E. Friar and Herman B. Leonard, *The Federal Budget and the States: Fiscal Year 1994* (Cambridge, MA, and Washington, DC: John F. Kennedy School of Government and the Office of Senator Daniel Patrick Moynihan, 1995), p. 51.

22. Ibid., p. 86.

23. See, for example, the table in David C. Saffell, *State and Local Government: Politics and Public Policies*, 5th ed. (New York: McGraw-Hill, 1993), p. 20.

24. Liebschutz, "Political Conflict," p. 51.

25. Advisory Commission, *Significant Features of Fiscal Federalism*, p. 32.

26. Friar and Leonard, *Federal Budget*, p. 51.

27. Timothy J. Conlan, James D. Riggle, and Donna E. Schwartz, "Deregulating Federalism? The Politics of Mandate Reform in the 104th Congress," *Publius* 25 (Summer 1995): 27.

28. Timothy J. Conlan and David R. Bream, "Federal Mandates: The Record of Reform and Future Prospects," *Intergovernmental Perspective* 18:7 (March 1992).

29. Martha Derthick, "Preserving Federalism: Congress, the States, and the Supreme Court," *Brookings Review* 4 (November 1986): 36.

30. Joseph F. Zimmerman, "Financing National Policy through Mandates," *National Civic Review* (Summer–Fall 1992): 368.

31. Ibid.

32. Nathan, "The 'Devolution Revolution,'" p. 13.

33. Warren Moscow, *Politics in the Empire State* (New York: Alfred A. Knopf, 1948), p. 218.

34. Joseph F. Zimmerman, *The Government and Politics of New York State* (New York: New York University Press, 1981), p. 339.

35. George E. Pataki and Patricia A. Woodworth, *State of New York Executive Budget 1995–96* (Albany: State of New York, 1996), p. 50.

36. Steven D. Gold and Sarah Ritchie, "The Role of the State in the Finances of Cities and Counties in New York," in Stonecash, et al., *Governing New York State*, p. 65.

37. Frank J. Mauro, "Financing Public Education and Local Government in the Twenty-First Century: Reducing Reliance on the Property Tax," unpublished paper, Fiscal Policy Institute, Albany, January 1994, p. 13.

38. According to Census Bureau figures compiled in 1996 by the office of State Senator Franz Leichter.

39. *City of Clinton v. Cedar Rapids and Missouri Railroad Company* 24 Iowa 455 (1868), 471.

40. *Curtis v. Eide* (1963) 19 AD2nd 507; 244 NYS, 2nd 330.

41. Management Resources Project, *Governing the Empire State: An Insider's Guide* (Albany: Rockefeller Institute, 1988), p. 194.

42. This quote and the surrounding discussion of mandate types is taken from ibid., pp. 192–93.

43. Mauro, "Financing Public Education," p. 12.

44. These figures are taken from a May 1996 memorandum from the office of state Senator Franz Leichter, p. 3.

45. Frank B. Moore, "Early History of Town Government in New York State,"

introduction to Book 61, *Town Law*, of *McKinney's Consolidated Laws of New York Annotated* (St. Paul, MN: West Publishing, 1965), p. vii.

46. Ibid.

47. The full panoply of these overlaps are detailed in the report of State Comptroller H. Carl McCall, *Overlapping Real Property Taxes* (Albany: Bureau of Municipal Research and Statistics, 1996).

48. Ibid., p. iii.

49. Keith M. Henderson, "Other Governments: The Public Authorities," in Stonecash, et al., *Governing New York State*, p. 212.

50. Ibid., p. 220.

51. C. Herman Pritchett, *The Federal System in Constitutional Law* (Englewood Cliffs, NJ: Prentice Hall, 1978), p. 298.

52. Ibid., p. 299.

53. G. Alan Tarr and Mary Cornelia Aldis Porter, *State Supreme Courts in State and Nation* (New Haven: Yale University Press, 1988), p. 8.

54. Daniel C. Kramer and Robert Riga, "The New York Court of Appeals and the U.S. Supreme Court, 1970–76," in eds. G. Alan Tarr and Mary Cornelia Aldis Porter, *State Supreme Courts: Policymakers in the American Federal System* (Westport, CT: Greenwood Press, 1982), p. 196.

55. Herbert Jacob, *Law and Politics in the United States*, 2nd ed. (New York: Harper, Collins, 1995), p. 272.

56. Ibid.

57. Robert W. Kastenmeier and Michael J. Remington, "A Judicious Legislator's Lexicon to the Federal Judiciary," in ed. Robert A. Katzmann, *Judges and Legislators: Toward Institutional Comity* (Washington, DC: The Brookings Institution, 1988), p. 61.

58. Harry A. Stumpf and John H. Culver, *The Politics of State Courts* (New York: Longmans, 1992), p. 3.

59. George A. Mitchell, ed., *The New York Red Book, 1995–1996*, 93rd ed. (Guilderland, NY: New York Legal Publishing Corp., 1995), p. 427.

60. Stumpf and Culver, *Politics of State Courts*, pp. 23–24.

61. James Willard Hurst, *The Growth of American Law: The Lawmakers* (Boston: Little, Brown, 1950), pp. 85–197. Harry P. Stumpf, *American Judicial Politics* (New York: Harcourt, Brace, Jovanovich, 1988), p. 74.

62. Tarr and Porter, *State Supreme Courts*, p. 28.

63. Harold J. Spaeth, *Supreme Court Policy Making* (San Francisco: W.H. Freeman, 1979), pp. 6–7.

64. 4 Dallas (1789), 1.

65. Lawrence M. Friedman, *A History of American Law*, 2nd ed. (New York: Simon and Schuster, 1985), pp. 661–62.

66. *Garcia v. San Antonio Metropolitan Transit Authority* 490 U.S. 552 (1985).

67. Grodzins, "Centralization and Decentralization in the American Federal System," in Goldwin, *A Nation of States*, p. 9.

Notes to Chapter 3

1. Alex Rose, a founder of the Liberal Party, as quoted by Robert J. Spitzer, "Third Parties in New York State," in eds. Jeffrey M. Stonecash, John Kenneth White, and Peter W. Colby, *Governing New York State*, 3rd ed. (Albany: State University of New York Press, 1994), pp. 83–84.

2. Chao-Chi Shan, "The Decline of Electoral Competition in New York State Senate Elections," unpublished doctoral dissertation, Syracuse University, 1991, as cited in ibid., p. 108.

3. Spitzer, "Third Parties," p. 107.

4. Chris McNickle, *To Be Mayor of New York: Ethnic Politics in the City* (New York: Columbia University Press, 1993), p. 196.

5. Howard A. Scarrow, *Parties, Elections, and Representation in New York State* (New York: New York University Press, 1983), p. 25.

6. Ibid., p. 26.

7. Center for Voting and Democracy, *Dubious Democracy* (Washington, DC: Center for Voting and Democracy, 1998), unpaged.

8. Nebraska's unicameral legislature was not included in the rankings. Alan Rosenthal, *The Decline of Representative Democracy* (Washington, DC: CQ Press, 1998), pp. 73–74.

9. Jeffrey M. Stonecash, "Political Parties and Partisan Conflict," in Stonecash, et al., *Governing New York State*, pp. 83–84.

10. Ibid., p. 84.

11. Scott Thomas, "The Tale of Two States," *Empire State Report*, January 1983, p. 34.

12. Ibid., p. 37.

13. Warren Moscow, *Politics in the Empire State* (New York: Alfred A. Knopf, 1948), p. 41.

14. Ralph Straetz and Frank Munger, *New York Politics* (New York: New York University Press, 1960) provide the classic description of these regional patterns.

15. Asher Arian, Arthur S. Goldberg, John H. Mollenkopf, and Edward T. Rogowsky, *Changing New York City Politics* (New York: Routledge, 1991), p.182.

16. Ibid., p. 186.

17. Stonecash, "Political Parties," p. 96.

18. Robert K. Merton, *Social Theory and Social Structure* (Glencoe, IL: Free Press, 1957), p. 71.

19. Frank S. Robinson, *Machine Politics: A Study of Albany's O'Connells* (New Brunswick, NJ: Transaction Books, 1977). Under the heading "Albany Democrats: 75 Years of Power" the Albany *Times Union* compiled an excellent analysis of the machine's history and political legacy. See the issue of December 8, 1996, pp. A-1, 6 and 7.

20. For a good description of the Schenectady County Organization and the reform coalition that challenged it see James A. Reidel, "Boss and Faction," *Annals of the American Academy of Political and Social Science* 353 (1964): 14–26.

21. Alexander B Callow, Jr., ed., *The City Boss in America* (New York: Oxford University Press, 1976), p. 269.

22. Daniel P. Moynihan, "When the Irish Ran New York," in Callow, pp. 120–21.

23. Robert F. Pecorella, *Community Power in a Postreform City: Politics in New York City* (Armonk, NY: M.E. Sharpe, 1994), p. 35.

24. Rachel Sady, *District Leaders: A Political Ethnography* (Boulder, CO: Westview Press, 1990), p. 130.

25. Most important election statistics in New York state can be found in various editions of the official *New York Red Book* (Guilderland, NY: New York Legal Publishing Co., various years). For some local races, those taking place since 1996, and some primaries, we have relied—unless otherwise noted—on the official records provided by the state and New York City boards of elections.

26. This synthesis is implicit in Frances Fox Piven and Richard Cloward, *Why Americans Don't Vote* (New York: Pantheon Books, 1988) and spelled out in their remarks in a symposium in the June 1990 issue of *PS: Political Science and Politics*.

27. The record of the New York City Board of Elections in failing to facilitate voter turnout is well-documented in Ronald Hayduk, *Gatekeepers of the Franchise: Election Administration and Voter Participation in New York* (Unpublished doctoral dissertation, The Graduate Center, City University of New York, 1996).

28. City of New York, Voter Assistance Commission, *1994 Annual Report* (New York: Voter Assistance Commission, 1994), p. 44.

29. These were the figures provided to the courts by the Puerto Rican Legal Defense and cited by Judge McLaughlin in *Diaz v. Silver*, slip opinion, United States District Court, Eastern District of New York, 95–CV-2591 (February 26, 1997), p. 8.

30. Voter Assistance Commission, p. 69.

31. Ibid.

32. Moscow, *Politics in the Empire State*, p. 167. It is perhaps worth noting that since the method of selecting delegates to future constitutional conventions was to be election from these same upstate-biased senate districts, the possibilities of change by that route were also limited.

33. 369 U.S. 186 (1962).

34. 328 U.S. 549 (1946), 565–66.

35. *Reynolds v. Sims*, 377 U.S. 533 (1964), 568.

36. Joseph F. Zimmerman, *The Government and Politics of New York State* (New York: New York University Press, 1981), pp. 118–19.

37. For a more extended argument and examples of pre-*Baker v. Carr* gerrymanders, see Edward V. Schneier and Bertram M. Gross, *Congress Today* (New York: St. Martin's, 1993), pp. 39–41. On the original New York case, see Calvin B.T. Chin, *One Man, One Vote: WMCA and the Struggle for Equal Representation* (New York: Scribners, 1967).

38. Peter A. A. Berle, *Does the Citizen Stand a Chance: Politics of a State Legislature: New York* (Woodbury, NY: Barron's Educational Series, 1974), pp. 9–10.

39. For a good summary of these issues see Gerald Benjamin, "The Political Relationship," in eds. Gerald Benjamin and Charles Brecher, *The Two New Yorks: State-City Relations in the Changing Federal System* (New York: Russell Sage Foundation), pp. 139–42.

40. 509 U.S. 630 (1993).

41. *Miller v. Johnson* 115 S. Ct. 2475 (1995), 2486.

42. *Diaz v. Silver*, p. 79.

43. Ibid., p. 33.

44. In the current 72nd Assembly District, 69 percent of those classified as Hispanic are over 18 as compared with 77 percent of the non-Hispanics. New York State Legislative Task Force on Demographic Research and Reapportionment, *Congressional and Legislative Districts: State Senate and State Assembly* (New York: Legislative Task Force, 1994), p. A-180.

45. *Diaz v. Silver*, p. 66.

46. Scholars have actually developed workable measures of how relatively bizarre, or lacking in compactness, varying districting schemes are. See Richard H. Pildes and Richard G. Niemi, "Expressive Harms, 'Bizarre Districts,' and Voting Rights: Evaluating Election-District Appearances After *Shaw v. Reno*," *Michigan Law Review* (1993), 92: 483–566. A similar measure of compactness, accepted by all parties in *Diaz v. Silver* was developed in a special report to congress in 1994 by David C. Huckabee of the Congressional Research Service.

47. Interview with John F. Haggerty, in Gerald Benjamin and Robert T. Nakamura, *The Modern New York State Legislature: Redressing the Balance* (Albany: Rockefeller Institute, 1991), p. 290.

48. For a good discussion of national realignments see Walter Dean Burnham, *Critical Elections and the Mainsprings of American Electoral Politics* (New York: W.W. Norton, 1970).

49. Moscow, *Politics in the Empire State*, p. 167.

50. Stonecash, "Political Parties," p. 87.

51. Morris Fiorina, *Divided Government* (New York: MacMillan, 1992), p. 24.

52. David R. Mayhew, *Divided Government* (New Haven: Yale University Press, 1991), p. 179.

53. Bob Gurwitt, "Joseph L. Bruno: Nobody's Puppet," in ed. Thad L. Beyle, *State Government: CQ's Guide to Current Issues and Activities 1995–96* (Washington, DC: CQ Press, 1995), p. 117.

54. Jeffrey M. Stonecash, "The Legislature: The Emergence of an Equal Branch," in Stonecash, et al., p. 154.

55. Ibid., p. 155.

56. John Hull Mollenkopf, *A Phoenix in the Ashes: The Rise and Fall of the Koch Coalition in New York City Politics* (Princeton, NJ: Princeton University Press, 1994), p. 88.

57. Richard C. Wade, "The Withering Away of the Party System," in eds. Jewell Bellush and Dick Netzer, *Urban Politics New York Style* (Armonk, NY: M.E. Sharpe, 1990), p. 282.

58. Ibid., p. 283.

59. Mollenkopf, *A Phoenix in the Ashes*, p. 170.

60. Ibid., p. 181.

61. Ibid., p. 199.

62. Ibid., p. 214.

63. Arian, et al., *Changing New York City Politics*, p. 199.

64. Schneier and Gross, *Congress Today*, p. 23.

65. Cornelius P. Cotter, James L. Gibson, John F. Bibby, and Robert J. Huckshorn, *Party Organizations in American Politics* (Pittsburgh, PA: University of Pittsburgh Press, 1989), p. 28.

66. Raymond Wolfinger, "Why Political Machines Have Not Withered Away and Other Revisionist Thoughts," *Journal of Politics* 34 (May 1972): 365–98.

67. Mollenkopf, *A Phoenix in the Ashes*, pp. 77–78.

Notes to Chapter 4

1. Clarence N. Stone, *Regime Politics: Governing Atlanta, 1946–1988* (Lawrence: University Press of Kansas, 1989), p. 219.

2. Robert F. Pecorella, *Community Power in a Postreform City: Politics in New York City* (Armonk, NY: M.E. Sharpe, 1994), pp. 14–15.

3. Wallace B. Sayre and Herbert Kaufman, *Governing New York City* (New York: Russell Sage Foundation, 1960). On the rise of the "new machines" see Theodore J. Lowi, "Machine Politics: Old and New," *The Public Interest* 9 (Fall 1967): 83–92.

4. Paul Peterson, *City Limits* (Chicago: University of Chicago Press, 1981), p. 209.

5. John Hull Mollenkopf, *A Phoenix in the Ashes: The Rise and Fall of the Koch Coalition in New York City Politics* (Princeton, NJ: Princeton University Press, 1992), p. 200.

6. E. E. Schattschneider, *The Semisovereign People: A Realist's View of Democracy in America* (New York: Holt, Rinehart, and Winston, 1960), p. 40.

7. David C. Nice, *Federalism: The Politics of Intergovernmental Relations* (New York: St. Martin's Press, 1987), pp. 29–30.

8. Elizabeth Drew, "Charlie," in eds. Allen J. Cigler and Burdett A. Loomis, *Interest Group Politics* (Washington, DC: CQ Press, 1983), p. 230. Originally published in *The New Yorker*, January 9, 1978.

9. Clem Miller, quoted in John W. Baker, ed., *Member of the House* (New York: Charles Scribner's Sons, 1962), pp. 137–140.

10. Nice, *Federalism*, p. 31.

11. Clive S. Thomas and Ronald J. Hrebenar, "Interest Groups in the States," in eds. Virginia Gray and Herbert Jacob, *Politics in the American States: A Comparative Analysis*, 6th ed. (Washington, DC: CQ Press, 1996), p. 149.

12. Schattschneider, *The Semisovereign People*, p. 35.

13. Theodore J. Lowi, *The Politics of Disorder* (New York: Basic Books, 1971), p. 31.

14. An excellent summary and analysis of the literature comparing the American states in this regard can be found in Sarah M. Morehouse, "Interest Groups, Parties and Policies in the American States," unpublished paper delivered at the 1997 Annual Meeting of the American Political Science Association, Washington, DC, August 28–31, 1997.

15. David L. Cingranelli, "New York: Powerful Groups and Powerful Parties," in eds. Ronald J. Hrebenar and Clive S. Thomas, *Interest Group Politics in the Northeastern States* (State College: Pennsylvania State University Press, 1993), p. 276.

16. Clive C. Thomas, "The Changing Nature of Interest-Group Activity in the Northeast," in Hrebenar and Thomas, *Interest Group Politics in the Northeastern States*, pp. 383–84.

17. Virginia Gray and David Lowery, "Reflections on the Study of Interest Groups in the States," in eds. William Crotty, Mildred A. Schwartz, and John C. Green, *Representing Interests and Interest Group Representation* (Lanham, MD: University Press of America, 1994), pp. 57–66.

18. John W. Kingdon, *Agendas, Alternatives, and Public Policies*, 2nd ed. (New York: HarperCollins, 1995), p. 150.

19. Cingranelli, "New York," p. 271.

20. Some people who thought they were giving money to help Republicans maintain control of the senate might have been upset to learn that their contributions had been diverted to such local races, but there is nothing illegal about such a transfer. What would have been illegal—and there is no evidence that this happened—is if an individual who had already given the maximum amount allowed to the candidates for judge had made a contribution to the Republican Senate Campaign Committee *knowing* that it would be diverted back to the state. Of course if he or she made such a contribution without *knowing* that the funds would be diverted, it is legal.

21. Frank J. Sorauf, "Political Action Committees," in eds. Anthony Corrado, Thomas E. Mann, Daniel R. Ortiz, Trevor Potter, and Frank J. Sorauf, *Campaign Finance Reform: A Sourcebook* (Washington, DC: The Brookings Institution, 1997), p. 124.

22. Technically, candidates are supposed to use their campaign accounts only for their own campaign expenses. As with most campaign finance regulations in New York, the definitions of expenditure categories are so loose as to make this rule virtually inoperative. A series of exposés in various May 2000 issues of the Albany *Times*

Union, which found members using their campaign accounts for anything from trips to Israel to building a backyard swimming pool, were shrugged off by most politicians as routine.

23. Alan Rosenthal, *The Decline of Representative Democracy: Process, Participation, and Power in State Legislatures* (Washington, DC: CQ Press, 1998), p. 223.

24. Richard L. Hall and Frank W. Wayman, "Buying Time: Moneyed Interests and the Mobilization of Bias in Congressional Committees," *American Political Science Review* 84 (September 1990): 797–820.

25. Warren Anderson in Gerald Benjamin and Robert T. Nakamura, eds., *The Modern New York State Legislature: Redressing the Balance* (Albany: Rockefeller Institute, 1991), p. 64.

26. Perry B. Duryea, Jr., in ibid., p. 42.

27. Jeffrey M. Stonecash, "Working at the Margins: Campaign Finance and Party Strategy in New York Assembly Elections," *Legislative Studies Quarterly* XIII (November 1988): 485.

28. Ibid., p. 490.

29. Daniel M. Shea, *Transforming Democracy: Legislative Campaign Committees and Political Parties* (Albany: State University of New York Press, 1995), p. 167.

30. Ibid., p. 170.

31. As quoted in Kevin Sack, "The Great Incumbency Machine," *New York Times Magazine*, September 27, 1992, p. 60.

32. David Morgan, *The Capitol Press Corps: Newsmen and the Governor of New York State* (Westport, CT: Greenwood Press, 1978), p. 15.

33. *The Red Book, 1995–96*, p. 405.

34. Morgan asked a sample of Albany correspondents whether "political news from the State level suffers by contrast with the frequency and immediacy of local and/or Washington news?" 78.3 percent answered yes. Morgan, *Capitol Press Corps*, p. 112.

35. Martin Linsky, "Legislatures and the Press: The Problems of Image and Attitude," *State Government* 59 (Spring 1986): 159.

36. Nicholas Goldberg as quoted in Jeffrey M. Stonecash, "Media Coverage of State Politics," p. 201.

37. Morgan, *Capitol Press Corps*, p. 21.

38. Linsky, "Legislatures and the Press," p. 158.

39. Morgan, *Capitol Press Corps*, p. 39.

40. Ibid., p. 106.

41. Ibid.

42. Jeffrey Stonecash, "Critics of Legislature Are Failing to See Democracy," Syracuse *Gazette*, October 9, 1994, p. F-4.

Notes to Chapter 5

1. *Wein v. State*, 383 NYS 2nd 225 (1976), p. 228.

2. Richard Briffault, "State Constitutions in the Federal System," in ed. Gerald Benjamin, *The New York State Constitution: A Briefing Book* (Albany: Nelson A. Rockefeller Institute of Government, 1994), p. 11.

3. Ibid., p. 12.

4. Peter J. Galie, *Ordered Liberty: A Constitutional History of New York* (New York: Fordham University Press, 1996), p. 24.

5. Ibid.

6. Ibid., p. 36.

7. Ibid., p. 89.

8. Ibid., p. 112.

9. Vernon O'Rourke and Douglas Campbell, *Constitution-Making in a Democracy: Theory and Practice in New York State* (Baltimore: Johns Hopkins University Press, 1943).

10. Thad L. Beyle, "Enhancing Executive Leadership in the States," *State and Local Government Review* 27 (1995): 18–25.

11. Thad Beyle, "Governors: The Middlemen and Women in Our Political System," in eds. Virginia Gray and Herbert Jacob, *Politics in the American States: A Comparative Analysis* (Washington, DC: CQ Press, 1996), p. 237.

12. Council of State Governments, *The Book of the States: 1994–95 Edition* (Lexington, KY: The Council of State Governments: 1994), p. 66.

13. Joseph F. Zimmerman, *The Government and Politics of New York State* (New York: New York University Press, 1981), p. 188. The Peyser case shows that competency and honesty are not the sole criteria, at least when important political feathers are ruffled; but Zimmerman's general statement remains pretty much the prevailing norm.

14. Beyle, "Governors," p. 228.

15. Quoted in Gerald Benjamin and Robert C. Lawton, "The Governorship in an Era of Limits," in eds. Jeffrey M. Stonecash, John Kenneth White, and Peter W. Colby, *Governing New York State*, 3rd ed. (Albany: State University of New York Press, 1994), p. 134.

16. Ibid.

17. George Weeks, "A Statehouse Hall of Fame," *State Government* (Fall 1982), as cited in Benjamin and Lawton, p. 134.

18. *People v. Miner*, 2 Lansing 396 (New York Appellate Division, 1868). A useful compendium of material on the office can be found in Lynne M. Ross, *State Attorneys General: Powers and Responsibilities* (Washington, DC: Bureau of National Affairs, 1990).

19. Louis Galambos, *The New American State: Bureaucracies and Policies since World War II* (Baltimore: Johns Hopkins University Press, 1987), p. 2.

20. Management Resources Project, *Governing the Empire State* (Albany: Rockefeller Institute, 1988), p. 18. This rather dry guide to state government has an especially sensitive analysis of the governor's office which we draw upon here.

21. Quoted in ibid., p. 22.

22. Ibid., p. 27.

23. As quoted in Richard Rose, *Managing Presidential Objectives* (New York: Free Press, 1976), p. 151.

24. Michael Martinez, "Government Makeover," *Empire State Report* (June 1997), p. 24.

25. Keith M. Henderson, "Other Governments: The Public Authorities," in Stonecash, et al., p. 220.

26. Benjamin and Lawton, "The Governorship," p. 141.

27. Ibid.

28. David Osborne and Ted Gaebler, *Reinventing Government: How the Entrepreneurial Spirit Is Transforming the Public Sector* (New York: Penguin Books, 1993).

29. James Bryce, *The American Commonwealth*, vol. I (New York: Macmillan, 1906), p. 539.

30. Nelson W. Polsby, "The Institutionalization of the U.S. House of Representatives," *American Political Science Review* 62 (March 1968): 144–68.

31. Ibid., p. 145.

32. These and other figures on the house are taken from Polsby.

33. Jeffrey M. Stonecash, "The Legislature: The Emergence of an Equal Branch," in Stonecash and Colby, p. 153.

34. Gerald Benjamin and Robert T. Nakamura, *The Modern New York State Legislature: Redressing the Balance* (Albany: Nelson A. Rockefeller Institute, 1991), p. xv.

35. Stonecash, "The Legislature," p. 155.

36. Benjamin and Nakamura, *Modern New York State Legislature*, p. xxiv.

37. Stanley Fink, as quoted in ibid., p. 117.

38. Arthur J. Kremer, as quoted in ibid., p. 157.

39. Stonecash, "The Legislature," p. 156.

40. Ibid., p. 158.

41. Quoted in Leonard Ruchelman, *Political Careers: Recruitment through the Legislature* (Rutherford, NJ: Fairleigh Dickinson University Press, 1970), p. 153.

42. Stonecash, "The Legislature," p.159.

43. Ibid., p. 158.

44. Zimmerman, *Government and Politics of New York State*, p. 132.

45. Michael B. Berkman, Suzanna De Boef, and Sarah Poggione, "Legislative Modernization in Comparative Perspective: Economic Change, Political Ambition, and American State Legislatures," paper delivered at the 1995 Annual Meeting of the American Political Science Association in Chicago, August 31–September 3, Figure 3A.

46. Kremer interview in Benjamin and Nakamura, *Modern New York State Legislature*, p. 157.

47. Malcolm E. Jewell and Marcia Lynn Whicker, *Legislative Leadership in the American States* (Ann Arbor: University of Michigan Press, 1994), Chapter 1.

48. Alan Rosenthal, "The Legislative Institution: In Transition and at Risk," in ed. Carl Van Horn, *The State of the States*, 2nd ed. (Washington, DC: CQ Press, 1993), p. 136–37.

49. Jewell and Whicker, *Legislative Leadership*, p. 8.

50. As quoted in Benjamin and Nakamura, *Modern New York State Legislature*, p. 70.

51. John F. Haggerty, in ibid., p. 293.

52. Galie, *Ordered Liberty*, p. 156.

53. Nancy Burns, *The Formation of American Local Governments* (New York: Oxford University Press, 1994), p. 31.

54. Ibid., p. 53.

55. Ibid., p. 6.

56. *1995 New York State Statistical Yearbook* (Albany: Rockefeller Institute, 1995), p. 202.

57. Ibid., p. 203.

58. Theodore J. Lowi, *The End of Liberalism: The Second Republic of the United States*, 2nd ed. (New York: W.W. Norton, 1979), p. 175.

59. Burns, *Formation of American Local Government*, p. 114.

60. Ibid., pp. 114–15.

61. John Caher, "Court Marks 150 Years," Albany *Times Union*, September 8, 1997, p. A-5.

62. Eddie Borges, "Courting Change," *Empire State Report* (June 1997), p. 37.

63. *People ex. rel. Arcara v. Cloud Books*, 68 NY2d 553 (1986), p. 558.

64. Peter J. Galie, *The New York State Constitution: A Reference Guide* (Westport, CT: Greenwood Press, 1990), p. 57.

65. Burton C. Agata, "Criminal Justice," in Benjamin, *New York State Constitution*, p. 200.

66. Ibid., p. 199.

67. Gerald Benjamin and Melissa Cusa, "Amending the New York State Constitution through the Legislature," in Benjamin, *New York State Constitution*, p. 63.

68. Ibid., p. 64.

69. Edward V. Schneier and Bertram Gross, *Congress Today* (New York: St. Martins, 1993), pp. 485–87.

70. Richard Briffault, "State Constitutions in the Federal System," in Benjamin, *New York State Constitution*, p. 4.

Notes to Chapter 6

1. Interview with Stanley Fink in Gerald Benjamin and Robert T. Nakamura, *The Modern New York State Legislature: Redressing the Balance* (Albany: Rockefeller Institute, 1991), p. 117.

2. Tom Loftus, *The Art of Legislative Politics* (Washington, DC: CQ Press, 1994), p. 52.

3. Malcolm E. Jewell and Marcia Lynn Whicker, *Legislative Leadership in the American States* (Ann Arbor: University of Michigan Press, 1996), p. 63.

4. Ibid., p. 70.

5. Loftus, *The Art of Legislative Politics*, p. 52.

6. Fink in Benjamin and Nakamura, *The Modern New York State Legislature*, p. 119.

7. Alan G. Hevesi, *Legislative Politics in New York State: A Comparative Analysis* (New York: Praeger, 1975), p. 60.

8. Ibid.

9. Ralph Wright, *All Politics Is Personal* (Manchester, VT: Marshall Jones, Co., 1996), pp. 24–25.

10. Alan Rosenthal, *The Decline of Representative Democracy* (Washington, DC: CQ Press, 1998), p. 258.

11. A pay raise law, enacted in a special session in December of 1998, raised these figures by roughly a third.

12. Cited in Rosenthal, *The Decline of Representative Democracy*, p. 275.

13. Charles O. Jones, "Joseph Cannon and Howard W. Smith: An Essay on the Limits of Leadership in the House of Representatives," *Journal of Politics* 30 (Fall 1968): 617.

14. Jeffrey M. Stonecash, "The Legislature: The Emergence of an Equal Branch" in eds. Jeffrey M. Stonecash, John Kenneth White, and Peter W. Colby, *Governing New York State* (Albany: State University of New York Press, 1994), p. 150.

15. Michael Bragman, New York State Assembly *Record of Proceedings*, May 22, 2000, p. 31.

16. Jewell and Whicker, *Legislative Leadership in the American States*, p. 125.

17. Ibid., p. 129.

18. Ibid., p. 130.

19. David W. Rohde, *Party Leaders in the Postreform House* (Chicago: University of Chicago Press, 1991), p. 35.

20. Jewell and Whicker, *Legislative Leadership in the American States*, p. 127.

21. Ibid., pp. 130–35.

22. Rosenthal, *The Decline of Representative Democracy*, p. 137.

23. Wayne L. Francis and James W. Riddlesperger, "U.S. State Legislative Committees: Structure, Procedural Efficiency, and Party Control," *Legislative Studies Quarterly* VII (November 1982): 457.

24. Rosenthal, *The Decline of Representative Democracy*, p. 141.

25. For patterns in other states a comprehensive survey of the literature can be found in Keith R. Hamm and Ronald D. Hedlund, "Committees in State Legislatures," in ed. Joel H. Silbey, *Encyclopedia of the American Legislative System* (New York: Scribners, 1994), p. 693.

26. John J. Pitney, Jr., "Leaders and Rules In the New York State Senate," *Legislative Studies Quarterly* VII (November 1982): 496.

27. As quoted in ibid.

28. Frank Mauro in Benjamin and Nakamura, *The Modern New York State Legislature*, p. 331.

29. Ibid., p. 229.

30. Richard E. Neustadt, *Presidential Power: The Politics of Leadership* (New York: Wiley, 1960), p. I.

31. Ibid., p. 58.

32. Thad Beyle, "Governors: The Middlemen and Women in Our Political System," in eds. Virginia Gray and Herbert Jacob, *Politics in the American States: A Comparative Analysis* (Washington, DC: CQ Press, 1996), p. 222.

33. Allen Schick, "The Budget Bureau That Was: Thoughts on the Rise, Decline and Future of a Presidential Agency," *Law and Contemporary Problems* LV (Summer 1970): 22.

34. Martha Wagner Weinberg, *Managing the State* (Cambridge, MA: MIT Press, 1977), p. 210.

35. As quoted in Daniel C. Kramer, *The Days of Wine and Roses Are Over: Governor Hugh Carey and New York State* (Lanham, MD: University Press of America, 1997), p. 323.

36. Ibid.

37. Neustadt, *Presidential Power*, p. 58.

38. Herbert London in Kramer, *The Days of Wine and Roses Are Over*, p. 319.

39. Interview with Norman M. Adler in Benjamin and Nakamura, *The Modern New York State Legislature*, p. 479.

40. Rosenthal, *The Decline of Representative Democracy*, p. 295.

41. Nelson W. Polsby, *Political Innovation in America: The Politics of Policy Initiation* (New Haven, CT: Yale University Press, 1984), p. 3.

42. Warren Anderson in Benjamin and Nakamura, *The Modern New York State Legislature*, p. 64.

43. Perry B. Duryea, Jr. in ibid., p. 43.

44. Kevin Sack, "The Great Incumbency Machine," *New York Times Magazine*, September 27, 1992; p. 49.

45. Herbert Jacob, "Courts: The Least Visible Branch," in eds. Virginia Gray and Herbert Jacob, *Politics in the American States: A Comparative Analysis*, 6th ed. (Washington, DC: CQ Press, 1996), p. 253.

46. Bradley Cannon, "The Impact of Formal Selection Processes on Characteristics of Judges—Reconsidered," *Law and Society Review* (May 1972): 62–65.

47. Craig F. Emmet and Henry R. Glick, "The Selection of State Supreme Court Justices," *American Politics Quarterly* XVI (October 1988): 445–65; and Barbara Luck Graham, "Do Judicial Selection Systems Matter? A Study of Black Representation on State Courts," *American Politics Quarterly* XVIII (July 1990): 316–36.

48. M.L. Henry, Jr., *Characteristics of Elected versus Merit-Selected New York City Judges, 1977–92* (New York: Fund for Modern Courts, 1992), pp. 1–2. In a 1998 follow-up study, described in a July 14 press release, the Fund found a dramatic increase in diversity with the proportion of female judges initially elected and appointed increasing from 28 percent in 1977–91 to 53 percent in 1992–97, and minority judges increasing from 21 to 41. Differences between elected judges and those appointed by the mayor were not significant.

49. Interview with Sol Wachtler, as quoted in John M. Caher, *King of the Mountain: The Rise, Fall, and Redemption of Chief Judge Sol Wachtler* (New York: Prometheus Books, 1998), p. 55.

50. Ibid., p. 52.

51. *1995 New York State Statistical Yearbook*, 20th ed. (Albany: Rockefeller Institute, 1995), p. 260. Roughly, a million of these cases were filed in civil courts, and 1.5 million in criminal courts, with the bulk of the remainder in parking and traffic courts.

52. As cited in Lawrence M. Friedman, *A History of American Law*, 2nd ed. (New York: Simon and Schuster, 1985), p. 573.

53. Ibid., p. 576.

54. Ibid., p. 574.

55. Patterson, "Historical and Evolutionary Theories of Law," reprinted in William D. Popkin, *Materials on Legislation: Political Language and the Political Process* (Westbury, NY: Foundation Press, 1993), p. 38.

56. Ibid., pp. 38–39.

57. Ibid., p. 39.

58. Ibid.

59. *McKinney's* has been published annually since 1943 by the West Publishing Company of Minneapolis, MN.

60. William Lasser, *The Limits of Judicial Power: The Supreme Court in American Politics* (Chapel Hill: University of North Carolina Press, 1988), p. 263.

61. *United States v. Richardson*, 418 U.S (1974), 166, 192.

62. Caher, *King of the Mountain*, p. 164.

63. G. Alan Tarr, *Judicial Process and Judicial Policymaking* (St. Paul, MN: West Publishing, 1994), p. 316.

64. Caher, *King of the Mountain*, p. 115.

65. Ibid., p. 117.

Notes to Chapter 7

1. Management Resources Project, *Governing the Empire State: An Insider's Guide* (Albany: Rockefeller Institute of Government, 1988), p. 118.

2. These figures are compiled each year by the legislative bill drafting commission and published in the annual *Legislative Digest* available for inspection in the senate and assembly public information offices.

3. James David Barber, *The Lawmakers: Recruitment and Adaptation to Legislative Life* (New Haven, CT: Yale University Press, 1965) uses the term "spectators" to describe those members of the legislature who play little active role in policy making.

4. These figures were compiled in 1986 by Professor Jeffrey Stonecash and first published in the 1986 handbook of the Assembly Internship Committee.

5. Frank E. Horack, Jr., "The Common Law of Legislation," *Iowa Law Review* 23 (1937): p. 42.

6. Figures on the sources of legislation and much of the argument which follows are taken from a random sample of 100 bills studied by Schneier and his students in the Assembly Internship Program in 1985–86 and reported in an unpublished paper, "On the Origins of Legislative Issues" delivered at the 1988 annual meeting of the Southwestern Political Science Association in San Antonio, Texas.

7. James Anderson, *Public Policy Making* (New York: Holt, Rinehart, and Winston, 1982), p. 37.

8. Arthur T. Johnson, "Potential Groups and Agenda Responsiveness," *Polity* 12 (Winter 1979): 349.

9. George C. Edwards, III, *At the Margins: Presidential Leadership of Congress* (New Haven, CT: Yale University Press, 1989), p. 223.

10. On this point, see especially Nelson W. Polsby, *Political Innovation in America: The Politics of Policy Initiation* (New Haven: Yale University Press, 1984).

11. Harry Jones, "Some Reflections on a Draftsman's Time Sheet," reprinted in Frank C. Newman and Stanley S. Surrey, eds., *Legislation: Cases and Materials* (Englewood Cliffs, NJ: Prentice-Hall, 1965), p. 535.

12. Edward V. Schneier and Bertram Gross, *Legislative Strategy: Shaping Public Policy* (New York: St. Martin's Press, 1993), p. 118. The quotations in this paragraph are taken from Aaron Wildavsky, *The Politics of the Budgetary Process* (Boston: Little, Brown, 1974), p. 22.

13. Robert A. Caro, *The Power Broker: Robert Moses and the Fall of New York* (New York: Random House, 1974), p. 174.

14. Murtaugh, knowing he had the votes to win in the higher education committee, once refused a request from his good friend Ed Sullivan to hold a bill. The bill passed over Sullivan's objections, but although Sullivan never mentioned it again the bill somehow died in the rules committee.

15. Nebraska, because it has a unicameral or one-house legislature, does not have conference committees, nor does Delaware, which relies upon joint committees instead. An excellent comparison of New York and other states was prepared by Assemblyman Dan Feldman and is available on the assembly's web site at http://www.assembly.state.ny.us.

16. Joseph F. Zimmerman, *The Government and Politics of New York State* (New York: New York University Press, 1981), p. 203.

17. Gerald Benjamin, "The Governorship," in Peter Colby, ed., *New York State Today* (Albany: State University of New York Press, 1985), p. 134.

18. William K. Muir, Jr., *Legislature: California's School for Politics* (Chicago: University of Chicago Press, 1982), p. 169.

19. Alan Rosenthal, *The Decline of Representative Democracy: Process, Participation, and Power in State Legislatures* (Washington, DC: CQ Press, 1998), p. 297.

20. Perhaps the best known and most eloquent of these theses is Theodore J. Lowi, *The End of Liberalism*, 2nd ed. (New York: W.W. Norton, 1979).

21. Francis F. Rourke, *Bureaucratic Politics and Public Policy* (Boston: Little, Brown, 1984), p. 37.

22. Charles T. Goodsell, *The Case for Bureaucracy: A Public Administration Polemic* (Chatham, NJ: Chatham House, 1983), p. 65.

23. James L. Perry, *Facing the Bureaucracy: Living and Dying in a Public Agency* (San Francisco: Jossey-Bass, 1993), p. 33.

24. A very good short history of studies in this area can be found in Chapter 2 of B. Dan Wood and Richard V. Waterman, *Bureaucratic Dynamics: The Role of Bureaucracy in a Democracy* (Boulder, CO: Westview Press, 1994).

25. Randall Ripley and Grace Franklin, *Policy Implementation and Bureaucracy* (Chicago: Dorsey Press, 1986), p. 41.

26. Herbert London and Edwin S. Rubenstein, *From the Empire State to the Vampire State: New York in a Downward Transition* (Lanham, NY: University Press of America, 1994), p. 99.

27. Robert F. Pecorella, "Federal Mandates, State Policy Coalitions, and Waste Management in New York State," in eds. Jeffrey M. Stonecash, John Kenneth White, and Peter W. Colby, *Governing New York State*, 3rd ed. (Albany: State University of New York Press, 1994), p. 343.

28. Zimmerman, *The Government and Politics of New York State*, p. 251.

29. Herbert Kaufman, *Red Tape: It's Origins, Uses, and Abuses* (Washington, DC: The Brookings Institution, 1977), pp. 58–59. For a timeless and enduringly excruciating case study—its subtitle lays it out—of how discouraging the process can be, see Jeffrey L. Pressman and Aaron B. Wildavsky, *Implementation: How Great Expectations in Washington Are Dashed in Oakland; Or, Why It's Amazing That Federal Programs Work at All, This Being the Saga of the Economic Development Administration as Told by Two Sympathetic Observers Who Seek to Build Morals on a Foundation of Ruined Hopes* (Berkeley: University of California Press, 1973).

30. Cornelius M. Kerwin, *Rulemaking: How Government Agencies Write Law and Make Policy* (Washington, DC: CQ Press, 1994), p. 4.

31. Ibid., p. 3. On state administrative practices see Arthur Bonfield, *State Administrative Rulemaking* (Boston: Little, Brown, 1986).

32. Management Resources Project, *Governing the Empire State: An Insider's Guide* (Albany: Rockefeller Institute, 1988), p. 166.

33. Ibid.

34. Ibid., p. 167.

35. Kerwin, *Rulemaking*, p. 209.

36. Ibid., p. 161.

37. Alice Sardell, "Health Policy in New York State: Health Care Needs and System Reform," In Stonecash, White, and Colby, p. 308.

38. Albert Gore, *From Red Tape to Results: Creating a Government That Works Better and Costs Less*. Report of the National Performance Review (Washington, DC: U.S. Government Printing Office, 1993), p. 14.

39. William Riordan, *Plunkitt of Tammany Hall* (New York: Dutton, 1963), p. 23.

40. Frank Anechiarco and James B. Jacobs, *The Pursuit of Absolute Integrity: How Corruption Control Makes Government Ineffective* (Chicago: University of Chicago Press, 1996), p. 200. Many administrators work hard to exempt their agencies or departments from rigid purchasing policies. Such devices as using subcontractors to

purchase most supplies have become so commonplace that true competitive bidding is no longer the norm (if it ever was).

41. Ibid., p. 135.

42. Kermit Gordon, as quoted in Kaufman, *Red Tape*, p. 14.

43. Ibid., p. 60.

44. The exception is Louisiana whose roots are essentially in the Napoleonic Code.

45. Lawrence M. Friedman, *History of American Law*, 2nd ed. (New York: Simon and Schuster, 1985), p. 92.

46. Abraham S. Blumberg, *Criminal Justice* (Chicago: Quadrangle Books, 1969), p. 110.

47. Harry P. Stumpf and John H. Culver, *The Politics of State Courts* (New York: Longman, 1992), pp. 22–34.

48. Ibid., pp. 77–78.

49. The New York Constitution allows the legislature to provide for trials without jury in many cases, but the U.S. Supreme Court has held that defendants have a federal right under the Sixth Amendment to jury trials in all cases where the potential punishment exceeds six months in jail. *Baldwin v. New York*, 399 U. S. 66 (1970).

50. Herbert Jacob, *Law and Politics in the United States*, 2nd ed. (New York: Harper and Collins, 2nd ed., 1995), p. 171.

51. Ibid.

52. Harry Kalven, Jr. and Hans Zeisel, *The American Jury* (Boston: Little, Brown, 1966), p. 21.

53. Cited in Zimmerman, p. 297.

54. G. Alan Tarr, *Judicial Process and Judicial Policymaking* (St. Paul, MN: West Publishing, 1994), p. 166.

55. Jacob, *Law and Politics in the United States*, pp. 172–73.

56. *1995 New York State Statistical Yearbook* (Albany: Rockefeller Institute, 1996), p. 255.

57. Ibid., p. 269.

58. Ibid., p. 260.

59. Tarr, *Judicial Process and Judicial Policymaking*, p. 251.

60. Jacob, *Law and Politics in the United States*, p. 180.

61. Tarr, *Judicial Process and Judicial Policymaking*, p. 240.

62. Ibid., p. 241.

63. Ibid., p. 242.

64. These figures are reported in ibid., p. 253.

65. Richard Neely, *Why Courts Don't Work* (New York: McGraw-Hill, 1983), p. 10.

66. James A. Gardner, "The Failed Discourse on State Constitutionalism," *Michigan Law Review* 90 (February 1992): 270.

67. From an unpublished paper by Craig Emmert cited in Henry R. Glick, "Policy Making and State Supreme Courts," in eds. John B. Gates and Charles A. Johnson, *The American Courts: A Critical Assessment* (Washington, DC: CQ Press, 1991), pp. 87–88.

68. Dorothy J. Samuels, "Mistaken Identity: Bum Rap against New York Court," *New York Times*, March 18, 1996, Section 5, p. 16.

69. These figures were compiled by Professor Norman Olch of John Jay College and reported in ibid.

70. Quoted in Zimmerman, *Government and Politics of New York State*, p. 277.

71. John M. Caher, *King of the Mountain: The Rise, Fall, and Redemption of Chief Judge Sol Wachtler* (Amherst, NY: Prometheus Books, 1998), p. 154.

72. Ibid., p. 157.

Notes to Chapter 8

1. Aaron Wildavsky, *The Politics of the Budgetary Process*, 4th ed. (Boston: Little, Brown, 1984), p. 4.

2. Dall W. Forsythe, *Memos to the Governor: An Introduction to State Budgeting* (Washington, DC: Georgetown University Press, 1997), p. 7.

3. A long-time budget technician quoted in Roy T. Meyers, *Strategic Budgeting* (Ann Arbor: University of Michigan Press, 1994), p. 19.

4. Wildavsky, *The Politics of the Budgetary Process*, pp. 1–2.

5. Quoted in ibid., p. 10.

6. Ibid.

7. Ibid.

8. Robert D. Behn, as quoted in Meyers, *Strategic Budgeting*, p. 11.

9. Wildavsky, *The Politics of the Budgetary Process*, p. 17.

10. Ibid., p. 15.

11. Ibid., p. 17.

12. Meyers, *Strategic Budgeting*, p. 17.

13. State of New York, Management Resources Project, *Governing the Empire State: An Insider's Guide* (Albany: Rockefeller Institute of Government, 1988), p. 39.

14. Ibid., p. 41.

15. Forsythe, *Memos to the Governor*, p. 26.

16. George E. Pataki, *1999–2000 New York State Executive Budget* (Albany: Division of the Budget), Appendix I, p. 13.

17. Forsythe, p. 28.

18. Alan Rosenthal, *The Decline of Representative Democracy: Process, Participation, and Power in State Legislatures* (Washington, DC: CQ Press, 1998), p. 309.

19. Forsythe, *Memos to the Governor*, p. 39.

20. Management Resources Project, p. 59.

21. Forsythe, *Memos to the Governor*, p. 51.

22. Kenneth Shapiro interview in Gerald Benjamin and T. Nakamura, *The Modern New York State Legislature: Redressing the Balance* (Albany: Rockefeller Institute, 1991), p. 221.

23. Forsythe, *Memos to the Governor*, p. 75.

24. Assembly Minority Leader John Faso as quoted in the Albany *Times Union*, April 20, 1998, p. 12.

25. New York State Assembly, *Record of Proceedings*, May 22, 2000, p. 29.

26. Frank Mauro interview in Benjamin and Nakamura, *The Modern New York State Legislature*, p. 340.

27. *New York Times*, February 8, 1999, p. B1.

28. As quoted in Rosenthal, *The Decline of Representative Democracy*, p. 307.

29. Management Resources Project, p. 51.

30. *County of Oneida v. Berle* 398 NY Supp. 2nd, 600.

31. Mauro in Benjamin and Nakamura, *The Modern New York State Legislature*, p. 332.

32. Management Resources Project, pp. 52–53.

33. Unless otherwise noted, most of the budget numbers used here are from those reported for 1998–99 in Governor Pataki's *2000–2001 Executive Budget.*

34. Albany *Times Union,* April 27, 2000, p. B2.

35. H. Carl McCall, *2000–01 Budget Analysis: Review of the Enacted Budget* (Albany: Office of the Comptroller, 2000), p. 2.

36. Jonathan Bowles, "In One Pocket and Out the Other," a May 1996 report from the office of Senator Franz Leichter, p. 3.

37. Jeffrey M. Stonecash, "Taxes and Policy Debates in New York State," in eds. Jeffrey M. Stonecash, John Kenneth White, and Peter W. Colby, *Governing New York State,* 3rd ed. (Albany: State University of New York Press, 1994), p. 239.

38. The cycles of financial collapse and their political repercussions in New York City are richly detailed in Robert F. Pecorella, *Community Power in a Postreform City: Politics in New York City* (Armonk, NY: M.E. Sharpe, 1994), Chapter 2.

39. Dick Netzer, "The Economy and the Governing of the City," in eds. Jewell Bellush and Dick Netzer, *Urban Politics New York Style* (Armonk, NY: M.E. Sharpe, 1990), p. 46.

40. Assembly Ways and Means Committee, *Fiscal Change, Financial Sense: Budgetary and Financial Reform in New York State* (Albany: The State Assembly, 1989).

41. Raymond J. Keating, *New York by the Numbers* (Lanham, MD: Madison Books, 1997), p. 17.

42. Alberta M. Sbragia, *Debt Wish: Entrepreneurial Cities, U.S. Federalism, and Economic Development* (Pittsburgh, PA: University of Pittsburgh Press, 1996), pp. 214–15.

43. Penelope Lemov, "Taxes: The Struggle for Balance," *Governing* (August 1994): 32.

44. Forsythe, *Memos to the Governor,* p. 2.

45. Edward Regan, as quoted in an interview in Herbert London and Edwin S. Rubenstein, *From the Empire State to the Vampire State: New York in a Downward Transition* (Lanham, MD: University Press of America, 1994), p. 107.

46. Alice Sardell, "Health Policy on New York State: Health Care Needs and System Reform," in Stonecash, et al., *Governing New York State,* p. 309.

47. Ibid., p. 309.

48. These figures, for 1996, are taken from a February 1998 report of the United Hospital Fund, "Trends in the Distribution of Health Insurance Coverage among New Yorkers."

49. Sardell, p. 302. That these pathologies are found more frequently in New York City does not mean that they necessarily originate in the city. Drug addicts, alcoholics, and the homeless are often drawn to major urban areas where drugs, alcohol, and places to keep warm at night are easier to find than they are in many smaller towns.

50. New York Temporary State Commission on Lobbying, *2000 Annual Report* (Albany: State Commission on Lobbying, 2000), Appendix G.

51. Most of the data in this section are taken from the state education department report, *New York: The State of Learning, Statewide Profile of the Educational System* (Albany: The University of the State of New York, 1997). A more extensive presentation of this material can be found in Chapter 12 "The State of Education" (by Edward Schneier) of Jeffrey Stonecash, ed., *Governing New York State* (Albany: State University Press, forthcoming).

52. State Education Department, 1997 Report, p. 34.

53. www.ci.rochester.ny.ns and www.co.monroe.us.aboutmc.

54. Robert H. Connery and Gerald Benjamin, *Rockefeller of New York: Executive Power in the Statehouse* (Ithaca, NY: Cornell University Press, 1979), p. 298.

55. Helen F. Ladd, "Big City Finances," in ed. George E. Peterson, *Big City Politics, Governance and Fiscal Constraints* (Washington, DC: The Urban Institute Press, 1994), p. 244.

56. Ibid., p. 249.

57. Sharon D. Gold and Sarah Ritchie, "The Role of the State in the Finances of Cities and Counties in New York," in Stonecash, et al., *Governing New York State*, p. 71.

58. The presidents of each of New York City's five boroughs, which are, in a sense, counties by another name, do have small budgets of their own, but they comprise an essentially trivial proportion of the overall city budget. Boroughs do not have anything near the scope of authority enjoyed by county governments in the rest of the state where, in rural areas in particular, they often provide such basic services as police, sanitation, and health.

59. These figures, and those following on New York City finances are taken from Mayor Giuliani's 2000 executive budget.

60. Figures on Rochester were downloaded from the 2000 city of Rochester and Monroe County budget summaries available on the city and county websites.

61. The state education department, from which these numbers were obtained, calculates a combined wealth ratio for each school district that combines property value and personal income figures divided by the per-pupil state average. In 1992–93, the per-pupil ratio for New York City was 99.1 percent of the state average; Rochester's was 67.6 percent, but per-pupil expenditures were $9,659 as compared with $7,921 in New York City. State Education Department, *New York the State of Learning: Statistical Profiles of Public School Districts* (Albany: The State University of New York, 1995), Table 2.

62. Ibid.

Notes to Epilogue

1. Paul C. Light, *Thickening Government: Federal Hierarchy and the Diffusion of Accountability* (Washington, DC: The Brookings Institution, 1995), p. 1.

2. Ibid., p. 7.

3. George A. Mitchell, ed., *The New York Red Book, 1997–98*, 94th ed. (Guilderland, NY: New York Legal Publishing Co., 1997), passim.

4. The classic description of how President Roosevelt pitted one agency against another is found in Richard E. Neustadt, *Presidential Power* (New York: Wiley, 1976), Chapter 2.

5. Light, *Thickening Government*, p. 63.

6. Ibid., p. 62.

7. John F. Bibby and Thomas M. Holbrook, "Parties and Elections" in eds. Virginia Gray and Herbert Jacob, *Politics in the American States*, 6th ed. (Washington, DC: CQ Press, 1996), p. 110.

8. Austin Ranney, *The Doctrine of Responsible Party Government* (Urbana: University of Illinois Press, 1962), p. 12.

9. Jarol B. Manheim, *All of the People, All of the Time* (Armonk, NY: M.E. Sharpe, 1992), pp. 4–5.

10. McKinney's, for those who missed earlier references, are the annually updated, official repositories of statute law published by the West Publishing Company.

Index

Edward Schneier is professor of Political Science at the City College of New York and the graduate center of the City University. Before coming to City in 1968, he taught at Princeton and Johns Hopkins Universities, was a research fellow at the Brookings Institution, and worked as legislative assistant to U.S. Senator Birch Bayh. From 1985 to 1987 he served as professor-in-residence for the Internship Committee of the New York State Assembly. He has long been active in New York politics, running for Congress in 1976, serving as president of the Downtown Independent Democrats, and vice president of the state's New Democratic Coalition. For the past five years, he has been state legislative director of Americans for Democratic Action and a registered lobbyist for the Citizens for Equity in Educational Funding. His publications include *Party and Constituency* (1969); *Vote Power* (1974); and *Legislative Strategy* (1993).

John Brian Murtaugh works within the united court system of New York state in the office of court administration and is an adjunct professor of political science at the City College of New York. He has had extensive political experience in New York politics, having been the legislative aide to a New York City Council member and Democratic District Leader from the Northern Manhattan 72nd Assembly District in the 1970s. He was elected to the New York State Assembly in 1980 and served eight terms representing the 72nd Assembly District (1981–96). Murtaugh chaired the Assembly Standing Committee on Alcoholism for eight years (1988–96) and sponsored over 100 laws in the housing, health care, mental health, and alcoholism and substance abuse fields. He also served as chair of the Democratic Study Group and chair of the Speaker's Office on State–Federal Relations.